# JAVASCRIPT COOKBOOK

**Yosef Cohen**

**WILEY COMPUTER PUBLISHING**

JOHN WILEY & SONS, INC.

New York • Chichester • Weinheim • Brisbane • Singapore • Toronto

*To Maddy, Jeremiah, Michael, and Moriah*

*Executive Publisher:* Katherine Schowalter
*Editor:* Tim Ryan
*Assistant Editor:* Kathryn A. Malm
*Managing Editor:* Brian Snapp
*Text Design & Composition:* Pronto Design & Production, Inc.

Designations used by companies to distinguish their products are often claimed as trademarks. In all instances where John Wiley & Sons, Inc., is aware of a claim, the product names appear in initial capital or ALL CAPITAL LETTERS. Readers, however, should contact the appropriate companies for more complete information regarding trademarks and registration.

This publication is designed to provide accurate and authoritative information in regard to the subject matter covered. It is sold with the understanding that the publisher is not engaged in rendering legal, accounting, or other professional service. If legal advice or other expert assistance is required, the services of a competent professional person should be sought.

*Library of Congress Cataloging-in-Publication Data:*
Cohen, Yosef, 1946-
        JavaScript cookbook/Yosef Cohen.
        p. cm.
        Includes index.
ISBN 0-471-18145-5 (pbk./CD:alk.paper)
1. JavaScript (Computer program language) I. Title.
QA76.73.J39C64  1997                          97-1559
005.2'762--cc21                               CIP

Printed in the United States of America

10 9 8 7 6 5 4 3 2 1

# Contents

**Introduction**

Who Should *not* Read This Book . . . . . . . . . . . . . . . . . xiii
Who *Should* Read this Book . . . . . . . . . . . . . . . . . . . . xiii
The Approach . . . . . . . . . . . . . . . . . . . . . . . . . . . . . xiv
How to Read This Book . . . . . . . . . . . . . . . . . . . . . . . xv
What's in the Book . . . . . . . . . . . . . . . . . . . . . . . . . . xvi
What's on the Enclosed CD-ROM . . . . . . . . . . . . . . . xvii
Notation Conventions . . . . . . . . . . . . . . . . . . . . . . . . xviii
Acknowledgments . . . . . . . . . . . . . . . . . . . . . . . . . . . xix

**PART I** OVERVIEW . . . . . . . . . . . . . . . . . . . . . . . . . . . . . 1

**Chapter 1** An Introduction to JavaScript . . . . . . . . . . . 3
JavaScript in Perspective . . . . . . . . . . . . . . . . . . . . . . 3
What You Should Expect . . . . . . . . . . . . . . . . . . . . . . 10
Getting Started . . . . . . . . . . . . . . . . . . . . . . . . . . . . 11
The "Hello World" Example . . . . . . . . . . . . . . . . . . . . 15
Analysis of the "Hello World" Example . . . . . . . . . . . . 18
"Hello World" Example with a Button and
    an Alert Window . . . . . . . . . . . . . . . . . . . . . . . . . 23
How to Use JavaScript in an HTML Page . . . . . . . . . 25
The "Last Modified" Example . . . . . . . . . . . . . . . . . . 26

**Chapter 2** Programming in JavaScript . . . . . . . . . . . . . 31
Programming Discipline . . . . . . . . . . . . . . . . . . . . . . 31
Function Definitions and Calls . . . . . . . . . . . . . . . . . . 33
Events and Event Handlers . . . . . . . . . . . . . . . . . . . . 38
Arrays and Strings . . . . . . . . . . . . . . . . . . . . . . . . . . 48
Miscellaneous Programming Topics . . . . . . . . . . . . . . 55

**Chapter 3** Objects . . . . . . . . . . . . . . . . . . . . . . . . . . . . 57
Object Hierarchy . . . . . . . . . . . . . . . . . . . . . . . . . . . 57
Automatically Created Objects . . . . . . . . . . . . . . . . . . 62

**Chapter 4** Windows, Frames,
    Documents, and Forms . . . . . . . . . . . . . . . . . . . . . 75
The `window` Object . . . . . . . . . . . . . . . . . . . . . . . . . 77
The `frame` Object . . . . . . . . . . . . . . . . . . . . . . . . . . 97

The `document` Object . . . . . . . . . . . . . . . . . . . . . . . . . . 99
The `form` Object and the `forms` Array . . . . . . . . . . . 106
The JavaScript Repertoire of User Interface
    Objects in a `form`. . . . . . . . . . . . . . . . . . . . . . . . . . 108

**Chapter 5** The JavaScript Language. . . . . . . . . . . . . . . . 117
Data Types . . . . . . . . . . . . . . . . . . . . . . . . . . . . . . . . . 117
Literals . . . . . . . . . . . . . . . . . . . . . . . . . . . . . . . . . . . . 121
Expressions. . . . . . . . . . . . . . . . . . . . . . . . . . . . . . . . . 122
Operators. . . . . . . . . . . . . . . . . . . . . . . . . . . . . . . . . . . 123
Statements . . . . . . . . . . . . . . . . . . . . . . . . . . . . . . . . . 133
Braces . . . . . . . . . . . . . . . . . . . . . . . . . . . . . . . . . . . . 142

**Chapter 6** What's New Since Navigator 2.0 . . . . . . . . 145
A Word about Object Names . . . . . . . . . . . . . . . . . . . . 145
Navigator JavaScript New Features . . . . . . . . . . . . . . . 147
New Objects. . . . . . . . . . . . . . . . . . . . . . . . . . . . . . . . . 149
New Properties . . . . . . . . . . . . . . . . . . . . . . . . . . . . . . 149
Two Ways to Index an Object's Properties. . . . . . . . . 150
New or Modified Methods, Forms,
    and Form Elements. . . . . . . . . . . . . . . . . . . . . . . . . . 151
Events and Event Handlers . . . . . . . . . . . . . . . . . . . . . 151
HTML Tags and Attributes. . . . . . . . . . . . . . . . . . . . . . 154
Added and Modified JavaScript
    Language Features . . . . . . . . . . . . . . . . . . . . . . . . . . 157

**PART II** REFERENCE. . . . . . . . . . . . . . . . . . . . . . . . . . . . . 159

**Chapter 7** Objects Reference. . . . . . . . . . . . . . . . . . . . . 161
About the Reference Format. . . . . . . . . . . . . . . . . . . . . 161
`anchor` and `anchors` array. . . . . . . . . . . . . . . . . . . . . 163
`applet` and `applets` array. . . . . . . . . . . . . . . . . . . . . 167
`Area` . . . . . . . . . . . . . . . . . . . . . . . . . . . . . . . . . . . . . . 170
`Array` . . . . . . . . . . . . . . . . . . . . . . . . . . . . . . . . . . . . . 173
`button`. . . . . . . . . . . . . . . . . . . . . . . . . . . . . . . . . . . . . 176
`checkbox`. . . . . . . . . . . . . . . . . . . . . . . . . . . . . . . . . . . 179
`Date` . . . . . . . . . . . . . . . . . . . . . . . . . . . . . . . . . . . . . . 184
`document`. . . . . . . . . . . . . . . . . . . . . . . . . . . . . . . . . . . 187
`elements` array . . . . . . . . . . . . . . . . . . . . . . . . . . . . . 191

FileUpload .............................. 193
form and forms array.................... 196
frame and frames array ................. 198
Function................................ 205
hidden.................................. 209
history................................. 212
Image and images array ................. 215
link and links array................... 221
location ............................... 227
Math ................................... 230
mimeTypes .............................. 232
navigator .............................. 234
Option ................................. 237
password ............................... 239
Plugin and embeds array ................ 242
plugins array .......................... 243
radio .................................. 246
reset .................................. 249
select and options array............... 253
String ................................. 259
submit.................................. 263
text ................................... 268
textarea................................ 271
window ................................. 277

**Chapter 8** Methods and Functions Reference ....... 283
Introduction to Methods and Functions ........... 283
abs(*number*) ............................ 285
acos(*number*) ........................... 285
alert([*argument*]) ...................... 287
anchor(*anchorNameAttribute*) ............ 289
asin(*number*) ........................... 290
atan(*number*) ........................... 292
atan2(*xCoordinate, yCoordinate*) .......... 293
back() ................................. 295
big() .................................. 295
blink() ................................ 296
blur() ................................. 297

bold() ................................ 300
ceil(*number*) ....................... 300
charAt(*position*) ................... 301
clearTimeout(*idFrom_setTimeout*) ........ 303
click() .............................. 305
close() .............................. 308
confirm([*argument*]) ................ 311
cos(*angle*) ......................... 314
escape(*aString*) .................... 315
eval(*aString*) ...................... 317
exp(*x*) ............................. 320
fixed() .............................. 322
floor(*number*) ...................... 323
focus() .............................. 324
fontcolor(*color*) ................... 325
fontsize(*integer*) .................. 329
forward() ............................ 330
getDate() ............................ 332
getDay() ............................. 334
getHours() ........................... 334
getMinutes() ......................... 335
getMonth() ........................... 335
getSeconds() ......................... 336
getTime() ............................ 336
getTimezoneOffset() .................. 337
getYear() ............................ 338
go(*relativePosition* | "*url*") ...... 339
indexOf(*searchForString*[, *startFrom*]) .... 340
isNaN(*aValue*) ...................... 343
italics() ............................ 345
javaEnabled() ........................ 346
join() ............................... 348
lastIndexOf(*searchForString*
  [, *startFrom*]) .................... 349
link(*hrefAttribute*) ................ 352
log(*x*) ............................. 352
max(*x1*, *x2*) ...................... 353
min(*x1*, *x2*) ...................... 353

open([*mimeType*]).............................. 354
open([*URL, windowName*
    [, *windowFeatures*]) ..................... 355
parse(*aDate*)................................. 357
parseFloat(*aString*) ........................ 359
parseInt(*aString*[, *radix*]) ............... 361
pow(*base, exponent*)......................... 364
prompt([*argument*][, *defaultArgument*]).... 365
random() ..................................... 367
reload([*true*]) ............................. 372
replace(*URL*) ............................... 374
reset() ...................................... 375
reverse() .................................... 377
round(*x*) ................................... 380
scroll(*x, y*) ............................... 381
select() ..................................... 384
setDate(*dayOfTheMonth*) ..................... 385
setHours(*hourOfTheDay*) ..................... 386
setMinutes(*minuteOfTheHour*) ............... 388
setMonth(*monthOfTheYear*) .................. 390
setSeconds(*secondOfTheMinute*) ........... 391
setTime(*millisecondsSinceEpoch*) ........ 393
setTimeout(*expression, milliseconds*)..... 395
setYear(*yearInteger*) ...................... 395
sin(*angle*) ................................. 397
small() ...................................... 397
sort([*sortOrderFunction*]) ................. 398
split([*separator*]) ........................ 400
sqrt(*aNumber*) .............................. 402
strike() ..................................... 403
sub() ........................................ 405
submit() ..................................... 406
substring([*beginIndex*][, *endIndex*]) ...... 406
sup() ........................................ 408
taint(*aProperty*) ........................... 409
tan(*anAngle*) ............................... 409
toGMTString() ................................ 411
toLocaleString() ............................. 412

toLowerCase() ............................. 413
toString([*radix*]) ....................... 414
toUpperCase() ............................. 417
unescape() ................................ 418
untaint(*aProperty*) ...................... 418
UTC() ..................................... 419
write() ................................... 420
writeln() ................................. 421

**Chapter 9** Properties Reference .................... 423
Introduction............................... 423
action .................................... 424
alinkColor ................................ 426
anchors ................................... 428
appCodeName ............................... 430
appName ................................... 431
appVersion................................. 433
arguments ................................. 435
bgColor ................................... 436
border .................................... 439
checked ................................... 440
complete .................................. 444
cookie .................................... 445
defaultChecked ............................ 449
defaultSelected ........................... 452
defaultStatus ............................. 456
defaultValue .............................. 457
description ............................... 459
E ......................................... 461
elements .................................. 462
enabledPlugin ............................. 463
encoding .................................. 465
fgColor ................................... 468
filename .................................. 468
forms ..................................... 470
frames .................................... 472
hash ...................................... 473
height .................................... 474

host ........................................ 475
hostname ................................... 478
href ....................................... 479
hspace ..................................... 480
index ...................................... 480
lastModified ............................... 483
length ..................................... 485
linkColor .................................. 486
links ...................................... 488
LN2 ........................................ 489
LN10 ....................................... 489
location ................................... 490
LOG2E ...................................... 490
LOG10E ..................................... 491
lowsrc ..................................... 491
method ..................................... 494
name ....................................... 494
opener ..................................... 496
options .................................... 498
parent ..................................... 498
pathname ................................... 499
PI ......................................... 500
port ....................................... 501
protocol ................................... 502
prototype .................................. 503
referrer ................................... 505
search ..................................... 508
selected ................................... 508
selectedIndex .............................. 509
self ....................................... 510
SQRT1_2 .................................... 511
SQRT2 ...................................... 511
src ........................................ 512
status ..................................... 513
suffixes ................................... 513
target ..................................... 514
text ....................................... 515
title ...................................... 517

top ........................................ 519
type ....................................... 519
URL ........................................ 521
userAgent .................................. 522
value ...................................... 524
vlinkColor ................................. 529
vspace ..................................... 531
width ...................................... 531
window ..................................... 532

**Chapter 10** Event Handlers Reference ........... 535
Introduction ............................... 535
onAbort .................................... 536
onBlur ..................................... 537
onChange ................................... 539
onClick .................................... 540
onError .................................... 542
onFocus .................................... 546
onLoad ..................................... 548
onMouseOut ................................. 550
onMouseOver ................................ 551
onReset .................................... 552
onSelect ................................... 553
onSubmit ................................... 554
onUnload ................................... 556

**Chapter 11** Statements ....................... 557
Introduction ............................... 557
break ...................................... 558
Comment .................................... 561
continue ................................... 561
for ........................................ 562
for...in ................................... 564
function ................................... 566
if...else .................................. 568
new ........................................ 570
return ..................................... 572
this ....................................... 574
var ........................................ 574

```
while ..................................... 575
with ..................................... 576
```

**PART III** APPLICATIONS ............................. 579

**Chapter 12** The Internet Store—Preliminaries ....... 581
Introduction...................................... 581
Project Design and Implementation .............. 582
The Internet Store............................... 585
Data Design .................................... 588
Specifying the Stereo Component Database ...... 590
Global Variables................................. 591
The Stereo Components Selection Lists........... 592
Building the Stereo System Description
    and Computing Its Price ...................... 595
The Data to Submit ............................. 598

**Chapter 13** Data Validation......................... 601
Introduction...................................... 601
Strategies for Data Validation .................... 602
Validating the Stereo System Configuration....... 604
Validating a First Name .......................... 604
Validating Letter Data............................ 607
Validating a Last Name .......................... 608
Validating a Street Address ...................... 608
Validating Alphanumeric Data..................... 610
Validating a Digit ............................... 611
Validating a Positive Integer...................... 612
Validating a Negative Integer..................... 613
Validating an Integer............................. 614
Validating a Floating-Point Number............... 614
Validating a Number Less Than
    a Maximum Number ........................... 615
Validating a Number Greater Than
    a Minimum Number............................ 616
Validating a Number Less Than or
    Equal to a Maximum Number .................. 617
Validating a Number Greater Than or
    Equal to a Minimum Number .................. 617
```
```

Validating a Number in Range . . . . . . . . . . . . . . . . . . . . 618
Validating a Phone Number . . . . . . . . . . . . . . . . . . . . . . 619
Validating a State . . . . . . . . . . . . . . . . . . . . . . . . . . . . . 620
Validating an Exact Number of
    Characters in a String . . . . . . . . . . . . . . . . . . . . . . . 622
Validating a Maximum Number of
    Characters in a String . . . . . . . . . . . . . . . . . . . . . . . 623
Validating a Minimum Number of
    Characters in a String . . . . . . . . . . . . . . . . . . . . . . . 623
An Alternative Way to Validate the State . . . . . . . . . . 624
Validating a Zip Code . . . . . . . . . . . . . . . . . . . . . . . . . . 626
Validating a Date . . . . . . . . . . . . . . . . . . . . . . . . . . . . . 627

**Chapter 14** The Internet Store—
    Communicating with the User . . . . . . . . . . . . . . . . 629
Communicating with the User . . . . . . . . . . . . . . . . . . . 629
Putting It All Together . . . . . . . . . . . . . . . . . . . . . . . . . 636
Suggestions for Extensions . . . . . . . . . . . . . . . . . . . . 641
Testing and Debugging the Application . . . . . . . . . . . 643

**Chapter 15** Drawing with JavaScript—A Bar Graph . 647
Introduction . . . . . . . . . . . . . . . . . . . . . . . . . . . . . . . . . 647
Global Variables . . . . . . . . . . . . . . . . . . . . . . . . . . . . . 648
The `maxOfArray()` and
`minOfArray()` Functions . . . . . . . . . . . . . . . . . . . . . 649
The `computeBarWidths()` Function . . . . . . . . . . . . . 650
The `doBar()` Function . . . . . . . . . . . . . . . . . . . . . . . . 651
Some Extensions . . . . . . . . . . . . . . . . . . . . . . . . . . . . 653

**PART IV** APPENDICES . . . . . . . . . . . . . . . . . . . . . . . . . . 657

    **A. Glossary** . . . . . . . . . . . . . . . . . . . . . . . . . . . . . . . . 659

    **B. JavaScript Reserved Keywords** . . . . . . . . . . . . . 663

    **C. Color Names and Values** . . . . . . . . . . . . . . . . . . 665

    **D. Internet Resources** . . . . . . . . . . . . . . . . . . . . . . . 671

    **E. The CD-ROM** . . . . . . . . . . . . . . . . . . . . . . . . . . . . 673

    **Index** . . . . . . . . . . . . . . . . . . . . . . . . . . . . . . . . . . . . . 675

# *Introduction*

- Who I wrote this book for
- My approach
- How to read this book
- What is this book and the CD-ROM

This section is intended to whet your appetite, or—depending on your wishes, aspirations, desires, and political orientation—mess it up. I also want to quickly get you used to my style of writing (which might not be all that different from that of others).

##  Who Should *not* Read This Book

If one of the conditions below meet yours, this book is *not* for you:

- If you think you are dummy, this book is not for you; there are lots of JavaScript books for dummies. In writing this book, I assumed that readers have self-respect!

- If you want to learn JavaScript quickly and superficially, and are not interested in working with it further, this book is not for you. There are lots of "learn-in-a-week" JavaScript books. In writing this book, I assumed that you want to see (quickly) what could be done with JavaScript, do some work, and then come back to the book when needed for deepening your knowledge and reference.

- Finally, if you know absolutely nothing about HTML, you should pick up at least a cursory knowledge of it, and then come back.

##  Who *Should* Read This Book

This book was written for readers with varying levels of skills in programming in general, and JavaScript in particular. If you are here, you have already gone through the first filter in the previous section. This book *is* for you if:

- You know absolutely nothing about JavaScript, but are eager to learn.

- You know a lot about JavaScript, and need a reference to rely on.
- You know absolutely nothing about programming in general, and object-oriented programming in particular, but wish to learn.
- You know a lot about object-oriented programming, and wish to extend your knowledge to JavaScript.
- You want to see full-fledged JavaScript applications, and learn how to develop your own applications.
- You want to learn about general programming, software development, data validation, and debugging strategies and their implementation in JavaScript.
- You want to bring your HTML documents to life, and communicate with the user through forms, menus, dialog windows, animation, and so on (all of these, without having to rely on the good will of Internet server mediation).

# The Approach

In writing this book I made no assumptions about your knowledge of programming—any kind of programming. Yet (for some reasons you can probably guess and others that you cannot) I wanted to provide a text that would appeal to as broad an audience as possible. Thus, I organized the text into three distinct parts: Overview, Reference, and Applications. This will allow you to decide quickly which material to pay attention to, and also develop your JavaScript skills as you go along.

Learning to program and developing software, whether simple or complex, is not a linear process: You need to know everything before you start, but you also need to start before knowing everything. This calls for what I call the slippery spiral climbing approach (see Chapter 1 for more). This means that I have to expose you to some issues without going through details, and then come back to these time and again, at ever-increasing levels of detail and complexity. This also means that if you know nothing, you should start from the beginning; if you know something, start from the middle; and if you know a lot, go to the appropriate sections to refresh and polish your knowledge.

Another cornerstone of teaching (and learning) programming is this: Smart people learn from their own experiences; wise people learn from those of others. Looking at it differently, the difference between a smart person and a wise person is that a smart person knows how to get out of trouble, a wise person never gets into trouble in the first place. I therefore included hundreds of examples and code listings. Some of these use tricks of the trade; others use simple and not-so-tricky code.

I have tried to minimize what I call arm-waving: "Here is some code snippet, that you can easily modify to suit your own needs." Being a scripting language in a rapidly evolving milieu, JavaScript still has a lot of idiosyncrasies and some inconsistencies. It sometimes does not behave as you expect it to. I therefore went through every topic presented (objects, methods, functions, properties, and so on), and wrote code that produces tangible results. To let you know what to expect, I have also included numerous figures that display these results.

When teaching programming, explanations sometimes complicate things more than necessary. Thus in most cases, I followed the format of presenting code, and explaining it by line numbers. Where I thought the ideas were simple, I did not even explain the code.

Finally, programming is not an abstract topic. It is factual and tangible. It should produce desirable results, and these results should be demonstrated.

#  How to Read This Book

To get the most out of this book, follow these guidelines.

## For the Novice

Start by reading Part I. As you go through the chapters, be sure to do the exercises. Some of the exercises require nothing more than cutting and pasting the code to your own HTML document and then loading the document to your browser. Others ask you to modify the code and examine the results.

Next, move to Part III. See what can be done with JavaScript and how a full-fledged (albeit not fancy) application is designed and implemented.

As you go through Parts I and III, if you want to learn more about an object, a method, a function, a property, an event handler, or a language feature, go to the appropriate reference section in Part II.

To learn the vocabulary and be aware of the potential of JavaScript, look at the topic headings in Part II. These will give you a clue to what is available. You can then read about those topics that you fancy.

## For the Intermediate

Survey Part I. Here, you may just want to look at the topic headings, and read thoroughly those topics that you think you need. Part II is a detailed and formal reference. Go through the topics as needed. I suggest you read these every now and then to refresh your memory and remind yourself what can be done with JavaScript. Take a close look at the examples and the accompanying listings.

Part III presents a full-fledged application. Read it in detail. You will learn how to develop software, strategies for data validation and debugging, and how to communicate with the user without reverting to a server's services.

## For the Experienced

If you are a programmer experienced in both JavaScript and object-oriented programming, skip Part I. Use Part II for reference. Pay special attention to the examples. I used some of them to test for JavaScript inconsistencies and counter-intuitive results. In Part III you will find a full-fledged application that may be useful to you. There are ideas there on how to establish a communication loop with the user (via forms and formatted e-mail replies) without relying on server processing with, for example, Java or CGI.

#  What's in the Book

By the time you are done with Part I you should have a good working knowledge of JavaScript and what object-oriented programming is all about.

Part II is a complete reference for JavaScript, as it functions with Netscape's Navigator Version 3.0. All of the available objects, methods and functions, properties, event handlers, and language features are presented formally. The behavior of objects is detailed, along with lists of their methods and properties. Methods are detailed, along with lists of the objects to which they belong. Differences among implementations of identically named methods and properties in different objects are highlighted. Properties are listed along with objects to which they belong. A similar approach is taken in discussing event handlers. For all of these, examples demonstrate implementation and what results to expect.

Part III presents the Internet store and a bar graph drawing applications. The Internet store application presents the user with a choice of stereo components. The user can then design his or her own stereo system. Once done, the user fills in an information form (name, address, comments, etc.), and submits the form. Submission sends the information (the system the user desires, its price, and the user information) to your e-mail address. The message, which is formatted for easy readability, can be saved as a file and then parsed into a database.

Part III also looks at strategies for data validation (how to validate a name, a phone number, a state, etc.). Strategies for debugging and software quality assurance testing are discussed as well. Finally (and this is the place where I do some arm-waving), I suggest some potential extensions: how to modify the application to run, for example, a video store or, a bookstore, and to draw scatter plots and various shapes with JavaScript.

All of the listings in the book are given in separate files in the enclosed CD. When you wish to run an example or listing, go to the enclosed CD and cut and paste the code to your own file. Then open the example in your browser and play with it. Once you know what to expect in terms of the code's behavior, go back to the appropriate section and read the explanation of the code.

#  What's on the Enclosed CD-ROM

The CD-ROM contains all of the listings in the book organized by chapter.

One more thing about the listings: a few of them (less than a handful) load images that reside in a directory other than the listing's directory. In such cases, I use a standard like this:

```
<IMG SRC = '.\\images\\image.jpg' ...>
```

where image.jpg is the image filename and images is a subdirectory of the directory in which the invoking HTML document resides. These lines need to be changed as follows so that your browser can find the images:

- If you are using a UNIX-based platform, change the double backslashes (\\) to a single forward slash (/).

- If you are using MacOS, change the double backslashes (\\) to a single colon (:).

#  Notation Conventions

Throughout, we shall stick with the notations shown in Table I.1. Take a few moments to familiarize yourself with the vocabulary. Later, as you go

through your first few syntax examples, come back to Table I.1 and read it
again; it will make better sense.

**TABLE I.1** Notation conventions.

| Notation | Definition | Example |
|---|---|---|
| x \| y | x is the menu bar in your browser, and y is its submenu. This means, click on x and then on y to do something. | `File | Open File`<br>`in Browser...` |
| *italics* | When a concept appears first, and then explained in the Glossary, it will be italicized, using the norma text font. | *function* |
| `Courier New` | Statements and text that you type as shown, or that show on your screen, appear in mono space type using the Courier New font. | `<SCRIPT>` |
| `Courier New Italics` | Statements that represent variables XE variable—words that take a value of your choice—will appear in italicized monotype using the Courier New font. | *AStringVariable* **You may enter** `"Hello World"` **for** *aStringVariable*. |
| Line-numbered paragraphs | Lines of JavaScript listings will be numbered. The line numbers are not part of the script listing. | `1 //a JavaScript comment`<br>`2 document.write(aStr)` |

| Notation | Definition | Example |
|---|---|---|
| | Each number, designates a single line of code, even if that code wraps to the next line. | |
| a [b \| c] | Syntax statements; square brackets delineate optional part of the statement, and \| indicates "or" b or c. | `function functionName ([argument, ...]) {[statements]}` |

In addition, wherever I use a function name, I will follow the name with () to emphasize the fact that it is a function. For example, interpret `write()` to mean "the function `write`".

Be aware that some of the examples in the book are intended to demonstrate the use of colors in background, foreground, links, and so on. The resulting figures in the book are in grayscale. When you invoke the listings through your browser, colors will show up (except where indicated).

#  Acknowledgments

Special thanks to the Wiley publishing team:

Kathryn Malm, the assistant editor, who had to put up with my insulting jokes.

Brian Snapp, the managing editor, who actually laughed at some.

Jodi Beder, the copyeditor for her superb and careful editing.

Frank Grazioli, the senior managing editor.

Katherine Schowalter, the executive publisher.

Tim Ryan who initiated the project.

Tom Hyland, who being in charge of manufacturing never gets mentioned.

Thanks to George Spangler, who provided the "Soaring Eagle" image and some fish (images).

Finally, to my family. Without you, this book would have been impossible!

# PART ONE

# OVERVIEW

# AN INTRODUCTION TO JAVASCRIPT

- ⮑ A brief history of Java, JavaScript, VBScript, and JScript
- ⮑ Intended audience and what you should expect
- ⮑ Why you should bother to learn JavaScript
- ⮑ How to organize your work and develop JavaScript-enhanced HTML pages
- ⮑ JavaScript versus Java
- ⮑ Introductory examples

## ⮑ JavaScript in Perspective

This section is devoted to some general remarks about programming languages, interpreters, Java, the Internet, and where JavaScript fits in. If you are anxious to get going, skip it. I use the word Internet to loosely indicate everything that allows communication among computers. These include communication protocols (http, FTP, TCP/IP, etc.), software (servers, browsers, etc.), the hardware (optic fibers, ethernet, etc.), and the Web. The precise meaning of the word Internet should be clear from the context within which it is used.

The Internet has grown exponentially, and is now a widespread communication medium primarily because it offers quick and effective access to a large number of information sources. The communication of this information is effective for at least three important reasons: The medium is largely visual, it allows the user a measure of passivity (something between participating in a discussion and watching TV), and it affords anonymity. Information on the Internet is increasingly presented through *HTML* (Hypertext Markup Language) documents. HTML has its advantages (simplicity, shallow learning curve, and so on), and its disadvantages. One of its major disadvantages is the fact that HTML alone does not make documents particularly interactive. To make HTML pages interactive, authors have had to rely on server-based applications, and creating these is still the domain of professionals. Java, an object-oriented computer language, can remedy these problems.

## A Brief History of Java and JavaScript

In 1990, Sun Microsystems decided to embark on a new project. The fundamental idea was that microchips are already anywhere: They control your refrigerator, microwave oven, conventional oven, toaster, TV, door locks, and so on. This begets a multitude of programs, written for different processors, with no standard in sight. "So," reasoned Sun's officials, "we should build a generalized operating system that will run on all computers, even those that do not exist yet." A team of talented programmers was then assembled, a daughter company, FirstPerson Inc., was created, and the Oak operating system was born. For various reasons, Oak never got off the ground, and in 1994 FirstPerson was dissolved.

Yet, the idea lingered. Instead of designing a consumer-electronic operating system, Sun modified the goal to deal with PCs: to create a programming language that is written for any PC or workstation operating system, and that, when compiled (we'll talk about compilation later), will run on any PC, with the Internet in mind. This is a marked departure from traditional programming languages such as C, C++, FORTRAN, Pascal, or BASIC. In such languages, you write the code (software) for a specific operating system. If you want your software (for example, a word processor) to run on a different operating system, you will have to modify the code substantially, and you will usually lose both some of the standard and familiar user interface in the process, and sleep. Also, writing code to deal with information exchange (among different computers with different operating systems) over the Internet in traditional programming languages is not a trivial task. The goal was to create a new language that would trivialize this task as much as possible.

Oak was modified, facilities to deal with the Internet were added, and by 1995, Java as we know it was born. Java is not an operating system; it is a so-called high-level object-oriented computer language. This means that it allows mortals to write program code in ways that can be relatively easily interpreted on first reading. Wisely enough, Java's designers kept the C++ language syntax; but make no mistake, Java is not C++. Because Java was designed such that programs written in Java would run on any PC or workstation running on any operating system (UNIX, Solaris, Windows 95, MacOS, etc.), it was necessary to create an interface (a layer) between the Java program and the operating system it runs on. The interface itself, would, of course, be operating system–specific. This interface layer is sometimes called an *interpreter*. This idea is shown in Figure 1.1.

"What's the big deal?" you might ask, "after all, interpreted languages such as BASIC are not new!" Take a look at Figure 1.1 again. Interpreters

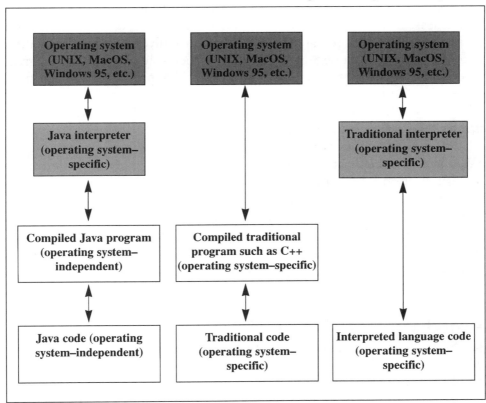

**FIGURE 1.1** The difference between Java and traditional computer languages, and traditional interpreted languages.

for such languages (middle right box) are operating system–specific, but they do not allow you to write code that is independent of the operating system; Java does! This by itself is quite an accomplishment. But the Java designers did not stop there. They integrated a wealth of Internet-specific facilities with the language. For example, you can easily write a Java program that allows information exchange between two computers running any operating systems, using the TCP/IP and FTP protocols (TCP/IP, FTP—it does not matter what they stand for—are a set of rules by which computers talk to each other). You can do this in C++, for example, but I do not recommend it, even if you are highly paid.

Because the designers were developing Java for Internet, they were faced with a challenge: Java-written programs must be robust and safe—robust to avoid system crashes, safe because if you allow others to write programs that you routinely download and run on your computer, you are increasing your vulnerability to viruses and other malicious acts. Details aside, the designers did, at least in theory, make Java extremely safe—"in theory" because after its first release, some researchers at Princeton University found a security hole that allowed an innocent-looking but maliciously written Java program to erase all of the files on a user's hard disk. This problem has been fixed since then. Common sense dictates that sooner or later, another dark mind will poke a hole in Java's security; but as it stands now, Java-written software is safer than software written in other languages.

Java, like any other computer language, takes time and desire to learn. Writing a Java application, although simpler than, for example, writing a C++ application for any operating system, can still be a daunting task—particularly for the uninitiated. To bring the technology closer to the everyday casual user, Java teamed up with Netscape (which at the time was developing its version of Internet scripting language, called LiveScript). Together, they pared down Java, designed an easy interface with HTML documents, and called the product JavaScript. So if you like, you can view JavaScript as a subset of Java.

## What Is JavaScript?

JavaScript is an object-based scripting language. It is used in developing client and server Internet applications. JavaScript programs are embedded in an HTML page; a JavaScript-aware browser interprets the JavaScript code and executes it. JavaScript provides you, the script writer, with compact pre-built tools that enhance interactions between users and an HTML page. These tools allow response to mouse clicks, form input, page navigation, and other events. Responses to user actions can be invoked by JavaScript without network transmissions. This, incidentally, is a major advantage of JavaScript over scripting languages such as *CGI* (Common Gateway Interface): If the user's interactions with your page are processed on the user's computer (as happens with JavaScript), then excess Internet traffic is avoided. With CGI, interactions with the user are processed on the host (server) computer, and must be transmitted, processed, and then transmitted back to the guest computer.

## Visual Basic Scripting Edition (VBScript) and JScript

With the release of Microsoft's Internet Explorer, Version 3.0, in August 1995, a JavaScript-like scripting was provided. VBScript is a subset of the Visual Basic language. It allows linking with Web page objects, including Java applets and other ActiveX controls. VBScript is intended to be fully compatible with Visual Basic and Visual Basic for Applications. Microsoft made the VBScript source code available under license free of cost to browser and application vendors who wish to support VBScript in their applications.

JScript is Microsoft's flavor of JavaScript. It is intended to provide the same functionality as VBScript. At the time of this writing, JavaScript and JScript are not entirely compatible.

## JavaScript vs. Java

Java is a full-fledged object-oriented programming language (we will talk about object-oriented programming later). By "full-fledged programming language" we mean a language that is capable of reading a program code, which resides in a *text file* (also called an *ASCII file*), *compile* and *link* it to create the so-called *executable*. Java is an object-oriented language, and although different, it has syntax that resembles C++.

As with any other programming language, you use a text editor (or perhaps your word processor) to create Java program files. These text files are given the filename extension java. In the program files you assemble a set of statements, *functions*, control structures, and other typical programming constructs that somehow relate to each other in accomplishing a variety of tasks such as word processing tasks. Now any programming language (Java included) provides you with the ability to compile these files into *object files* (in Java, these files are given the filename extension class). The object files are binary files that contain sequences of 0 and 1. The sequential arrangement of the 0s and 1s is such that the computer itself (mainly the central processor, usually called the *CPU*) recognizes as commands to be executed. The object files are then linked together into a single file, the executable file. The user purchases, downloads, borrows, or otherwise obtains the executable, and runs it with operating system–specific commands: by double clicking its name or icon, using the Run dialog box, and so on. The program thus invoked can be as complex as a drawing program, or as simple as a clock.

JavaScript, on the other hand, is a scripting language. You do not create an executable file with scripts. They are usually invoked by software that is already running, and are tailored to be interpreted by that software. The running software may have a module that recognizes script statements and "knows" how to execute them. Such software or software modules are called *interpreters*. They may be stand-alone applications, or part of a large collection of software. For example, Netscape has a JavaScript interpreter that the user can turn on or off. Scripts are rarely compiled and linked to create executable files.

Scripts are very much like macros. A sequence of commands that you type in your spreadsheet, for example, can be named and then executed by invoking the macro name. No compiling and linking is involved, and the macro can run only when your spreadsheet application is running. Be aware, however, that some scripts can be compiled (but not linked into an executable), and even here, the difference between scripts and programs is becoming less distinct with time. In your browser, the JavaScript script is a set of programming constructs that are executed by the browsing program itself.

Table 1.1 summarizes the major differences between JavaScript and Java. Some of the differences will make little sense to you at this time. Most will be clear by the time you are done with this book. To see an example of a Java application in action, visit http://turtle.gis.umn.edu.

Hard-core programmers, especially the arrogant breed, like to make a distinction between scripting (inferior) and programming (superior). So, what is the difference between programming and scripting? Not much. After all, a computer program is a set of instructions designed to make a CPU accomplish some well-defined tasks. These instructions are arranged logically, and allow the programmer to control the flow of execution through repetitions (loops), conditional statements (if-then-else), and so on. This is precisely what characterizes scripts as well. So, from now on, I shall not distinguish between programming and scripting—both terms will be used interchangeably.

**TABLE 1.1**  A comparison of JavaScript and Java.

| JavaScript | Java |
|---|---|
| Interpreted rather than compiled. This means that you do not need a compiler, but you do need an interpreter. | Compiled on server; executed on client. To develop Java applets (or applications), you need a compiler that translates the code you write to machine recognizable instructions. |
| You can create relatively simple applications, and easily interact with HTML documents. You cannot create stand-alone applications. | You can create simple and complex applications. The applications are executed from within the interpreter (Netscape, Hot Java, etc.) or as stand-alone. |
| Object-based and extensible. Neither classes nor inheritance are available. | Object-oriented, with classes and inheritance. |
| Code embedded in HTML, and execution depends on availability of interpreter. | Applets and applications can be independent of HTML documents. |
| JavaScript is a loosely typed language: variables can be used without declaring their data type first. | Variable data types must be declared before their use. |
| Object references are checked at run-time; this is called dynamic binding. | Object references must exist at compile-time; this is called static binding. |
| Because of these attributes, JavaScript is simple to program, but is prone to bugs and errors. | Java is more complicated to work with, but bugs and errors are easier to detect and fix. |

## Why JavaScript?

There are several reasons for using JavaScript scripts in your HTML document. They allow you to do things with your page that are difficult (and sometimes impossible) to accomplish otherwise. In some cases you can use CGI—and sometimes, particularly when you communicate with the server, you will have to—instead of JavaScript, but CGI is hard to learn, and requires additional knowledge of perl, a programming/scripting language.

Suppose you wish to add *buttons* to your HTML document, and attach some actions to them. You may wish to cycle through various possibilities, change the content of your HTML page based on user input (this is sometimes called changing on the fly or changing at run-time), do calculations inside your HTML document, and so on. Some of these tasks require *arrays* (we shall talk about these later), others require *program control structures* (if-then-else; we will talk about these later as well). JavaScript, like any other traditional programming language, provides these facilities. Furthermore, being in its infancy, JavaScript is evolving rapidly; its capabilities are expanding and will (sooner rather than later) exceed those of CGI.

Suppose you wish to build an HTML document that caters to as many users as possible. There are a number of browsers and browser versions currently in use, and they differ in how they interpret HTML code and tags. If you develop your page for one browser, it may not show well in another. You may then wish to display different versions of your HTML document based on the browser that a visitor is using. This means that you need to access information about the browser that is accessing your site, and based on the browser identification, display the appropriate HTML document. This can be done with JavaScript.

Perhaps the best way to see "why JavaScript" is simply to learn it and visit Internet sites that include pages with JavaScript code. You can then download the code, modify it, and insert it in your HTML file. One of the most effective ways to learn programming is to look at other people's code. As you proceed with JavaScript, "why" will become an increasingly irrelevant question.

# What You Should Expect

This book is designed to familiarize you with JavaScript. By the time you are done, you should be able to:

- Read and understand JavaScript code that you care to explore in a *URL* (Universal Resource Locator). This is a good way to learn JavaScript.

- Enliven your HTML page with *scripts* that can produce automatic dating, create frames within a window, create additional windows, and add menus and buttons to your HTML document

- Create forms and queries that interact with visitors to your HTML page.

- Implement computations and drawing within your HTML page.

- Create and implement small applications that enhance interactions with users.

Learning to program and writing programs is like climbing a slippery spiral. You crawl up, and slide back some, and crawl up again. As you crawl up, the same ideas repeat themselves, and every repetition exposes more of the complexities of these ideas. This is the spirit in which this book was written. We will look at examples and discuss issues that may seem unfathomable at first. Later we will come back to these ideas and examine them from a different perspective, and with new levels of complexity. It is important that you encounter the same topics in different contexts. Be patient with yourself.

Throughout, I shall assume that you are familiar with HTML and with how to use your browser. The examples were all developed with Netscape Navigator Version 3.0, and tested with under Windows 95, MacOS, and Solaris operating systems. There are other Internet browsers. Be sure to verify that your particular browser supports JavaScript. Your browser may also implement JavaScript in ways other than Netscape. However, efforts are underway to standardize JavaScript. You can therefore expect your scripts to work across browsers (with minor changes).

Believe it or not, part of the fun of programming is the process of backsliding and then climbing again. If you get regularly frustrated with *bugs*, unclear ideas, and programs that refuse to execute as expected, you will never learn to enjoy the process. When you embark upon a JavaScript project (or any programming project, for that matter), and when faced with self- or otherwise-imposed deadlines, always quadruple the amount of time within which you originally expected to finish the project, and then maybe quadruple it again.

Programming (and writing scripts in JavaScript is as legitimate programming as writing programs in C++ or Java) is a creative process. Some people never considered themselves creative until they started programming.

#  Getting Started

In this section, I shall discuss the hardware and software you will need to be able to write, debug, test, and run JavaScript programs. I shall also suggest a way to formalize the development cycle. If you have already installed whatever is necessary to accomplish these tasks, and if you have developed your own working habits (and you do not wish to change these habits), skip this section.

## What You Need to Develop, Test, and Run JavaScript Programs

Here is a list of hardware and software components you need to be able to proceed.

### Hardware and Operating Systems

You will need a PC or a workstation with an operating system capable of running a JavaScript-aware Internet browser.

If you are using a workstation, any *GUI* (Graphical User Interface) workstation operating system will do. Typical workstations are the Sparcs provided by Sun Microsystems, and workstations of Silicon Graphics, Hewlett Packard, Digital Equipment Corporation, IBM, and a score of other companies. All of these provide GUI-based (usually also UNIX-based) operating systems. Microsoft offers the Windows NT operating system, which runs on most of these workstations.

If you are using a PC, you will have to be a bit more careful. Older PCs (for example, Intel 386 and lower) will not do. You should have a 32-bit operating system for Intel-based computers (for example, Windows 3.1), or a Macintosh capable of running MacOS version 7 or later.

### Software

You should have a JavaScript-aware Internet browser. Two that will work fine are Netscape and Hot Java. Others may or may not work (I have not tested them). Microsoft, in line with its old tradition, is going its own way: using Internet Explorer for a browser, and developing J++ (as a substitute for Java), VBScript (as a substitute for JavaScript), and ActiveX. Much of the JavaScript development was done with Netscape's Navigator Version 3.0; occasionally I shall point to other Internet software for comparison.

Here are some places that will get you to the site where you can download the latest Internet browser for free:

- Netscape's Navigator

    http://www.netscape.com

    http://www.netscape.home.com

- Microsoft's Internet Explorer

    http://www.microsoft.com/ie/

- Sun's Hot Java

http://java.sun.com:80/java.sun.com/HotJava/CurrentRelease/

Of course, you may have a Catch-22 problem here: If you have no browser, how are you to download a browser? For those of you who have FTP (File Transfer Protocol) software, you may use it to download the appropriate Internet browser. Most mail programs provide FTP capabilities. To download the appropriate browser, you need to log into one of the sites in Table 1.2. You normally do that by issuing the command:

```
ftp ftp-site
```

where *ftp-site* is one of the sites in Table 1.2. Next, in response to the request for your login name, answer

```
anonymous
```

You will then be asked to enter your e-mail address as a password. Once logged into the site, change to the appropriate directory by issuing the command

```
cd directory
```

where *directory* stands for the appropriate directory in Table 1.2. Once in the appropriate directory, download the file you need by issuing the command

```
get filename
```

where *filename* is the filename (usually with extension exe or zip) that contains the browser you need. Most of these sites have README or INDEX text files that contain information about files in the site and their contents.

I know that the instructions are incomplete; but things change so quickly around the Internet that it will be worth your while to find the exact way of doing things on your own. Learning to deal with the Internet is not learning facts, it is learning to deal with ever-changing facts.

Here is an example of an FTP session downloading HotJava for Solaris from Sun's FTP site. Boldface type is what you type; italics indicate variable information that depends on your particular situation. The rest is the machine's prompts:

```
$ ftp ftp.javasoft.com
Name (ftp.javasoft.com): anonymous
```

```
331 Guest login ok, send your complete e-mail address as password.
Password: user@machine
<< informational messages >>
ftp> binary
200 Type set to I.
ftp> cd pub
250 CWD command successful.
ftp> get hotjava-1_0prebeta1-solaris2-sparc.tar.Z
ftp> quit
```

**TABLE 1.2**  FTP sites to download Internet browsers.

| Browser | FTP Site | Directory |
|---|---|---|
| Netscape in: | | |
| USA | ftp7.netscape.com | |
| Japan | ftp.leo.chubu.ac.jp | /pub/WWW/netscape |
| Hong Kong | ftp.sunsite.ust.hk | /pub/WWW/netscape |
| Israel | ftp.sunsite.huji.ac.il | /Netscape |
| Australia | ftp.adelaide.edu.au | /pub/WWW/Netscape |
| United Kingdom | ftp.sunsite.doc.ic.ac.uk | /computing/information-systems/www/Netscape |
| Germany | ftp.informatik.rwth-aachen.de | /pub/mirror/ftp.netscape/com |
| USA | ftp.wuarchive.wustl.edu | /packages/www/Netscape |
| USA | ftp.sunsite.unc.edu (USA) | /packages/infosystems/WWW/clients/Netscape |
| HotJava | ftp.javasoft.com | /pub |

## Setting Up for Work

As I said, writing programs in general, and JavaScript in particular, is an iterative spiraling process. You write some code, check to see that it does what you want, debug, rewrite, and so on. Often you need to go through this cycle many times until you achieve a desired result. Here is one suggestion on how to organize your work in the Windows 95 environment:

1. Verify that your particular browser supports JavaScript. For example, in Netscape 3.0, enable JavaScript by clicking on the Options |

`Network Preferences...` menu. When the Preferences dialog shows up, click on the Languages tab and check the `Enable JavaScript` checkbox.

2. Start your browser, and set its window to a size that fits your needs.

3. Start your favorite word processor or text editor. This is where you write the code. Some word processors and Internet browsers provide facilities that help develop HTML pages. In such environments you are relieved of some of the chores of coding an HTML page.

4. Type in the HTML code and save the file. Make sure that the file is saved as a text file.

5. Switch to your browser, and load the HTML page. If it is already loaded, reload it. In Netscape, you load the file using the `File | Open File in Browser...` menu.

6. Did you achieve the desired result? If not, you have just slid down the spiral. Start climbing again.

A word about using a text editor: You can use any editor, as long as it saves your file in an ASCII or "text" format. JavaScript is a programming language, and as we shall see later, careful organization of the code through use of things like braces, indentations, and line breaks, will go a long way towards simplifying your programs, avoiding bugs, and debugging. If you have programmed in the past, you are probably aware of the various editors that are available for other languages in the so-called integrated development environment (to make life hard, computer buffs call this IDE). Such programs usually will organize your code as much as possible. If you anticipate using JavaScript (or other programming languages) extensively, I recommend that you use such an IDE.

Now that we have disposed of some preliminaries, let us move on to our first example.

# The "Hello World" Example

To get you started, here is a first JavaScript example. In the programming world, you usually start by writing a simple (and sometimes very complex) program that prints "Hello World" somewhere (the "somewhere" is what often makes the difference between complex and simple programs). So let us start with "Hello World" as shown in Listing 1.1. As you go through the code, do not worry if you do not "understand" something. Just be patient with yourself. Many novices think of themselves as fools if they cannot decipher code on first reading. Remember, it is a language, and languages take time and practice to learn. You would surely not feel stupid if you know no French, ask a Frenchman for directions to the Eiffel Tower, and the person answers in melodious French. Why should you expect to know what code means at first reading?

This example is designed to show you where, in the HTML page, JavaScript fits, and how to fit it in there, and to give you a first look at functions and built-in functions. Do not worry if you do not fully know what is going on; we shall get back to these ideas time and again (remember the slippery spiral metaphor?). Just follow the instructions given below.

**EXERCISE 1.1** "HELLO WORLD."

1. Start your favorite word processor or text editor.

2. Type the code shown in Listing 1.1, *without the line numbers*, and save it as L1-1.HTML (in Windows 95, MacOS, or UNIX), or L1-1.HTM (in Windows 3.1), or any other name of your choice. Remember that all listings can also be found on the accompanying CD; so instead of typing the code, you can simply copy and paste.

3. Start your browser. Be sure that it recognizes JavaScript code. To see that it does, check Options | Network preferences... and in Languages, check Enable JavaScript.

4. Load L1-1 to your browser. In Netscape's Navigator, use the File | Open File in Browser. . . .

5. Do you see Figure 1.2 in your browser window? If not, go back to step 2, correct the code, and try again.

**LISTING 1.1** "Hello World."

```
1    <HTML>
2    <HEAD>
3    <TITLE>
4        Hello World Example
5    </TITLE>
6    </HEAD>
7    <H1> Hello World Example </H1>
8    <BODY>
```

```
 9    <BR>
10    <BR>
11       Here you may put your usual HTML stuff.
12    <BR>
13    <BR>
14    <SCRIPT LANGUAGE = "JavaScript">
15       <!- This is HTML comment; it hides code from old browsers
16       //and this is JavaScript comment
17       document.write("From JavaScript: Hello World!") //inline
      JavaScript comment
18    //stop hiding JavaScript code->
19    </SCRIPT>
20    <BR>
21    <BR>
22       Here you may put more HTML stuff.
23    </BODY>
24    </HTML>
```

Note that line 17 in the HTML file spans two lines in Listing 1.1. That is why the line following line 17 is not numbered. In short, a line that is not

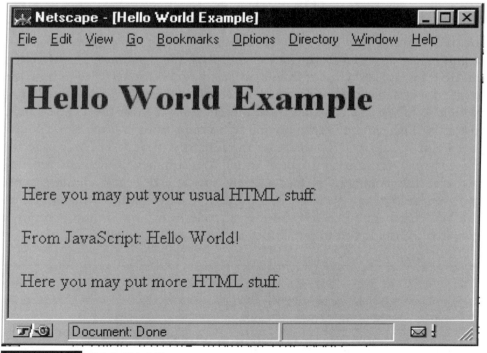

**FIGURE 1.2**   "Hello World."

numbered is a continuation of the preceding line and should appear on the same line with the preceding line in the HTML code file. And now for the analysis of Listing 1.1.

## Analysis of the "Hello World" Example

To begin with, you may ask: "Why should I go through the pain of writing this silly program? After all, I can just type 'Hello World' in the <BODY> of my HTML page—instead of these unfamiliar and complicated constructs—and obtain the same result." True, you could do that. But could you open another window and write "Hello World" to it, without creating a different HTML page and asking the user to open it? How about querying the user for her name, and then saying Hello name where name stands for any name the user entered? You will see how to accomplish these tasks later.

### The <SCRIPT> Tag

The code up to the <SCRIPT> tag (line 14) should be familiar to you—it is standard HTML. When the browser sees the <SCRIPT> tag it knows that from here on, some code must be interpreted as JavaScript. This interpretation will revert back to HTML when the browser application meets the </SCRIPT> tag (line 19). As with other HTML tags, you can use lowercase for the tag, but this is not recommended. Following the tag, line 15 is the beginning of an HTML comment. You place this comment line after the <SCRIPT> tag, and close it in line 18, just before </SCRIPT>, to hide the JavaScript code. Some browsers (or old versions of existing browsers) do not recognize JavaScript code, and will therefore print it on the HTML page just as is. This can be very annoying to a visitor using a browser without a JavaScript interpreter. To maintain the integrity of your HTML page for these visitors, enclose the script in an HTML comment; but again, remember that the comment is enclosed by the SCRIPT tag. Because most browsers recognize JavaScript by now, and to save space, I will not use an HTML comment to enclose JavaScript code from now on. So here are a couple of rules for you to remember:

Include JavaScript in your code by using the <SCRIPT>. . . </SCRIPT> tag or by including event handlers.

Hide the JavaScript code in your HTML document by enclosing it in a HTML comment, or use the <NONSCRIPT> tag.

## The <NOSCRIPT> Tag

The <NOSCRIPT> tag is similar to the <NOFRAMES> tag for frames. HTML text within the tag is displayed by a non-JavaScript browser, while code enclosed within the tag is hidden and ignored by Navigator. This tag is used to specify alternate content for browsers that do not support JavaScript, or in case the user has disabled JavaScript in `Options | Network prefer-ences...` in Netscape's Navigator. Instead of using the JavaScript code–hiding approach using HTML comments (as in lines 15 and 18 in Listing 1.1), we can use the approach in Listing 1.2. To examine the effect of the <NOSCRIPT> tag, do Exercise 1.2.

**EXERCISE 1.2** "HELLO WORLD" WITH THE `<NOSCRIPT>` TAG.

1. Start your favorite word processor or text editor.

2. Type the code shown in Listing 1.2, *without the line numbers*, and save it as `L1-2.HTML` (in Windows 95, MacOS, or UNIX), or `L1-2.HTM` (in Windows 3.1), or any other name of your choice. Remember that all listings can also be found on the accompanying CD; instead of typing the code, you can simply copy and paste.

3. Start your browser. Be sure that it recognizes JavaScript code. To see that it does, check `Options | Network preferences...` and in `Languages`, check `Enable JavaScript`.

4. Load L1-2 to your browser. In Netscape's Navigator, use the `File | Open File in Browser. . . .`

5. Do you see Figure 1.3? If not, go back to step 2, correct the code, and try again.

**LISTING 1.2** "Hello World" with the `<NOSCRIPT>` tag.

```
1    <HTML>
2    <HEAD>
3    <TITLE>
4    Hello World Example
5    </TITLE>
6    </HEAD>
7    <H1> Hello World Example </H1>
8    <BODY>
9    <BR>
10   <BR>
11   Here you may put your usual HTML stuff.
12   <BR>
13   <BR>
14   <SCRIPT LANGUAGE = "JavaScript">
```

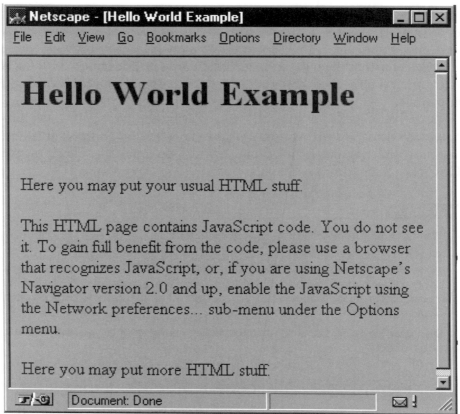

**FIGURE 1.3** "Hello World" with the <NOSCRIPT> tag.

```
15    <!- This is HTML comment; it hides code from old browsers
16    //and this is JavaScript comment
17    document.write("From JavaScript: Hello World!") //inline
      JavaScript comment
18    //stop hiding JavaScript code->
19    </SCRIPT>
20    <NOSCRIPT>
21    This HTML page contains JavaScript code. You do not see it. To
      gain full benefit from the code, please use a browser that rec-
      ognizes JavaScript, or, if you are using Netscape's Navigator
      version 2.0 and up, enable the JavaScript using the Network
      preferences... sub-menu under the Options menu.
22    </NOSCRIPT>
23    <BR>
24    <BR>
25    Here you may put more HTML stuff.
26    </BODY>
27    </HTML>
```

Personally, I prefer the <NOSCRIPT> approach I use an editor that colors HTML keywords, literals, strings and so on (we'll talk about literals, strings, and so on later); with the HTML comment approach I lose this programming aid, and wind up with more bugs than necessary. Now back to Listing 1.1.

### The LANGUAGE Keyword

With the `<SCRIPT>` tag (line 14) you need to specify what scripting language you are using. Already some browsers include interpreters for other scripting languages. Microsoft, for example, encourages the use of VBScript and JScript. So, enter `LANGUAGE = "JavaScript"`.

### Comments in JavaScript Code

Next, notice the double slashes (//) in lines 16 and 17 of Listing 1.1. Double slashes in JavaScript tells the interpreter, "everything to the right and to the end of the line is a comment; ignore it!" As line 16 shows, you can insert // at the beginning of the line, and thus the whole line is considered a JavaScript comment; line 17 shows that you can also insert // anywhere within a line, and thus the remainder of the line to the right of // is considered a JavaScript comment. To extend comments over two or more lines, you will have to start each line with //. Or better yet, if you wish to comment a block of contiguous lines, you can use the forward-slash-star star-forward-slash pair like this:

```
/* everything from forward-slash-star to
star-forward-slash is a JavaScript comment,
regardless of how many lines it extends over */
```

// indicates a JavaScript comment: Everything to the right up to the end of the line is ignored.

/*...*/ is a JavaScript comment: Everything between the slash-star and the star-slash is ignored, regardless of how many lines it spans.

### The document.write Function

The `document.write("Hello World!")` code in line 17 of Listing 1.1 is recognized by the browser as a built-in JavaScript *function* (a collection of statements that perform some well-defined task). It is recognized as such because `document.write` is followed by ( ) with something inside the parenthesis—

here, the string `"From JavaScript: Hello World!"`. By a *string* we mean a sequence of characters (including punctuation marks and spaces) that we want the JavaScript interpreter to recognize as is. The value inside the parenthesis is called a parameter or argument, and it can change. Whatever string you put inside the parenthesis will be shown on the HTML page.

"What does this peculiar `document.write` notation in line 17 of Listing 1.1 mean? Why the dot between `document` and `write`? Did you miss the space after the period?" you might ask. Good questions! This is crucial to know, and we will discuss it in due time. For now, suffice it to say that the dot tells whoever needs to know that `write` belongs to `document`; and that the sooner you get used to the jargon the better. Remember, you do not have to get to the bottom of things the first time you see them; just hold your horses.

## Embedding a String Within a String

Once you start using JavaScript regularly, you will quickly realize that much of your time in developing scripts is spent manipulating strings of characters. This is particularly true when you communicate with your HTML page visitor. To get you started on strings, do Exercise 1.3 and see what happens. Exercise 1.3 is designed to teach you some fundamental string manipulation tricks. Be sure to run the various parts of the exercise and examine differences among the resulting HTML pages.

**EXERCISE 1.3**　STRING WITH A STRING.

1. Start your favorite word processor or text editor.
2. Change line 17 in Listing 1.1 to read:

   ```
   document.write("Goodbye " + '<BR>"World!"')
   ```

   and save the file.
3. Start your browser. Be sure that it recognizes JavaScript code.
4. Load the file to your browser and study the output.
5. Repeat steps 2–4 for the following:

   ```
   document.write("Goodbye " + '<BR>"World!"')
   document.write("Goodbye " + "<BR>\"World!\"")
   ```

We want "World" to appear in quotes, but we must provide it within a string as an argument to the write function: thus we have to embed quotes within quotes. As Exercise 1.3 demonstrates, you can do that in two ways.

To embed a quotation mark inside a quotation use ' ' when the string is quoted with " ", or " " when the string is quoted with ' '.

You can instead use \" for embedded quotes. See Exercise 1.3.

#  "Hello World" Example with a Button and an Alert Window

To whet your appetite some more, let us take a look at a slightly more elaborate example. Here, I want to demonstrate how easy it is to communicate with your visitor using JavaScript. Follow the instructions in Exercise 1.4. We shall discuss the code momentarily.

**EXERCISE 1.4** "HELLO WORLD" WITH A BUTTON AND AN ALERT WINDOW.

1. Start your favorite word processor or text editor.
2. Type the code shown in Listing 1.3, without the line numbers, and save it under a filename of your choice (with the extension HTML; or HTML if you are using Windows 3.1).
3. Start your browser. Be sure that it recognizes JavaScript code.
4. Load the file to your browser.
5. Click on the Click here... button. Do you see Figure 1.4? If not, go back to step 2 and correct the code.

**LISTING 1.3** "Hello World" with a button and an alert window.

```
1    <HTML>
2    <HEAD>
3    <H3> A Button and an Alert Window </H3>
4    </HEAD>
5    <BODY>
6    <FORM>
7    <INPUT TYPE = "button"
8           NAME = "helloButton"
9           VALUE = "Click here..."
10          onClick = "alert('From JavaScript through a button and
     an alert window:\r\rHello world')">
11   </FORM>
12   </BODY>
13   </HTML>
```

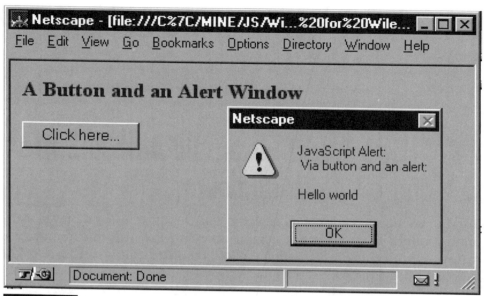

**FIGURE 1.4** "Hello World" with a button and an alert window.

## Analysis of the "Hello World" Example with a Button and an Alert Window

Lines 1 through 6 should be familiar to you; lines 7–9 maybe. The code INPUT TYPE = "button" in line 7 creates a button in your HTML document. The code NAME = "helloButton" in line 8 assigns a name to the button, while VALUE = "Click here..." in line 9 defines the text that appears in the button. If you have never used JavaScript, line 10 needs some explanation.

*Objects*—such as buttons, text entry boxes, pop-up lists, and menus—that you create in JavaScript (in our example a button) normally have actions associated with them. These actions are triggered by *events*: The user clicks on the object, enters text in a text box, checks an items in a checkbox, clicks a radio button, and so on. The actions themselves are called *event handlers* and you, the programmer, must write JavaScript code that reacts to these user inputs. Thus, in line 10 of Listing 1.3, the Click event occurs when the user clicks on the Click here... button. The "alert(...)" part of the statement handles the event itself through the onClick event handler. It calls a built-in JavaScript function, alert(), with a string that you send as an argument to the function. We shall talk about all of these things in more details in due time.

As you can see, using the built-in capabilities of JavaScript allows you to minimize the amount of code that you need to write, and provides quick access to user interface modules. It is important to realize that although the use of JavaScript in this listing is not explicit, the statement in lines 7 to 10 is recognized as JavaScript and is executed by the JavaScript interpreter.

Now that we have looked at a couple of examples, you should be starting to develop a feel for JavaScript and how to use it. So let me explain where JavaScript code fits into an HTML page. Note that I use the word "page" to specify an HTML file that is loaded into your browser. This is sometimes called an HTML "document," but document is an object in JavaScript, which can cause confusion. So just remember that when I say "HTML page" I mean an HTML file that you normally load onto your browser.

# How to Use JavaScript in an HTML Page

There are two ways to embed JavaScript code in an HTML document:

- As event handlers, using HTML tags

- As code enclosed in the SCRIPT tag

The first case is demonstrated in Listing 1.3. The event handler is shown in line 10 of Listing 1.3. The event handler simply tells the JavaScript interpreter what you wish it to do in reaction to an event.

The second way of incorporating JavaScript code in an HTML page is shown in Listing 1.1. In particular, note the following in Listing 1.1:

- The script section begins with `<SCRIPT>` and of course ends with `</SCRIPT>`.

- The `<SCRIPT>` section does not have to be included in the `<BODY>` section. There are some rules to observe here, and we shall discuss them later. When the script appears in the `<BODY>`, then (unless it is a *function* definition) it is executed by the interpreter as it is loaded into memory, and the results of the execution are placed exactly where the script is in the HTML page. We shall talk about functions and definitions in due time.

- The `document.write(...)` statement in line 17 of Listing 1.1 does the work for us. In particular, note the parenthesis, the text inside the parenthesis, and the fact that it is enclosed with quotation marks.

- Because the code is enclosed within the `<SCRIPT>` tag, the browser knows what to do with `document.write(...)`—it recognizes this as a function to be executed, and will look for it in its known repertoire of JavaScript functions.

# ↳ The "Last Modified" Example

The last in this sequence of examples may be useful to you. The "Hello World" example achieved the status of folklore in the programming world; the so-called "Last Modified" example in JavaScript is rapidly achieving such status.

Often you may be interested in providing yourself and the reader of your Internet page with information about the last time that the page was modified—that is, the last time the HTML file was saved on the system where it resides. When a computer file is saved, all operating systems (UNIX, Windows 95, MacOS, etc.) stamp the file with the date and time. This information is often important, and can be retrieved in one way or another. Exercise 1.5 shows how to include this information in your HTML page.

**EXERCISE 1.5**  LAST MODIFIED.

1. Start your favorite word processor or text editor.
2. Type the code in Listing 1.4 and save it as an HTML file.
3. Start your browser. Be sure that it recognizes JavaScript code.
4. Load the HTML file that you created in step 2.
5. Do you get something like Figure 1.5?

**LISTING 1.4**  Last Modified.

```
1    <HTML>
2    <HEAD>
3    <TITLE>
4    Last Modified Example
```

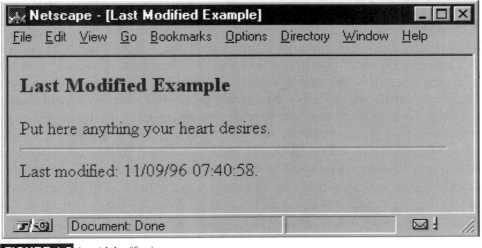

**FIGURE 1.5** Last Modified.

```
5    </TITLE>
6    </HEAD>
7    <H3> Last Modified Example </H3>
8    <BODY>
9    Put here anything your heart desires.
10   </BODY>
11   <HR>
12   <SCRIPT LANGUAGE = "JavaScript">
13      document.write("Last modified: " +
14      document.lastModified + ".")
15   </SCRIPT>
16   </HTML>
```

## Analysis of the "Last Modified" Example

There is nothing new from line 1 down to the <SCRIPT> tag in line 12 of Listing 1.4. What is new is the statement in lines 13 and 14.

This is somewhat more complex than the "Hello World" string in Listing 1.1, so let us parse it. Remember that functions are recognized as such by the *function-name* followed by (), with or without argument(s) inside the parenthesis. The function-name may be built in, in which case the browser will automatically execute whatever that function is telling it to do. If it is not built in, you will have to supply it (the function)—we shall see how later. By now you should recognize document.write(...) as a built-in function that simply writes whatever is inside the parenthesis to the HTML page on which it appears.

## String Addition and the lastModified Property

"What does this weird sequence of quotations and + signs in lines 13 and 14 of Listing 1.4 mean?" you might ask. You have seen how to include a string as an argument to a function in Listing 1.1 (line 17). Here we are constructing a new string, using the + sign and a property of the document called `lastModified`. It turns out that JavaScript concatenates (pastes together in sequence) strings separated by the + sign. When JavaScript sees a + sign placed between two strings, it simply takes the second string and appends it to the first. As you can imagine, you cannot use the inverse of addition (subtraction) with strings, as it has no meaning. A space (the so-called blank character) inside a string is just another character. Thus, in JavaScript `"this"` + `"That"` will result in `thisThat`, while `"this "` + `"That"`, or `"this"` + `" That"` will evaluate to `this That`. The last two results are what you usually want; so do not forget the space character.

The `lastModified` part of the statement in Listing 1.4, line 14 is a *property* of the document. We shall discuss properties and documents more formally later. For now, just realize that a property is a kind of a variable—in this case, one in which the date that the file that contains the document was last saved is stored. This property is an integral part of the data that identify a document, and is recognized by the document as such.

I want to say a few introduction words about properties, variables, and assignments. If you are not an experienced programmer, understanding these concepts will help you understand and debug your own code later. If you are an experienced programmer, you may wish to skip the rest of this chapter.

### A First Encounter with Properties, Variables, and Assignments

We say a property is a kind of a variable because every time you save the document, a new date and time will be stored in the `lastModified` property of the document. Do not let this wording confuse you. You will recognize, for example, the statement x = 5. This means that you assign the value 5 to the variable x. You can later assign the value 10 to x. In JavaScript (and other programming and scripting languages) you can also assign a string to a variable. Thus, you can say x = "Hello there". Next time you use x, you will be using the value that was last stored in it, whether it is 5 or `Hello there`. Among other things, this saves a lot of typing.

What are we really saying when we write x = 5 in a computer program? Essentially, we are reserving a physical location somewhere in the computer memory and we are calling this location x. It is important to realize that we give the location an address, named x. The physical location of the address can contain almost any data that we care to put there. Now, when we write x = 5 we are telling the CPU: "Go to the physical location whose address is labeled x, and put the number 5 in there." Incidentally, x = 5 is called an *expression*, and the = sign is an *assignment*: 5 is assigned to x. Note we can also say that the expression evaluates to 5 (an expression must always evaluate to something).

If we subsequently say y = x, we store 5 in the physical memory location whose address is denoted by y. We may next write x = 10, which tells the CPU to go to the physical memory location whose address is labeled x, and overwrite whatever value that is there with the value 10. Note that we have said nothing about y now, so the value of y remains 5. The addresses labeled x and y are called variables in the programming jargon; they hold values. Just to tantalize you, let us point out that x (the address label) itself must be somewhere in the computer's physical memory, so x itself has an address that somehow must be labeled, and so on.

Now JavaScript (and other programming languages) can, in addition to numbers, store strings in a block of memory locations. For example, we may write x = "how are you doing?", then write y = x, and then print y. The printed text will say how are you doing?. If you realize that document.lastModified in Listing 1.4 plays the role of x in this example, you not only have the hang of it, you have also gone a long way toward becoming a programmer.

## Why 5 + 10 = 15 While "5" + 10 = 510

One more thing: The result of x = 5 + 10 is 15, while the result of x = "5" + "10" is 510. Why? Because in the first case, 5 and 10 are recognized as numbers (integers, to be more precise); in the second, they are recognized as strings (sequences of characters). Actually, JavaScript is a forgiving language: It sometimes tries to figure out what you mean. For example, if you say x = 5 + "10", you will get 510 again (but we shall talk about this later).

The upshot of all this is that the statement in lines 13–14 of Listing 1.4 constructs part of the HTML page shown in Figure 1.5 by concatenating three strings. The first and last strings are constants (sometimes called *literals*), and the middle string is a value stored in the variable lastModified, which the JavaScript interpreter (part of your browser) provides you with.

# PROGRAMMING IN JAVASCRIPT

- How to write well-structured programs
- How to define and call functions in your JavaScript code
- Events and event handlers
- Interfacing with your home page visitor
- Dealing with arrays and strings

Now that I have made some general remarks and you have seen a few examples, you need to learn how to program in JavaScript. In this chapter we shall discuss the important features of JavaScript, and the various facilities that it provides. In reading this chapter, remember that a computer program of any kind does nothing more (and nothing less) than manipulating data and displaying it. JavaScript goes a long way in helping you, the programmer, to accomplish this task.

##  Programming Discipline

Before we start, a few words about programming discipline. Experienced programmers settle on their own style; but take a look at their code, and you will realize that regardless of styles, the code is well organized, with indentations, comments, and so on. The sooner you develop a consistent and clear style of programming, the faster you learn to work with JavaScript and avoid repeated (and often frustrating) bugs. Here are some important tips to remember:

- Comment your code profusely, but keep the comments concise and self-explanatory. As you develop your programming skills, you will be writing code with ever-increasing complexity. Do not worry about what people think about your program; you are inserting comments for yourself. When inserting comments in your code, assume that they are intended for somebody who sees the program for the first time, and tries to figure out what it does (that's you in a few weeks after writing the code).

- Indent blocks of code. We shall talk about statements and nested statements later. For now, just remember that as you compound statements, use indentation levels to give you a clue about the structure of your program. For example, when you write a function or a loop, be sure to clearly identify where it begins and where it ends. Keep the different levels of indentation consistent.

- Use spaces abundantly. For example, always write x = y, not x=y. This will make your code more readable, and you will catch syntax errors more easily.

- Some programmers isolate the opening and closing braces of statements on separate lines. Others like to put the opening braces at the end of the line that opens a block of code. Whichever way you choose, be consistent, and always indent the code between the opening and closing braces.

- If a single statement spans more than one line of code, indent the lines following the first line more than once. This will cue you to the fact that the next line is a continuation of the present line.

- Christen variables (placeholders for values) with names that give you a clue about what they do. Because variable names cannot include spaces, you can separate words in a variable name by using an underscore, or by starting successive words with uppercase letters (for example, `firstVariable` or `first_variable`). Do the same with functions.

To reemphasize:

As you read the examples throughout, pay attention to the programming style, and see how it fits (or does not fit) with these suggestions. I will stick

Comment your code profusely.

Indent nested statements.

Be consistent with braces.

Use spaces abundantly.

Give variables and functions meaningful names.

with these suggestions for a short while, and then abandon them, in order to save trees.

#  Function Definitions and Calls

Functions are blocks of code that are designed to accomplish specific tasks. It is important to realize that the `<SCRIPT>` tag tells the browser to evaluate the script delimited by the tag after the entire HTML page is loaded. Before you call a function, you must define it. Defining a function means giving it a name, and a code that determines what the function is supposed to do. Calling a function means telling the function to execute its code. Contrary to intuition, you can actually define and call a function at the same time. This leads to the so-called recursive functions.

A function is recognized as such by the fact that its name is followed by ( ). Inside the parenthesis, you may include one or more variables or constants. These are called function *arguments*, and serve as a way to pass data to the function. We shall see numerous examples, and these ideas will become clear as we proceed. But to get you started, let us look at an example. As you go through the examples, go back to the programming discipline suggestions and see how they are implemented in the code.

**EXERCISE 2.1**    FUNCTION CALL WITH ARGUMENT AND RETURN VALUE.

1. Start your favorite word processor or text editor.
2. Type the code in Listing 2.1 and save it as an HTML file. Do not type the line numbers.
3. Start your browser. Be sure that it recognizes JavaScript code.
4. Load the file created in step 2.
5. Do you get something like Figure 2.1?

**LISTING 2.1** Function call with argument and return value.

```
1    <HTML>
2    <HEAD>
3    <TITLE>Area of a Circle</TITLE>
4    <SCRIPT LANGUAGE = "JavaScript">
5    <!- Hide the code from browsers that
6    // do not recognize JavaScript
7    //
8    //Calculate area of a circle
9    //Arguments:
10   //   radius  - the radius of the circle
11   //Return value:
12   //   the area of the circle
13   function cArea(radius)
14   {
15      document.write("radius = ", radius,"<BR>")
16      return (Math.PI * radius * radius)
17   }
18   // we are done hiding the script  ->
19   </SCRIPT>
20   </HEAD>
21   <BODY>
22   <H3>Area of a Circle</H3>
23   <SCRIPT LANGUAGE = "JavaScript">
24   document.write("area = ",cArea(2.5),".")
25   </SCRIPT>
26   </BODY>
27   <HTML>
```

## Analysis of Listing 2.1

Here is how to interpret the code in Listing 2.1:

- We indicate that the JavaScript code begins in line 4 with the tag `<SCRIPT LANGUAGE = "JavaScript">`

- As shown in line 19, we tell the browser that we are done with JavaScript code with `</SCRIPT>`.

- Everything between these two tags is interpreted as JavaScript code, not as HTML code. If a user's browser does not recognize JavaScript, then the `<SCRIPT>` tag is ignored, and the JavaScript code will appear on the HTML page as if it were HTML text—not a pleasing experience to a visitor of your page.

- To avoid such a problem, Line 5 in Listing 2.1 begins an HTML comment. It is used to hide the JavaScript code from browsers that do not recognize it. So we close the comment just before closing the JavaScript code with `</SCRIPT>` (line 18).

- Lines 8–12 tell what the function does, what arguments it takes, and what value (if any) it returns. Not all functions return values; and some functions take no arguments, while others take more than one argument.

- Lines 13 to 17 constitute the function definition—the code that dictates what the function actually does.

- In lines 23 to 25 we put another JavaScript section (this time not commenting it out), including a call to the built-in function `document.write()`.

Let us see what the function does, and how. We start with a short comment about what the function is intended to accomplish (line 8). Next, we comment about the function's arguments, and about the function's return value, if any. Line 13 starts the function definition. Whenever you define a function, you must follow this syntax:

```
function name ([arg1, arg2, ..., argN])
{
    [statements]
}
```

The function definition syntax requires the keyword `function`. Next comes a function name of your choice (`cArea` in this example), followed by parenthesis. In the parenthesis you include zero or more arguments. You start the function body with { and end it with }. Inside the braces you code whatever it is you want the function to do.

Now back to Listing 2.1. In line 13 we name the function `cArea` (for circle area) and tell it to expect a call with one argument, the circle's `radius`. We want to display the value for the radius that the function "sees," and so in line 15 we call `document.write()` (we'll talk about this peculiar notation more later). This is a good debugging technique; remember it! Often you will write functions and send values as argument to these function. What the function actually sees may be different from what you think it should see. This is a common *run-time* error that is difficult to decipher. Run-time errors are errors that occur during the program execution. They are different from *syntax errors*, which occur when the interpreter tries to interpret your JavaScript code.

In the return statement in line 16 we calculate the circle's area. The syntax Math.PI means that PI (a constant known to JavaScript) is a property of the object Math (we will talk more about objects and properties later).

In the second JavaScript section of our program (lines 23 to 25) we call document.write() again (line 24), but this time we call cArea() from inside document.write(). Note that the call is cArea(2.5). This means that when cArea() starts to execute, it assigns 2.5 to its argument radius. It is important to understand what gets executed when. Recall that functions are loaded to memory and are not executed until called. So by the time you call cArea() in line 24, the interpreter knows what to do with the call, because the function has already been defined. Because document.write() is a built-in function, it is executed as soon as the interpreter encounters.

All of this can be confusing, but the sooner you get used to the language the better. So let us go through line 24 one more time:

- We call the function document.write(). This function writes to the HTML page in which it appears whatever is inside the parentheses.

- In parentheses, we write
  ```
  "area = ",cArea(2.5),"."
  ```

- This means that we send to document.write() three arguments: "area = ", then cArea(2.5), and finally ".".

- Now it so happens that a call to a function as an argument to another function—in our case cArea() is an argument to document.write()—is executed first. In other words, cArea() is executed, and the value that it returns (the circle area) becomes the second argument to document.write(). Note that because cArea is defined with a single argument, radius (line 13 in Listing 2.1), the call cArea (2.5) is interpreted as "execute the function cArea with radius=2.5".

- Finally, we add a period at the end (as a string).

- document.write() then constructs a single string from these three arguments and displays it on the screen, as shown in Figure 2.1.

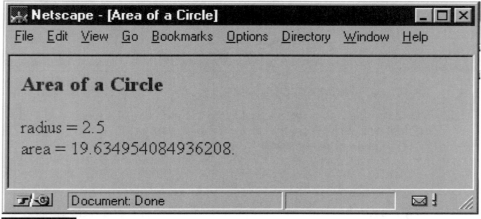

**FIGURE 2.1** Function call with argument and return value.

The HTML code in Listing 2.1 should be familiar to you. A few more comments about Listing 2.1:

- First, note that we put the function definition in the `<HEAD>` section of the document. This ensures that the function is loaded to memory first, and the interpreter will know what to do with it when it sees a call to it.

- Second, note the indentation inside the function definition. This isolates the code inside the function and allows us to understand the code more readily. Indentation is not required by the JavaScript language, but it is good programming practice.

- Third, `cArea` knows what the value of `radius` is when it calculates the circle area (on line 15) because it is an argument whose value we have passed to the function.

Some rules to remember when writing functions:

1. Make your function definitions as general as possible; this will allow you to reuse them.
2. Have a function accomplish one specific task; if you need to accomplish a few tasks in a function, break the function into different functions, and have them call each other.
3. Define functions in the HEAD portion of the document.

To gain some more experience with using functions, go through Exercise 2.2.

---

**EXERCISE 2.2** | FUNCTIONS FOR THE AREA OF A SQUARE AND THE VOLUME OF A SPHERE.

1. Start your favorite word processor or text editor.
2. Modify the code in Listing 2.1 to calculate the area of (i) a square, and (ii) the volume of a sphere. Recall that the volume of a sphere is

$$\frac{4}{3}\pi r^3$$

where *r* is the sphere's radius.
3. Display the result of the function calls from the `<BODY>` of the document, not from its `<HEAD>`.
4. Run the scripts and see what you get (running a script means loading the HTML file that contains it to memory).

---

# Events and Event Handlers

One of the greatest incentives to use JavaScript is the fact that it allows you to easily react to a user's actions in your HTML document without having to communicate with the server. Keep in mind that:

- Events occur in reaction to some user action, such as a click on a button, a move from one text entry field to another, moving the browser's window to the desktop background, and so on.

- Event handlers call scripts (usually functions) that are executed in reaction to an event.

- The JavaScript interpreter recognizes a specific set of events.

- You implement event handlers in a document as attributes of HTML tags, usually as calls to event handler functions.

These distinctions among events, event handlers, and actions that are executed as a reaction to events can be confusing. To clarify these ideas and lodge the distinctions in your mind, take a look at Figure 2.2:

- An event occurs (top box) due to user action or other Navigator activities such as loading or unloading a document or an image, clicking on a button, checking a checkbox, and so on.

- This triggers an event handler; event handler names usually start with on, as in `onClick, onAbort, onLoad,` and so on.
- The event handler triggers a JavaScript code that you write.

In some cases, event handlers are associated with objects that react to user actions. Here, the sequence of links in Figure 2.2 is represented in an HTML document this way:

```
<INPUT TYPE = "inputType" ... onEvent = "someFunction(arguments)">
```

where:

- *inputType* is the type of input object, such as a button, checkbox, radio button, or selection list.
- *onEvent* is one of the events recognized by *inputType*.
- *someFunction(arguments)* is the function that is triggered by the event handler.

In other cases event handlers are associated with the browser's actions, such as loading a document or an image, moving to another URL, and so on.

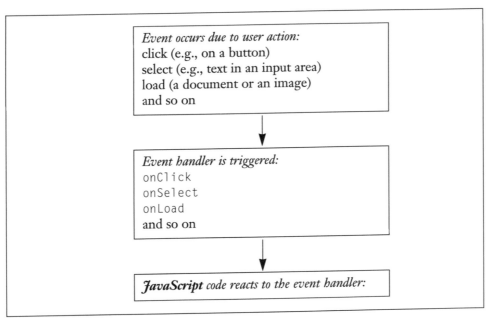

**FIGURE 2.2** Events, event handlers, and reactions to event handlers.

In these cases *onEvent* is associated with HTML tags such as <BODY>, <IMG>, and so on.

To see how events and event handlers work hand in hand, let us look at Exercise 2.3.

**EXERCISE 2.3** EVENTS AND EVENT HANDLERS: A SIMPLE CALCULATOR.

1. Start your favorite word processor.
2. Type the code in Listing 2.2, save it as an HTML file, and load it in your browser.
3. Does your browser window look like Figure 2.3? If not, try again.
4. In Listing 2.2, change the names of the text fields and the button (but not the text in the button). Also change the name of the function. Save the page, reload it, and see what you get.

**LISTING 2.2** Events and event handlers: a simple calculator.

```
1    <HTML>
2    <HEAD>
3    <TITLE> Simple Calculator </TITLE>
4    <SCRIPT LANGUAGE = "JavaScript">
5    //Function to do simple calculations
6    //Arguments:
7    //    theForm -    the form in which a text field
8    //                 that contains the input resides
9    //Return value:
10   //      the answer, written in the text area
11   //       that resides in theForm
12   function simpleCalculator(theForm)
13   {
14       if ( confirm("Calculate?") )
15       {
16           theForm.answer.value = eval(theForm.expression.value)
17       }
18       else
19       {
20           alert("No calculation done.")
21       }
22   }
23   </SCRIPT>
24   </HEAD>
25
```

```
26    <BODY>
27    <H3> Simple Calculator </H3>
28    <FORM>
29    <B>Expression:
30    <BR>
31    <INPUT    TYPE = "text"
32              NAME = "expression"
33              SIZE = 15>
34    <INPUT    TYPE = "button"
35              VALUE = 'Calculate'
36              onClick = "simpleCalculator(this.form)">
37    <BR>
38    Result:
39    <BR>
40    <INPUT    TYPE = "text"
41              NAME = "answer"
42              SIZE = 15>
43    <BR>
44    </B>
45    </FORM>
46    </BODY>
47    </HTML>
```

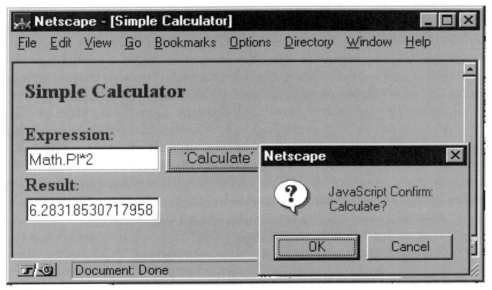

**FIGURE 2.3** Events and event handlers: a simple calculator.

## Analysis of Listing 2.2

Listing 2.2 demonstrates a few important ideas, so let us spend some time discussing it and associated issues. Down through line 11 things should be familiar to you by now. Just note again my insistence on commenting the functions uniformly. Incidentally, later I will abandon this insistence for the sake of brevity.

The interesting stuff begins on line 12. Here, we are using a form (an object), which we call `theForm`, as an argument to the function `simpleCalculator()`. We will have more to say about forms later. For now, just remember that a form is an object in your HTML document that is tagged as such. The form object in an HTML document can contain a variety of other objects, such as buttons and text entry boxes. When a form is built, these objects become properties (data) of that form. So when you send an object of type form to a function, all of its data become known to the function in its definition. For example, `theForm`—the argument to `simpleCalculator()`—knows about the input fields and the button in the form (see Figure 2.3).

Lines 14–21 use the `if-else` JavaScript control structure. The code is interpreted this way: If whatever is inside the parenthesis following the `if` keyword evaluates to `true`, then execute the statement that follows the `if`. Otherwise, execute the statement that follows the `else`. Now inside the parenthesis of the `if` in line 14 we are calling a JavaScript built-in function called `confirm()`. This function takes a single string argument—here, the string `"Calculate?"`. The function `confirm` evaluates to (returns) a *Boolean* result—that is, either true or false. The function `confirm()` displays a confirm dialog window (see Figure 2.3, for example); it returns true if the user clicks on the `OK` button, false if the user clicks on the `Cancel` button.

Suppose your visitor clicks on the OK button. Then the if in line 14 evaluates to true, and the statement on line 16 is evaluated. The right-hand side of the statement on line 16 calls another built-in function, `eval()`. This function takes a single argument, a string, and treats it as an evaluation expression. An evaluation expression is something that is evaluated to a value; for example `4 + 5` is an evaluation expression.

What is it that `eval()` in line 16 of Listing 2.2 is evaluating? Recall that `theForm` is an argument to the function `simpleCalculator()`, and that it is a `form` object. Objects in general, and form objects in particular, have properties. For `form` objects, these properties are, among others, objects that reside in the form.

The syntax `theForm.expression` in line 16 says that the `INPUT` object called `expression` (as defined in lines 31–33) is a property of `theForm`.

Furthermore, `theForm.expression.value` evaluates to `value` (a property of an `INPUT` object which holds the value in the input area) that belongs to `expression` that belongs to `theForm`. Thus, `theForm.expression.value` contains the string that was entered in the `Expression` text box (see Figure 2.3). That is how the interpreter finds out what the user put in the `expression` input box. So once `theForm.expression.value` is evaluated to the string in the `INPUT` object called `expression` (`Math.PI*2` in Figure 2.3), the function `eval` parses the string to an expression and attempts to compute it. The result of the computation is returned by `eval()`. And yes, I shall explain this `Math.PI` thing in a moment.

Finally, the value that `eval()` returns is assigned to the value of the `INPUT` `text` object we named `answer` (in line 41), which is part of the form called `theForm`. The object we called answer (an input text that belongs to the `form` object) knows how to display its `value`. Thus, you see the result in Figure 2.3.

A lot of "activity" is going on behind the scene when line 16 is encountered by the interpreter. It is crucial that you know what is going on, and how the statement in line 16 is interpreted. So let us summarize what happens both verbally and visually. First, verbally:

`theForm.expression.value` **is the string that is stored in a** `text`**-input object called** `expression`.

`theForm.expression` **means that** `expression` **is a property (data) of** `theForm`.

`theForm` **is a** `form` **object.**

Next, visually: Figure 2.4 summarizes the state of affairs. `theForm` is the container object. It is defined in Listing 2.2 lines 28–45. It contains two `text` objects, one named `expression` (defined in lines 31–33) and the other named `answer` (defined in lines 40-42). These objects are properties of the form object named `theForm`. The `text` objects named `expression` and `answer`, each has a property called `value`. For both objects, `value` is not defined—it does not appear in the object definitions. The statement

```
eval(theForm.expression.value)
```

takes the string `"Math.PI*2.333333"`, interprets it as the expression `Math.PI*2.333333`, computes it, and transforms the result back to the string

"6.28318530717958", which is then returned by eval(). The expression theForm.answer.value = eval(...) assigns the string "6.28318530717958" to the value of the answer object. All of this activity occurs when the JavaScript interpreter stumbles upon line 16.

Now suppose that your visitor clicks on the button Cancel (see Figure 2.3). In this case, confirm("Calculate?") in line 14 is evaluated to false, and line 20 is executed. Line 20 simply displays the familiar alert dialog window; once the visitor clicks on the OK button (see Figure 2.5), we reach the end of the function simpleCalculator(), and therefore code execution returns to the end of line 36.

Line 36 in Listing 2.2 is where the click on the Calculate button event is handled. It conforms to the general syntax

```
<TAG ... eventHandler = "JavaScript Code">
```

where

- *TAG* is some HTML tag that has event handlers associated with it
- *eventHandler* is the name of the event handler
- *JavaScript Code* is the code—enclosed in quotes—that executes when *eventHandler* is triggered

In our example, we are assigning the function simpleCalculator() to the event handler onClick. The click event itself occurs when the object to which the event handler belongs—in this case, the button Calculate—is clicked.

Note the syntax this.form in line 36. It says: Send the argument this.form to the function simpleCalculator(). The keyword this refers to the current object. The current object, a text input object named expres-

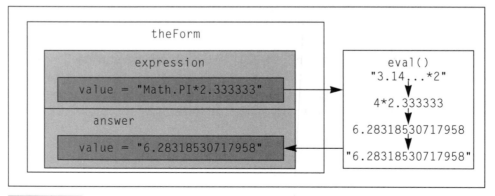

**FIGURE 2.4** How objects are referenced (see line 16 of Listing 2.2).

**FIGURE 2.5** An alert dialog window.

sion, has a property `form`, and this property contains data: the content of the form. Thus, we are in effect sending the form to which the `text` object (named `expression`) belongs to the function `simpleCalculator()`.

> Study Listing 2.2; it will go a long way in helping you become a good JavaScript programmer.

You may put any JavaScript statements inside the quotes following `onClick`. These statements get executed when the user clicks on the button. If you put two or more statements inside the quotes, separate them with a semicolon (;). When possible, handle the event via calls to functions, not via direct statement execution. This will increase the modularity of your program and will enable you to use your handler function in different parts of your HTML document, as well as in other documents.

I still owe you an explanation of what `Math.PI` means (see Figure 2.3). Like any other object, the built-in JavaScript `Math` object has properties. One of them is the constant `PI` (3.14 . . . .).

## The Repertoire of JavaScript Events

For your reference, Table 2.1 lists details about events, the event handlers, the objects that can trigger such events, and brief explanation of these events. The event handlers themselves are named by adding an action verb to the event name: `onFocus`, `onClick`, and so on. To avoid common bugs (and for other reasons), JavaScript has built-in functions that are called by event handlers. These functions do nothing, so if you put a button in your document, for example, and click on it, nothing will happened, and your page will function properly.

**TABLE 2.1** The repertoire of JavaScript events and event handlers.

| Event | Event Handler | Applicable Objects | Comments |
|---|---|---|---|
| Abort | onAbort | image | Occurs when the user aborts loading an image. |
| Blur | onBlur | frame, select, text, textarea, window | Triggered when the object loses focus (the browser window is no longer at the top of the desktop, the user clicks on another frame, etc.). |
| Change | onChange | select, text, textarea | Triggered when input alue for the object changes, or when selection changes for select objects. |
| Click | onClick | button, checkbox, radio, link, reset, submit | Triggered when the user clicks on the object. |
| Error | onError | image, window | Triggered when an error occurs while loading an image or an HTML document. |
| Focus | onFocus | frame, text, textarea, window | The opposite of blur. Triggered when the user activates the object by click or keyboard actions (such as tab). |
| Load | onLoad | image, window | The opposite of abort. Triggered when an HTML document or an image finishes loading. |
| Mouse-out | onMouseOut | area, link | Triggered when the mouse pointer leaves an area or a link in the document. |
| Mouse-over | onMouseOver | area, link | The opposite of onMouseOut. Triggered when the mouse pointer moves over the object. |
| Reset | onReset | form | Triggered when a form is reset. |
| Select | onSelect | text, textarea | Triggered when text in the input area of the object is selected. |
| Submit | onSubmit | form | Triggered when a form is submitted. |
| Unload | onUnload | window | The opposite of onLoad. Triggered when the user unloads an HTML document. |

When you want to incorporate event handling in your document, that is, when you want to interact with the user, you need to know which HTML tags (and often their TYPE attribute) signify the object that triggers the event and event handler. For example, the abort event is triggered from within the <IMG> tag by adding onAbort to it, like this:

```
<IMG ... onAbort = "some JavaScript code">
```

where "some JavaScript code" should usually be a call to a function. For such details, refer to Table 2.2. You should refer to Table 2.2 when you ask yourself questions such as: "What events can I handle in my interaction with the user for a particular object?" For example, does an image react to onClick event? From Table 2.2, the answer is, no.

**TABLE 2.2**  Events and the HTML tags they apply to.

| Event | HTML Tags |
| --- | --- |
| Abort | <IMG> |
| Blur | <BODY> when related to window; <FRAME>; <INPUT> with TYPE attribute set to text , textarea, or select |
| Change | <INPUT> with TYPE attribute set to text, textarea, or select |
| Click | <INPUT> with TYPE attribute set to button, checkbox, radio, submit, reset; <A> |
| Error | <BODY> when related to window; <IMG> |
| Focus | <BODY> when related to window; <FRAME>; <INPUT> with TYPE attribute set to text, textarea |
| Load | <BODY> when related to window; <IMG> |
| Mouse-out | <A>; <MAP> |
| Mouse-over | <A>; <MAP> |
| Reset | <FORM> |
| Select | <INPUT> with TYPE attribute set to text, textarea |
| Submit | <FORM> |
| Unload | <BODY> when related to window |

# 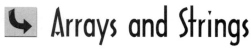 Arrays and Strings

Arrays and strings are used extensively in JavaScript. As a scripter, you should learn to take advantage of the JavaScript facilities that enhance dealing with these.

## Dealing with Arrays

An array is an ordered collection of values. The location of an element in the collection is its *index*. You specify the index using square brackets. Arrays in JavaScript are objects. Thus, to create an array, you need to create an array object. We will talk about objects later. For now, you will just learn how to create and populate an array.

To create an array, JavaScript provides you with a special function called a constructor. The constructor is identified by a keyword called `new`. Thus, to create an array of 77 elements, you simply write:

```
anArray = new Array(77)
```

In this statement, `anArray` is an object of type `Array`, `Array()` is an array object constructor, and 77 is the number of elements in the array.

In working with arrays, keep the following in mind:

- Array objects have a property called length. To access the number of elements of an array, you write, for example:

```
arrayLength = anArray.length
```

The JavaScript expression above will assign the value 77 to `arrayLength`.

- The index of the first element of an array is zero; thus, to refer to the first element in `anArray`, you write, for example:

```
firstElement = anArray[0]
```

This JavaScript expression assigns the value of the first element in `anArray` to the variable `firstElement`.

- The index of the last element of an array is one less than the array's length. To refer to the last element, you write, for example:

```
lastElement = anArray[anArray.length - 1]
```

This JavaScript statement assigns the value of the last element in `anArray` to the variable `lastElement`.

- Array elements can be of any type: numbers, strings of characters, and other objects (including other arrays).

You will save yourself many a headache if you remember this:

1. The index of the first element of an array in JavaScript is zero.
2. The index of the last element of an array is the number of elements in the array −1.

Born arrays and their elements are objects; you can create arrays of any kinds of objects. This capability can be used to create some very clever data structures in your scripts. Suppose you write a script to follow prices of several stocks in the last few days (since you are smart, you decide to buy or sell not on the basis of the stock price, but rather on the basis of change in the stock value). Then you may define an object as shown in Listing 2.3.

**LISTING 2.3** Defining an object.

```
1    function twoDayStockPrice(stockName, dayMinus1, dayMinus2)
2    {
3        this.stockName = stockName
4        this.dayMinus1 = dayMinus1
5        this.dayMinus2 = dayMinus2
6    }
```

Here an object is defined (not created yet) with three properties: `stockName`, `dayMinus1`, and `dayMinus2`. Next, you would create an array of stock prices as shown in Listing 2.4.

**LISTING 2.4** Populating an array of objects.

```
1    stockPrices = new twoDayStockPrice(3)
2    stockPrices[1] = new twoDayStockPrice("great stock", 100, 200)
3    stockPrices[2] = new twoDayStockPrice("so-so stock", 80, 110)
4    stockPrices[3] = new twoDayStockPrice("bad stock", 200, 150)
```

To make this script snippet useful, you would write a JavaScript to automatically download stock prices from the Internet, update the array in real time, and flag good stocks for buying, with the computer belching and whistling—but we shall not show you how to do that.

## Dealing with Strings

You will spend much time working with strings. In fact, dealing with strings will undoubtedly be one of your most common (and often time-consuming) programming chores. Following is an example more elaborate than those we have looked at thus far. Use this example to learn more about strings and string manipulations. Remember, the more you see examples, even if you do not know what they mean at first sight, the more you learn (recall the slippery spiral metaphor).

**EXERCISE 2.4**  DEALING WITH STRINGS.

1. Start your favorite word processor or text editor.

2. Type the code in Listing 2.5 and run it. Do not type line numbers.

3. Does your browser window looks like Figure 2.6? If not, try again.

4. Change the string in line 29, and include in it the following characters:
   `"\"H\r\nello there\""`.
   Examine the results.

**LISTING 2.5** Dealing with strings, controlling program flow, and use of functions.

```
1    <HTML>
2    <HEAD>
3    <TITLE>Working with Strings</TITLE>
4    <SCRIPT LANGUAGE = "JavaScript">
5    //Function to go through characters in a string
6    function testFunction(aString)
7    {
8        var startValue = 0
9        var endValue = aString.length
10
11       //Show one character at a time
12       for (var i = startValue; i < endValue; i++)
13       {
14           //Build the string to show
15           alert( "aString["+i+"] = " +
16                   aString.charAt(i) )
```

```
17        }
18    }
19    </SCRIPT>
20    </HEAD>
21
22    <BODY>
23    <H3>Working with Strings</H3>
24    Who said: "customers are our enemies, competitors are our
      friends" (Hint: supermarket of the world)
25    <FORM>
26    <INPUT    TYPE = "button"
27              NAME = "testButton"
28              VALUE = "Test"
29              onClick = "testFunction('From ADM archives')">
30    </FORM>
31    </BODY>
32    </HTML>
```

## Analysis of Listing 2.5

The script displays the characters embedded in a string, one character at a time, in an alert window. Sometimes strings may contain characters that do

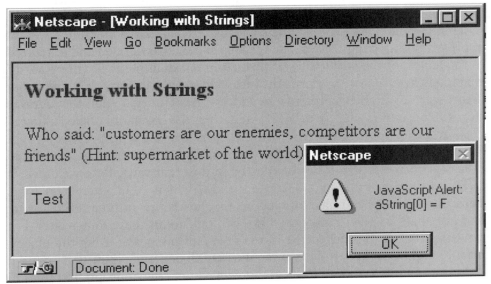

**FIGURE 2.6** Netscape view of Listing 2.5.

not show in your editor, but are processed by the script. When you examine such strings, the outcome may baffle you. Use Listing 2.5 to see what your browser actually "sees" as it processes your string. Note the generous use of the alert dialog window. You may use this approach for debugging, but avoid using it in a page designed for visitation. Because the alert dialog waits for user response, it throws off the flow of execution, and may be confusing to the end-user.

Between `<FORM>` and `</FORM>` (lines 25 and 30), the `<INPUT>` tag (lines 26 to 29) sets up a button, with the string `Test` shown in it. When the button is pressed, `testFunction()` is called. The call to the function includes a string argument, `'From ADM archives'`. Recall that HTML documents are loaded into memory as they are read by the browser; also, that the `<HEAD>` section of a document is loaded first. Thus, when the document in Listing 2.5 is loaded into memory, the function definition (that is, code of what it actually does) is loaded before the call to the function. Therefore, by the time the call to `testFunction()` is made in line 29, the interpreter knows what to do with the call. The call to the function tells the interpreter to go to line 6 and start executing the function code.

The keyword var in line 8 tells the interpreter that the next word—`startValue` in this case—identifies a placeholder (also called a variable), an address where a value is normally stored. On the same line the zero is also assigned to the variable `startValue` (remember our discussion of variables in the section titled "A First Encounter with Properties, Variables, and Assignments" in Chapter 1?). The constant zero is called a literal or constant in programming jargon. Next, the variable `endValue` is defined and initialized to the length of the string `aString`, which in the example is 17 (there are 17 characters in `aString`). To clarify the idea of literal versus variable, think about it this way: a variable represents an address in memory. When that address stores a constant (say 5, 10, `Math.PI`, etc.), then the constant is called a literal.

How is the number 17 arrived at? `aString.length` is a property of strings. When you create a string, its length (the number of characters in it) is stored in this property. A string can be created in different ways; here we create it by just using its value `From ADM archives`, which is 17 characters long. Because `aString` is an object of type `String`, JavaScript automatically creates and initializes its `length` property. We will talk about these things later. For now, just realize that this is one of the great advantages of using the object-oriented approach. `aString` is treated as an object, and when you create it (here by assigning a value to it), the object assigns the appropriate values to its properties, including the `length` property.

After declaring and initializing the necessary variables, we move on to the `for` loop in line 12. The first line in the loop is a standard statement, and it really does not take much to get used to it. The statement

```
for (i = startValue;  i < endValue;  i++)
{
    ...
}
```

Agree means: Do everything inside the braces for `i = startValue`, which in this case is zero. Next, increment `i` by 1 (this is the meaning of `i++`); then do everything inside the braces again, and so on; when the value of `i` is no longer less than `endValue`, stop execution of the statements inside the braces, and go to the next statement following the closing braces. (Usually, you will be doing something with `i` inside the loop, (as in lines 15 and 16.)

Before we discuss what is actually being done inside this loop, let us look more closely at variables and names. Recall that variable names are addresses where you wish to store some values. When you choose names for the variables, be sure to use names that do not conflict with JavaScript reserved words. A *reserved word* is a name of something that is reserved by the language and has a special meaning. For example, `var` is a reserved word; it indicates that the word following `var` denotes an address of a value. Choosing `var` instead of `endValue` will result in ambiguity, and JavaScript cannot allow that. Most computer languages (including JavaScript) use a small set of reserved words, and it does not take long to learn them. You do not have to learn all of the language-specific reserved words before you start; just enrich your vocabulary as you need and use these words. In order to avoid potential conflicts with reserved words, simply name your variables in a way that will avoid conflict. For example, most computer languages reserve words like `end`, `exit`, `break`, `int`, `for`, `do`. Instead of using `end`, we chose `endValue`. Because most reserved words are short and in lowercase, we will have no conflict here, even if we do not remember all of the reserved words. See "Appendix B: JavaScript Reserved Words" for a full list of JavaScript reserved words.

Now back to what is done in the `for` loop in Listing 2.5. The call to an `alert` dialog on lines 15 and 16 consists of the function name, `alert`, and a parameter inside the parenthesis, which, when all is said and done, must resolve to a string. `alert` is like any other function that you have seen thus far, except that it is built in. It takes a string for an argument, and knows how to display it in an alert dialog window. Inside the parenthesis, we start the string argument with `"aString["`. Next, we add to the string the value of `i` by writing the expression `"aString[" + i`. Most programmers will be baffled by this expression. "After all," they will say, "`aString[` is a string, and `i` is a number; how can you add a number to a string?" The answer is that unlike many other programming languages, JavaScript will do the necessary conversion before the addition (recall our discussion in the section titled "Why 5 + 10 = 15 While "5"+10 = 510" in Chapter 1).

The first time you go through the loop, the value of `i` is zero. Thus, on the first journey around the loop we now have constructed the string `aString[0`. The next part of the expression adds `] =` to the string, giving us the string `aString[0] =`.

Finally, we add `aString.charAt(i)` to the value of the literal string we have constructed thus far in line 15. Recall that `aString` is an object whose type (`String`) is known to JavaScript. When JavaScript constructs this object, it assigns values to its properties (for example, `length`). In addition to properties, objects also have *methods*. These are functions that act on properties or other arguments that you supply. Thus, `charAt()` is a method (function) that belongs to an object of type `string`. Because `aString` is an object of type `string`, when you write `aString.charAt(i)`, JavaScript knows what to do with it. It turns out that `charAt(aNumber)` is one of the string methods. It returns the character that is located in position `aNumber`. In our example, because `aString` equals `From ADM archives`, `F` is returned the first time we go through the loop. Note that the first time we loop, `i = 0`. This means that the character at position zero (`F`) is returned by `aString.charAt(0)`. Let me remind you again that JavaScript starts counting indices from zero, not from one. Thus, the position (also called index) of the last character is `length - 1`.

Going through the loop for the first time, the complete the string that we have built as parameter to the alert function is thus `aString[0] = F`.

Listing 2.5 results in Figure 2.6. The window in which the alert appears is often called a dialog window. When you load the HTML file that holds Listing 2.5 and click on the `Test` button, the JavaScript alert dialog window appears. Every time you hit the `OK` button in the alert window, the next letter in the string you sent to the `testFunction()` will show up, along with its index (in the square brackets). Go through the script a few times, and you will quickly realize how annoying the use of the alert dialog window can be. The reason is that until the user gets rid of the window (by pressing `OK` as many times as there are characters in the string being examined), nothing else can be done. This is so because alert dialog windows are *modal*: Some condition must be satisfied to make the window go away before the user can continue with any other action in the invoking application. Windows 95 is full of modal windows! Another rule to get used to:

> Minimize the use of modal dialog windows in your application; they annoy your guests.

Now back to the reason we are looking at Listing 2.5 in the first place: Note the comments and indentations. The indentations highlight the fact that some code is inside the function, and the comments are concise and explanatory. Thanks to the indentations, even a cursory look at the code reveals that the function begins in line 6 and ends in line 18, and that the `for` loop runs from lines 11 to 18. The comments remind us what the function does, and some other details.

#  Miscellaneous Programming Topics

This section describes various useful scripting techniques and other details that may prove important in your scripting work.

## Updating Pages

JavaScript formats the HTML page as it loads it to memory, moving sequentially through the code. Once the page is loaded in memory, you cannot change the page format, unless you reload the document. You can update sub-windows in a frame independently of the document. If you attempt to update a page in your script, nothing will happen.

Keep in mind that data persistence is not a straightforward issue with Navigator: Information may persist between loads and re-load of the same document, and sometimes between loading and re-loading the Navigator application. This can be confusing. So take my advice: When you debug your JavaScript code and things do not work the way you think they should, do not assume immediately that your code is at fault. Try the `View | Reload` menu; if the code still does not behave, try `File | Open File in Browser....` If your code still does not behave, you can assume (almost for sure) that your code is at fault. If you look and look and look and still you cannot isolate an error, try to exit Navigator and start it again, and then load the HTML file that holds your script. Now if the code does not behave, you can assume (this time for sure) that your code is at fault.

If after all this you still cannot find your code error, you have two options:

- Ask a friend to take a look at your code.

- Start from scratch, with a different approach, (not the same approach for you are likely to repeat the same mistake).

## Printing

JavaScript does not provide the ability to print.

## Using Quotes

If you need to nest quotes, you can use any one of these approaches:

- `"a string with 'quotes' in an HTML page."`

- `'a string with "quotes" in an HTML page.'`

- `"a string with \"quotes\" in an HTML page."`

## Defining Functions in the HEAD

The `<HEAD>` section of your HTML document is always loaded to memory before any part of the page is displayed. Put functions in the `<HEAD>`. When the page is loaded and there is a call to a function, the interpreter then will know what to do. Otherwise, for example, if you have event handlers in your document and you define functions in places other than the HEAD, the event may attempt to execute before the function is known to the interpreter. This can be annoying.

⤷ Objects and their hierarchy

⤷ Objects that you need to know about

⤷ How to work with key objects

⤷ How JavaScript creates objects

# ⤷ Object Hierarchy

Object hierarchy is not difficult to understand. The basis for it is in some underlying concepts of programming in general, and object programming in particular.

Recall that variables are placeholders (addresses) for some values. The values themselves can be of various data types. For example, an integer is a data type, and so is a string. Thus, one attribute of variables is the type of data they hold. In programming languages such as C++ and Java, you must tell the compiler what type of data a variable is to hold before you use that variable. Thus, your program will often include statements such as

```
int i
```

which says that i is a type of integer. You can then say i = 10 and the compiler will "understand" what you mean.

In the object programming world, we often deal with *classes*. A class can be viewed as an extension of data type. For example, just as an integer is defined as a data type that denotes whole numbers, a particular class may denote a collection of integers, other data types, and functions. A variable can then be defined as a particular class type. Let's say that we define a class and call it `IntegerClass`. We define `IntegerClass` such that it includes two integers, and a set of functions that deal with these integers (sum, subtract, etc.). Next, in our program we may say

```
IntegerClass i
```

and the compiler will know what to do with `i`. Now in the object programming jargon, `i` is an object of class `IntegerClass`. The "variable" `i` is also called an instance of the class `IntegerClass`. We could say

```
IntegerClass i, j
```

in which case we have two instances of `IntegerClass`: `i` and `j`—both objects. In the JavaScript world we say that `i` and `j` are objects of type `IntegerClass`. To use the objects in our program, we employ the by-now-familiar dot notation. For example, if one of the properties of `IntegerClass` is the value of an integer, called `val`, then we can write

```
i.val = j.val
```

which formally says: "Assign the value stored in the property `val` of object instance `j` to the value stored in property `val` in object instance `i` where both `i` and `j` are objects of type `IntegerClass`."

In the object programming world, understanding class hierarchy is absolutely crucial. Class hierarchy allows you to create new classes which have all of the properties (data and methods) of existing classes, and then some. This is called *inheritance*. Because of inheritance, you can build new classes based on existing classes, without having to re-code the whole class. For example, suppose that in our class `IntegerClass` we defined a method (a function) to sum two integers that are members of this class. Next, we want to define a different class that will know how to subtract these integers. We can define a new class, call it, for example, `ChildInteger`, and add the method to subtract the two integers (that are members of the class). Because `ChildInteger` is a subclass of `IntegerClass`, all we have to do is program the method for subtraction. All of the other methods of `IntegerClass` automatically become methods of `ChildInteger`. Inheritance is one of the major advantages of object programming. Inheritance also leads to the concept of class hierarchy, because now `ChildInteger` is a subclass of `IntegerClass`, and `IntegerClass` is the parent of `ChildInteger`.

As you have probably guessed by now, some of these concepts apply to JavaScript. Being a scripting language, JavaScript does not allow you to work with classes; you work with objects. Yet, the class structure is preserved in the relationships among objects. Thus we arrive at the concept of object hierarchy. A good grasp of the hierarchy will allow you to understand and manipulate objects in your programs. When you learn about objects, you need to learn facts: what properties and methods are part of the object, what names are given to these, and how to call them. Remember that methods are functions that are defined as part of the object, and that properties (variables that are defined as part of the object) store data. To work with an object, you need to know its properties, including its parent objects and sometimes its descendants, and its methods.

The JavaScript interpreter has numerous built-in objects. As an HTML page is constructed, object instances are constructed which reflect the structure of the HTML page. For example, if you have two `<INPUT TYPE ="BUTTON"...>` tags in your HTML document, the interpreter builds two button objects. If you use an experienced object-oriented programmer, you should be aware that the hierarchy we are talking about is instance (object) hierarchy, not class hierarchy. This allows us to do two important things:

- We can define an object as a property of another object. For example, a `form` is a property of a `document` that includes it, and a `text` object is a property of the `form` in which it appears.

- We can also define the same object to be a property (or a daughter) of another object. For example, the `frames` array is a daughter of both the `window` and the `frame` objects (note that `frames` is an array, while `frame` is not).

## The JavaScript Object Hierarchy

Figure 3.1 shows the Netscape Navigator object hierarchy from the first to the third generation. To draw the full object hierarchy in the same figure is cumbersome, so I continued the hierarchy from the third to the fifth generation in Figure 3.2. It will (truly) be worth your while to study these figures, and come back to them frequently. One of the most common programming errors in JavaScript is to try to access objects in an incorrect hierarchical order; in such cases JavaScript will frequently alert you that *something* is not a property of *something else*. These error messages can be baffling. This is when you should refer to both of these figures.

From the object hierarchy in Figure 3.1 and Figure 3.2 you can deduce that to refer to the full name of a `text` object named `textObjectName` that resides in a form named `formObjectName`, you use the syntax

```
window.document.formObjectName.textObjectName
```

Note that because `window` is the topmost object, and an HTML document usually has one top-most window, you do not need to append the window's name at the top of the hierarchy when you wish to access an object (there are some exceptions to this rule, and they are discussed in the

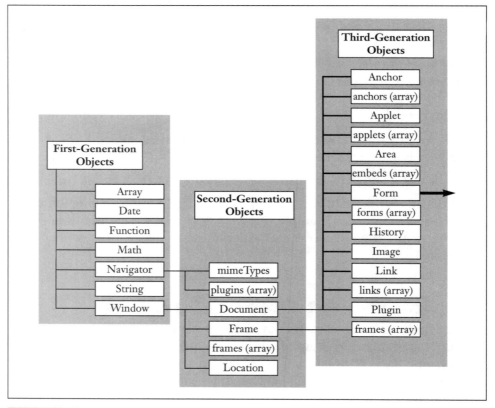

**FIGURE 3.1**  JavaScript object hierarchy—from first to third generation.

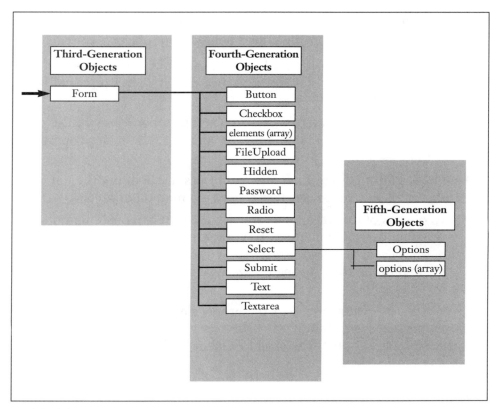

**FIGURE 3.2** JavaScript object hierarchy—from third to fifth generation.

appropriate object reference in Chapter 7). Thus, the statement above is equivalent to

```
document.formObjectName.textObjectName
```

Because forms is an array whose parent is document, you can access the text object with yet another variation:

```
document.forms[i].textObjectName
```

where i is the index of the desired form in the array of forms in documents.

Each of the objects in Figure 3.1 and Figure 3.2 has properties and methods, and it is these that you need to learn to work with. These properties can be variables of any kind: numbers, strings, arrays, and other objects. For example, one of the properties of the text object is value, which is a string variable that stores the value that the text displays.

## Objects and the Dot Notation

To summarize, let us go over the salient points about object hierarchy:

- A daughter object is associated with its parent by the dot notation; for example, `document.formObjectName` means that `formObjectName` is the daughter of the object `document`.

- Objects own properties; to access an object's property, use the dot notation: `textObjectName.value` means that `value` is a property of `textObjectName`.

- Objects own methods; to access an object's method, use the dot notation: `window.blur()` means that `blur()` is a method of `window`.

- Two objects of different type can have identically named methods and properties; yet, these methods and properties are distinct. For example, `window.focus()` and `textObjectName.focus()` are two distinct methods; they do different things (one brings a `window` object to focus, the other a `text` object).

- Objects can own arrays, and the arrays elements can be objects. For example, `document.forms[1].elements[0].name` is a way to access the name property of the first object element in the second `form` object in the `document` object.

I know that at first look all of this can be confusing (it was to me when I first learned about object-oriented programming). But as you use the language, and make many errors (hopefully most of them syntax, not run-time errors), you will learn.

#  Automatically Created Objects

When a browser creates an HTML page, it automatically creates a few objects that you can work with; Table 3.1 lists these objects.

Of the objects listed in Table 3.1, `document` is the richest. This is so because it contains the content of the HTML page, and pages are usually unique. A document that contains two forms will have two `form` objects stored in its `forms` array property (see Figure 3.1).

To see how these ideas work, take a look at Exercise 3.1. This example teaches how to examine the properties of objects in your page. Use this technique for debugging, and for clarifying to yourself what is going on with objects (behind the scenes) in the HTML page you are working on. We will present Exercise 3.1 and the code that produced it in a moment.

**TABLE 3.1** Objects created when an HTML page is displayed.

| Object | Comments |
|--------|----------|
| window | This is the topmost object in the hierarchy (see Figure 3.1). It contains properties that apply to the entire window. |
| location | Contains properties about the current URL. |
| history | Contains properties representing recently visited URLs. |
| document | Contains document-specific properties which themselves are objects (e.g., forms, applets), title, background color, etc. |

## Examining Object Properties

Often you run into the following problem in JavaScript coding: You refer to a property in your code, and the property does not exist. For example, run Listing 3.1. You should get a window similar to Figure 3.3. Before showing you how to deal with such situations, let me explain what happens in Listing 3.1:

- In lines 9 through 13 we insert JavaScript code in the document's body.

- In line 10, we write to the document a property of the document object. The syntax in this line tells us that document.write() is a method of document, and that aProperty is, presumably, a property of document.

- In line 11 we write to the document the lastModified property of the current document.

- In line 13 we write to the current document the lastModified property of window.

- Because aProperty is not a property of document, JavaScript responds with the word undefined (see Figure 3.3).

- Because lastModified is a property of document, the response is the value stored in this property (third line in Figure 3.3).

- Because lastModified is not a property of the window object, the response is undefined (fourth line in Figure 3.3).

LISTING 3.1 Referring to the wrong properties.

```
1    <HTML>
2    <HEAD>
3    <TITLE>Referring to the Wrong Properties</TITLE>
4    </HEAD>
5
6    <BODY>
7    <H3>Referring to the Wrong Properties</H3>
8    <BODY>
9    <SCRIPT LANGUAGE = "JavaScript">
10   document.write(document.aProperty)
11   document.write("<BR>" + document.lastModified)
12   document.write("<BR>" + window.lastModified)
13   </SCRIPT>
14   </BODY>
15   </HTML>
```

You should realize that "undefined" is not really a value, it is JavaScript's way of telling you that it does not know about something.

Another common situation that arises while coding with JavaScript is that you are not sure what properties a particular object owns. To learn how to examine the properties of objects, do Exercise 3.1.

**EXERCISE 3.1**   EXAMINING BUTTON AND TEXT PROPERTIES.

1. Start your favorite word processor or text editor.

2. Type the code in Listing 3.2 and run it. Do not type line numbers.

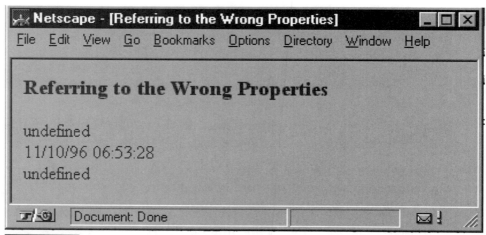

**FIGURE 3.3**   Referring to the wrong properties.

3. Does your browser window looks like Figure 3.4? If not, try again.

4. Click on the `button` object and examine its properties. Do you get something like Figure 3.5?

5. Click on the `text` object and examine its properties. Do you get something like Figure 3.6?

6. Feeling venturesome? Insert another object in Listing 3.2—say, a `textarea`, or a `checkbox`; implement the appropriate event handler, and examine the object's properties.

**LISTING 3.2** Examining button and text properties.

```
1     <HTML>
2     <HEAD>
3     <TITLE>Examining Object Properties</TITLE>
4     <SCRIPT LANGUAGE = "JavaScript">
5     function inspectProperties(theObject, theObjectName)
6     {
7       var theProperties = ""
8
9       for (var i in theObject)
10      {
11        theProperties += theObjectName + "." + i +
12                         " = " + theObject[i] + "\n"
13      }
14      alert(theProperties)
15    }
16    </SCRIPT>
17    </HEAD>
18
19    <BODY>
20    <H3> Examining Object Properties </H3>
21    <FORM>
22    <INPUT TYPE = "button"
23           NAME = "buttonObject"
24           VALUE = "Click here..."
25           onClick =
              "inspectProperties(buttonObject,'buttonObject')">
26    <P> Enter some text:
27    <INPUT TYPE = "text"
28       NAME = "textObject"
29       VALUE = "Put the cursor anywhere in here"
30       SIZE = 40
31       onFocus = "inspectProperties(this, this.name)">
32    </FORM>
33    </BODY>
34    </HTML>
```

**FIGURE 3.4** Examining button and text properties.

Netscape

JavaScript Alert:
buttonObject.type = button
buttonObject.name = buttonObject
buttonObject.form = [object Form]
buttonObject.value = Click here...
buttonObject.defaultValue = null
buttonObject.length = null
buttonObject.options = null
buttonObject.selectedIndex = null
buttonObject.checked = null
buttonObject.defaultChecked = null

OK

**FIGURE 3.5** Examining button object properties.

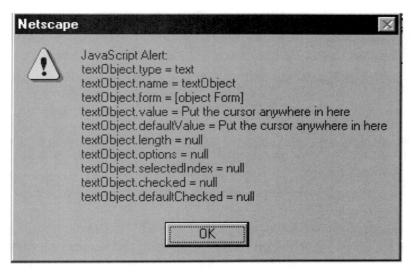

JavaScript Alert:
textObject.type = text
textObject.name = textObject
textObject.form = [object Form]
textObject.value = Put the cursor anywhere in here
textObject.defaultValue = Put the cursor anywhere in here
textObject.length = null
textObject.options = null
textObject.selectedIndex = null
textObject.checked = null
textObject.defaultChecked = null

OK

**FIGURE 3.6**  Examining `text` object properties.

## Analysis of Listing 3.2

Let us analyze the code in Listing 3.2. In line 5, we begin with the definition of a function we call `inspectProperties()`. Data to work on is passed to this function in two arguments: `theObject` and `theObjectName`. Before getting further into the function definition, let us look at these arguments. In lines 22 to 25 we define a button object. The object name is `buttonObject`. So in the call to `inspectProperties()`, we specify `buttonObject` as the object (it is an object of type `button`). The second argument is the name of the object, `"buttonObject"`. There is a subtlety here that you need to know about: `buttonObject` is the name of the variable which represents an object of type `button`. Thus, we cannot enclose `buttonObject` in quotes when we pass it as an argument to `inspectProperties()`. The variable name itself, however, is a string, and we pass it to the function as a string because we want to display it (the object name) in front of its properties.

We now go back to line 5. Based on our call to `inspectProperties()` in line 25, `theObject = buttonObject`, and `theObjectName = "buttonObject"`. In line 7 we specify a string variable that will hold the properties and will then be displayed, and call it `theProperties`. Note the initialization of `theProperties` to `""`. You'll see why we do that in a moment.

Line 9 needs some explanation:

The statement

```
for ( var i in theObject)
{
   ...
}
```

tells the interpreter to cycle through all of the properties in theObject using the index i, and every time i is incremented, to execute the statements nested in the braces. Furthermore, i represents the property name.

This is an extremely convenient language construct. It is made possible because JavaScript stores the object properties in an array, and these properties can be accessed by either their names (if you know them) or by the index i.

Inside the for loop (lines 11 and 12), we construct the theProperties string that holds the properties. Note the use of the += assignment. It means the following:

The assignment

```
x += y
```

is a shorthand notation for the assignment

```
x = x + y
```

Thus, every time we go through the for loop, we add the object name followed by a period (see line 11 in Listing 3.2). Then we add i, which represents the property name, followed by " = ". We then add the value of the property, which is stored in theObject[i]. Finally we add the special character \n. Note that \n is a single character, sometimes called a special character. This character is not printed, but is interpreted as an end of line.

We needed to initialize theProperties to an empty string in line 7. Because we are adding to theProperties in the for loop, we must add a value to an existing value. The statement in line 11, expanded, says

```
theProperties = theProperties + ...
```

but when we go through the loop the first time we have not allocated storage for `theProperties` yet, and JavaScript does not know what `theProperties` on the right-hand side of the assignment means. This causes an error. That is why we initialize `theProperties to ""` in line 7. If you do not believe me (and even if you do), and to get you started on a journey all too familiar, comment out line 7 from the code (just type // at the beginning of the line), and run the code again. You should get the window similar to the one shown in Figure 3.7.

Once we are done with construction of `theProperties` string, we display it with `alert()` (line 14 of Listing 3.2) and that is what we see in Figure 3.5 after we click on the `Click here...` button shown in Figure 3.4.

Let us now examine the outcome of clicking on the `Click here...` button. The `inspectProperties()` function builds a list of the properties and displays it (Figure 3.5). Only the first four properties are of interest to us:

- The object type, stored in the property `buttonObject.type`, is `button`.

- The object name, stored in the property `buttonObject.name`, is `buttonObject`.

- The `object buttonObject` is embedded in a `form` object, and you can access all of this `form`'s properties by the construct `buttonObject.form.form`*PropertyName*, where *formPropertyName* is one of the form object properties. This is an example in which `form` is the parent of `button`, but it is also a property of `button`; so the construct `formName.buttonName.formName` refers to the same `form` object.

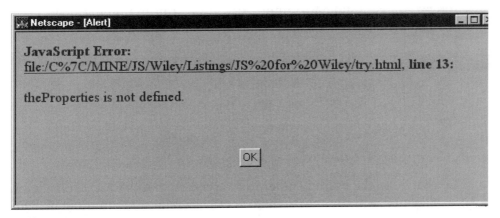

**FIGURE 3.7** A JavaScript error displayed in an alert window.

- The value of the object is `Click here...`; for `button` objects, the value of the `value` property is displayed on the face of the button.

Let us turn back to the second element in the form, the `text` object. It is defined in lines 27 to 31 of Listing 3.2. There, we do the following:

- endow the object of type `text` with the name `textObject`;

- assign the value `Put the cursor anywhere in here` to it; and

- the user calls `inspectProperties()` again.

The result of endowing `textObject` (a form element of type `text`) with focus is to trigger the `onFocus` event handler, which in turn calls `inspectProperties()`, and displays a window as shown in Figure 3.6.

"But wait a minute," you say, "how come when you call `inspectProperties()` in line 25 you give it two arguments, the object and its name, whereas in line 31 you send `inspectProperties()` these two weird arguments `this` and `this.name`?" The answer is quite simple: `this` refers to the current object, and `this.name` is the name of the current object. The current object is the object from within which we make the call (the object of type `text` whose name is `textObject`).

"But aside from confusing me, why in the world do you want to make a call like this?" The answer this time is simple again. When I make use of `this` and `this.name` (as in line 31), instead of the object and its name (as in line 25), I am making the code modular. I can replace the arguments in line 25 with `this` and `this.name`, and the code will still work, regardless of the object type and object name.

Exercise 3.2 is designed to improve your skill in examining properties, and will also expose you to properties of a very important object: the `window`.

---

**EXERCISE 3.2** EXAMINING WINDOW PROPERTIES.

1. In Listing 3.2, replace
   ```
   onClick = "inspectProperties(buttonObject,'buttonObject')"
   ```
   with
   ```
   onClick = "inspectProperties(parent.document, 'window')"
   ```
2. Examine the results. Do they look like Figure 3.8?

---

The change to the event handler in Exercise 3.2 needs some explanation. This explanation will illuminate the object hierarchy some more. The window (the background in Figure 3.4) is created by the browser (your Navigator). Inside the window resides a `document` object. Inside the docu-

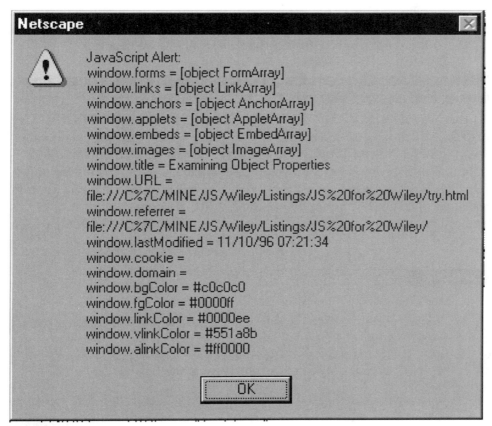

**FIGURE 3.8** Window properties.

ment resides a `form` object, and inside the form reside the `button` and `text` objects. So the `document` object is known to the interpreter. The parent of the document is a `window` object. Examine its properties in Figure 3.8; most of the properties names are self-explanatory. To understand the hierarchy we just illustrated, refer back to Figure 3.1 and Figure 3.2.

Some of the more interesting properties of the `window` object are:

- `forms`—this holds an array of forms (as many as there are on the HTML page). In this case it has a length of 2. The values of `forms[0].name` and `forms[1].name`, for example, are `buttonObject` and `textObject` respectively.

- `links`—all the links on the HTML page are collected into this property and can be referred to by their index.

- URL—the URL for the window object.

We will discuss some of these properties more as we proceed.

## When Do Objects Become Available for Use in JavaScript?

As the browser application reads HTML code, it builds the HTML page display sequentially, from the top of the HTML file. This process is called *layout*: The browser figures out how to lay out various elements in the document. As the browser lays out whatever elements it is responsible for on the page, it also creates the appropriate objects. This means that if you attempt to use an object in JavaScript before the HTML element that constitutes this object has been laid out, you will get an error message. To see this, do Exercise 3.3.

**EXERCISE 3.3**  LAYOUT AND OBJECTS

1. Start your favorite word processor or text editor.
2. Type the code in Listing 3.3 and run it. Do not type line numbers. Do you get something like Figure 3.9?
3. Next, move lines 11—14 to follow right after line 4. Run again and see what happens. Do you get something like the window shown in Figure 3.10?

Note line 12 in Listing 3.3. Remember object hierarchy? The full hierarchy should start with window.document.... However, because window is the topmost object, you do not need to indicate it. Going down the hierarchy, we see that the document object includes a form object called valueless, which in turn contains a text object called aPolitician, which in turn has a property value. In the value property of the object named aPolitician (of type text) of the form object named valueless, we store the string What do they mean? (note the difference between the value and the data it holds).

**LISTING 3.3**  Layout and objects.

```
1    <HTML>
2    <TITLE> Layout </TITLE>
3    <BODY>
4    <H3>Layout</H3>
5    <FORM NAME = "valueless">
6    <INPUT TYPE = "text"
7        NAME = "aPolitician"
```

```
8        size = 20
9        VALUE = "Values?">
10   </FORM>
11   <SCRIPT>
12   document.valueless.aPolitician.value = "What do they mean?"
13   document.write(document.valueless.aPolitician.value)
14   </SCRIPT>
15   </BODY>
16   </HTML>
```

The reason that step 3 in Exercise 3.3 resulted in an error (shown in Figure 3.10) is the layout sequence. You tried to use both valueless and aPolitician before they were actually created by the layout sequence. The objects do not exist yet, you get an error message, and your script bombs. So keep this in mind:

Objects (page components) are created by the browser as they are encountered in the HTML source code.

Do not use an object in your JavaScript before it was created on the page.

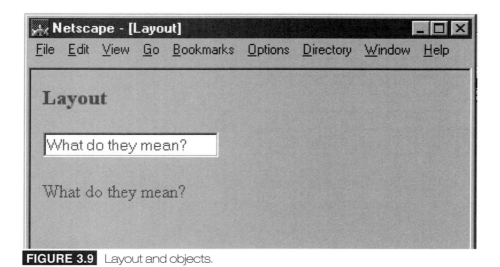

**FIGURE 3.9** Layout and objects.

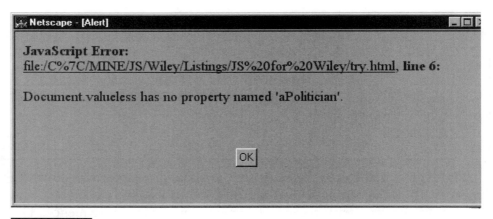

**FIGURE 3.10** Layout error.

There are actually two things to take care of when you think about layout:

- You cannot call a JavaScript function (from a page element), before the function is loaded into memory; so put in the <HEAD> section of your document those JavaScript functions that you intend to call later in your code.

- You cannot access an object from a JavaScript code before the object has been laid out on the HTML page; so if you must use an object in JavaScript code that resides inside the <BODY> section of your document, be sure to put the <SCRIPT> tag after the HTML code that creates the object.

# WINDOWS, FRAMES, DOCUMENTS, AND FORMS

↳ The `window`, `frame`, `document`, and `form` objects are discussed

↳ How to use these objects

↳ The methods, properties, and event handlers of these objects

↳ Examples of implementing these objects, their methods, and their event handlers

We have looked at the `window`, `frame`, `document`, and `form` objects in numerous examples. We now take a closer look at these four important objects. As you go along, keep in mind the object hierarchy (see Figures 3.1 and 3.2 in Chapter 3). To be slightly more formal than we have been thus far, in some cases we shall commence the discussion of an object with a table that describes its properties, methods, and event handlers. Use these tables as references in your future work with JavaScript.

Recall that properties of an object are variables (including objects) that hold data. Thus, if you have two objects as properties of the same object (for example, two buttons in a form), you access the data for these objects (for example, their `value`) by the dot notation. To wit, if part of your HTML document looks like this:

```
<FORM NAME  = "formObjectName">
<INPUT TYPE = "button"
```

```
        NAME = "buttonObjectName"
        VALUE = "Click on me ...">
<INPUT TYPE = "text"
        NAME = "textObjectName"
        VALUE = "I am a default string">
</FORM>
```

and you wish to access the objects in your JavaScript code, you could do this:

```
aValue = document.formObjectName.buttonObjectName.value
anotherValue = document.formObjectName.textObjectName.
value
```

In these two statements `aValue` stores the string `Click on me...` and `anotherValue` stores the string `I am a default string`.

Methods are functions that belong to objects; they essentially *do* something in the script. To continue our example, we can simulate a click on `buttonObjectName` with the statement

```
document.formObjectName.buttonObjectName.click()
```

We can select the text in the `textObjectName` input field (to simulate a double-click, or mouse drag on text) with the statement

```
document.formObjectName.textObjectName.select()
```

Event handlers are the actions that are taken in response to an event (usually a user's action such as a clicks on a button). Thus, we could expand on the example and write

```
<FORM NAME  = "formObjectName">
<INPUT TYPE = "button"
      NAME = "buttonObjectName"
      VALUE = "Click on me ..."
      onClick = "reactEventToHandler(this)">
<INPUT TYPE = "text"
      NAME = "textObjectName"
      VALUE = "I am a default string">
      onSelect = "reactEventToHandler(this)">
</FORM>
```

In this example, when the user clicks on the button, the `onClick` event handler triggers `reactEventToHandler()`, which takes one argument, the `button` object that triggered the function (this is the meaning of the keyword this). In the case of the `text` object, `reactEventToHandler()` reacts to selecting text in the `text` object input field, and again, the argument to the function is the text object named `textObjectName`. In `reactEventToHandler()` your JavaScript code can determine who the calling object was and thus invoke the appropriate portion of the code.

In the spirit of the climbing spiral, the exposition of the objects in this chapter is not complete. Next time you meet the `window`, `frame`, `document`, and `form` objects, it will be in the reference chapters, where the discussion of each of the objects, methods, and properties introduced here is complete, with examples for each and every one of them. For now, we just need to develop a feel for the language and its important objects, methods, properties, and event handlers.

#  The `window` Object

Everything starts with the `window` object. Because it is the topmost object (in the object hierarchy; refer to Figure 3.1 in Chapter 3), you do not need to use its name in object references when you access its and its descendants' properties. Thus, even though the full path of the document object's `close()` method is `window.document.close()`, when you call `close()` from the current document you can just write `document.close()`. Be aware that there are exceptions to this rule—in some cases you will have to include window in your "dot path." These exceptions are discussed in the reference chapters.

A `window` object is created for you when you start the browser. You can create your own windows with the `window` object's method `open()`. For reference, the properties, methods, and event handlers of the `window` object are listed in Table 4.1.

**TABLE 4.1** Properties methods and event handlers of the window object.

| Properties | Methods | Event Handlers |
|---|---|---|
| defaultStatus, document, focus, frame, frames, length, location, name, opener, parent, self, status, top, window | alert(), blur(), clearTimeout(), close(), confirm(), focus(), open(), prompt(), scroll(), setTimeout() | onBlur, onError, onFocus, onLoad, onUnload |

## Properties of the `window` **Object**

The following sections list and describe some of the `window`'s properties.

### defaultStatus

The default message is displayed in the status bar at the bottom of the Navigator window. You can set the default status by statements such as

```
window.defaultStatus = "A message"
```

which will cause the string on the right to display in the bottom of the window. This message will appear anytime nothing else is specified to appear there; something can be specified to appear there by setting another `window` object's property called `status`.

Set this property to a string value that you wish to display in the status line when the mouse is not over an object that sets the status line with the `status` property. The use of this property is demonstrated in Exercise 4.3.

### document

Use this property to access the document that is loaded into the current window.

### frames

This property holds data about the sub-windows inside a window. The differences between `frames` and `window` objects is the fact that a window is the top object, and a few methods, such as setting the status line—see below—are not available to `frames`. Frames allow you to divide the window into sub-regions, and build different interfaces (that interact with the user) among frames. Frames form an array that is a property of the window. Thus, you can refer to the first frame in a window as

```
parent.frames[0]
```

where parent specifies the parent of frames (the window in which `frames[0]` resides). To find how many frames you have in a window, use

```
parent.frames.length
```

To refer to the last frame in a window, use

```
parent.frames[parent.frames.length-1]
```

Frames, like windows, have as one of their properties a document (see Figure 3.1 in Chapter 3). Thus, to refer to the title of a document in the first frame, you write

```
parent.frames[0].document.title
```

and so on. JavaScript allows you to use names for indexes. For example, if the name of a frame is `frameOne`, and you are not sure about its index in the array of frames, you can refer to its document title thus:

```
parent.frames["frameOne"].document.title
```

## length

Use this property to find out how many frames a `window` contains. You can access this property with a statement like this:

```
numberOfFrames = windowReference.length
```

## location

The URL from which the window was loaded is stored in this property.

## name

You can use this property to access the name of a window or of a frame in a window. The name is usually given with the appropriate tag. For example, if you create a window with a statement like this:

```
aWindow = window.open("","windowName")
```

you can then access the window name this way:

```
aName = aWindow.name
```

If you create a frame in a window with the HTML tag

```
<FRAME NAME = "aFrame" ...>
```

and if the frame named `aFrame` is the first frame in the window, then you can refer to the frame's name with the following statement:

```
aName = aWindow.frames[0].name
```

In this case `aName` will be assigned the value aFrame.

## opener

This property tells you which window opened the current window. If, for example, the statement

```
aWindow = window.open("", "windowName")
```

appears in another window, then the URL of the other window will be stored in `aWindow.opener`. You can thus discover the URL of the window that was used to created the current window.

## parent

Windows (in particular, frames) may have `parent` windows that you may need to refer to. For example, the parent property allows you to access the window that includes the two child windows as shown in Figure 4.1. We will see an example in a minute. In the figure, we have a parent window, the one that sets the frames, and two child windows, the frames themselves. To be able to refer to a property or data of the parent window from one of the child windows, you use the `parent` property. Before looking at an example, and because these properties are related, we next talk about the `self` and `top` properties.

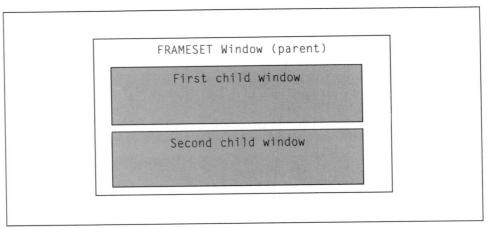

**FIGURE 4.1** FRAMESET and child windows.

### self

This property allows you to access properties and methods of the current object in use. Exercise 4.1 demonstrates the use of this property.

### status

This property refers to the status line that appears at the bottom of the Navigator window. Use this property to temporarily control the content of this status line. The use of this property is demonstrated in Exercise 4.3.

### top

This property refers to the topmost window in the Navigator hierarchy. Use this property to access other objects that are included in the HTML document. In Figure 4.1, for example, the FRAMESET window is the top window. If the first child window needs to refer to some object (say, a button) in the second child window, you will need to use the dot hierarchy to access properties of the button through top. We will see an example momentarily.

### window

Use this property as yet another way to refer to the current window. This property allows you to deal with accessing properties that in some situations may confuse the browser. For example, the document and window objects have some methods (open(), close(), and so on) that have identical names. To remove ambiguity from your code, you need to use window.close() when you want to close a window. If you just write close(), this will (in most cases) close the document, not the window. This is so because of variable and function *scoping*.

To clarify (a little) the idea here, suppose that you have a single-frame window. You wish to access some property of the window. The following statements are all equivalent and will access the said property:

```
window.someProperty
self.someProperty
someProperty
```

As I said, *someProperty* will work in most but not all cases.

To see how some of the window properties relate to each other, and gain some practice in using them, we next go through a series of exercises and examples.

# Using window Properties—Examples

Exercise 4.1 demonstrates the use and access of window properties such as frames, self, top, window, and parent.

**EXERCISE 4.1** WINDOWS AND FRAMES.

1. Start your favorite word processor or text editor.

2. Type the code in Listing 4.1; do not type the line numbers. Save this text file as FramesAndWindows.HTML (or some other filename) if you are running under Windows 95 or MacOS; otherwise, save the listing with a filename of your choice.

3. Type Listing 4.2 and save it as window1.HTML.

4. Type Listing 4.3 and save it as window2.HTML.

5. Load FramesAndWindows.HTML to your browser, press the buttons, and examine the results. You should get a display that corresponds to Figure 4.2.

6. Change the filenames window1.HTML and window2.HTML to names of your choice; implement these changes in the appropriate place in the code, and load the file that sets up the frames into your browser. You should get the same results as in step 5.

**LISTING 4.1** Frames and windows, setup file.

```
1    <HTML>
2    <HEAD>
3    <TITLE>Parents and Children</TITLE>
4    <SCRIPT LANGUAGE = "JavaScript">
5    function someWindowProperties(frameIndex)
6    {
7      var theProperties = ""
8      theProperties +=
9       "top:  " + top + "\n"
10     theProperties +=
11      "window:  " + window + "\n"
12     theProperties +=
13      "self:  " + self + "\n\n"
14     theProperties +=
15        "self.document.title:  " + self.document.title + "\n"
16     theProperties +=
17        "parent:  " + parent + "\n"
18     theProperties +=
19        "parent.document.title:  " + parent.document.title + "\n"
20     theProperties +=
21        "this.frames["+frameIndex+"].document.title:  " +
22        this.frames[frameIndex].document.title + "\n"
```

```
23        alert(theProperties)
24    }
25    </SCRIPT>
26    </HEAD>
27    <FRAMESET ROWS="50%,50%">
28      <FRAME  NAME = "firstFrame"
29          SRC = "window1.html">
30      <FRAME  NAME = "secondFrame"
31          SRC = "window2.html">
32    </FRAMESET>
33    </HTML>
```

**LISTING 4.2** Frames and windows; `window1.html`. The frame setup is shown in Listing 4.1.

```
1     <HTML>
2     <HEAD>
3     <TITLE>First Frame Title</TITLE>
4     </HEAD>
5     <BODY>
6     <FORM>
7     <INPUT  TYPE  = "button"
8          NAME  = "firstFrame"
9          VALUE = "First frame properties..."
10         onClick = "parent.someWindowProperties(0)">
11    </FORM>
12    </BODY>
13    </HTML>
```

**LISTING 4.3** Frames and windows; `window2.html`. The frame setup is shown in Listing 4.1.

```
1     <HTML>
2     <HEAD>
3     <TITLE>Second Frame Title</TITLE>
4     </HEAD>
5     <BODY>
6     <FORM>
7     <INPUT  TYPE  = "button"
8          NAME  = "secondFrame"
9          VALUE = "Second frame properties..."
10         onClick = "parent.someWindowProperties(1)">
11    </FORM>
12    </BODY>
13    </HTML>
```

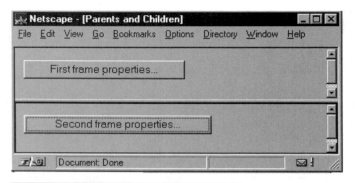

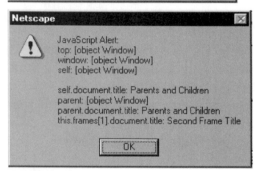

**FIGURE 4.2** Windows and Frames: (a) window with two frames; (b) first frame properties; (c) second frame properties.

From the perspective of object hierarchy, Listing 4.1 creates the top window (the FRAMESET window in Figure 4.2); Listing 4.2 corresponds to the First child window in Figure 4.2; and Listing 4.3 corresponds to the Second child window in Figure 4.2. Because we wish to demonstrate the idea of hierarchy and the access of properties, we put the function someWindowProperties() in the top window. We could have, alternatively, put copies of the function in each of the child windows, in which case access will be less tortuous but more cumbersome.

In line 5 of Listing 4.1 we start the definition of the function someWindowProperties(). The function takes a single argument, the index of the frame that calls the function. Recall that windows have a frames property, which is an array of frames (starting the count from zero). So if we call someWindowProperties() from a frame, we simply send to the function the index of that frame. This will be clarified momentarily.

In line 7 of Listing 4.1 we initialize a string variable, theProperties, to an empty value (which, remember, is different from a NULL value). We later use this variable to collect the properties and display them in the JavaScript alert window. Next, we put the value of the top property in the theProperties string (lines 8 and 9). The remaining code of the function (lines 10 through 24) is self-explanatory—it simply builds the array that lists all of the window properties. Study these lines and make sure that you are able to predict what theProperties will eventually look like in the alert window.

In lines 27 through 32 of Listing 4.1 we set up the two frames. We now have the object hierarchy shown in Figure 4.1.

Listings 4.2 and 4.3 are almost identical. The important difference between them is the call to the function someWindowProperties(): In the former we use an index value of 0 (the first frame), and in the latter we use a value of 1 (the second frame). Note the use of the parent property in line 10 of both Listing 4.2 and Listing 4.3. Without it, we cannot access someWindowProperties(). This is so because someWindowProperties() is a function in the parent of both frames. To understand what happens, try Exercise 4.2.

---

**EXERCISE 4.2**   HOW THE PARENT PROPERTY WORKS.

1. Remove "parent." (the word "parent" as well as the following period) from the code in both window1.HTML and window2.HTML.

2. Reload FramesAndWindows.HTML (you may have to quit and restart your browser). What happened? Do you understand why?

---

When you first load FramesAndWindows.HTML using Exercise 4.1, the window shown in Figure 4.2 appears. Soon after you click on the First frame properties... button, you should see the alert window shown in Figure 4.2. Note that the top, window, self, this, and parent properties all produce the same result: These are properties of the FRAMESET window (see Figure 4.1). To access properties of a frame, you use its index (or its name as a string, instead of the numerical value of the index). Thus, the document titles of frame[0] and frame[1] appear correctly (see Figure 4.2).

It is important to realize that each of the frames in Figure 4.2 has its own `document` object, and that the title that appears in the HTML text file (for example, line 3 in both Listing 4.2 and Listing 4.3) is a property of the `document` object that belongs to the frame, not of the frame. The `document` object is created by the browser and is populated by the components of the HTML document.

As a final example in this section, let us take a look at the `status` and `defaultStatus` properties. To see how these work, do Exercise 4.3.

**EXERCISE 4.3** The status and defaultStatus properties.

1. Create an HTML file for Listing 4.4.

2. Load the file into your browser and move the mouse around. In particular, move over the message and Netscape Home words, and watch the status line.

3. You should get three different messages; one of them is shown in Figure 4.3. Did you?

**LISTING 4.4** The `status` and `defaultStatus` properties.

```
1    <HTML>
2    <HEAD>
3    <TITLE> The status and defaultStatus Properties </TITLE>
4    </HEAD>
5    <H3> The status and defaultStatus Properties </H3>
6    <BODY onLoad = "window.defaultStatus = 'Here is the default
status.'">
7    Move the mouse around, and watch the
8    <A HREF = "message"
9      onMouseOver = "window.status = 'Put a message here.'; return
true">
10   message</A>
11   on the status line changing.
12   <P>
13   <A HREF = "http://home.netscape.com"
14     onMouseOver = "window.status = 'Go to Netscape Home page.';
return true">Netscape Home</A>
15   </BODY>
16   </HTML>
```

Once you go through Exercise 4.3 you will understand the `status` and `defaultStatus` properties. There is one peculiarity in the code that must be pointed out here. Look at lines 9 and 14 in Listing 4.4. The semicolons in

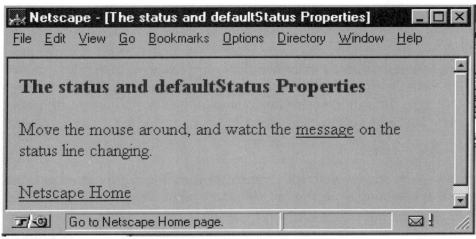

**FIGURE 4.3** The status and defaultStatus properties.

these lines separate two statements that go with the event handler onMouseOver. The first statement in line 14, for example, is

```
window.status = 'Go to Netscape Home page.'
```

and the second is

```
return true
```

This event handler requires an expression that returns true as its last expression, and the statement return true in lines 9 and 14 do just that.

## Methods of the window Object

### alert(aString)
This method creates an alert window and returns no value. The window displays the value of aString. It is a modal window, which means that the user cannot do anything with the browser application before clicking on the OK button. Lest you annoy your visitors, use this window sparingly!

### blur()
This method sends the window to the desktop background (in most window systems). In the call to the method you need to explicitly state the window or the frame reference, like this:

```
windowReference.blur()
```

or

```
frameReference.blur()
```

where *windowReference* and frameReference are valid ways to refer to a `window` object or a `frame` object. A valid way to refer to a `window` is by creating a reference to the window with (for example) the `(open)` method (discussed below). Thus, the statement

```
aWindow = open(...)
```

creates a valid window reference named `aWindow`. You can create a frame reference by assigning a value to the `NAME` attribute of the `<FRAME>` tag like this:

```
<FRAME SRC = "source"
    NAME = "frameReference">
```

where `source` is the URL of the HTML file you want to load to the frame.

### clearTimeout(*timeOutID*)

This method clears a previously created time-out with `setTimeout()` (see below). The method `setTimeout()` returns a `timeOutID`, an internal number by which the call to `setTimeout()` is identified.

### close()

This method closes an open window. There are some subtleties involved with the use of this method, and they are discussed following Exercise 4.5.

### confirm(*aString*)

This method creates a so-called confirm dialog window with `aString` displayed in it. It returns true if the user clicks on the `OK` button and false if she clicks on the `Cancel` button. Use this method sparingly. To see how it works, go through Exercise 4.4. You may use the technique shown in Exercise 4.4 for debugging.

---

**EXERCISE 4.4**  THE CONFIRM WINDOW

1. Create an HTML file for Listing 4.5.
2. Load the file into your browser and click the `Click here...` button.
3. You should get results as shown in Figure 4.4.
4. Experiment with the `OK` and `Cancel` buttons and verify that `confirm()` returns `true` or `false`, based on the button you click.

**LISTING 4.5** The `confirm` dialog window.

```
1    <HTML>
2    <HEAD>
3    <TITLE>Confirm</TITLE>
4    <SCRIPT LANGUAGE = "JavaScript">
5    function returnValue()
6    {
7      var trueOrFalse =
8       confirm("Click OK or Cancel to see the return value")
9      alert("confirm() returned " + trueOrFalse)
10   }
11   </SCRIPT>
12   </HEAD>
13   <BODY>
14   <H3>Confirm</H3>
15   <FORM>
16   <INPUT  TYPE = "button"
17        NAME = "aButton"
18        VALUE = "Confirm..."
19        onClick = "returnValue()">
20   </FORM>
21   </BODY>
22   </HTML>
```

Let us look at the code in Listing 4.5 briefly:

• In lines 5 through 10 we define the function `returnValue()` because we wish to see the value that `confirm()` returns.

**FIGURE 4.4**  The confirm dialog window.

- In line 7 we declare the variable `trueOrFalse`, and assign to it the value returned from `confirm()` in line 8.
- In line 9 we display `trueOrFalse` with an alert dialog window.
- Figure 4.4 shows the confirm dialog window, and Figure 4.5 shows the return value from `confirm()` when the user clicks on the `OK` button of the confirm dialog window in Figure 4.4.
- In lines 16 to 19 we set up a `button` object named `aButton`, and assign `returnValue()` to its `onClick` event handler.

## focus()

This method does the opposite of what `blur()` does: It brings the desired `window` to focus. To work with `focus()`, use the following syntax:

```
windowReference.focus()
```

or

```
frameReference.focus()
```

`windowReference` and `frameReference` are explained in the discussion of the `blur()` method above.

## open("*URL*", "*windowName*"[, "*aStringOfFeatures*"])

This method returns a newly created window object, or null if the function fails to create the object. Recall that the square bracket notation indicates optional elements; the call to `open()` must have at least two arguments, *URL* and *windowName*. These appear in italics because they take a value that you assign (or a variable with a name of your choice and the appropriate value assigned to that name).

**FIGURE 4.5** Return value from `confirm()`.

The *URL* argument specifies the HTML document you wish to populate the window with. Although you cannot omit this argument, you can specify nothing for it, that is, you can give it the value `""`. If you do that, an empty window will be created and you can then populate it with a document that is created via JavaScript (see Exercise 4.5).

Use the *windowName* argument to name the newly created window. The third (optional) argument to the function is a single string that contains a variety of features you can use to create the window. You can, for example, create the window with or without a toolbar, with or without location field, and so on. The available features are detailed in Table 4.2.

The syntax for the call is simple: All Boolean features are set to false, and you name those that you wish to set to true. Thus, if you wish to create a new window with a toolbar and scrollbars, and using the default width and height, make the call as follows:

```
window.open("index.html", "My Window",
"toolbar,scrollbars")
```

This will load the `index.html` file from the local directory, will name the newly created window `My Window`, and will endow it with a toolbar and scrollbars.

A more thorough call might look like this:

```
window.open("", "",
"toolbar,scrollbars,height=100,width=200")
```

**TABLE 4.2** Window features in the call to `window.open()`.

| Feature | Type | Comments |
|---------|------|----------|
| toolbar | Boolean | If true, creates the familiar toolbar buttons. |
| location | Boolean | If true, displays the current URL. |
| directories | Boolean | If true, displays browser specific directory buttons. |
| status | Boolean | If true, displays the status line. |
| menubar | Boolean | If true, displays the menubar with the window (not on Macintosh). |
| scrollbars | Boolean | If true, displays scrollbars, if necessary. |
| resizable | Boolean | If true, the window is resizable. |
| copyhistory | Boolean | If true, the Go menu history is duplicated. |
| width | integer | Window width, in pixels. |
| height | integer | Window height, in pixels. |

To see how `open()` and `close()` work, follow the instructions in Exercise 4.5.

**EXERCISE 4.5** | OPENING AND CLOSING WINDOWS.

1. Create an HTML file for Listing 4.6.

2. Load the file into your browser and open and close the window.

3. You should get results as shown in Figure 4.6.

4. Change the window features in line 9 of Listing 4.6 to create a variety of window features. In particular, figure out what the default width and height are.

**LISTING 4.6** Opening and closing windows.

```
1    <HTML>
2    <HEAD>
3    <TITLE> Open and Close a Window </TITLE>
4    <SCRIPT LANGUAGE = "JavaScript">
5    var anotherWindow = null
6    function createWindow()
7    {
8      // window.open returns a window object
9       anotherWindow = window.open("", "", "width=200,height=100")
10     // does the window exist?
11     if (anotherWindow != null)
12     {
13      // create the HTML
14      var newContent =
15        "<HTML><HEAD><TITLE>Another Window</TITLE></HEAD>"
16      newContent +=
17        "<BODY><H3>Another Window</H3>"
18      newContent +=
19        "<FORM><INPUT TYPE = 'button' VALUE = 'Close' onClick =
'self.close()'></FORM>"
20      newContent +=
21        "</BODY></HTML>"
22      // write the HTML
23      anotherWindow.document.write(newContent)
24     }
25   }
26   </SCRIPT>
27   </HEAD>
28   <BODY>
29   <H2> Open and Close a Window </H2>
30   <FORM>
```

```
31    <INPUT TYPE = "button"
32        NAME = "openWindow"
33        VALUE = "New Window"
34        onClick = "createWindow()">
35    <INPUT TYPE = "button"
36        NAME = "closeWindow"
37        VALUE = "Close Window"
38        onClick = "anotherWindow.close()">
39    </FORM>
40    </BODY>
41    </HTML>
```

Let us discuss Listing 4.6 for a moment. First, note the declaration of a global variable in line 5. By declaring `anotherWindow` outside a function, we are telling the JavaScript interpreter to recognize this variable name wherever it appears in the script. If we were to declare it inside the function braces, it would be recognized only inside the function. This, in programming jargon, is called variable *scope*.

*Scope* refers to the duration of existence of a variable. Let's look at a variable declared within a function. A function, "exists" for as long as it is executed—once execution is complete, the function no longer exists. (The word "exist" here has a precise meaning having to do with things such as memory, stacks, loading order, and so on, but we shall not pursue it further.) Thus, when you declare a variable inside a function and assign a value to it, that value is accessible everywhere in the function by using the variable name; but you can access neither the variable value from outside the function by using the variable name, nor the variable itself (because it no longer exists). We then say that the scope of the variable is inside the function. When you declare a variable outside a function (as we did in line 5 of Listing 4.6), you can access the value of the variable by using the variable name from anywhere in your script.

We next define the `createWindow()` function. In line 9 a `window` object is created by the function `window.open()` and is assigned to the variable `anotherWindow`. If the window has been created successfully, the value of `anotherWindow` is no longer null, and we can go ahead and design the HTML page (lines 14–21). The instructions to construct the new HTML page are stored in the `newContent` variable. This variable exists only inside the function `createWindow()`, and cannot be referred to outside the function. "Inside the function" means inside the braces that delineate the function (opening in line 7 and closing in line 25).

Finally, in line 23 we write the HTML page to the new window's document. Note that in the newly created HTML page we are adding code to create a button in the new window, and the action of this button is to close the window itself. This is done with a call to `self.close()` in line 19.

In lines 31 to 34 we create a button that will open the new window by calling `createWindow()`. Again, we are creating a button that allows the user to close the new window from the top window (lines 35 to 38). Note the difference in the call to `close()` in line 19 vs. line 38: In line 19 we are calling `close()` from within the new window, and therefore use the `self` property to tell the interpreter which window to close. In line 38, we are closing a `window` object, which is stored in the global variable `anotherWindow`. Here again the dot notation and object hierarchy "conspire" to confuse us, but by now we know what we are doing.

The results of running the code in Listing 4.6 are demonstrated in Figure 4.6.

## prompt(aString[, defaultValue])

Calling `prompt()` creates a modal window on the screen. In the window, `aString` is displayed with an input field where the user can type input. If *defaultValue* is specified, it is displayed as the default value in the input field. When the user clicks `OK` (returns from the window), the method returns the value in the input field. If the user clicks the `Cancel` button, the function returns `null`. If nothing is entered in the field, an empty string (`""`) is returned. Use this method to acquire information from the user. Keep in mind that the return value is always a string; if you wish to obtain a numer-

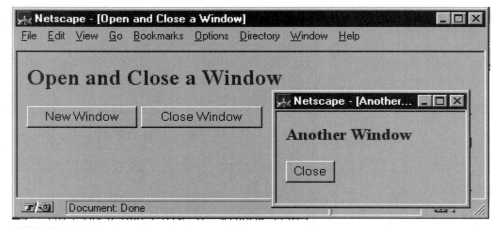

**FIGURE 4.6** Opening and closing windows.

ical value from the user, you will have to use string processing functions to convert the return value to the appropriate data type. An example of how to use the prompt window is given in Exercise 4.6.

EXERCISE 4.6 THE PROMPT WINDOW.

1. Create an HTML file for Listing 4.7.

2. Load the file into your browser and click the Click here... button.

3. You should get results as shown in Figure 4.7.

4. Experiment with the OK and Cancel buttons with and without something entered in the input area of the prompt window. Examine the return values. Be sure to understand the difference between null and an empty string.

**LISTING 4.7** The prompt window.

```
1     <HTML>
2     <HEAD>
3     <TITLE>Prompt</TITLE>
4     <SCRIPT LANGUAGE = "JavaScript">
5     function returnValue()
6     {
7       var returnValue =
8        prompt("Enter something and click OK or enter nothing and
         click OK or click Cancel","")
9       alert('prompt() returned "' + returnValue + '"')
10    }
11    </SCRIPT>
12    </HEAD>
13    <BODY>
14    <H3>Prompt</H3>
15    <FORM>
16    <INPUT TYPE = "button"
17        NAME = ""
18        VALUE = "Click here..."
19        onClick = "returnValue()">
20    </FORM>
21    </BODY>
22    </HTML>
```

Here is what the code in Listing 4.7 does:

- In lines 5 to 10 we define the function returnValue() because we wish to see what prompt() actually returns.

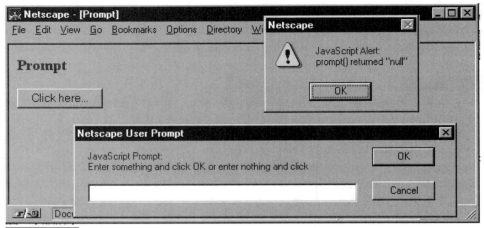

**FIGURE 4.7** The prompt window.

- In lines 7 and 8 we assign the return value from `prompt()` to `returnValue`.
- Then, in line 9 we `prompt()` the `returnValue`.
- The results are shown in Figure 4.7.

## scroll(*x,y*)

Use this method to scroll a window to specified *x,y* coordinates. The coordinates are specified in pixels. To specify which window to scroll, use the syntax

```
windowReference.scroll(x,y)
```

where *windowReference* is a valid way to refer to a window, as explained in the discussion of the `blur()` method above. Note that `scroll()` does not move the cursor; it just scrolls the window. Unfortunately, you cannot control the cursor position from JavaScript. This, I am sure, will change in the future.

## setTimeout("expression", millisecondsToWait)

This function returns a value that is used in `clearTimeout()`. Use this function to specify the amount of time in milliseconds that you wish to wait before *expression* is evaluated. In *expression*, put whatever you wish to execute. For example, you may wish to create a scrolling banner. If the banner moves too fast, you can slow it down with this function. There are some subtleties involved here, but we shall just leave it at that.

## Event Handlers of the window Object

### onBlur

When focus is removed from a window so that it is no longer the top window (when, for example, the user clicks on another window), a blur event occurs, and it, in turn, triggers the onBlur event handler. You can simulate the event handler with the blur() window method.

### onError

When an error occurs as Navigator loads a window, an error event occurs, and it, in turn, triggers the onError event handler. You can use this event handler to deal with errors that occur during activities such as loading a window or an image.

### onFocus

When a window receives focus (when, for example, the user clicks on the window and brings it to the top of the desktop), a focus event occurs, and it, in turn, triggers the onFocus event handler.

### onLoad

When the browser finishes loading the document, this event is sent to the current window. You can use this event to display a message on the status line, for example. Do not use this event to activate one of the modal windows discussed above; this may cause delays for users that automate (use macros for) navigation on the Internet.

### onUnload

Just before a document is cleared from view, an unload event is sent to the current window. If you need to process some information just before the document disappears, use this event handler.

 # The frame Object

A frame is created as part of a FRAMESET by another document. Other than this fact, which leads to a different hierarchy, a frame object behaves exactly like a window. Its properties, methods, and event handlers are identical to those shown in Table 4.1. Like a window object, a frame object can point to its own URL, and can be targeted by other URLs. Being an experienced HTML user, you should know how to create frames.

Here we need to discuss hierarchy again. Consider the code snippet shown in Listing 4.8. It will create the object hierarchy shown in Figure 4.8 and a window skeleton shown in Figure 4.9. You access the various frames and their properties and methods as shown in Figure 4.8. Note that all frames have the same parent, regardless of how they were defined within a FRAMESET. The following rules will save you grief (and debugging time) in the future:

A frame's parent is its parent window.

A frame defines a window.

A FRAMESET does not define a window.

**LISTING 4.8** frames hierarchy.

```
1    <FRAMESET ROWS="90%,10%">
2      <FRAMESET COLS="30%,70%">
3      <FRAME SRC = file1.html NAME = "northEastFrame">
4      <FRAME SRC = file2.html NAME = "northWestFrame">
5      </FRAMESET>
6      <FRAME SRC = file3.html NAME = "southFrame">
7    </FRAMESET>
```

To further clarify the idea of frames, windows, and hierarchies, consider the code snippet in Listing 4.9, and supose that file1.html in line 2 includes the code snippet in Listing 4.10. This will create the object hierarchy shown in Figure 4.10 and the window skeleton shown in Figure 4.11. You access the

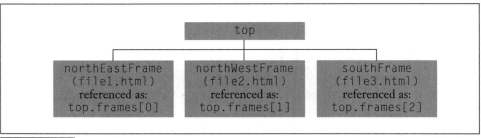

**FIGURE 4.8** frames hierarchy. The shading illustrates the hierarchy from topmost dark to bottom light.

Chapter 4

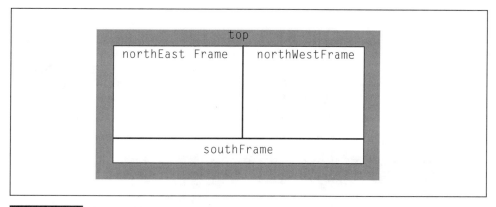

**FIGURE 4.9** frames hierarchy in a window.

various `frames`, their properties, and methods as shown in Figure 4.10. Compare the shading in Figure 4.9 to that in Figure 4.11—it highlights the idea of hierarchy.

**LISTING 4.9** Another frames hierarchy.

```
1    <FRAMESET ROWS="90%,10%">
2       <FRAME SRC = file1.html NAME = "northFrame">
3       <FRAME SRC = file2.html NAME = "southFrame">
4    </FRAMESET>
```

**LISTING 4.10** Yet another frame hierarchy.

```
1    <FRAMESET COLS="30%,70%">
2       <FRAME SRC = file1a.html NAME = "eastFrame">
3       <FRAME SRC = file1b.html NAME = "westFrame">
4    </FRAMESET>
```

# ⤷ The document Object

The `document` object is one of the richest objects in JavaScript. Take a look at the object hierarchy in Figures 3.1 and 3.2 in Chapter 3, and examine it closely to see which objects are daughters of `document`. For your reference, Table 4.3 details the properties, methods, and event handlers of the `document` object.

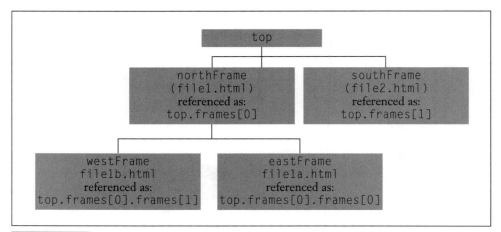

**FIGURE 4.10** Yet another frames hierarchy. The shading illustrates the hierarchy from topmost dark to bottom light.

**TABLE 4.3** Properties, methods, and event handlers of the document object.

| Properties | Methods | Event Handlers |
|---|---|---|
| alinkColor, anchor, anchors, Applet, applets, Area, bgColor, cookie, embeds, fgColor, form, forms, history, Image, images, lastModified, link, linkColor, links, Plugin, referrer, title, URL , vlinkColor | close(), open(), write(), writeln() | None |

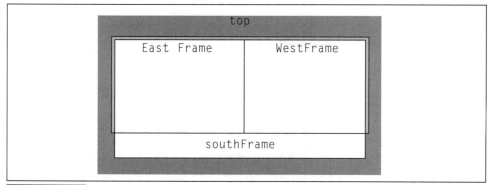

**FIGURE 4.11** Yet another frames hierarchy in a window.

To understand where the document object sits physically, not only in terms of the object hierarchy shown in Figures 3.1 and 3.2, but also take a look at Figure 4.12. Here a frameset `window` object has created two `frame` objects. Each of these objects contains an HTML document which actually determines what is displayed in the window. This hierarchy is also depicted by shading from light in the background to dark in the foreground. A structure like the one shown in Figure 4.12 could have been created by code such as this:

```
<FRAMESET COLS = "50%, 50%">
  <FRAME SRC = FILE1.HTML NAME = "north">
  <FRAME SRC = FILE2.HTML NAME = "south">
</FRAMESET>
```

What we have then is a top window which contains two `frame` objects, that are, for all practical purposes, two `window` objects. When the browser loads each of the HTML files to their respective frames, it creates two instances of the `document` object. These `document` objects interpret the HTML code and display it in the window. In terms of hierarchy, one way to refer to the individual `document` objects that were inserted in the `north` and `south` frame objects is to say

```
window.frames[0].document
```

and

```
window.frames[1].document
```

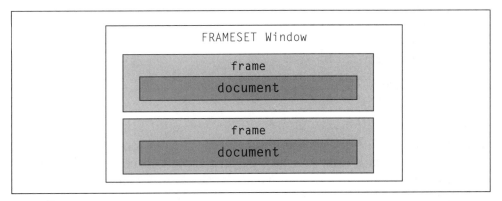

**FIGURE 4.12** The document objects in the physical hierarchy of a Navigator window. Light is background, dark is foreground.

respectively. If you insist, you could create an even more complicated structure, including another `frameset` in the `north` and `south` frames by including the `<FRAMESET>` tag in `FILE1.HTML` and `FILE2.HTML`.

## Properties of the document Object

### alinkColor

This property determines the color of an active link in your document. Colors can be specified as a combination of three hexadecimal numbers that indicate the mix of red, green, and blue (hence the convention RGB). Each color value is specified in the range from 00 to FF (255 decimal). For example, FF0000 is pure red, 00FF00 is pure green, and 00FFFF is the color named aqua. You can also specify colors with their literal names, such as "aqua" (see Appendix C for a list of recognized color names).

### anchor

An `anchor` object is created with the `<A>` tag. When such an object is created in the document, it becomes its property.

### anchors

This is an array property that holds all of the anchors in a `document`. You can thus use the `length` property of arrays to find how many anchors there are in your document by a statement such as:

```
aCount = document.anchors.length
```

The `anchors` array is automatically constructed as the HTML document is laid out. Each `anchor` object is added as an element to the `anchors` array in the order it is encountered in the HTML source code. So if you have three anchors in your document (three <A> tags), and you want to refer to the second `anchor` object, you can write

```
document.anchors[1]
```

### Applet

Instances of `Applet` objects can be created in your document with the `<APPLET>` tag. This is how you include Java applets in your HTML document. Suppose that you included two applets in your document, and that the code for the second one looks something like this:

```
<APPLET ... NAME = "myApplet" ...>
```

To access the `name` property of `myApplet`, you can write

```
appletName = document.applets[1].name
```

The last statement will assign the string `myApplet` to the variable `appletName`.

## applets

This is an array that is built for you as the page is laid out and `<APPLET>` tags are encountered in the HTML source code.

## Area

You can define an area of an image as an imagemap.

## bgColor

This specifies the `document` background color (see `alinkColor` for further details about colors).

## cookie

The browser creates a so-called `cookie` file on the client's PC. You can store and retrieve some information from this file using JavaScript. For security reasons, your control over the file is limited, and it is largely maintained by the browser. The cookie property is discussed in detail in the reference section.

## embeds

The `<EMBED>` tag creates a plug-in object in the document. Each `<EMBED>` tag in the document is added to the `embeds` array in the order it is encountered in the source code. To access the *i*-th plug-in, you use the statement

```
document.embeds[i]
```

where *i* is the index of the desired plug-in the `embeds` array.

## fgColor

This property holds the document's foreground color (the color of text). See the discussion of `alinkColor` for details about color specifications.

## forms

The `forms` property is an array of forms that are included in the `document` object. A `form` object inside a document is created whenever you use the FORM tag. If you name the form `<FORM NAME = "someName"`... then you refer to the form as `document.someName`. We have also seen examples in which forms are referred to using the array notation: `document.forms[0]`.

### history

The `history` object is a linked list of URLs the user has visited. You can use it to navigate back and forth with methods such as `history.go(-3)` (to go three links backward in your sequence of visits). Use this property to emulate the actions of the Go | Back or Go | Forward Navigator menu options.

A linked list, incidentally, is like an array, except that each element in the list also has the address (in memory) where the next element of the list is.

### image

For each `<IMG>` tag an `image` object is created. This object can be accessed via the document hierarchy.

### images

Each `<IMG>` tag that is encountered is added to the images array in the source order. `image` properties can be accessed the usual way. For example, you can write in your document the name of the first `image` object in your document by a statement like this:

```
document.write(document.images[0].name)
lastModified
```

We have used the `lastModified` property in Exercise 1.5 in Chapter 1.

### link

Each `<A>` HTML tag that is encountered in your code causes a creation of a new `link` object (see `links` below).

### linkColor

This property specifies the color of the document hyperlinks. See discussion of the `alinkColor` property for color specifications.

### links

Items that are created with the `<A HREF = ...>` tag are links in an HTML page. They accumulate in the `links` array. You can thus find, how many links there are in a page with the statement:

```
lCount = document.links.length
```

## plugin

Each `<EMBED>` tag that is encountered in your HTML code triggers creation of a `plugin` object that is also added to the `embeds` array (see the `embeds` property above).

## referrer

This property holds the URL of a document that refers to a link in the current document. This provides a good way to spy on your visitors.

## title

The string between the `<TITLE>` and `</TITLE>` tags in your HTML document is stored in this property.

## URL

This property stores the document object URL, and you access it like this, for example:

```
document.write(document.URL)
```

## vlinkColor

This property stores a string that specifies the color of visited links (see discussion of `alinkColor` for color specification).

# Methods of the document Object

## close()

This function returns nothing; the complement of `open()`, it closes a document. When you write to a document using, for example `write()`, you should `close()` the document in order to see the result.

## open(["*mimeTypes*"])

This returns nothing. If you wish to use `document.write()` to write to a document object that does not yet exist, you first need to open it. Mime type specifies what kind of data the document is going to receive. Some of the values that JavaScript accepts for *mimeTypes* are:

- text/HTML
- text/plain

- image/gif
- image/jpeg
- image/xbm
- plugIn

See the discussion of the `mimeTypes` object in the reference section for further details.

### write(["*aString*"]) **and** writeln(["aString"])

This returns `true` if successful. We have seen examples of `document.write()`. The `document.writeln()` behaves just like `document.write()`, except that it adds a carriage return to the end of *aString*. Be aware that the carriage return may not be added, depending on the HTML code in which `writeln()` is embedded. To cause the next `write` to actually start at the beginning of the next line, you can enclose `writeln()` in the `<PRE>` tag like this:

```
<PRE>
  <SCRIPT LANGUAGE = "JavaScript">
   writeln("Campaign contributions = bribes!")
  </SCRIPT>
</PRE>
```

or more simply, just add a `<BR>` in `write()`—for example:

```
write("Campaign contributions = bribes!<BR>")
```

#  The `form` Object and the `forms` Array

Rather than go through the same format I used in discussing the `window` and `document` objects, I want to introduce you to the `form` object in a more narrative way. To see exactly how it works, and what its properties, methods, and event handlers are, refer to the appropriate reference chapters.

The `form` object is the way to build an interactive HTML page. All of the elements of the form are designed to facilitate interaction. We shall talk about form elements in a moment. For now, just remember that any user interface elements (`button`, `text`, `textarea`, `radio`, `select`, and `checkbox` objects) must be embedded in the `form`, and become elements in the `forms` array. You can collect data through these objects, and then use the data to react to user input.

You create a form object with the `<FORM>` tag. To build on the physical hierarchy we introduced in Figure 4.12, we add another layer in Figure 4.13. The darkest layer is in front of the other objects (it is at the bottom of the hierarchy).

In Figure 4.13 we have a window with two frames in it. Each `frame` has one `document`, and each document has one `form`. You could have more if you wish; however, keep your page and JavaScript code simple—neither you nor your visitor need complicated HTML documents. Here is one way to refer to the bottom form in Figure 4.13 all the way from the top object (the `window`):

```
window.frames[1].document.forms[0]
```

Now suppose that you add two buttons to the bottom form in Figure 4.13, naming them `politician` and `bribes` like this:

```
<FORM>
<INPUT                TYPE = "button"
                      NAME = "politician"
                      VALUE = "Democrat">
<INPUT                TYPE = "buttons"
                      NAME = "anotherPolitician"
                      VALUE = "Republican">
</FORM>
```

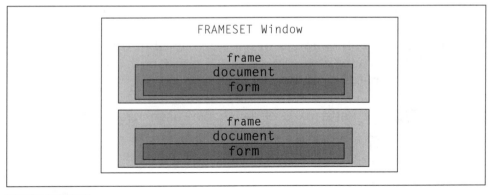

**FIGURE 4.13** The `form` objects in the physical hierarchy of a Navigator window. Light is background, dark is foreground.

Then if you want to store the `value` of the `button` object named `politician`, you write

```
partyAffiliation =
window.frames[1].document.forms[0].elements[0].value
```

and if you want to store the `value` of the `anotherPolititian` button, you write

```
partyAffiliation
window.frames[1].document.forms[0].elements[1].value
```

If you happen to name the frames and the forms (with the tag `NAME`), you can refer to these elements with their names, instead of through their location in the respective arrays. We shall see many examples as we proceed.

#  The JavaScript Repertoire of User Interface Objects in a form

In the final section of this chapter I want to expose you to the repertoire of user interface objects that JavaScript makes available to you. Intimate knowledge of these objects will improve your communication skills with the user. This, remember, is a first exposure to these objects. They are discussed in much more detail in the reference section (along with many examples).

To produce, in a single window, all of the JavaScript user-interface objects, do Exercise 4.7. You can use the accompanying listing and figures for future reference. If you want to remind yourself of what you can do to interact with the visitor of your page, take a glance at the figures, and then go to the appropriate line in the code that produces the object in question.

---

**EXERCISE 4.7** THE REPERTOIRE OF JAVASCRIPT USER-INTERFACE OBJECTS.

1. Create an HTML file for Listing 4.11.
2. Load the file into your browser.
3. You should get results as shown in Figure 4.14 and Figure 4.15.
4. Click on each of the objects shown in the figures. You should get an alert dialog box that tells you about the object and its attributes as implemented in the HTML tags.

5.  Use this exercise and figures for future reference; when in doubt about what you can do with user-interface objects, take a quick glance at the figures and the listing.

**LISTING 4.11** The repertoire of JavaScript user-interface objects.

```
1      <HTML>
2      <TITLE>The Repertoire of User Interface Objects</TITLE>
3      <BODY>
4      <H3>The Repertoire of User Interface Objects</H3>
5      <FORM   NAME = "aForm">
6      A button:
7      <INPUT   TYPE = "button"
8              NAME = "aButton"
9              VALUE = "Click me..."
10             onClick =
"alert(this);alert(this.form.elements[2].value)">
11     <INPUT   TYPE = "checkbox"
12             NAME = "aCheckBox"
13             VALUE = "Check me:"
14             onClick = "alert(this)">A checkbox
15     <P>Hidden: "You won't see me"
16     <INPUT   TYPE = "hidden"
17             NAME = "aHidden"
18             VALUE = "You won't see me">
19     <P>A password:
20     <INPUT   TYPE = "password"
21             NAME = "aPassword"
22             VALUE = "myPassword"
23             SIZE = 25>
24     <SCRIPT LANGUAGE = "JavaScript">
25     alert(document.aForm.elements[3])
26     </SCRIPT>
27     <P>A radio:
28     <INPUT TYPE = "radio"
29            NAME = "r"
30            VALUE = "Radio 1"
31            onClick = "alert(this)"
32            CHECKED> Radio 1
33     <INPUT TYPE = "radio"
34            NAME = "r"
35            VALUE = "Radio 2"
36            onClick = "alert(this)"> Radio 2
37     <INPUT TYPE = "radio"
38                       NAME = "r"
39                       VALUE = "Radio 3"
```

Windows, Frames, Documents, and Forms       **109**

```
40       onClick = "alert(this)"> Radio 3
41  <INPUT TYPE = "reset"
42       NAME = "aReset"
43       VALUE = "I\'m a Reset button"
44       onClick = "alert(this)">
45  <P>Select:
46  <SELECT NAME = "occupation"
47       onFocus = "alert(this)">
48       <OPTION SELECTED> Politician
49       <OPTION> Actor
50       <OPTION> JavaScripter
51       <OPTION> Irrelevant
52       <OPTION> Politician
53       <OPTION> Administrator
54  </SELECT>
55  Multiple select:
56  <SELECT NAME = "occupation"
57       MULTIPLE
58       onFocus = "alert(this)">
59       <OPTION SELECTED> Politician
60       <OPTION> Actor
61       <OPTION> JavaScripter
62       <OPTION> Irrelevant
63       <OPTION> Politician
64       <OPTION> Administrator
65  </SELECT>
66  <P>Submit:
67  <INPUT TYPE = "submit"
68       NAME = "aSubmit"
69       onClick = "alert(this)">
70  Text:
71  <INPUT TYPE = "text"
72       NAME = "aText"
73       VALUE = "Text value"
74       onFocus = "alert(this)">
75  <P>Textarea:
76  <TEXTAREA
77       ROWS = 3
78       COLS = 25
79       NAME = "aTextarea"
80       onFocus = "alert(this)">
81  </TEXTAREA>
82  </FORM>
83  </BODY>
84  </HTML>
```

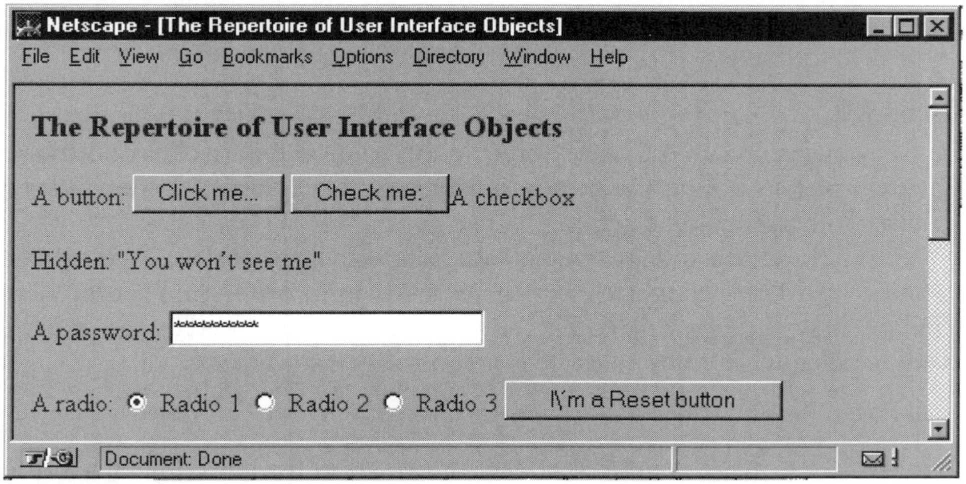

**FIGURE 4.14** The repertoire of JavaScript user-interface objects.

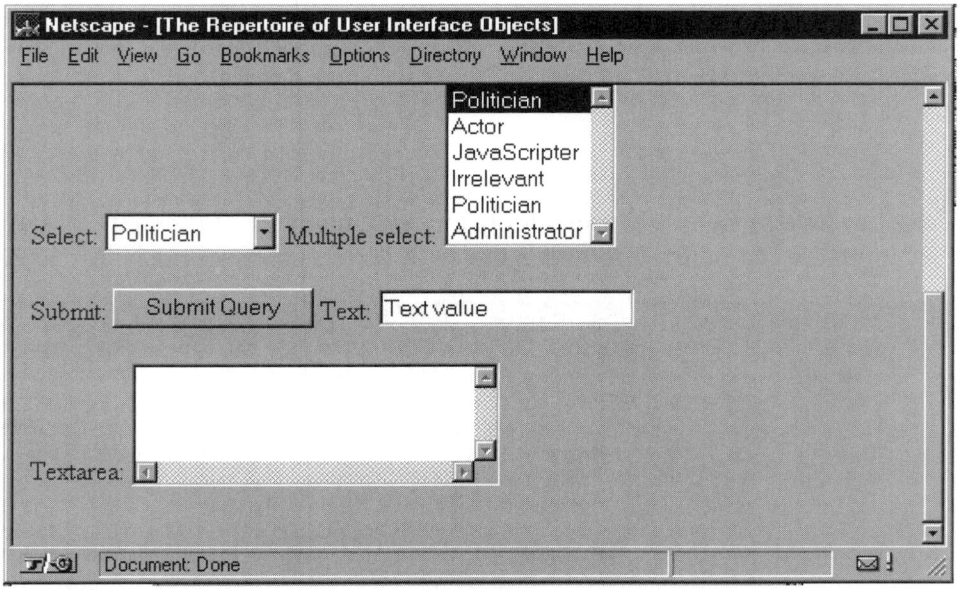

**FIGURE 4.15** The repertoire of JavaScript user-interface objects, continued.

The following discussion of each user-interface object refers to the code in Listing 4.11.

## button

Button objects are used to take some action when the user clicks on them. For example, a click on the button may bring up a confirm window asking the user to confirm some action.

The button object in Figure 4.14 (with its face saying Click me...) is created in lines 7 to 10 in Listing 4.11. When you click on it, you should get the alert window shown in Figure 4.16. This alert window was produced by the onClick event handler, which calls alert(this), and this is just what it is: this.

## checkbox

The checkbox object is used to collect information from the user when the information can be displayed as multiple choices. The user can click more than one checkbox (in contrast to the radio object, which allows a selection of only a single option from a list of options). When checkbox is checked, its value is true.

The checkbox object in Figure 4.14 (accompanied with the text Check me...) is created in lines 11 to 14 in Listing 4.11. When you click on it, you should get an alert window displaying what JavaScript knows about the object—in particular, its attributes. This alert box has the same format as that in Figure 4.16.

## file

Use this element to let the user supply an input filename. This element creates a FileUpload object and is created with code as shown in Listing 4.12.

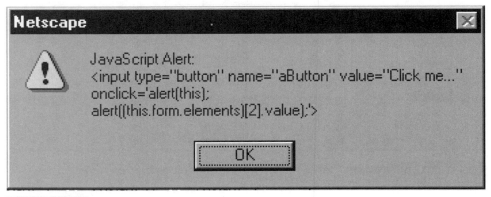

**FIGURE 4.16** The button object attributes.

The user interface looks as in Figure 4.17. The user can either type in a filename in the input area, or click on the Browse... button. When the user does do the latter in Windows 95, the File Upload dialog appears, as shown in Figure 4.17. The user can then interactively browse for the file he or she wishes to specify.

**LISTING 4.12** The `file` user-interface.

```
1    <HTML>
2    <TITLE>FileUpload</TITLE>
3    <BODY>
4    <H3>FileUpload</H3>
5    <FORM  NAME = "aForm">
6    FileUpload:
7    <INPUT  TYPE = "file"
8         NAME = "fileUploadName">
9    </FORM>
10   </BODY>
11   </HTML>
```

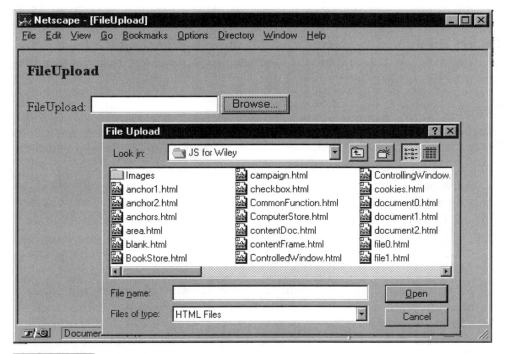

**FIGURE 4.17** The file user-interface.

### hidden

Hidden objects are normally used to collect information in a form; the value stored for the object is then relayed back to the server when the user submits the form. In the Internet Store application in Chapter 12, the hidden object is used to collect the order information and mail it back to the store when the user submits the form.

The hidden object (not shown Figure 4.14; it is hidden) is created in lines 16 to 18 in Listing 4.11. When the user clicks on Click me..., information about the object is shown in the next alert.

### option

The option object is discussed with the Select object below.

### password

Password objects are normally used to collect information in a form and verify it. Without access to a server there is little you can do with this object, except to verify a given password. As you can see in Figure 4.14, the text the user types in is masked.

The password object (shown Figure 4.14) is created in lines 20 to 23 in Listing 4.11. The script code in line 25 produces information about the object when the document is loaded. When you first load the file listed in Listing 4.11, you should identify the alert dialog window that shows information about this object.

### radio

Radio objects are normally used to collect information when the user has to make a single choice among several choices (in contrast to the checkbox object, where the user can pick more than one choice).

The radio object (shown Figure 4.14) is created in lines 28 to 40 in Listing 4.11. JavaScript knows that a group of radio buttons belong to a single radio object by the fact that all of the radio buttons have identical values for their NAME attribute (r in our example).

### reset

Reset objects are used to reset all of the information in a form to its default values. The user can use this button to erase all of the information entered in a form in a single click.

The reset object (shown Figure 4.14) is created in lines 41 to 44 in Listing 4.11.

## select

The `select` object is used to present the user with a list of selection items (options); the user can select on one or more items in the list by clicking on them. The `select` object has two versions. One version is created as shown in lines 46 to 54. Here, a drop-down list is created and the user can select a single item. The second version of the `select` object is created with the `MULTIPLE` attribute, as shown in lines 56 to 65. Here the user can select more than one option with the Shift-click combination.

Both versions of the `select` object are shown in Figure 4.15. Note also that each `option` in the `select` object is an object itself.

## submit

The `submit` button object is used to submit the data in a form using the `ACTION` attribute of the `<FORM>` tag. When the user clicks on the `submit` button, the specified `ACTION`—such as mailing the data to a specified e-mail address by using the `mailto` action—takes place.

The `submit` button object is created in lines 67 to 69 and is shown in Figure 4.15. Note that we do not specify `VALUE` for the object; JavaScript puts a default string, `Submit Query`, on the `submit` button's face.

## text

A `text` object is used to obtain one-liners from the user. The `text` object is created in lines 71 to 74 and is shown in Figure 4.15. It is different from the `textarea` object (see below).

## textarea

A `textarea` object is used to obtain multiple-line textual information from the user. The `textarea` object is created in lines 76 to 81 and is shown in Figure 4.15. It is different from the `text` object (see above).

# THE JAVASCRIPT LANGUAGE

⤵ Data types

⤵ Expressions

⤵ Operators and order of precedence

⤵ Some formal definitions of the JavaScript language

Now that you have learned about some of the important objects and have gone through numerous exercises that demonstrate how to implement these, you are ready for a more detailed and formal description of the JavaScript language. Many of the topics in this lesson repeat and reinforce previous discussions (remember the slippery spiral metaphor in Chapter 1?). We shall also discuss some general ideas that will enhance your understanding of programming issues in general.

# ⤵ Data Types

All programs are written to do something. In order to do something, you have to have substance—that is, the material with which you work in order to do. In programs, the substance is data. Without data, a program will have nothing to work on. You should realize that not all data are created equal.

Although more permissive than other programming languages, JavaScript still requires that you specify what kind of data you wish to work in. The data type creates a context for the script to work in. One of the difficult aspects of working with computers is the fact that being machines, they do not understand context—you have to create it.

Data types provide some of the context computers need in order to work. For example, 5 may represent a quantity (5 apples), or a symbol that represents that quantity (when you want to communicate "five apples," you write "5 apples"). If you want 5 to represent a quantity, as opposed to a character, you must say so. The data types that JavaScript recognizes are given in Table 5.1.

**TABLE 5.1** JavaScript data types.

| Type | Examples | Comments |
|------|----------|----------|
| Null | `null` | This means a quantity that has no value. |
| Boolean | `true, false` | Often the result of comparison of values. |
| Number | `5, 5.5` | This type includes numbers with and without decimal points. |
| Function | `write("a")` | Usually associated with an object; an object's method. |
| Object | `document` | Usually includes properties and methods (functions). |

The `null` data type is needed on those occasions when you wish to specify some data as having no value. For example, when you work with numerical data, you will often need to distinguish between zero and missing data. It makes a big difference whether on January 1, 2000 the temperature "was" zero, or, in fact, the weather station did not operate on that day.

The Boolean data type plays an important role in comparisons. For example, when $x = 5$ and $y = 6$, comparing these two will result in the Boolean value of false. The comparison symbol is ==. Remember this.

For $x = 5$ and $y = 6$,

$x$ == $y$ returns false, while

$x$ = $y$ assigns the value 6 to $x$.

Numerical data are handled in JavaScript in a peculiar way. In most programming languages there is a distinction between a floating-point number and an integer. A floating-point number is a number that includes a decimal point; an integer does not. JavaScript treats both integers and floats as a single data type, and tries to do the best it can to interpret what you mean, as you will see.

Functions and object data types are discussed further below.

## Numbers

JavaScript treats both integers and floats as a single data type, called number. It then tries to interpret expressions appropriately. Thus, in JavaScript 5 + 6 = 11 (note that no decimal points appear with the numbers; this indicates that they are integers), whereas 5 + 6.1 = 11.1 (approximately, because floating point numbers in computers are always approximations). That is, when JavaScript sees an operation on numbers, if one of the numbers is a float, all other numbers become floats. However, if numbers sum to an integer, the result is an integer. Thus, 5.9 + 6.1 = 12, not 12.0.

## Strings and Special Characters

We have already discussed some of the JavaScript peculiarities in dealing with mixes of strings and numbers. To reiterate, 5 + 6 = 11; however, 5 + "6" = "56" (where 56 is a string, not a number) and 5 + 6 + "6" = 116. Although confusing at first, the rules are simple. JavaScript reads an expression from left to right and computes results as soon as it can. Thus, when it reads 5 + 6 + "6" it recognizes the first two numbers as such, and sums them to 11. Next, 11 + "6" evaluates to the string "116".

## Variable Names and Scope

Variable names must start with a letter—A-Z, or a-z—or an underscore ("_"). The remaining characters can also be digits (0-9). Remember that JavaScript is case sensitive. Here are some examples of variable names:

- aVariable
- avariable
- _aVariable
- a_variable
- variable1

Each and every variable name in this list is distinct.
The following are invalid variable names:

- `a variable`
- `1variable`
- `variable+1`
- `"avariable"`

Recall that variable scope is essentially where you can refer to a specific variable (or its value) in a script. JavaScript provides only two variable scopes:

- global—the variable may be used anywhere in the script
- local—the variable can be used in the current function only

To declare a variable as global, use (or declare) it anywhere outside a function. Declare your global variables at the beginning of your script; they will be loaded to memory first and known to functions and script parts that may wish to use them. To declare variables as local, define or use them in a function. The code snippet in Listing 5.1 illustrates these ideas (see the comments in the code).

**LISTING 5.1**  Variables and scope.

```
1    <HTML>
2    <HEAD>
3    <SCRIPT LANGUAGE = "JavaScript">
4    var a1 = "Hello there" //a1 is a global variable
5    a2 = "Hello here" + 22 //and so is a2
6    function returnValue()
7    {
8       var a3 //a3 and a4 are local; you can use neither
9       a4 = 5.5 //outside the braces
10      ...
11   }
12   </SCRIPT>
13   </HEAD>
14   <BODY>
15   ...
16   </BODY>
17   </HTML>
```

# Literals

Literals are constants that represent actual values—they are not placeholders. Here are some examples:

- 5
- 5.5
- "The value 5.5 is a string literal here"

## Integers

Integers can be expressed in various bases (if you do not anticipate using these, just skip this section). In JavaScript notation, the base is indicated as follows:

- decimal (base 10)—any sequence of digits with no decimal point. For example, 13 is a decimal integer.

- octal (base 8)—any sequence of digits that starts with zero. For example, 013 is an octal integer.

- hexadecimal (base 16)—any sequence of digits and the letters A-F or a-f that starts with 0x or 0X (0 stands for zero). For example, 0xfff, 0xFFF, and 0x13 are all hexadecimal integers.

## Floating Point

Here are some examples of floating point literals:

- 13.1
- 1.1e3
- -.1E4
- 11e5

## Boolean

Here are the only possible literals for the Boolean data type:

- true
- false

## Strings

Here are some possible literals for the string data type:

- `"abc"`
- `'abcd'`
- `"123"`
- `"abac\n123"`

## Special Characters

You can embed the following special characters in a string to control text format in JavaScript:

- `\b`—backspace
- `\f`—form feed (usually means top of next page)
- `\n`—new line
- `\r`—carriage return
- `\t`—tab

# ↳ Expressions

Now that we have discussed literals formally, we can define expressions thus: An expression is any valid set of literals, variables, operators, and expressions that evaluates to a single value. The value can be any of the JavaScript data types. For example

```
x = 5
```

is an expression, and so is

```
2 + 3
```

Expressions are classified according to the data type they evaluate to, and sometimes how they are evaluated:

- Arithmetic expressions—evaluate to numbers; for example, `x = 13`, and `7 + 6` are both arithmetic expressions.

- String expressions—evaluate to strings; for example, `x = "Hi"`, `"Hello"`, and `'1024'` are all string expressions.

- Logical expressions—evaluate to `true` or `false`.

- `null` expressions—evaluate to `null`; for example, `x = null` is a null expression.

- Conditional expressions—evaluate to one of two values based on a condition. These have a special syntax:

```
(condition) ? value1 : value2
```

or

```
x = (condition) ? value1 : value2
```

Read the syntax above as follows: If the condition is `true`, the expression evaluates to `value1`, otherwise, it evaluates to `value2`. For example, the conditional expression

```
x = (true) ? 5 : "I will never be evaluated"
```

evaluates to 5, while

```
y = (false) ? "I will never be evaluated":"But I always will"
```

evaluates to `But I always will`. The expression

```
profit = (income > 0) ? "We had a profit" : "We had a loss"
```

evaluates to `We had a profit` if the value of the variable `income` is positive; otherwise, the value of `profit` is `We had a loss`.

# ↳ Operators

An operator is a shorthand notation for an instruction to do something with an expression. There are binary and unary operators. Binary operators require the sequence

```
operand1 operator operand2
```

while the unary operator sequence can be

```
operator operand
```

or

```
operand operator
```

We shall see examples of these below.

# Assignment Operators

These assign the value of the right operand to the value of the left operand. JavaScript uses the familiar arithmetic operators, and some additional operators with special meanings. The assignment operators are given in Table 5.2.

**TABLE 5.2** Assignment operators.

| Operator | Action | Example |
|---|---|---|
| = | The value of the right operand is assigned to the value of the left operand. | For y having the value of 5, x = y assigns the value of 5 to x. |
| += | The value of the right operand is added to the value of the left operand and the result is assigned to the left operand. | For x = 5 and y = 6, x += y assigns 11 to the value of x. |
| −= | The value of the right operand is subtracted from the value of the left operand and the result is assigned to the left operand. | For x = 5 and y = 6, x -= y assigns -1 to the value of x. |
| *= | The value of the right operand is multiplied with the value of the left operand and the result is assigned to the left operand. | For x = 5 and y = 6, x *= y assigns 30 to the value of x. |
| /= | The value of the left operand is divided by the value of the right operand and the result is assigned to the left operand. | For x = 15 and y = 3, x /= y assigns 5 to the value of x. |
| %= | The value of the left operand is divided by the value of the right operand and the remainder is assigned to the left operand. | For x = 15 and y = 7, x %= y assigns 1 to the value of x. |

The assignment operators below are called bitwise operators, because they operate on bits, not on the whole value of variables. We will not discuss these here; they are presented only for the sake of completeness:

- x <<= y

- x >>= y

- x >>>= y
- x &= y
- x ^= y
- x |= y

## Arithmetic Operators

When used in an expression, arithmetic operators result in a single numerical value. The most familiar arithmetic operators are addition (+), subtraction (-), multiplication (*), and division (/). The JavaScript repertoire of arithmetic operators is listed in Table 5.3.

**TABLE 5.3** Arithmetic operators.

| Operator | Action | Example |
|---|---|---|
| +,-,*,/ | Addition, subtraction, multiplication, and division. | |
| Modulus (%) | Results in the remainder of integrally dividing `operand1` by `operand2`. | For x = 12 and y = 5, `x % y` results in 2. |
| Increment (++) | `operator operand++` implements the `operator` and then increments the `operand` by 1; `operator ++operand` increments the `operand` by 1 and implements the `operator`. | For y = 6, `x = y++` assigns 6 to the value of x and increments y by 1, while `x = ++y` increments y by 1 and assigns the value 7 to x. |
| Decrement (—) | `operator operand --` implements the `operator` and then decrements the `operand` by 1; `operator -- operand` decrements the `operand` by 1 and implements the `operator`. | For y = 6 `x = y --` assigns 6 to the value of x and decrements y by 1, while `x = --y` decrements y by 1 and assigns the value 5 to x. |
| Unary negation (-) | Precedes the `operand` and makes it negative. | For x = 6, `x = -x` assigns -6 to the value of x. |

The + arithmetic operator can be used with strings. Thus, as we discussed before,

```
"abc" + "DEF"
```

evaluates to `"abcDEF"`, and

```
"abc = " + 15
```

evaluates to

```
"abc = 15"
```

## Comparison Operators

A comparison operator compares two operands and returns a logical value. The JavaScript comparison operators are listed in Table 5.4.

**TABLE 5.4** Comparison operators.

| Operator | Action | Example |
|----------|--------|---------|
| Equal (==) | operand1 == operand2 **returns** true **if the** operands **are equal.** | For x = 1 and y = 1, z = (x == y) assigns true to z. |
| Not equal (!=) | operand1 != operand2 **returns** true if operand1 **is not equal to** operand2. | For x = 1 and y = 1, z = (x != y) assigns false to z. |
| Greater than (>) | operand1 > operand2 **returns** true **if** operand1 **is greater than** operand2. | For x = 1 and y = 1, z = (x > y) assigns false to z. |
| Greater than or equal to (>=) | operand1 >= operand2 **returns** true if operand1 **is greater than or equal to** operand2. | For x = 1 and y = 1, z = (x >= y) assigns true to z. |
| Less than (<) | operand1 < operand2 **returns** true if operand1 **is less than** operand2. | For x = 1 and y = 1, z = (x < y) assigns false to z. |
| Less than or equal to (<=) | operand1 <= operand2 **returns** true if operand1 **is less than or equal to** operand2. | For x = 1 and y = 1, z = (x <= y) assigns true to z. |

Notice the difference between = and ==: The former is an assignment, and returns the appropriate data type in the statement in which it is used; the latter is a comparison, and returns `true` or `false` only. This is one of the major sources of confusion for beginners (and programmers experienced in, for example, dBase), and often causes nasty run-time errors. You will do well to remember this:

= is an assignment operator, while == is the equal-to comparison operator. They mean two different things!

Keep in mind that all of the comparison operators can be (and often are) used with strings. Thus,

```
"ABC" == "ABc"
```

evaluates to `false` and

```
"125" == "125"
```

evaluates to `true`. Yet,

```
"125.0" == "125"
```

evaluates to `false`, while

```
eval("125.0") == eval("125")
```

evaluates to `true`. We will discuss the JavaScript function `eval()` later (see `eval()` in Chapter 8).

You can also use comparisons like these: for x = "abc" and y = "ab", x > y evaluates to `true`, while x < y evaluates to `false`. For x = "abc" and y = "ab", x > y evaluates to `false`.

## Logical Operators

When used in an expression, logical operators result in a single logical value. There are only two logical values: `true` or `false`. The JavaScript logical operators are described in Table 5.5.

**TABLE 5.5** Logical operators.

| Operator | Action | Example |
|---|---|---|
| And (&&) | expression1 && expression2 **returns** true **if both** expression1 **and** expression2 **are** true. | **For** x = 1 **and** y = 2, z = (x == 1) && (y == 2) **assigns** true **to** z. |
| Or (\|\|) | expression1 \|\| expression2 **returns** true **if either** expression1 **or** expression2 **are** true. | **For** x = 1 **and** y = 2, z = (x == 1) && (y == 3) **assigns** true **to** z. |
| Not (!) | !expression **returns** true **if** expression **is** false **and** false **if** expression **is** true. | **For** x = 1, z = !(x == 1) **assigns** false **to** z **and** z = !(x == 2) **assigns** true **to** z. |

It is important to know that && is evaluated from left to right, and the evaluation returns false as soon as the first expression in the evaluation is evaluated to false. This can cause some debugging headaches. For example,

```
expression1 && expression2
```

evaluates to false if expression1 is false; **unless** expression1 is true, expression2 is not evaluated. In your script, do not expect expression2 to do anything.

Similarly, || in a statement evaluates to true as soon as the first expression in the statement evaluates to true. For example

```
expression1 || expression2
```

evaluates to true if expression1 is true; **unless** expression1 is false, expression2 is not evaluated.

## The typeof **Operator**

You use this operator in one of two ways:

- typeof *operand*
- typeof (*operand*)

where operand is the string, variable, keyword, or object for which the type is to be returned. You can use this operator to find out the type of something.

For example, Listing 5.2 produces the `typeof` shown in Figure 5.1. Note the distinction between a data type of `string`, and a `string` object: Lines 8 and 9 cause `typeof` to return `object` and `string`, respectively (see Figure 5.1).

**LISTING 5.2** The `typeof` operator.

```
1    <HTML>
2    <TITLE>typeof</TITLE>
3    <BODY>
4    <H3>typeof</H3>
5    <FORM NAME = "aForm">
6    <SCRIPT LANGUAGE = "JavaScript">
7    var aFunction = new Function("Math.sin(Math.PI)")
8    var aString = new String("I am a string object")
9    var bString = "I am a string"
10   var aNumber = 1
11   var aDate = new Date()
12   document.write("typeof(aFunction)) = ", typeof(aFunction))
13   document.write("<BR>typeof(aString)) = ", typeof(aString))
14   document.write("<BR>typeof(bString)) = ", typeof(bString))
15   document.write("<BR>typeof(aNumber)) = ", typeof(aNumber))
16   document.write("<BR>typeof(aDate)) = ", typeof(aDate))
17   document.write("<BR>typeof(document.aFrom)) = ",
18           typeof(document.aForm))
19   </SCRIPT>
20   </FORM>
21   </BODY>
22   </HTML>
```

## The void **Operator**

Use this operator when you want JavaScript to evaluate something, but return nothing. For example, if you want to include a hypertext link in your document that does nothing (say for debugging purposes, or to demonstrate a point), you can write

```
<A HREF = "javascript:void(0)"> Do nothing </A>
```

When the user clicks on `Do nothing`, `void` evaluates to `0` but nothing happens.

Another case is when you want to assign to an `<A>` tag an action other than going somewhere. Say you want to reset a form using hypertext instead of a button. Then you can write:

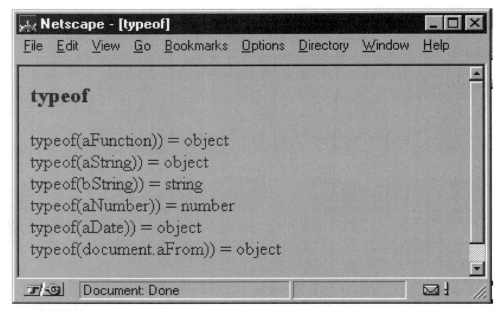

**FIGURE 5.1**  The typeof operator.

```
<A HREF = "javascript:void(document.forms[0].reset())">
Reset form data
</A>
```

In this case, when the user clicks on the hypertext, JavaScript will execute whatever is inside void(); but since it returns nothing, the user will not be referred to a nonexistent URL.

## Operator Precedence

Operator precedence is important in expressions that contain multiple operators. For example

```
5 + 5 * 6
```

evaluates to 35, while

```
(5 + 5) * 6
```

evaluates to 60. The first example shows that the multiplication operator takes precedence over the addition operator. When in doubt (and even when not), you should get into the habit of using parentheses to force whatever precedence you wish to occur. Thus, in the second example above, 5 + 5 is executed first, and the multiplication is done next.

Sooner or later you will have to construct complex expressions. One way to avoid precedence problems is to build the complex expression from a collection of simpler expressions, and try each simpler expression first. For example, suppose you wish to divide 10 by 5 and then multiply the result by 3. This should result in 6. If you are not sure about precedence, do this: First, write

```
10 / 5
```

and test that you get 2. Second, multiply by 3

```
(10 / 5) * 3
```

to get 6. In this example you will get the correct result if you write

```
10 / 5 * 3
```

because division and multiplication have the same order of precedence. When operators have the same order of precedence, the evaluation is done from left to right; that is, 10 is divided by 5 and the result is multiplied by 3. If you do not remember the fact that multiplication and division have the same level of precedence, writing (10 / 5) * 3 will ensure that you can always get what you want (contrary to the assertions by some famous singers).

Precedence order can be particularly nasty in if statements that include the && and || operators. Rather than try to figure out how expressions are evaluated based on precedence, just enclose them in parentheses (the less time you spend on syntax, the more complicated you can make your script— we always simplify so that we can make things more complicated later). For example, suppose you want to do something only if x has a value of 5 *and* y a value of 6. Instead of writing

```
if (x == 5 && y == 6)
```

write

```
if ( (x == 5) && (y == 6) )
```

This will ensure that if 5 is stored in the variable x, then true is returned; then, if 6 is stored in the address labeled y, a true is returned again. Only after both expressions are evaluated will the && evaluation be done, and true && true results in true.

For the sake of completeness, the formal and full JavaScript order of precedence is listed in Table 5.6. Some of the operators may not be familiar to you—these are rarely used, and we shall not discuss them. Except for the (), operators that have the same order of precedence in Table 5.6 are executed from left to right. The () are evaluated from innermost to outermost. Thus,

```
( (5 + 6) - (7 - 1) )
```

is first evaluated to

```
(11 - 6)
```

and then to 5.

**TABLE 5.6** Operator precedence.

| Precedence Level | Operator(s) |
|---|---|
| 1 | () [] function() |
| 2 | ! - ++ -- |
| 3 | * / % |
| 4 | + - |
| 5 | << >> >>> |
| 6 | < <= > >= |
| 7 | == != |
| 8 | & |
| 9 | ^ |
| 10 | \| |
| 11 | && |
| 12 | \|\| |
| 13 | ? |
| 14 | = += -= *= /= %= <<= >>= >>>= &= ^= != |
| 15 | , |

Although rarely used, you may see the comma (,) operator in expressions. Experienced programmers may use it to create terse expressions (mostly, to impress colleagues and inexperienced programmers). Just so you know what it means, here is an example. The expression

```
y = (x = 5, ++x)
```

will store 6 in y. Try to figure out why on your own. To help you understand what happens, and also convince you that ++x is different from x++, go through Exercise 5.1.

---

**EXERCISE 5.1** | THE "," AND "++" OPERATORS IN AN OPERATOR PRECEDENCE CONTEXT.

1. Create an HTML file for Listing 5.3.
2. Load the file into your browser.
3. You should get results as shown in Figure 5.2.
4. Experiment with some of the precedence operators in Table 5.6.

---

**LISTING 5.3** The "," and "++"operators in an operator precedence context.

```
1    <HTML>
2    <HEAD>
3    <TITLE>++ and ,</TITLE>
4    </HEAD>
5    <H3> "++" and "," </H3>
6    <BODY>
7    <SCRIPT LANGUAGE = "JavaScript">
8      document.write(y = (x = 5, ++x))
9      document.write("<BR>")
10     document.write(y = (x = 5, x++))
11   </SCRIPT>
12   </BODY>
13   </HTML>
```

# ↳ Statements

The official JavaScript guide defines a statement as a line of code that contains a keyword (see Appendix B for a list of JavaScript reserved words, and Table 11.1 in Chapter 11 for a list of JavaScript keywords). On occasions, a statement will mean a collection of lines that are related somehow. At any

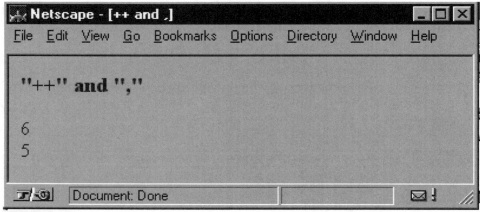

**FIGURE 5.2** The "," and "++" operators in an operator precedence context.

rate, the meaning of statement should be clear from its context. If the following code, for example:

```
function functionName(functionParameters)
{
 statement1
 statement2
 statement3; statement4
 ...
}
```

each line inside the braces is a statement. The statements are grouped by braces. This means that all of the statements from { to } are said to be sub- or nested statements.

The available set of statements provide you, the JavaScript writer, with powerful tools that facilitate interactive Web pages.

## Conditional Statements

The JavaScript conditional statement is if. The syntax is shown in Listing 5.4.

**LISTING 5.4** The if statement.

```
1    if (condition)
2    {
3      [statements...]
```

```
4    }
5    [else
6    {
7      statements...
8    }]
9    ...
```

From the convention we use, it should be clear that statements inside the if braces are optional, and so is the else statement. If *condition* in line 1 of Listing 5.4 is true, everything between lines 2 and 4 will be executed, and the script will continue execution at line 9. Otherwise, the nested statements between lines 6 and 8 are executed, and the script will continue execution from line 9. If you do not wish to include an alternative to the if condition, omit the else statement, along with its optional nested statements (lines 5 through 8). Remember this:

When checking for equality in an if statement, use the == operator, *not* the = operator.

## Loop Statements

A loop statement is executed repeatedly until a specified condition is met. The two available statements are for and while. Use the keywords break and continue with loops.

The syntax for the for statement is given in Listing 5.5.

**LISTING 5.5** The for statement.

```
1    for([initial-expression;][condition-expression;][increment-
     expression])
2    {
3      [statements...]
4    }
5    ...
```

The sequence of execution of the for loop in Listing 5.5 is as follows:

1. The *initial-expression*, if any, is executed. Here you usually initialize the loop counter.

2. The *increment-expression* is executed. Here you usually update a counter.

3. The *condition-expression* is evaluated. If the condition evaluates to true, the nested loop statements (line 3) are evaluated; otherwise, the script continues execution from line 5.

4. The loop nested statements are executed in sequence down to line 4 and control returns to step 2.

To see how this works, consider Exercise 5.2.

**EXERCISE 5.2** FOR LOOP DEMO.

1. Create an HTML file for Listing 5.6.
2. Load the file into your browser.
3. You should get results as shown in Figure 5.3.
4. Select a different number of options by using Shift-click and click on the button. You should get the number of options selected shown in the alert box (as shown in Figure 5.4).

**LISTING 5.6** for loop demo.

```
1    <HTML>
2    <HEAD>
3    <TITLE> for Loop</TITLE>
4    <SCRIPT>
5    function forLoopDemo(theObject)
6    {
7      var selected=0
8      for (i = 0; i < theObject.options.length; i++)
9      {
10     if (theObject.options[i].selected == true)
11     selected++
12     }
13     return selected
14   }
15   </SCRIPT>
16   </HEAD>
17   </BODY>
18   <H3> "for" Loop </H3>
19   <FORM NAME = "selectForm">
20   <P><B>
21   Choose one or more stocks:
```

```
22   </B> <BR>
23   <SELECT NAME = "stocks" MULTIPLE>
24    <OPTION SELECTED> GM
25    <OPTION> Texaco
26    <OPTION> 3M
27    <OPTION> Netscape
28    <OPTION> Microsoft
29    <OPTION> Apple Computer
30    <OPTION> IBM
31   </SELECT>
32   <P>
33   <INPUT TYPE = "button"
34    VALUE = "Number of stocks selected..."
35    onClick = "alert('Number of stocks selected:' +
forLoopDemo(document.selectForm.stocks))">
36   </FORM>
37   </BODY>
38   </HTML>
```

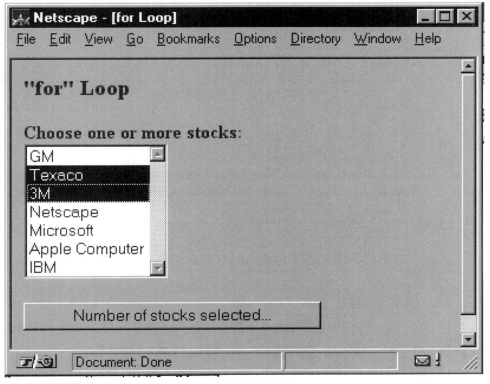

**FIGURE 5.3** for loop demo.

**FIGURE 5.4** The number of stock options selected.

Another JavaScript loop control is the while statement, and its syntax is shown in Listing 5.7. Before executing the nested statements inside the loop, *condition* is checked. If it is true, *statements...* are executed, and the condition is tested for true again. If it is, *statements...* are executed again, and so on. When *condition* becomes false (if ever), script execution continues from line 5.

**LISTING 5.7** The while statement syntax.

```
1    while(condition)
2    {
3      [statements...]
4    }
5    ...
```

One of the nastiest run-time (logical) program bugs is setting *condition* such that it never becomes false. Another programming tip to remember:

In a while loop, always make sure that either *condition* eventually becomes *false*, or that you *break* out of the loop.

## The break and continue Statements

The break statement terminates the current while or for loop and program execution continues from the statement following the terminated loop (the loop is usually terminated with }). For example, in Listing 5.8 we let `while` repeat itself infinitely. Inside `while`, we test *aCondition*; if it is `true`, the flow of execution is transferred to line 6. Be sure to verify that *aCondition* will, sooner or later, be evaluated to true. Otherwise . . .

**LISTING 5.8** The `break` statement.

```
1    while(true)
2    {
3     if(aCondition) break
4     statements...
5    }
6    ...
```

The `continue` statement in a `while` loop jumps back to the *condition*. In a `for` loop the `continue` statement causes execution to jump to the *increment-expression*.

## Object Manipulation Statements

Object manipulation statements ease work with objects considerably. The available object manipulators are:

- `for ... in`
- `new`
- `this`
- `with`

The `for ... in` statement iterates a specified variable over all of the object properties. For each property, the specified statement is executed. The syntax is:

```
for (variable in object)
{
 statements...
}
...
```

Listing 5.9 demonstrates how `for . . . in` can be used to inspect object properties.

Here is what the code does:

- In line 4 we specify two arguments for the function `objInspector()`. The argument `theObj` is the object whose properties we wish to examine. The argument `theObjName` is the name of the object.

- In line 6 we initialize the `prop` string.

- Line 7 causes execution to loop through all `theObj` properties.

- In line 9 and 10 we store `theObj` properties and its name in `prop`. Note the new line (`\n`) after each of the properties. This will cause each of `theObj` properties to be displayed on a new line.

- Line 12 causes the list of `theObj` properties to be shown in an alert window.

- Lines 19 to 22 demonstrate a call to `objInspector()`. This call will display all of the properties of the button object named `theButton` in an alert window.

**LISTING 5.9** The object-inspector function.

```
1    <HTML>
2    <HEAD>
3    <SCRIPT LANGUAGE = "JavaScript">
4    function objInspector (theObj, theObjName)
5    {
6         var prop = ""
7         for (var i in theObj)
8         {
9              prop += theObjName + "." + i +
10                             " = " + theObj [i] + "\n"
11        }
12        alert (prop)
13   }
14   </SCRIPT>
15   </HEAD>
16
17   <BODY>
18   <FORM>
19   <INPUT> TYPE = "button"
20        NAME = "theButton"
21        VALUE = "Click to see my properties . . ."
22        onClick = "objInspector (this, 'theButton')">
23   </FORM>
24   </BODY>
25   </HTML>
```

You create an instance of a user-defined object type with the `new` operator. The syntax is:

```
objName = new objType( arg1[, arg2] ... [, argN])
```

The this keyword allows you to refer to the current object; we have used it on numerous occasions. The syntax is:

```
this.[propertyName]
```

For example, suppose you create one of the INPUT objects in your HTML page, and you wish to pass the whole object to a function that does something with it. Then you may write the code according to the framework shown in Listing 5.10. In Listing 5.10 we send the INPUT text object called someName to someFunction() using the keyword this.

**LISTING 5.10** The this keyword.

```
1    ...
2    function someFunction(theObject)
3    {
4      do something with theObject here
5      ...
6    }
7    <INPUT TYPE = "text"
8      NAME = "someName"
9      onChange = "someFunction(this)">
```

The with statement establishes a default object for a set of statements. This relieves you from the need to repeat the object name in a sequence of statements. The syntax is:

```
with (objectName)
{
  statements...
}
```

For example, many of the familiar mathematical functions that are available in programming languages (such as C, Pascal, FORTRAN, and Basic) are provided in JavaScript as methods (or properties) of the Math object. Instead of writing

```
var x, y, z
x = Math.PI * x
y = x * Math.cos(PI)
z = x * Math.sin(PI)
...
```

you could write

```
var x, y, z
with Math
{
 x = PI * x
 y = x * cos(PI)
 z = x * sin(PI)
}
...
```

where PI is the familiar constant π, and cos and sin are the familiar trigono-metric functions.

## Comment Statements

In-line or single-line comments start with //, and multiple-line comments start with /* and end with */.

 # Braces

You may use braces anywhere you want to isolate statements. In some places they are required. For example,

```
for (var i = 0; i < 10; i++)
{
 statement1
 statement2
 statement3; statement4
 ...
}
```

will cause execution of all four nested statements once, each in its turn down the lines; then again, and so on, ten times in all. However,

```
for (var i = 0; i < 10; i++)
 statement1
 statement2
 statement3; statement4
 ...
```

will cause execution of *statement1* ten times, and *statement2* to *statement4* only once. This again emphasizes the value of indenting, for if instead of the example above we were to write

```
for (i = 0; i < 10; i++)
   statement1
statement2
statement3; statement4
  ...
```

the state of affairs would be less ambiguous.

# WHAT'S NEW SINCE NAVIGATOR 2.0

- ⤷ New objects
- ⤷ New properties
- ⤷ New methods
- ⤷ New language features
- ⤷ Examples of the new features

Since the release of Navigator 2.0, there have been numerous changes to JavaScript. These changes, summarized in Table 6.1, are discussed in the current chapter. The new and changed features have also been incorporated into the detailed reference discussion of objects, methods and functions, properties, event handlers, and statements (Chapters 7–11).

If you have old JavaScript code with bugs that refuse to be fixed, read this chapter. You may find the reason here. Use Table 6.1 as a reference. And when your JavaScript includes code that makes use of some of the new or changed features, you should read this chapter.

## ⤷ A Word about Object Names

Object names in JavaScript sometimes appear with an initial capital letter and sometimes they do not. Some of the reasons for this inconsistency are:

- Tags in HTML files are case insensitive, and often result in creating objects. Yet, JavaScript is case sensitive.

- Compiled functions (we shall talk about them later) need to be in all lower case.

Thus, in general, it is not possible to come up with a simple rule of when you need to use initial capitals in object names and when not. The naming convention should be clear from the context. One rule that is simple to remember and implement is this: Any time you use the keyword new to create a new object, use an initial capital for the object name. For example, when you wish to create a string object, use the convention

```
aString = new String ("abcdefg").
```

**TABLE 6.1** New and changed JavaScript features.

| New Features | Changed Features |
|---|---|
| **Event Handlers** | |
| onAbort, onError, onMouseOut, onReset | onBlur, onClick, onFocus onMouseOver, onLoad |
| **Functions:** | |
| atan2(), javaEnabled(), join(), scroll(), sort(), split(), reset(), reverse(), taint(), toString(), untaint() | blur(), close(), focus(), random() |
| **Objects:** | |
| Area, Array, FileUpload, Image, mimeTypes, Option, plugins | Button, Checkbox, Date, Document, Form, Hidden, Link, Location, Math, navigator, Password, Radio, Select String, Reset, Submit, Textobject, Textarea, Window |
| **Properties:** | |
| border, complete, description, enabledPlugin, filename, height, hspace, lowsrc, opener, prototype src, suffixes, type, typeof, vspace, width | defaultSelected, hash, host, hostname href, index, length, name, pathname, port, protocol, search, selected, target, textproperty, value |

#  Navigator JavaScript New Features

Here we discuss the new features that enhance communication between JavaScript and Java applets, the improved ability to deal with plug-ins, and improved security with data tainting.

## LiveConnect **Communication Between Java and JavaScript**

LiveConnect enables two-way communication between JavaScript and Java applets in an HTML page, and between JavaScript and loaded plug-ins. With it, you can access Java variables, methods, classes, and packages directly from JavaScript code. You can thus control the behavior of Java and Navigator plug-ins with JavaScript code. It is a two-way communication; you can also access JavaScript methods and properties from within Java code. To use this feature, you need to know Java, and we shall not discuss this topic any further; just be aware that you can use LiveConnect to enhance your JavaScript considerably. For example, if you wish to access files, databases, and other guest (or host) system features, you can use a Java applet, and then use JavaScript in your HTML page to invoke and control the behavior of the Java applet.

## Determining Installed Plug-ins

You can now use JavaScript to determine what plug-ins are available in the browser that is accessing the script. You can also control some aspects of the behavior of these plug-ins. You can also determine whether a client is capable of handling a particular MIME (Multipart Internet Mail Extension) type. To facilitate work with these, new objects—mimeTypes and plugins—were introduced (and will be discussed later). These objects are properties of the Navigator.

## Data Tainting

Data tainting is an advanced topic, and we shall not dwell upon it. If you are an experienced JavaScript programmer you may find the information in this section useful. For security reasons, JavaScript code on one server cannot access properties of documents on another server. Occasionally, you will need to access Navigator information on another server (for example, frames properties). To access window properties on another server, you can activate data tainting. Note, however, that it is up to the visitor of your page to allow you to access properties of his window.

Activating data tainting allows JavaScript in one window to access properties of another window, regardless of where the other window's document was loaded from. When JavaScript code in the first window attempts to send data derived from the second window's properties to a server, a confirmation dialog window allows the user to cancel the operation. Data are tainted by default.

The way you enable data tainting is system specific and requires knowledge of the system:

- On UNIX, use the `setenv` command.

- On Windows, use the `set` command.

- On Macintosh, you need a resource editor. Then, edit the resource with type `'Envi'` and number 128 in the Netscape application by removing the two ASCII slashes "//" before the `NS_ENABLE_TAINT` text at the end of the resource.

Individual properties can be tainted or untainted with the `taint()` and `untaint()` functions:

- `taint(aProperty)` taints *aProperty*.

- `untaint(aProperty)` untaints *aProperty*.

Suppose you have a `document` with a `form` named `aForm`, and a text element named `aText` in the form. You wish to send the value of `aText` in a URL or post it by other scripts (say, a script from another window). Then you can write:

```
untaintedProperty = untaint(document.aForm.aText.value)
```

You can now manipulate `untaintedProperty` as you wish. To later taint the property—say, when the value of `aText` is posted, and you do not want to grant access to it anymore—you can write

```
untaintProperty = taint(document.aForm.aText.value)
```

Of course, to maintain security, a script can taint or untaint its own data only.

You may wish to taint or untaint properties from within some control flow statements (`if`, `for`, and `while`); for example, based on the user's response you want to taint a value of some property. To deal with such cases, each window has a taint accumulator associated with it. The accumulator holds taint tested in the condition part of the code (`if`, `for`, and `while` statements). The accumulator then mixes taint codes to create new codes that identify data from different origins with the appropriate tainting.

The taint accumulator accumulates until the document is unloaded. However, when the taint accumulator contains the current document's origin code, it is reset to identity. All windows that load documents from one origin (e.g., URL) share a single taint accumulator.

The taint and untaint topic has more subtleties than are described here. These advanced topics can be explored through Netscape's URL:

```
http://home.netscape.com/eng/mozilla/3.0/handbook/javascript/
```

#  New Objects

The following useful new objects have been introduced and are discussed in detail in Chapter 7:

- `Area`—Use this object to define specific areas (polygons and circles) in a displayed image. This allows you to interact with the user based on her interaction with regions of the image.

- `Function`—Use this object to specify functions that you wish to compile as strings.

- `Image`—Use this object to facilitate JavaScript-created animation, and to manipulate images.

#  New Properties

Several properties have been added to the window object. Here are some of the more important ones:

- `opener`—This new property allows you to reference the window of a calling document.

- `type`—This new property allows you to determine the value assigned to the TYPE attribute of those HTML tags that use it. For example, you can determine if the object type that your JavaScript is dealing with is a `text`, `textarea`, `button`, `checkbox`, `radio`, and so on.

- `prototype`—This new property allows prototyping of those objects that can be created with the `new` keyword. These objects are `Date`, `String`, and user-defined objects.

 # Two Ways to Index an Object's Properties

When you create an object with a constructor function and define individual properties for this object, you cannot refer to these properties by their ordinal index. If you define an object's property with an index, then you can access the property through the index, but not by its name. To summarize:

- If you initially define a property by its name, you must always refer to it by its name.

- If you initially define a property by an index, you must always refer to it by its index.

- Objects created via HTML elements can be referred to by name or by index.

To see these ideas in action, go through Exercise 6.1; it demonstrates the two ways to access properties of `MyObject`.

**EXERCISE 6.1    INDEXING PROPERTIES.**

1. Type (or copy and paste) the code shown in Listing 6.1 and save it.
2. Load the saved file and watch what happens.

In line 12 of Listing 6.1 we add `property3` to `MyObject`. Because we add it by name, the alert window invoked in line 13 will display `property added by name`, while the alert window specified in line 14 will display `null`.

In line 15 we add a fourth property to `MyObject`; the alert window invoked in line 16 will display `property added by index`.

**LISTING 6.1**  Referring to property by name and by index.

```
1    <HTML>
2    <TITLE>Property Index</TITLE>
3    <BODY>
```

**150**                                    Chapter 6

```
4    <H3> Property Index</H3>
5    <SCRIPT LANGUAGE = "JavaScript">
6    function MyObject(property1, property2)
7    {
8            this.property1 = property1
9            this.property2 = property2
10   }
11
12   MyObject.property3 = "property added by name"
13   alert(MyObject.property3)
14   alert(MyObject[2])
15   MyObject[3] = "property added by index"
16   alert(MyObject[3])
17   </SCRIPT>
18   </BODY>
19   </HTML>
```

#  New or Modified Methods, Forms, and Form Elements

The following are either new methods, or old methods with modified (or added) behavior: `blur()`, `focus()`, `close()`, `javaEnabled()`, `reload()`, `replace()`, `reset()`, `scroll()`, and `split()`. All of these are discussed in detail in Chapter 8.

The `Select` object has been modified. You can now add options to forms by using the `Option()` constructor. As mentioned above, a `type` property was added, and a `FileUpload` object is now available (see the appropriate chapters for objects and properties).

# Events and Event Handlers

Some events have been modified, and others added. Specifically:

- `onAbort`—This event handler allows you to execute JavaScript code when the user aborts loading an image.

- `onBlur`—This event handler can be applied to both windows and framesets.

- `onFocus`—This event handler can be applied to both windows and framesets.

- onError—Using the onError event, you can execute JavaScript code when document or image loading result in an error.

- onMouseOut—When the mouse pointer leaves an area of an image or a link, you can direct JavaScript code execution using the onMouseOut event handler.

- onReset—When a reset event occurs, you can use the onReset event handler to execute JavaScript code.

## Resetting Event Handlers with JavaScript Code

You can call event handlers explicitly by resetting an event handler in an HTML page. You can also change values on a form from within JavaScript code. These features are demonstrated in Exercise 6.2. Let us see what happens.

**EXERCISE 6.2** | RESETTING EVENT HANDLERS. |

1. Type (or copy and paste) the code shown in Listing 6.2 and save it.

2. Load the saved file and watch what happens. In particular, watch exactly when the event handlers switch.

3. Think about a typical situation where you need to change the action of a specific event handler based on some condition, and implement it with JavaScript.

In line 34 of Listing 6.2 we assign the string call originalEventHandler to the theButton object. In line 35 we assign originalEventHandler() to the onClick event handler. In originalEventHandler() we increment the global variable counter by 1 (line 10) and then check if it is divisible by 3 with no remainder (line 11). If it is, we reset the theButton value to call newEventHandler (line 13) and the onClick event handler (line 14)—instead of calling originalEventHandler() it is now calling newEventHandler(). The alert windows are called from the respective functions to inform us which function is called by the onClick event handler (lines 15 and 16). When newEventHandler() is called, we reset the value of theButton so that it calls originalEventHandler().

The ability to reset the event handler can be quite useful. You may often wish to execute different functions for the same event (e.g., button click) based on some condition.

**LISTING 6.2** Resetting event handlers.

```
1    <HTML>
2    <TITLE>Calling Event Handlers</TITLE>
3    <HEAD>
4    <SCRIPT LANGUAGE = "JavaScript">
5
6    var counter = 0
7
8    function originalEventHandler()
9    {
10   counter++
11     if (counter % 3 == 0)
12     {
13           document.theForm.theButton.value = "call
     newEventHandler"
14           document.theForm.theButton.onclick = newEventHandler
15     }
16     alert("counter = " + counter + " originalEventHandler()")
17   }
18
19   function newEventHandler()
20   {
21     counter++
22     document.theForm.theButton.value =
23           "call originalEventHandler"
24     document.theForm.theButton.onclick = originalEventHandler
25     alert("counter = " + counter + " newEventHandler()")
26   }
27   </SCRIPT>
28   </HEAD>
29   <BODY>
30   <H3> Calling Event Handlers</H3>
31   <FORM   NAME = "theForm">
32   <INPUT  TYPE = "button"
33           NAME = "theButton"
34           VALUE = "call originalEventHandler"
35           onClick = "originalEventHandler()">
36   </FORM>
37   </BODY>
38   <HTML>
```

# Canceling the Action of an Event Handler

Normally, you use an onClick to call a JavaScript function. If the function you call returns false, the onClick event is canceled. Here is an example:

**LISTING 6.3** Canceling onClick.

```
1    <SCRIPT LANGUAGE = "JavaScript">
2    function f()
3    {
4       return false
5    }
6    </SCRIPT>
7    <INPUT TYPE = "checkbox" NAME = "doNothing" VALUE = "do
     nothing" onClick = "f()">
```

In line 7 of the code snippet we are calling f() for the onClick event handler of the checkbox called doNothing. The onClick will do nothing because f() returns false.

# HTML Tags and Attributes

Here we discuss some new HTML tags and attributes. You will find a complete explanation of these in Chapters 7 and 8.

## Referring to JavaScript Entities in an HTML Attribute Value

You may wish to set up some HTML character entities as variables that JavaScript, for example, can reference. Recall that you can use HTML character entities in JavaScript code—for example, instead of using the less-than sign (<), you can use the so-called character entity &LT;. To specify a JavaScript entity, use the following syntax:

```
&{JavaScript expression};
```

In other words:

- start with an ampersand
- enclose the JavaScript expression with curly braces
- end with a semicolon

Insert a JavaScript entity wherever an HTML attribute value goes. Exercise 6.3 is designed to demonstrate this new facility. Listing 6.4 results in a window shown in Figure 6.1. Remember, though, that to change the display of an already loaded HTML page, you have to reload it. You can, however, change values of some already displayed elements (see Exercise 6.2).

1. Type (or copy and paste) the code shown in Listing 6.4 and save it.

2. Load the saved file. It should look like Figure 6.1.

3. Modify the code in Listing 6.4 to use at least two more JavaScript entities, and use each of these at least twice, each time with a different value.

**LISTING 6.4** Using JavaScript entities in HTML.

```
1    <HTML>
2    <HEAD>
3    <TITLE>JavaScript Entity</TITLE>
4    <SCRIPT LANGUAGE = "JavaScript">
5    var aWidth = 75
6    </SCRIPT>
7    </HEAD>
8
9    <BODY>
10   Here is one horizontal line
11   <HR WIDTH = "&{aWidth};%">
12   and here is another
13   <SCRIPT LANGUAGE = "JavaScript">
14   aWidth = 50
15   </SCRIPT>
16   <HR WIDTH = "&{aWidth};%">
17   </BODY>
18   <HTML>
```

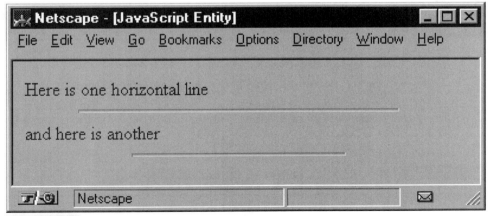

**FIGURE 6.1** Using JavaScript entities in HTML.

In line 5 of Listing 6.4 we are setting aWidth to 75. In line 11 we are drawing it (don't forget the % sign there). In line 14 we are resetting aWidth, and in line 16 we are drawing it again.

## The SRC **Attribute of the** <SCRIPT> **Tag**

The SRC attribute is a very welcome addition to JavaScript. Make use of it as much as possible. For example, when you have functions that you repeatedly use in a variety of projects (string manipulation functions, arrays, random number generators, and so on), put them in a file, and call that file whenever you need it. For the source, you can use any URL, relative or absolute.

Follow these rules for the source files:

- Do not include any HTML tags in the file; include only JavaScript code.

- Use .js for the filename extension.

- If you are including source files from a location other than "local" (the location of the file that calls the source) and things seem not to work, verify that the server where these files reside maps the .js filename suffix to the MIME type application/x-javascript; you may need help from your site administrator.

Exercise 6.4 is designed to demonstrate the use of JavaScript source files in an HTML file. Consider Listing 6.5: In line 4 we are telling the browser that in the same directory where the current HTML file resides there should be a file named CommonFunctions.js. Line 9 will be executed correctly if the .js file we specify contains the function aCommonFunction().

**EXERCISE 6.4**  USING THE SRC ATTRIBUTE OF THE <SCRIPT> TAG.

1. Type (or copy and paste) the code shown in Listing 6.5 and save it.

2. Type (or copy and paste) the code shown in Listing 6.6 and save it.

3. Modify the code in Listing 6.5 to use two JavaScript source files. Put some common functions in these two files. The file commonf.js (on the enclosed CD) includes a collection of useful functions.

**LISTING 6.5**  Using the SRC attribute of the <SCRIPT> tag.

```
1    <HTML>
2    <HEAD>
```

```
 3    <TITLE>Using SRC</TITLE>
 4    <SCRIPT LANGUAGE = "JavaScript" SRC = "CommonFunctions.js">
 5    </SCRIPT>
 6    </HEAD>
 7    <BODY>
 8    <SCRIPT LANGUAGE = "JavaScript">
 9      aCommonFunction("This is coming from a different file")
10    </SCRIPT>
11    </BODY>
12    </HTML>
```

The file `CommonFunctions.js` would then contain the code shown in Listing 6.6. Note that the file contains nothing but JavaScript code.

**LISTING 6.6** A JavaScript source file.

```
1    function aCommonFunction(aString)
2    {
3      document.write(aString)
4    }
```

### The <NOSCRIPT> Tag

We have discussed this tag (with an example) in Listing 1.2 in Chapter 1. It is listed here for the sake of completeness.

# Added and Modified JavaScript Language Features

Here are some welcome additions to JavaScript:

- An `Array` object—this object has some useful methods such as `join()`, `reverse()`, and `sort()`.

- The `Math` object's new random number generator, which works on all platforms. The file `commonf.js` (included on the enclosed CD) includes a portable random number generator.

- A new `String` object, including a `split()` method.

- The functions `isNaN()`, `parseFloat()`, and `parseInt()` work, according to Netscape, on all platforms.

- Using object prototypes, you can now share properties among all objects of the same type.

- You can use an associative array or a numerical index to refer to object properties. (You cannot mix these references for the same property.)

- A new `type` operator returns the data type of its operand.

- A new `void` operator allows you to specify an expression to be evaluated without having the expression return a value.

- A new `toString()` method converts objects, including function code, to strings.

# PART TWO

# REFERENCE

# O B J E C T S
# R E F E R E N C E

- ↳ Discussion of objects (new and old)
- ↳ Examples for each object
- ↳ Examples of forms and data submission
- ↳ Examples of testing for valid entries in forms
- ↳ Examples of controlling events and event handlers
- ↳ Animation examples

 **About the Reference Format**

Each object reference in Chapter 7 includes the following sections.

- **Title** gives the object's name. If the object has a related array, the array's name appears in the title. For example, form objects in a document are often collected in a forms array. Thus, the title is "form and forms array."

- **Purpose** includes a short statement about the purpose of the object.

- **Syntax** details the syntax of the object as it should appear in an HTML document. The syntax is followed by a table that lists the objects for which the current object is a property, the current object properties methods and event handlers, and related topics.

- **Access** lists whether you can modify the object's data (see below).

- **Discussion** gives details about how to use the object, and other relevant information.

- **Examples** lists examples of how to use the object.

In presenting the object syntax we follow the notation convention as explained in Table I.1 of the Introduction. For example, part of the syntax for the Image object looks like this:

```
<IMG
    [NAME = "imageName"]
    SRC = "highResLocation"
    [HEIGHT = "heighInPixels" | "heightInPercent"%]
    ...
>
```

This syntax means that:

- IMG must be typed exactly as shown.

- NAME is optional, but, if you include it, NAME must be typed as shown (you can use lower case if you wish), followed by the equals sign and an image name of your choice, enclosed in quotes.

- SRC must be typed as shown, followed by a string that specifies the location of the image, enclosed in quotes.

- HEIGHT is optional, but, if included, you must choose to specify the height in pixels or in percent (of the page height). If you choose to specify the height in percent, you must follow the height specification with the % sign.

Object acces is specified as read only or read and write. For read only objects, you can access the object property values, but you cannot change them. For read and write objects you can access property values, and also set them. Some objects may have properties that you can change, and other properties that you cannot. In such cases, I designated these objects as read and write. For example, the APPLET tag creates a read only applet object. You can access the name attribute of the applet with a staement like this:

```
appletName = theApplet.name
```

where `theApplet` is an applet object, and `name` is the applet name as specified by the `NAME` attribute of the `<APPLET>` tag. Because applet is a read only object, a statement such as

```
document.applets[0] = "fould.class"
```

has no effect.

Finally, keep in mind that JavaScript is an evolving language; I have tried to be as complete as possible. There may be some inconsistencies here and there. The final arbiter is the JavaScript Authors Guide, which can be accessed at:

```
http://home.netscape.com/eng/mozilla/3.0/handbook/javascript/
```

#  anchor and anchors array

## Purpose

Use the `anchor` text object as a hypertext link. Use the `anchors` array to handle anchors in your document.

## Syntax

```
<A [HREF = location]
 NAME = "anchorObjectName"
 [TARGET = "windowName"]>
 anchorText
</A>
```

where:

| | |
|---|---|
| HREF = | *location* identifies a destination anchor or URL. If this attribute is present, the `anchor` object is also a `link` object. See `link` for details. |
| NAME = | "*anchorObjectName*" specifies a tag that becomes an available hypertext target within the current document. |
| TARGET = | "*windowName*" specifies the window that the link is loaded into. This attribute is meaningful only if HREF = *location* is present. See `link` for details. |
| *anchorText* | specifies the text to display at the anchor. |

| | |
|---|---|
| **Property of** | document |
| **Properties** | None |
| **Methods** | None |
| **Event handlers** | None |
| **See also** | **Objects:** link, |
| | **Methods:** anchor() |

## Access

Read only. Thus, the assignment

```
document.anchors[0] = "anchorObjectName"
```

has no effect.

## Discussion

Anchors can be defined using the anchor() method. Each document's anchor is an entry in the anchors array. When a document is loaded, the browser builds an array of anchor objects in the document. The array contains an entry for each <A> tag containing a NAME attribute in the document, in the order it appears in the HTML source code. For example, a document that contains two named anchors has an anchors array with two entries. Each entry (an anchor object) can be referenced by its index; i.e., document.anchors[0], document.anchors[1]. Because anchors is an array, is has a length property. You can thus retrieve the number of anchors in your document with a statement like

```
numberOfAnchorsInDocument = document.anchors.length
```

Unless you build anchors naming them consecutively (as in Exercise 7.1 below), the value of anchors[i] (where *i* is the anchor's index) is null. Thus, the statement

```
anchorObjectName = anchors[0]
```

for example, will assign the value null to anchorObjectName.

## Examples

The HTML statement

```
<A NAME = "http://turtle.gis.umn.edu"><H2>My home page</H2></A>
```

assigns the URL http://turtle.gis.umn.edu to the text My home page. The text will be underlined, and when the user clicks on it, Navigator will connect the user to the appropriate URL.

Next, let us see how to deal with numbered links. Using this approach, you can use the hash property of location to refer to links as elements in the anchors array. To see what is going on, follow the instructions in Exercise 7.1.

---

**EXERCISE 7.1**    BUILDING AN ANCHORS ARRAY.

1. Type (or copy and paste) the code shown in Listing 7.1 and save it as ANCHORS.HTML.

2. Type (or copy and paste) the code shown in Listing 7.2 and save it as LINKS.HTML.

3. Load ANCHORS.HTML to your browser.

4. Click on the buttons. Why is it that the button Link 3 results in an error message, while buttons 1 and 2 do not? Why does button 4 result in an error message?

---

In line 7 of Listing 7.1 we are creating a new window. The HTML code for that window resides in LINKS.HTML. In line 10, we start the definition of a function that will pass the link number to the window that contains the links, the linksWindow. In lines 12–15 we use the hash property of location and the length property of anchors to connect to the appropriate link in the LINKS.HTML file (the latter's code is in Listing 7.2). Running the exercise should result in windows as shown in Figure 7.1 and Figure 7.2. Clicking on the button Link 3 results in an error because its anchor is not numbered.

**LISTING 7.1** Building an anchors array.

```
1     <HTML>
2     <HEAD>
3     <TITLE>Anchors Window</TITLE>
4     </HEAD>
5     <BODY>
6     <SCRIPT LANGUAGE = "JavaScript">
7     linksWindow = open("links.html","linksWindow",
8      "scrollbars = yes, width = 100, height = 100")
9     //
10    function seeLinksInOtherWindow(linkNumber)
11    {
12     if (linksWindow.document.anchors.length > linkNumber)
13     linksWindow.location.hash = linkNumber
14     else
```

```
15    alert("Anchor does not exist!")
16  }
17  </SCRIPT>
18
19  <B>Anchors</B>
20  <FORM>
21  <P>Click a button to see the corresponding anchor in
22  the Links windows
23  <P><INPUT TYPE = "button" VALUE = "0" NAME = "link0"
24   onClick = "seeLinksInOtherWindow(this.value)">
25  <INPUT TYPE = "button" VALUE = "1" NAME = "link0"
26   onClick = "seeLinksInOtherWindow(this.value)">
27  <INPUT TYPE = "button" VALUE = "2" NAME = "link1"
28   onClick = "seeLinksInOtherWindow(this.value)">
29  <INPUT TYPE = "button" VALUE = "Link 3" NAME = "link2"
30   onClick = "seeLinksInOtherWindow(this.value)">
31  <INPUT TYPE = "button" VALUE = "4" NAME = "link3"
32   onClick = "seeLinksInOtherWindow(this.value)">
33  </FORM>
34  </BODY>
35  </HTML>
```

**LISTING 7.2** The links HTML file.

```
1    <HTML>
2    <HEAD>
3    <TITLE>Links Window</TITLE>
4    </HEAD>
5    <BODY>
6    <A NAME = "0"><B>A List for Anchor 0</B></A>
7    <LI>0.1
8    <LI>0.2
9    <LI>0.3
10   <P><A NAME = "1"><B>A List for Anchor 1</B></A>
11   <LI>1.1
12   <LI>1.2
13   <LI>1.3
14   <LI>1.4
15   <LI>1.5
16   <P><A NAME = "2"><B>A List for Anchor 2</B></A>
17   <LI>2.1
18   <LI>2.2
19   <LI>2.3
20   <LI>2.4
21   <P><A NAME = "3"><B>A List for Anchor 3</B></A>
```

```
22   <LI>3.1
23   <LI>3.2
24   <LI>3.3
25   <LI>3.4
26   <LI>3.5
27   <LI>3.6
28   </BODY>
29   </HTML>
```

 # applet and applets array

## Purpose

Use this object to incorporate Java applets in a Web page.

## Syntax

```
<APPLET
  CODE = classFileName
  HEIGHT = heightInPixels
  WIDTH = widthInPixels
```

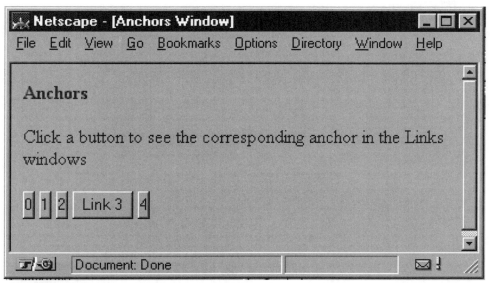

**FIGURE 7.1** Building an anchors array.

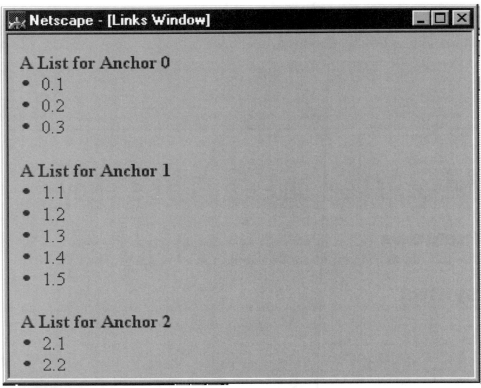

The `links` HTML file.

```
MAYSCRIPT
[NAME = "appletName"]
[CODEBASE = directory]
[ALT = "aString"]
[ALIGN = "left" | "right" |
"top" | "absmiddle" | "absbottom" |
"texttop" | "middle" | "baseline" | "bottom"]
[HSPACE = horizontalMarginInPixels]
[VSPACE = verticalMarginInPixels]>
[<PARAM NAME = parameterName VALUE = parameterValue>]
[ ... <PARAM>]
</APPLET>
```

where:

CODE =        *classFileName* is the filename of the Java applet. This
              file is generated by compiling Java code. The compila-

| | |
|---|---|
| | tion process produces a binary file of the same name with the extension .class. |
| HEIGHT = | *heightInPixels* is the height (in pixels) that you wish to allocate to the applet area in your HTML document. |
| WIDTH = | *widthInPixels* is the width (in pixels) that you wish to allocate to the applet area in your HTML document. |
| MAYSCRIPT | is used to prevent an applet from accessing JavaScript on a page without your knowledge. |
| NAME = | "*appletName*" is the name of the applet. |
| CODEBASE = | *directory* points to the directory where the .class file resides. Use it if the .class file resides in a directory other than the local directory (the directory from which the calling HTML file had been loaded). |
| ALT = | "*aString*" specifies a string that is displayed when the browser does do not recognize the <APPLET> tag. |
| ALIGN = | *alignment* is the alignment of the applet on the HTML page. |
| HSPACE = | *horizontalMarginInPixels* is the applet horizontal margin (in pixels) within the browser window. |
| VSPACE = | *verticalMarginInPixels* is the applet vertical margin (in pixels) within the browser window. |
| <PARAM> | defines a parameter for the applet. |
| NAME = | *parameterName* specifies the name of the parameter. |
| VALUE = | *parameterValue* specifies a value for the parameter. |

| | |
|---|---|
| **Property of** | document |
| **Properties** | name |
| **Methods** | None |
| **Event handlers** | None |
| **See also** | **Objects:** mimeTypes, Plugin  **Methods:** anchor() |

## Access

Read only. Thus, the assignment

```
document.applets[0]="foul.class"
```

has no effect.

## Discussion

To access an applet, use the MAYSCRIPT attribute of the APPLET tag. Without it, the applet will not work. For example, to run the foul.class applet, use the following:

```
<APPLET CODE = "foul.class" WIDTH = 200 HEIGHT = 200 NAME = "foul"
MAYSCRIPT>
```

In working with the applet object, keep the following in mind:

- When the browser loads the page with a number of <APPLET> tags, it builds an array of applets.
- If, for example, the HTML document includes two applets, you can access these with document.applets[0], document.applets[1] or with the associative array construct document.applets["appletName"].
- You can determine how many applets are included in your page with the property document.applets.length.

## Examples

The code

```
<APPLET CODE = "foul.class" WIDTH = 200 HEIGHT = 200 NAME = "foul"
MAYSCRIPT>
</APPLET>
```

will upload and run the foul application (to see what foul actually does, visit http://turtle.gis.umn.edu).

#  Area

## Purpose

Use it to define an area of an image as an imagemap. You can define a hypertext reference to the area; when the area is clicked, the reference is loaded.

## Syntax

```
<MAP NAME = "mapName">
  <AREA
```

```
    [NAME = "areaName"]
    COORDS = "x1,y1,x2,y2,..." | "x-center,y-center,radius"
    HREF = "location"
    [SHAPE = "rect" | "poly" | "circle" | "default"]
    [TARGET = "windowName"]
    [onClick = "onClickEventHandler"]
    [onMouseOut = "mouseOutHandler"]
    [onMouseOver = "mouseOverHandler"]>
</MAP>
```

where:

| | |
|---|---|
| NAME = | "*mapName*" is the name of the map. The map name can be identified with in the USEMAP attribute of the <IMG> tag. |
| AREA | Defines an area of an image as an imagemap. |
| NAME = | "*areaName*" gives the name of the Area object. Note, however, that you cannot refer to an Area object by name. |
| COORDS = | specifies the coordinates of the imagemap. |
| HREF = | "*location*" specifies the URL of the document to load when a user clicks the area. You must include this attribute if you use the onMouseOut and onMouseOver event handlers. |
| SHAPE | specifies the shape of the map. Use "default" to indicate a default region. If omitted, "rect" is used. |
| TARGET = | "*windowName*" specifies the window that the link is loaded into. *windowName* can be an existing window, a frame name, or one of the literal frame names _top, _parent, _self, or _blank. *windowName* cannot be a JavaScript expression. By convention, global variable names that are used internally by JavaScript begin with an underscore. Avoid using these as variable names in your code. |

| | |
|---|---|
| **Property of** | document |
| **Properties** | hash, host, hostname, href, pathname, port, protocol, search, target |
| **Methods** | None |
| **Event handlers** | onMouseOut, onMouseOver |
| **See also** | **Objects:** Image<br>**Operators:** void |

## Access

Read and write.

## Discussion

To access this object in a JavaScript code, use one of the following:

- `areaName.propertyName`
- `document.links[i].propertyName`
- `document.links["areaName"].propertyName`

where

- *areaName* is the value of the NAME attribute of an Area object
- *i* is an integer representing area in a document
- "*areaName*" is a string containing the name of an Area object
- *propertyName* is one of the object's properties (see above)

## Examples

To see the Area object in action, do Exercise 7.2. Be sure to go through step 4—it will clarify some issues to you. You should get something like Figure 7.3. If you do not get the figure, check that you have a subdirectory named images in the directory from which you load the HTML file and that the directory includes the file aworld.gif. Because the image does not use a hyperlink, we use the JavaScript operator void to return nothing in line 4 (Listing 7.3).

| EXERCISE 7.2 | USING THE AREA OBJECT. |
| --- | --- |

1. Type (or copy and paste) the code shown in Listing 7.3 and save it.
2. Load the file to your browser.
3. Move the cursor around, and watch the messages on the status line (see Figure 7.3).
4. Modify the exercise to inform the "mouse mover" that the move is one of the two circles (100,100,100) and (300,300,100), where the triplets are the x and y coordinates of circle center and the circle radius, respectively.

**LISTING 7.3** Using the Area object with onMouseOut and onMouseOver.

```
 1    <MAP NAME = "globe">
 2     <AREA NAME = "northHemisphere"
 3     COORDS = "0,0,400,200"
 4     HREF = "javascript:void(0)"
 5     onMouseOver = "self.status = 'You are in the Northern
       Hemisphere.'; return true"
 6     onMouseOut = "self.status = 'You have left the Northern
       Hemisphere.'; return true">
 7     <AREA NAME = "southHemisphere"
 8     COORDS = "0,200,400,400"
 9     HREF = "javascript:void(0)"
10     onMouseOver = "self.status = 'You are down under'; return
       true"
11     onMouseOut = "self.status = 'You are out of down under';
       return true">
12    </MAP>
13
14    <IMG SRC = "images\aworld.gif"
15     ALIGN = "top"
16     HEIGHT = "400"
17     WIDTH = "400"
18     USEMAP = "#globe">
```

 # Array

## Purpose

Use this object to create and work with arrays.

## Syntax

*arrayName* = new Array()

or

*arrayName* = new Array(arrayLength)

where

**FIGURE 7.3** Using the Area object with onMouseOut and onMouseOver.

*arrayName* is the name of the array object you wish to create.
*arrayLength* is the length of the array (the number of elements it contains).

| | |
|---|---|
| **Property of** | None |
| **Properties** | length, prototype |
| **Methods** | join (), reverse (), sort () |
| **Event handlers** | None |
| **See also** | **Objects:** Image |

## Access

Read and write.

## Discussion

You can use Array objects in one of two ways:

```
arrayName.propertyName
arrayName.methodName(arguments)
```

where *arrayName* is the name of an object or a property of an existing object, *propertyName* is one of the Array's properties, and methodName is one of the Array's methods.

For example, the statement

```
anArrayObject = new Array(7)
```

creates an Array object called anArrayObject with seven elements. Unless set, the values of the newly created array elements are all set to null. Note that A in Array must be capitalized. Whenever you use the new keyword to create an object, the object = type you create (Array in this case) must have an initial capital.

The length of an array can change dynamically. Thus, the statement

```
anArrayObject = new Array()
```

creates anArrayObject of length zero. As you assign indexed elements, the array length will automatically adjust if necessary. For example, the statement

```
anArrayObject[11] = "This is the 10th element of the array"
```

redimensions anArrayObject to a length of 11, and the tenth element value will equal the string shown above. Remember that the index of the first element in a JavaScript array is always zero, and the index of the last element is length −1.

JavaScript allows you to deal with dense arrays. These are arrays with each element having a value. To construct a dense array, assign values to each element at the time of creation, like this, for example:

```
aDenseArray = new Array("First element", 2.2)
```

This will create a dense array with two elements; the first (0th element) is a string and the second is a number. You can freely mix variable types in an array. If you now write

```
aDenseArray[99] = "The third element in the array, its index is 99"
```

then you in effect get what the string above explains. You can now assign a new value, say

```
aDenseArray[98] = 5.1
```

and continue treating the array as usual. The array will have only four elements, although to you, it has elements with indices 98 and 99.

## Examples

Listing 7.4 creates two arrays. In line 1 we create an array with no elements, in line 2 we add a zero element, and in line 3 we add 99 elements for a total of 100 elements. In line 4 we replace `null` with `2.3` in the 50th element. In line 5 we are creating a dense array with one element. In line 6 we are adding another element. The array now has two elements, but as far as you are concerned, it has 100. This saves space and yet allows you to index the array consistently without having to worry about the actual location of an element in the array. Dense arrays are sometimes also called sparse arrays.

**LISTING 7.4** Creating arrays.

```
1   newArray = new Array()
2   newArray[0] = "First element with index 0"
3   newArray[99] = "100-th element with index 99"
4   newArray[49] = 2.3
5   anotherArray = new Array("Dense Array")
6   anotherArray[99] = "99-th element, but array has only 2 elements"
```

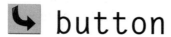 button

## Purpose

Use this object to create a push button in an HTML document.

## Syntax

```
<INPUT
  TYPE = "button"
```

```
NAME = "buttonName"
VALUE = "buttonText"
[onClick = "eventHandler"]>
```

where

| | |
|---|---|
| NAME = | "*buttonName*" names the button object. |
| VALUE = | "*buttonText*" specifies the text that appear in the button. |

| | |
|---|---|
| **Property of** | form |
| **Properties** | name, type, value |
| **Methods** | click() |
| **Event handlers** | onClick |
| **See also** | **Objects:** form, reset, submit |

## Access
Read and write.

## Discussion
To access a button's properties and methods, use one of the following:

- buttonName.propertyName

- buttonName.methodName(arguments)

- formName.elements[i].propertyName

- formName.elements[i].methodName(arguments)

where:

- *buttonName* is the value of the NAME attribute of the button

- *formName* is either the value of the NAME attribute of the form or an element in the forms array

- *i* is an integer index of a button on a form

- *propertyName* is one of the button's properties

- *methodName* is one of the button's methods

Because button is an element of a form object, it must be defined within a <FORM> tag. The button object is a custom button that you can use to perform an action you define. To associate an action with a button, associate JavaScript code with the `button`'s `onClick` event handler.

## Examples

In Exercise 7.3 we are creating a button. The text to appear on the button's face is `Press here...` (line 14); we can refer to the button by its name, `pressedButton` (as defined in line 15). The function `handleThisButton Click(...)` is called when the button is clicked (line 16). The argument we send to the function is the `form` object to which the button belongs. In the function (line 6) we can access whatever property of the form we wish; in this case we are accessing the name property of the `button`, which in turn is a property of the `form`.

---

**EXERCISE 7.3**    CREATING A BUTTON.

1. Type (or copy and paste) the code shown in Listing 7.5 and save it.

2. Load the file to your browser.

3. Press the button. Did you get the alert window as in Figure 7.4?

4. Modify the exercise to look at least two other properties of the `form` or the `window` objects to which the button belongs.

---

**LISTING 7.5** Creating a button.

```
1     <HTML>
2     <HEAD>
3     <SCRIPT LANGUAGE = "JavaScript">
4     function handleThisButtonClick(theForm)
5     {
6       alert(theForm[0].name)
7     }
8     </SCRIPT>
9     </HEAD>
10    <BODY>
11    <FORM NAME = "iHaveAButton">
12    <INPUT
13      TYPE = "button"
14      VALUE = "Press here..."
15      NAME = "pressedButton"
16      onClick = "handleThisButtonClick(this.form)">
17    </FORM>
```

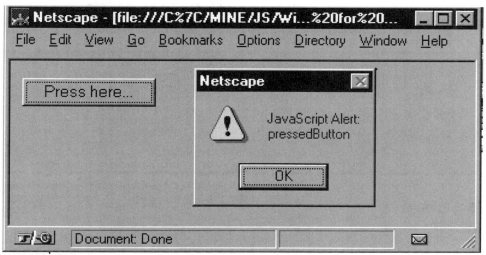

**FIGURE 7.4** Creating a button.

 # checkbox

## Purpose

Use this `form` element to present the user with a binary choice: yes or no, on or off.

## Syntax

```
<INPUT
 TYPE = "checkbox"
 NAME = "checkboxName"
 VALUE = "checkboxValue"
 [CHECKED]
 [onClick = "eventHandler"]>
 someText
```

where:

| | |
|---|---|
| NAME = | "*checkboxName*" is the name of the checkbox object. |
| VALUE = | "*checkboxValue*" is the value that is returned to the server when the checkbox is selected and the form is submitted. This defaults to "on". |

| | |
|---|---|
| CHECKED | causes the checkbox to be displayed with a check mark. |
| *someText* | is the label that appears beside the checkbox. |

| | |
|---|---|
| **Property of** | form |
| **Properties** | checked, defaultChecked, name, type, value |
| **Methods** | click() |
| **Event handlers** | onClick |
| **See also** | **Objects:** form, radio |

## Access
Read and write.

## Discussion
You access the checkbox properties and methods using one of the following:

- *checkboxName.propertyName*
- *checkboxName.methodName(arguments)*
- *formName.elements[i].propertyName*
- *formName.elements[i].methodName(arguments)*

where

- *checkboxName* is the value of NAME of the checkbox object
- *formName* is either the value of NAME of the form object or an element in the forms array
- *i* is an integer index of the checkbox object on a form
- *propertyName* is one of the properties of the checkbox object
- *methodName* is one of the methods of the checkbox object

Because a checkbox is a form element, it must appear within the <FORM> tag on your HTML page. The checked property is used to set the checkbox to checked. The defaultChecked property is used to set the checkbox to checked when the form is loaded.

## Examples
One of the most frequent uses of JavaScript is with forms and data entry. To get you started on this, let us take a look at a somewhat elaborate example.

The idea is to design a form with two kind of fields in it: a string field and a positive integer field. Data validation will amount to converting all the letters in a string to uppercase, and verifying that integers only are used in the positive integer fields. Checking the form can be done when the user is finished entering the data, or as data for each field is entered. These alternatives are triggered by a checkbox object on the form. To see how it all works, follow the instructions for Exercise 7.4.

**EXERCISE 7.4** USING CHECKBOX AND FORM VALIDATION.

1. Type (or copy and paste) the code shown in Listing 7.6 and save it.

2. Load the file to your browser.

3. Enter some data in the form. Try to enter data with the checkbox checked or unchecked; what happens to the data you enter in both cases, for the various fields? Did you get the window similar to that in Figure 7.5?

4. Modify the exercise to ask for a full name and full address of a user.

5. Change the isPositiveInteger() function to allow hyphens and parentheses to be entered in the telephone field.

**LISTING 7.6** Using checkbox and form validation.

```
1    <HTML>
2    <HEAD>
3    <TITLE>Using Checkbox and Form Validation</TITLE>
4    <SCRIPT LANGUAGE = "JavaScript">
5    function isPositiveInteger(theDatum)
6    {
7     aString = "" + theDatum
8     for (var i = 0; i < aString.length; i++)
9     {
10    if (aString.charAt(i) < "0" || aString.charAt(i) > "9")
11    return false
12    }
13    return true
14    }
15
16    function checkField(formElement, dataType) {
17     if (document.infoForm.validateForm.checked)
18     {
19     if (dataType == "string")
20     document.infoForm.elements[formElement].value =
21     document.infoForm.elements[formElement].value.toUpperCase()
22     if (dataType == "number")
```

```
23    {
24    if
      (!isPositiveInteger(document.infoForm.elements[formElement].value))
25    alert("Illegal datum: " +
      document.infoForm.elements[formElement].value)
26    }
27    }
28    }
29
30    function checkAll(fieldTypesArray)
31    {
32    for (var i = 0; i < fieldTypesArray.length; i++)
33    {
34    if (fieldTypesArray[i] == "string")
35    {
36    document.infoForm.elements[i].value =
37    document.infoForm.elements[i].value.toUpperCase()
38    }
39    if (fieldTypesArray[i] == "number")
40    {
41    if (!isPositiveInteger(document.infoForm.elements[i].value))
42    alert("Illegal datum: " + document.infoForm.elements[i].value)
43    }
44    }
45    }
46    </SCRIPT>
47    </HEAD>
48    <BODY>
49    <FORM NAME = "infoForm">
50    <SCRIPT LANGUAGE = "JavaScript">
51    fieldTypes = new Array("string", "string", "string", "string",
      "number", "number")
52    </SCRIPT>
53    Last name:
54    <INPUT TYPE = "text"
55     NAME = "lastName"
56     SIZE = 25
57     onFocus = "this.select()"
58     onChange = "checkField(0,'string')">
59    <BR>First name:
60    <INPUT TYPE = "text"
61     NAME = "firstName"
62     SIZE = 25
63     onFocus = "this.select()"
64     onChange = "checkField(1,'string')">
65    <BR>City:
66    <INPUT TYPE = "text"
67     NAME = "cityName"
```

```
68    SIZE = 25
69    onFocus = "this.select()"
70    onChange = "checkField(2,'string')">
71  State:
72  <INPUT TYPE = "text"
73    NAME = "stateName"
74    SIZE = 3
75    onFocus = "this.select()"
76    onChange = "checkField(3,'string')">
77  Zip:
78  <INPUT TYPE = "text"
79    NAME = "zipCode"
80    SIZE = 10
81    onFocus = "this.select()"
82    onChange = "checkField(4,'number')">
83  <BR>Phone:
84  <INPUT TYPE = "text"
85    NAME = "phoneNumber"
86    SIZE = 10
87    onFocus = "this.select()"
88    onChange = "checkField(5,'number')">
89  <BR>
90  <INPUT TYPE = "checkBox"
91    NAME = "validateForm"
92    onClick = "if (this.checked) {checkAll(fieldTypes)}"
93    > Check form
94  </FORM>
95  </BODY>
96  </HTML>
```

Let us look at some key lines in Listing 7.6. In line 5 we start the definition of a function that verifies that a datum is a positive integer. Only the digits 0–9 are allowed in this field.

In line 16 we begin the definition of a function that checks a datum in a field. The function takes two arguments: the form element—an integer that represents the index of an element in the elements array of a form; and the dataType ("string" or "numeric"). In line 17 we determine the status of the checked button. If it is checked, we validate the data based on its type: a string or a number. For a string field type, we simply convert the characters to uppercase (this eases later parsing of the string). For numerical data, we verify that we in fact have a positive integer; if not, we alert the user to this fact.

Lines 30–45 validate all fields at once. This function is useful in case the user wishes to validate the form only after all fields were entered, as opposed to validating fields as the cursor leaves them.

**Netscape - [Using Checkbox and Form Validation]**

File  Edit  View  Go  Bookmarks  Options  Directory  Window  Help

Last name:

First name:

City:                                    State:        Zip:

Phone:

☐ Check form

Document: Done

---

**FIGURE 7.5**  Using checkbox and form validation.

We begin the form construction in line 49. First, we store the field types (by the order they appear on the form) in the fieldTypes array. Then we start laying out the form elements. To ease editing, we select the text in the field when the field receives focus (when the cursor enters the field). This is done with the call to select() in line 57. In line 58 we call the checkField() function with the field index in the elements array (this is an array of elements on the form), and with the field type (string or number).

In line 90 we insert the checkbox in the form, and in line 92 we call the checkAll() function to check all fields in the form if the box is checked.

# ↳ Date

## Purpose

Use the Date object whenever you need to work with date and time.

## Syntax

You create a Date object in one of the following ways:

- *dateObjectName* = new Date()

- *dateObjectName* = new Date("*month day, year hours:minutes:seconds*")

- *dateObjectName* = new Date(*year, month, day*)

- *dateObjectName* = new Date(*year, month, day, hours, minutes, seconds*)

where (see discussion for further details):

| | |
|---|---|
| *dateObjectName* | is the name of a new object or a property of an existing object. |
| *month* | is the month of the year. |
| *day* | is the day of the week. |
| *year* | is the year. |
| *hours* | is the hour of the day. |
| *minutes* | is the minute of the hour. |
| *seconds* | is the second of the minute. |

| | |
|---|---|
| **Property of** | None |
| **Properties** | prototype |
| **Methods** | getDate(), getDay(), getHours(), getMinutes(), getMonth(), getSeconds(), getTime(), getTimezoneOffset(), getYear(), parse(), setDate(), setHours(), setMinutes(), setMonth(), setSeconds(), setTime(), setYear(), toGMTString(), toLocaleString(), UTC() |
| **Event handlers** | None |
| **See also** | **Objects:** String |

## Access

Read and write.

## Discussion

As with Array, a date object is created with the new keyword. Thus, case is important—new date() will cause an error; new Date() will not. Except for the parse() and UTC() methods, you use the Date object with statements like this:

```
dateObjectName.methodName(arguments)
```

where

- *dateObjectName* is either the name of an existing Date object or a property of an existing object
- *methodName* is one of the Date object's methods

If *dateObjectName* is an existing object, a call to *methodName* with arguments will set the existing object. The parse() and UTC() methods are static, and you must access them using the following syntax:

```
Date.UTC(arguments)
```

or

```
Date.parse(arguments)
```

If you omit arguments in creation of a Date object, the current (computer) system date and time will be stored in the new object. For example, the statement

```
aDate = new Date()
```

stores the current (computer) system date and time in aDate. You can omit the hours, minutes, or seconds from the arguments to Date(); this will set them to zero.

Dates are stored as integers that indicate the amount of time that elapsed in milliseconds since January 1, 1970 00:00:00. Currently you cannot rely on results with dates prior to 1970.

## Examples

In line 1 of Listing 7.7 we store today's date in the Date object named today. The current date is obtained from the operating system clock. In line 2 we store the current year in the variable currentYear, and in line 3 we set the year to 2000 for the today object.

**LISTING 7.7** Working with the Date object.

```
1    today = new Date()
2    currentYear = today.getYear()
3    today.setYear(2000)
```

 document

## Purpose

Use the document object to access information about an HTML document, display it, and manipulate it.

## Syntax

```
<BODY
 BACKGROUND = "anImage"
 BGCOLOR = "backgroundColor"
 TEXT = "foregroundColor"
 LINK = "unfollowedLinkColor"
 ALINK = "activatedLinkColor"
 VLINK = "followedLinkColor"
 [onLoad = "eventHandler"]
 [onUnload = "eventHandler"]
 [onBlur = "eventHandler"]
 [onFocus = "eventHandler"]</BODY>
```

where:

| | |
|---|---|
| BACKGROUND = | "*anImage*" sets the background image. |
| BGCOLOR = | "*backgroundColor*" sets the background color. |
| TEXT = | "*foregroundColor*" sets the foreground color. |
| LINK = | "*unfollowedLinkColor*" sets the not-clicked-yet link color. |
| ALINK = | "*activatedLinkColor*" sets activated link color. |
| VLINK = | "*followedLinkColor*" sets the followed link color. |
| onLoad = | "*eventHandler*" causes execution of *eventHandler* when the onLoad event handler occurs. |
| onBlur = | "*eventHandler*" causes execution of *eventHandler* when the onBlur event handler occurs. |
| onFocus = | "*eventHandler*" causes execution of eventHandler when the onFocus event handler occurs. |
| onUnload = | "*eventHandler*" causes execution of eventHandler when the onUnload event handler occurs. |

| | |
|---|---|
| **Property of** | window |
| **Properties** | alinkColor, anchor, anchors, Applet, applets, Area, bgColor, cookie, embeds, fgColor, form, forms, history, Image, images, lastModified, link, linkColor, links, Plugin, referrer, title, URL, vlinkColor |
| **Methods** | close(), open(), write(), writeln() |
| **Event handlers** | None |
| **See also** | **Objects:** frame, window |

## Access
Read and write.

## Discussion
To work with a document object, use statements such as

document.*propertyName*

or

document.*methodName*(*arguments*)

where

- *propertyName* is one of the document object properties

- *methodName* is one of the document object methods

Specify colors in one of two ways:

- RGB triplet in hexadecimal following the format RRGGBB or #RRGGBB, where RR, GG, and BB are the hexadecimal values of red, green, and blue respectively. For example, FFFFFF specifies the color white—a full mix of red, green, and blue. The mix 00FF00 specifies the color green (0 value for red, 0 value for blue, and maximum value for green).

- A string literal (see Appendix C).

A document usually consists of <HEAD> and <BODY> sections. A document can be loaded by using the location object. A document includes anchors, forms, and links arrays that facilitate working with these entities via JavaScript.

These arrays are built by the browser as objects of the respective types as encountered in the HTML source code. Each of these objects has an entry in its respective array.

As with other document's event handlers, onBlur and onFocus are specified in the <BODY> tag but are actually event handlers for the window object.

In working with document, keep the following in mind also:

- If you wish to access information about the document's location, use document.URL, not document.location.

- the document's functions close(), open(), and write() clear the document pane and remove the text and form elements.

- You can omit the document.open() call if you are writing text or HTML.

## Examples

In Exercise 7.5 we create a table of contents frame and a contents frame. Topics in the table of contents are linked to headings in the contents frame. Each frame has its own document. The topics in the table of contents frame are linked to anchors in the contents frame. The file PARENTDOC.HTML defines the frame; the file TOCDOC.HTML defines the table of contents, and the file CONTENTDOC.HTML defines the contents. Do Exercise 7.5 and see how things work. In particular, notice when onLoad and onUnload are executed. Use these event handlers to do some preparations and house cleaning in your JavaScript work. Following steps 5 and 6 in Exercise 7.5 will improve your knowledge of the document object.

| EXERCISE 7.5 | WORKING WITH THE DOCUMENT OBJECT. |

1. Type (or copy and paste) the code shown in Listing 7.8 and save it as PARENTDOC.HTML.

2. Type (or copy and paste) the code shown in Listing 7.9 and save it as TOCDOC.HTML.

3. Type (or copy and paste) the code shown in Listing 7.10 and save it as CONTENTDOC.HTML.

4. Load PARENTDOC.HTML to your browser and watch what happens. Did you get the window similar to that in Figure 7.6?

5. Modify the exercise to add some text, headings, etc. that fit your needs.

6. Modify the colors using the RGB code and examine the effect of mixing various combinations of red, green, and blue.

**LISTING 7.8** PARENTDOC.HTML.

```
1    <HTML>
2    <HEAD>
3    <TITLE>Document Object Example</TITLE>
4    </HEAD>
5    <FRAMESET COLS = "25%,75%">
6    <FRAME SRC = "tocDoc.html" NAME = "tocFrame">
7    <FRAME SRC = "contentDoc.html" NAME = "contentFrame">
8    </FRAMESET>
9    </HTML>
```

**LISTING 7.9** TOCDOC.HTML.

```
1    <HTML>
2    <BODY
3     BGCOLOR = "lightblue"
4     TEXT = "darkblue"
5     LINK = "red"
6     ALINK = "green"
7     VLINK = "brown">
8    <P><H3>Table of Contents</H3>
9    <LI><A HREF = "contentDoc.html#Chapter1" TARGET =
     "contentFrame">Chapter 1</A>
10   <LI><A HREF = "contentDoc.html#Chapter2" TARGET =
     "contentFrame">Chapter 2</A>
11   <LI><A HREF = "contentDoc.html#Chapter3" TARGET =
     "contentFrame">Chapter 3</A>
12   <LI><A HREF = "contentDoc.html#Chapter4" TARGET =
     "contentFrame">Chapter 4</A>
13   <LI><A HREF = "contentDoc.html#Chapter5" TARGET =
     "contentFrame">Chapter 5</A>
14   </BODY>
15   </HTML>
```

**LISTING 7.10** CONTENTDOC.HTML

```
1    <HTML>
2    <BODY
3     BGCOLOR = "oldlace"
4     onLoad = "alert('Just finished loading')"
5     onUnload = "alert('Just finished unloading')"
6     TEXT = "navy">
```

```
7     <P><A NAME = "Chapter1"><H3>Chapter 1</H3></A>
8     <P><LI>1.1 <LI>1.2 <LI>1.3 <LI>1.4 <LI>1.5 <LI>1.6 <LI>1.7
9     <P><A NAME = "Chapter2"><H3>Chapter 2</H3></A>
10    <P><LI>2.1 <LI>2.2 <LI>2.3 <LI>2.4 <LI>2.5 <LI>2.6 <LI>2.7
<LI>2.8
11    <P><A NAME = "Chapter3"><H3>Chapter 3</H3></A>
12    <P><LI>3.1 <LI>3.2 <LI>3.3 <LI>3.4 <LI>3.5 <LI>3.6
13    <P><A NAME = "Chapter4"><H3>Chapter 4</H3></A>
14    <P><LI>4.1 <LI>4.2 <LI>4.3 <LI>4.4 <LI>4.5 <LI>4.6 <LI>4.7
15    <P><A NAME = "Chapter5"><H3>Chapter 5</H3></A>
16    <P><LI>5.1 <LI>5.2 <LI>5.3 <LI>5.5 <LI>5.5 17      <LI>5.6
<LI>5.7
17    </BODY>
18    </HTML>
```

# ⮯ elements array

## Purpose

An array of elements in a form object.

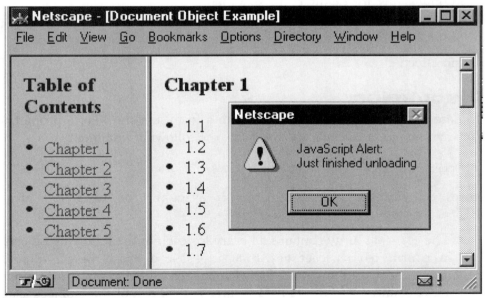

**FIGURE 7.6** Working with the document object.

## Syntax

```
formName.elements[i]
```

where

| | |
|---|---|
| formName | is the form name as specified in the NAME attribute of the <FORM> tag. |
| i | is the element index. Elements are placed in the array in the order they appear on the form in the HTML source code; i.e., the index of the first element is 0, and so on. |

| | |
|---|---|
| **Property of** | form |
| **Properties** | length |
| **Methods** | None |
| **Event handlers** | None |
| **See also** | **Objects:** form |

## Access

Read only. Thus, for example, the statement

```
aFrom.elements[0] = "anElement"
```

has no effect.

## Discussion

To determine the number of elements in a form, use the length property. For example, for a form named formName, the following statement

```
numberOfFormElements = formName.elements.length
```

stores the number of elements on formName in the variable number OfFormElements.

- The elements array contains an entry for each of the following objects in a form: button, checkbox, hidden, password, radio, reset, select, submit, text, and textarea. The elements are added to the array as they are encountered in the HTML source code. Each of these objects can also be referenced by its name, as defined by the NAME attribute of the element's tag. The `elements` array allows you to refer to these elements without necessarily knowing their names.

- Each radio button in a `radio` object has its own entry in the array.
- The value of each element in the `elements` array is the full HTML statement for the object.

## Examples

Suppose you wish to determine the names of elements in a particular form somewhere on the Internet. Listing 7.11 gives a JavaScript function to do just that. Replace *some URL* with a URL of your choice.

**LISTING 7.11** Using the `elements` array.

```
1    aWindow=window.open("some URL")
2
3    function elmentNames()
4    {
5     for (var j = 0; j < aWindow.document.forms.length; j++)
6     for (var i = 0; i <
7     aWindow.document.form[j].elements.length; i++)
8     alert(aWindow.document.form[j].elements[i].name)
9    }
```

# ↳ fileUpload

## Purpose

Use this object to upload a file from within an HTML document. A `fileUpload` object is an element in an HTML document.

## Syntax

```
<INPUT
 TYPE = "file"
 NAME = "fileUploadObjectName">
```

where

NAME =    "*fileUploadObjectName*" is the name of the `fileUpload` object.

| | |
|---|---|
| **Property of** | `form` |
| **Properties** | `name, type, value` |
| **Methods** | None |
| **Event handlers** | None |
| **See also** | **Objects:** `text` |

## Access
Read only.

## Discussion
You access `fileUpload` object properties with a statement such as

*fileUploadObjectName.propertyName*

where

- *fileUploadObjectName* is the name of the *fileUpload* object

- *propertyName* is one of the object's properties.

This object allows you to place a file in an HTML form. For security reasons, you cannot change the file you uploaded in any way via JavaScript.

## Examples
To see `fileUpload` in action, follow the instructions in Exercise 7.6.

**EXERCISE 7.6**    FILEUPLOAD.

1. Type (or copy and paste) the code shown in Listing 7.12 and save it.
2. Load the file to your browser and watch what happens. Did you get a window similar to that in Figure 7.7?
3. Press the `Browse...` button and observe what happens.
4. Change the filename in the text box, and press the `File Upload` properties... button. Observe the changes in the property values.

**LISTING 7.12** FileUpload.

```
1    <HTML>
2    <HEAD>
3    <TITLE> FileUpload Example </TITLE>
4    </HEAD>
5    <BODY>
6    <FORM NAME = "fileUploadForm"
7     METHOD = POST>
8    Upload:
9    <INPUT TYPE = "file"
10    NAME = "fileUploadObjectName">
11   <P>
12   <INPUT TYPE = "button"
13    VALUE = "File Upload Properties..."
14    onClick = "alert('FileUpload object name: ' +
15    document.fileUploadForm.fileUploadObjectName.name +
16    '\r' + 'FileUpload object value: ' +
17   document.fileUploadForm.fileUploadObjectName.value)">
18   </FORM>
19   <BODY>
20   </HTML>
```

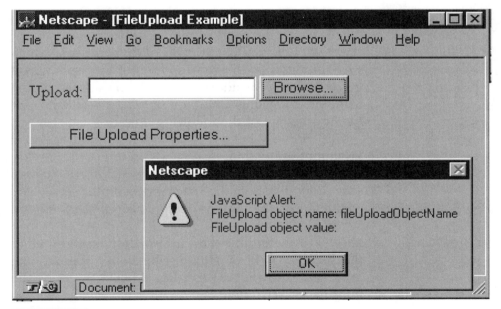

**FIGURE 7.7** FileUpload.

#  form and forms array

## Purpose

Use the `form` object to build interactive HTML documents, to obtain data, and to post the data to a server.

## Syntax

```
<FORM
    NAME = "formName"
    TARGET = "targetWindowName"
    ACTION = "URL"
    METHOD = GET | POST
    ENCTYPE = "dataEncodingType"
    [onReset = "onResetEventHandler"]
    [onReset = "eventHandler"]
    [onSubmit = "eventHandler"]>
</FORM>
```

where

| | |
|---|---|
| NAME = | "*formName*" is the name of the `form` object. |
| TARGET = | "*targetWindowName*" is the name of the window to which `form` responses go. Server responses to `form` submission go to the target window. *targetWindowName* can be the name of an existing `window` or `frame`. *targetWindowName* can also be one of the following literals: `_top`, `_parent`, `_self`, or `_blank`. *targetWindowName* cannot be a JavaScript expression. |
| ACTION = | "*URL*" is the URL of the server to which form data are sent. You can handle the arriving data on the server side with a CGI script, LiveWire application, or the `mailto` action. |
| METHOD = | GET \| POST determines how information is submitted to the server via the ACTION attribute. GET appends the information to the server URL, while POST sends the information separately. |
| ENCTYPE = | "*dataEncodingType*" is the MIME encoding of the data sent. This can be either the default "application/x-www-form-urlencoded" or "multipart/form-data". |

| Property of | document |
|---|---|
| **Properties** | `action, button, checkbox, elements, encoding, FileUpload, hidden, length, method, password, radio, reset, select, submit, target, text, textarea` |
| **Methods** | `reset( ), submit( )` |
| **Event handlers** | `onReset, onSubmit` |
| **See also** | **Objects:** `button, checkbox, hidden, password, radio, reset, select, submit, text, textarea` |

## Access

Read only. Thus, the statement

```
document.forms[0].name = "something"
```

will have no effect.

## Discussion

You can use a form and its properties with one of the following formats:

- *formName.propertyName*
- *formName.methodName(arguments)*
- *forms[i].propertyName*
- *forms[i].methodName(arguments)*

where

- *propertyName* and *methodName* are a `form` object property and method
- *i* is the index of the *form* in the forms array of the present *document*

Note that many of the `form` object properties are objects themselves.

When a `document` is loaded, the browser builds a `forms` array, where each form is added as an element to the array as it is encountered in the HTML source code. Thus, if a document contains two forms, as specified by the `<FORM>` tag, the first will be `document.forms[0]`, and the second `document.forms[1]`.

## Examples

For an example in the use of the form object, see Exercise 7.4.

 frame **and** frames **array**

## Purpose

Frames behave much like separate windows in the browser's window. Use frames to create areas in a window. Each area can have its own URL.

## Syntax

```
<FRAMESET
    ROWS = "listOfRowHeights"
    COLS = "listOfColumnsWidths"
    [onLoad = "eventHandler"]
    [onUnload = "eventHandler"]>
    [<FRAME SRC = "URL"
NAME = "frameName">]
    [onBlur = "eventHandler"]
    [onFocus = "eventHandler"]
</FRAMESET>
```

where:

| | |
|---|---|
| ROWS = | "*listOfRowHeights*" is a list of comma-separated integers specifying the respective row heights in pixels (the default). |
| COLS = | "*listOfColumnsWidths*" is a list of comma-separated integers specifying the respective column widths in pixels (the default). |
| <FRAME> | defines a frame. |
| SRC = | "*URL*" is the URL of the document to be displayed in the frame. The URL cannot be an anchor name. |
| NAME = | "*frameName*" is the name of the frame to jump to from a hyperlink. |

| | |
|---|---|
| **Property of** | window, frames (property of frame) |
| **Properties** | frames, name, length (property of frames), parent, self, window |
| **Methods** | clearTimeout(), setTimeout() |
| **Event handlers** | onBlur, onFocus |
| **See also** | **Objects:** document, window |

## Access

Elements in the `frames` array are read only. Thus, for example, the statement

```
parent.frames[0] = "newFrame"
```

has no effect.

## Discussion

Use one of the following methods to access frames and their methods and properties:

- `[windowReference.]frameName.propertyName`
- `[windowReference.]frames[i].propertyName`
- `window.propertyName`
- `self.propertyName`
- `parent.propertyName`

where

- *windowReference* is one of the following: a variable that stores a `window` definition, the synonym `top`, or the synonym `parent`.
- *frameName* refers to the value of the `NAME` attribute of the `<FRAME>` tag.
- *i* is the integer index of a frame object in the `frames` array.
- *propertyName* is one of the `frame` properties.

Note that the methods (or actions) associated with `onLoad` and `onUnload`, although they appear in the `<FRAMESET>` tag, are `window`, not `frame` methods (or actions). The `<FRAMESET>` tag is used to lay out the various frames in a page; a `frame` is actually a `window` object.

To communicate among various frames in the document, use the dot hierarchy notation (Figures 3.1 and 3.2 in Chapter 3). For example, if a document has two frames, one with `NAME = "firstFrame"` and the other with `NAME = "secondFrame"`, you can refer to properties of the second frame from the first frame thus, for example:

```
otherFrameName = parent.secondFrame.name
```

or

```
otherFrameName = parent.frames[1].name
```

To make your code modular, you can refer to the current `frame` using the `self` or `window` property. To navigate among frames in your code, you can also use the `top` property, which refers to the root frame (`window`) in which all other nested frame reside. To move one frame above in the hierarchy, use the `parent` property.

The `frames` array is constructed when the browser loads the HTML page. Each `<FRAME>` tag that is encountered is added as an element in the `frames` array. To determine the number of frame elements in a document (from within a `frame`), use the syntax

```
[parentOfFrame.]frames.length
```

where *parentOfFrame* is a `window` variable or the literal `top` or `parent`.

You access specific frames in the array using one of the following methods:

- `[theFrame.]frames[i]`
- `[windowVariable.]frames[i]`
- `[parent.]frames[i]`
- `[top.]frames[i]`

where

- *theFrame* is one of the ways you refer to frames
- *windowVariable* is a defined `window` variable in your code
- *i* is an integer representing the index of the frame in the *frames* array

The value of each element in the `frames` array is the frame's `NAME` attribute.

To use the `onBlur` and `onFocus` event handlers, use the following syntax (for frames, you cannot specify these event handlers in HTML):

- *frameReference*.`onblur` = *errorHandler*
- *frameReference*.`onfocus` = *errorHandler*

(note in particular the lowercase spelling of the event handlers) where

- *frameReference* is a valid way of referring to a *frame*
- *errorHandler* is the keyword `null`, the name of an error-handling function, or a variable or property that contains `null` or a valid function reference

# Examples

Exercise 7.7 demonstrates a somewhat elaborate use of `frame` objects and a `frames` array. Follow its instructions and the listings and you will understand how to work with `frames`, and how to access windows and frames from one another.

---

**EXERCISE 7.7**    WORKING WITH FRAME AND THE FRAMES ARRAY.

1. Type (or copy and paste) the code shown in Listing 7.13 and save it as `SETUP.HTML`.

2. Type (or copy and paste) the code shown in Listing 7.14 and save it as `WINDOW2.HTML`.

3. Type (or copy and paste) the code shown in Listing 7.15 and save it as `FILE0.HTML`.

4. Type (or copy and paste) the code shown in Listing 7.16 and save it as `FILE1.HTML`.

5. Type (or copy and paste) the code shown in Listing 7.17 and save it as `FILE2.HTML`.

6. Load `SETUP.HTML` to your browser and press the various frames elements. You should get windows as shown in Figure 7.8 and in Figure 7.9.

7. Change the messages that each of the buttons sends, and observe where the message appears.

---

**LISTING 7.13** Working with `frames`—SETUP.HTML.

```
1    <HTML>
2    <HEAD>
3    <TITLE>First Window</TITLE>
4    </HEAD>
5    <FRAMESET ROWS="50%,50%" COLS="50%,50%">
6    <FRAME SRC=file0.html NAME="frame0_window1">
7    <FRAME SRC=file1.html NAME="frame1_window1">
8    <FRAME SRC=file1.html NAME="frame2_window1">
9    <FRAME SRC=file1.html NAME="frame3_window1">
10   </FRAMESET>
11   </HTML>
```

The file `SETUP.HTML` in Listing 7.13 is responsible for setting up the frames in the first window to appear. There are four frames, named according to which window they belong to, and the order in which they are stored in the `frames` array.

**LISTING 7.14** Working with frames—WINDOW2.HTML.

```
1    <HTML>
2    <HEAD>
3    <TITLE>Second Window</TITLE>
4    </HEAD>
5    <FRAMESET ROWS="50%,50%" COLS="50%,50%">
6    <FRAME SRC=file1.html NAME="frame0_window2">
7    <FRAME SRC=file1.html NAME="frame1_window2">
8    <FRAME SRC=file1.html NAME="frame2_window2">
9    <FRAME SRC=file1.html NAME="frame3_window2">
10   </FRAMESET>
11   </HTML>
```

The file WINDOW2.HTML in Listing 7.14 sets up the frames in a window. FILE0.HTML in Listing 7.15 sets up the interface to all other frames, in both windows. Note that in it we open window2, whose HTML code resides in WINDOW2.HTML. Finally, FILE1.HTML and FILE2.HTML set up the frames in each of the windows (Listing 7.16 and Listing 7.17, respectively).

**LISTING 7.15** Working with frames—FILE0.HTML.

```
1    <HTML>
2    <BODY>
3    <A NAME = "frame0_window1"><H1>frame0_window1</H1></A>
4    <P>
5    <A HREF = "file2.html"
6     target=frame1_window1>
7     Click here</A>
8     to load a file3 into frame1_window1.
9    <SCRIPT LANGUAGE = "JavaScript">
10   window2 = open("window2.html","window2")
11   </SCRIPT>
12   <FORM>
13   <P>
14   <INPUT TYPE = "button"
15    VALUE = "Message to frame1_window1"
16    onClick =
17    "parent.frame1_window1.document.write('<P>I came from
       frame1_window1')">
18   <P>
19   <INPUT TYPE = "button"
20    VALUE = "Act on frame2_window1..."
```

```
21    onClick = "parent.frames[2].document.bgColor='red'">
22    <P>
23    <INPUT TYPE = "button"
24     VALUE = "Act on frame3_window1..."
25     onClick = "top.frames[3].document.bgColor='green'">
26    <P>
27    <INPUT TYPE = "button"
28     VALUE = "Act on frame1_window2..."
29     onClick =
30     "window2.frame1_window2.document.bgColor='blue'">
31    <P>
32    <INPUT TYPE = "button"
33     VALUE = "Act on frame2_window2..."
34     onClick =
35     "window2.frames[2].document.bgColor='yellow'">
36    <P>
37    <INPUT TYPE = "button"
38     VALUE = "Act on frame3_window2..."
39     onClick =
40     "window2.frames[3].document.bgColor='white'">
41    </FORM>
42    </BODY>
43    </HTML>
```

**LISTING 7.16** Working with frames—FILE1.HTML.

```
1    <HTML>
2    <BODY>
3    <P>This is frame2_window1 loaded from file1
4    </BODY>
5    </HTML>
```

**LISTING 7.17** Working with frames—FILE2.HTML.

```
1    <HTML>
2    <BODY>
3    <P>This is frame2_window1 loaded from file2
4    </BODY>
5    </HTML>
```

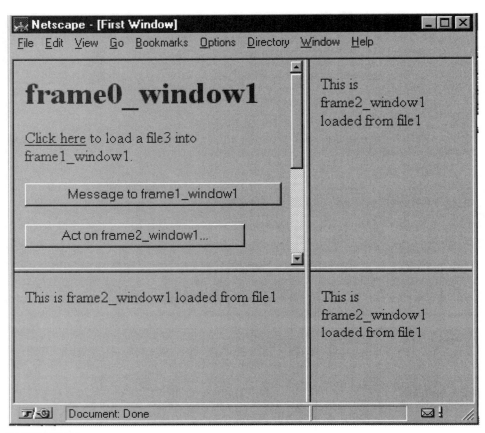

**FIGURE 7.8** Working with frames—first window.

**FIGURE 7.9** Working with frames—second window.

 # Function

## Purpose

Use this object to indicate that a string is actually JavaScript code that needs to be compiled as a function.

## Syntax

```
aVariable = new Function ([argument1, argument2, ... argumentN],
functionCode)
```

where

| | |
|---|---|
| *aVariable* | specifies the name of a variable, a property of an existing object, or an event handler of an object. |
| *argument1...argumentN* | are strings recognized by the function as its arguments. |
| *functionCode* | is a string that represent the function code. |

| | |
|---|---|
| **Property of** | None |
| **Properties** | arguments, prototype |
| **Methods** | None |
| **Event handlers** | None |
| **See also** | |

## Access

Read and write.

## Discussion

Because Function objects are compiled each time they are encountered, it is more efficient to declare functions only once and use them in your code.

To use a Function object in your code, assign the object to a variable and use the variable the way you use any function. For example, instead of using the function code in Listing 7.18, we can declare a variable called aFunction, assign a `Function` object to it, and then execute it in a script. Thus, the code in Listing 7.19 creates the `Function` object called `aFunction`. The object takes two arguments, `aString` and `aNumber`, and the function code displays an `alert` window with the number of times it was called. In line 3 we are calling the alert window three times.

**LISTING 7.18** `aFunction`.

```
1      function aFunction(aString, aNumber)
2      {
3       for (var i = 0; i < aNumber; i++)
4       alert(aString + i)
5      }
```

**LISTING 7.19** Using the `Function` object.

```
1      <SCRIPT LANGUAGE = "JavaScript">
2      var aFunction = new Function("aString", "aNumber", "for(var i
= 0; i < aNumber; i++) alert(aString + i)")
3      aFunction("This is call number: ",3)
4      </SCRIPT>
```

A function can be assigned to an event handler using the following syntax:

- `document.`*`formName.aValue`*`.onclick = `*`aFunctionObject`*

- `<INPUT NAME = "`*`aName`*`" TYPE = "`*`aType`*`" VALUE = "`*`aValue`*`" onClick = "`*`aFunctionObject`*`()">`

where

- *`formName`* is a `form` in the `document` with the NAME attribute *`formName`*

- *`aName`* is the name of an object of *`aType`*

- *`aType`* is an object that has the `onClick` event handler

- `aFunctionObject` is a `Function` object

Note that if you happen to combine the code in Listing 7.18 with the code in Listing 7.19 in the same script, the function `aFunction(...){...}` will be executed, not the `Function` object `aFunction`. A `Function` object can be called directly as in line 3 of Listing 7.19. To call a `Function` object that takes arguments via an event handler, you will have to assign the object value to a variable. This is so because event handler functions do not take arguments. For example, the statement in line 2 of Listing 7.20 will not work because event handlers do not take arguments, while the statement in line 4 will. Note in particular the use of lowercase for onfocus. You should use lowercase for all event handlers in calls like the ones in Listing 7.20.

**LISTING 7.20** The Function object and event handlers.

```
1    window.onfocus = new Function (argument1, functionCode)
2    window.onfocus()
3    window.onfocus = new Function (argument1, functionCode)
4    window.onfocus
```

## Examples

Exercise 7.8 demonstrates the use of the Function object. Note in particular the call to the object functions in lines 36, 42, 48, and 54. Without the assignment to document.calculator.z.value we cannot use the functions plus, minus, mult, and divide because the onClick event handlers cannot take arguments.

**EXERCISE 7.8** USING THE FUNCTION OBJECT TO BUILD A SIMPLE CALCULATOR.

1. Type (or copy and paste) the code shown in Listing 7.21 and save it.

2. Load the file to your browser; enter some numbers and calculate the results. In particular, enter a zero for the second operand, and use the divide operation. Do you get NaN (meaning Not a Number)? Do you get something like Figure 7.10?

3. In line 6 of Listing 7.21, replace the string return parseInt(x) + parseInt(y) with the string return x + y. What result do you get? Why?

4. Each of the functions in Listing 7.21 (plus, minus, mult, and divide) takes two arguments, x and y, and returns the result of the respective operation. The remaining code simply sets up the document's form, adds buttons to the form, and assigns the appropriate function to the button's onClick event handler.

**LISTING 7.21** Using the Function object to build a simple calculator.

```
1    <HTML>
2    <HEAD>
3    <TITLE>Calculator</TITLE>
4    <SCRIPT LANGUAGE = "JavaScript">
```

```
 5    var plus =
 6     new Function("x", "y", "return parseInt(x) + parseInt(y)")
 7    var minus =
 8     new Function("x", "y", "return x - y")
 9    var mult =
10     new Function("x", "y", "return x * y")
11    var divide =
12     new Function ("x", "y", "return x / y")
13    </SCRIPT>
14    </HEAD>
15    </BODY>
16    <H3>Calculator</H3>
17    <P>
18    <FORM NAME = "calculator">
19    <INPUT NAME = "x"
20     TYPE = "text"
21     VALUE = "0"
22     SIZE = 5>
23    <INPUT
24     NAME = "y"
25     TYPE = "text"
26     VALUE = "0"
27     SIZE = 5>
28    <INPUT NAME = "z"
29     TYPE = "text"
30     VALUE = ""
31     SIZE = 10>
32    <P>
33    <INPUT NAME = "plusButton"
34     TYPE = "button"
35     VALUE = " + "
36     onClick = "document.calculator.z.value =
37     plus(document.calculator.x.value,
38     document.calculator.y.value)">
39    <INPUT NAME = "minusButton"
40     TYPE = "button"
41     VALUE = " - "
42     onClick = "document.calculator.z.value =
43     minus(document.calculator.x.value,
44     document.calculator.y.value)">
45    <INPUT NAME = "multButton"
46     TYPE = "button"
47     VALUE = " * "
48     onClick = nt.calculator.z.value =
49     mult(document.calculator.x.value,
50     document.calculator.y.value)">
51    <INPUT NAME = "divideButton"
```

```
52    TYPE = "button"
53    VALUE = " / "
54    onClick = "document.calculator.z.value =
55    divide(document.calculator.x.value,
56    document.calculator.y.value)">
57    </FORM>
58    </BODY>
59    </HTML>
```

#  hidden

## Purpose

Use this object to hide form elements from the user, and for client-server communication.

## Syntax

```
<INPUT
  TYPE = "hidden"
  NAME = "hiddenName"
  [VALUE = "textValue"]>
```

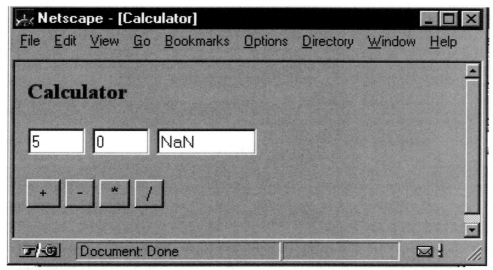

**FIGURE 7.10**  Using the Function object to build a simple calculator.

where

| NAME = | "*hiddenName*" is the object's name. |
| VALUE = | "*textValue*" the object's initial value. |

| | |
|---|---|
| **Property of** | form |
| **Properties** | name, type, value |
| **Methods** | None |
| **Event handlers** | None |
| **See also** | **Properties:** cookie |

## Access

Read and write.

## Discussion

Like all other form elements, you can access hidden elements with one of the following syntaxes:

- *hiddenName.propertyName*
- *formName.elements[i].propertyName*

where

- *hiddenName* is the value of the NAME attribute
- *formName* is either the value of the NAME attribute of a form object or an element in the forms array
- *i* is the integer index of the *hidden* object's position in the form's elements array
- *propertyName* is a hidden's object property

Being a form element, a hidden object must be defined inside the <FORM> tag.

## Examples

In Exercise 7.9 we assign the VALUE button objects on a form to a hidden object when a third button is clicked (lines 14–15 and 19–20, Listing 7.22). When the user clicks on the button to display the value of the hidden object, an alert window pops up (line 26). Were the user to submit the form, the value of the last clicked button would submitted.

1. Type (or copy and paste) the code shown in Listing 7.22 and save it.

2. Load the file to your browser. You should get a window similar to Figure 7.11. Click on Button 2 and then on Show hidden... (did you get a window similar to Figure 7.12). Next, click on Button 1 and then on Show hidden...

3. Feeling adventurous? Then add the ACTION mailto to the form, with a method POST, and send yourself an e-mail message with the value of the last clicked button.

**LISTING 7.22** Using the hidden object.

```
1    <HTML>
2    <HEAD>
3    <TITLE>Hidden Object</TITLE>
4    </HEAD>
5    <BODY>
6    Click an object and see its hidden value
7    <FORM NAME = "aForm">
8    <INPUT TYPE = "hidden"
9     NAME = "hObject"
10    VALUE = "None">
11   <INPUT TYPE = "button"
12    VALUE = "Button 1"
13    NAME = "Button1"
14    onClick =
15    "document.aForm.hObject.value = this.value">
16   <INPUT TYPE = "button"
17    NAME = "Button 2"
18    VALUE = "Button2"
19    onClick =
20    "document.aForm.hObject.value = this.value">
21   <P>
22   <INPUT TYPE = "button"
23    VALUE = "Show hidden..."
24    NAME = "Button3"
25    onClick =
26    "alert('hidden VALUE = ' + document.aForm.hObject.value)">
27   </FORM>
28   </BODY>
29   </HTML>
```

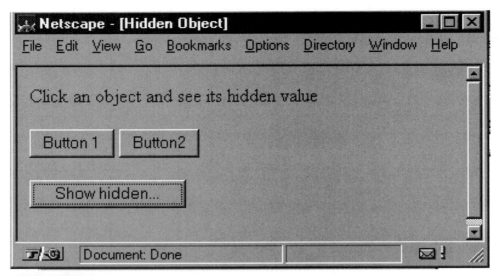

FIGURE 7.11 Using the hidden object.

# ↳ history

## Purpose

Use this object to retrieve information about the URLs that your HTML page user visited within a window. The Go menu uses the history list for navigation (e.g., Back, Forward).

## Syntax

- history.*propertyName*

FIGURE 7.12 Result of using the hidden object.

- history.*methodName(arguments)*

where:

*propertyName*   is one of the history's object properties.
*methodName*    is one of the history's object methods.

| | |
|---|---|
| **Property of** | document |
| **Properties** | length |
| **Methods** | back(), forward(), go() |
| **Event handlers** | None |
| **See also** | **Objects:** location |

## Access

Read only.

## Discussion

You can use the history object to emulate some of the behavior of the Go submenu items in Navigator. If you wish to go back n clicks ago in the current window, use the statement

history.go(*-n*)

where n is an integer. You can also move back and forth within a window with a statement like this:

*windowName*.history.back(*n*)

where *windowName* is a window name, and *n* is an integer. You can also move within a frame in a FRAMESET using statements such as:

parent.frames[i].history.back(*n*)

where *i* is the frame's entry in the frames array, and *n* is an integer.

## Examples

To observe the behavior of the history object, go through Exercise 7.10. The code is self-explanatory.

1. Type (or copy and paste) the code shown in Listing 7.23 and save it.

2. Load the file to your browser. You should get a window similar to Figure 7.13.

3. Modify the code in Listing 7.23 to query the user as to how many steps backwards or forwards she wishes to move. Hint: One way is to use the text object, and retrieve the number of steps by reading the value of the text object.

**LISTING 7.23** Using the history object.

```
1    <HTML>
2    <HEAD>
3    <TITLE>Using History</TITLE>
4    </HEAD>
5    <BODY>
6    <FORM NAME = "aForm">
7    <INPUT TYPE = "button"
8     VALUE = "Forward"
9     NAME = "Forward"
10    onClick = "history.go()">
11   <INPUT TYPE = "button"
12    NAME = "Backward"
13    VALUE = "Backward"
14    onClick = "history.back()">
15   </FORM>
16   </BODY>
17   </HTML>
```

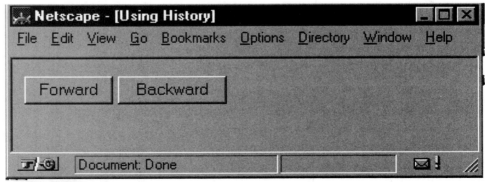

**FIGURE 7.13** Using the history object.

# Image and images array

## Purpose

Use the Image object to manipulate images in your HTML page.

## Syntax

```
<IMG
 [NAME = "imageName"]
 SRC = "highResLocation"
 [LOWSRC = "lowResLocation"]
 [HEIGHT = "heightInPixels" | "heightInPercent"%]
 [WIDTH = "widthInPixels" | "widthInPercent"%]
 [HSPACE = "imageHorizontalMarginsInPixels"]
 [VSPACE = "imageVerticalMarginsInPixels"]
 [BORDER = "imageBorderWidth"]
 [ALIGN = "left" | "right" |
 "top" | "absmiddle" | "absbottom" |
 "texttop" | "middle" | "baseline" | "bottom"]
 [ISMAP]
 [USEMAP = "imageLocation#mapName"]
 [onAbort = "abortEventHandler"]
 [onError = "errorEventHandler"]
 [onLoad = "loadEventHandler"]>
```

where

| | |
|---|---|
| NAME = | "imageName" is the name of the Image object. |
| SRC = | "highResLocation" is the URL location of the Image object. |
| LOWSRC = | "lowResLocation" specifies the URL of a low-resolution version of the Image object. If specified, Navigator will load this image first, and then replace it with the high-resolution image specified in SRC. |
| HEIGHT = | "heightInPixels" \| "heightInPercent"% gives the image height in either pixels or percentage of the window (or frame) height. If necessary, Navigator will scale the image to fit within the specified height. |
| WIDTH = | "widthInPixels" \| "widthInPercent"% gives the image width in either pixels or percentage of the window (or |

| | |
|---|---|
| | frame) width. If necessary, Navigator will scale the image to fit within the specified width. |
| HSPACE = | "*imageHorizontalMarginsInPixels*" gives the margin in pixels between the left and right edges of the image and the surrounding text. Applies only to images that use the ALIGN attribute. |
| VSPACE = | "*imageVerticalMarginsInPixels*" gives the margin in pixels between the top and bottom edges of the image and the surrounding text. Applies only to images that use the ALIGN attribute. |
| BORDER = | "*imageBorderWidth*" gives the image border width. |
| ALIGN = | "left" \| "right" \| "top" \| "absmiddle" \| "absbottom" \| "texttop" \| "middle" \| "baseline" \| "bottom" indicates the image alignment with respect to the surrounding text. |
| ISMAP | indicates that the image is a server-side imagemap. |
| USEMAP = | "*imageLocation#mapName*" indicates that the image is a client-side imagemap. |

| | |
|---|---|
| **Property of** | document |
| **Properties** | border, complete, height, hspace, length, (property of images array), lowsrc, name, prototype, src, vspace, width |
| **Methods** | None |
| **Event handlers** | onAbort, onError, onLoad |
| **See also** | **Objects:** Area, Link<br>**Event handlers:** onClick, onMouseOut, onMouseOver |

## Access

Elements in the images array are read only. Thus, statements like this:

```
document.images[0]="lion.gif"
```

have no effect.

## Discussion

Create an Image object using the following syntax:

```
imageName = new Image([width, height])
```

where `width` and `height` are the Image object width and height in pixels. You can then use the Image object in one of the following ways:

- `imageName.propertyName`
- `document.images[i].propertyName`
- `formName.elements[i].propertyName`

where

- `imageName` is the name specified for the NAME attribute or an Image object that is an attribute of another object
- `propertyName` is one of the Image object properties
- `images` is an array of images in the document
- `elements` is an array of elements in the `form` named `formName`
- `i` an integer specifying the index of the image in the respective array

The array of images is constructed during document loading, and each image is added as an entry to the array as it is loaded.

Use the following syntax to define event handlers for Image objects created with the Image() constructor:

- `imageName.onabort = eventHandlerFunction`
- `imageName.onerror = eventHandlerFunction`
- `imageName.onload = eventHandlerFunction`

Note that you must specify the event handlers in lowercase. The `eventHandlerFunction` can be one of the following:

- `null`
- the name of a function
- a variable whose value is `null` or a function reference
- a property whose value is `null` or a function reference

If you wish to have no border for the image, set BORDER to 0 (that is, zero). If the image appears within an anchor and you set the BORDER to 0, the color indicating a hyperlink will not appear.

If you set the ALIGN attribute to "left" or "right", the image will float into the next available space on the left or right side of the page, and the text will wrap around it. If you do not use the ALIGN attribute, the default ("bottom") will be used.

When you indicate that the image is a client-side image map, you must give the URL of the file that contains the image definition, and then give the name of the map using #; for example, the statement

```
USEMAP = "URL/MAPFILE.HTML#AMAP"
```

specifies that the file MAPFILE.HTML holds a list of imagemaps, AMAP is the specific map you wish to use, and the HTML file location is at the specified URL.

As with any other page layout element, you cannot change the Image layout: its position and size. You can, however, change the displayed image by manipulating the src and lowsrc properties. This gives you the ability to use JavaScript for animation. Be aware, however, that the animation will be slow, because changing the src or lowsrc properties uploads a file, and requires negotiations over the Internet for each change. If you wish to use event handlers (onClick, onMouseOut, onMouseOver) with an Image object, use the Area object. You can also use the <IMG> tag within a Link object. Then you can use the Area or Link event handlers.

If you need to load an image before displaying it in some element (e.g., frame) of your page, use the Image() constructor. When you need to actually display the image, set the src property to the appropriate value. This allows you to create smooth animation. For example, suppose you want to display an animation of a running lion. Then you can use code such as in Listing 7.24. The animation will be smooth because the images will be obtained from cache.

**LISTING 7.24** Using the Image() constructor for animation.

```
1    animalImage1 = new Image()
2    animalImage2 = new Image()
3    ...
4    animalImage1.src = "lion1.gif"
5    animalImage2.src = "lion2.gif"
6    ...
7    document.images[0].src = animalImage1.src
8    document.images[0].src = animalImage2.src
9    ...
```

The images array is constructed when the document is loaded. Each <IMG> tag is added to the array as it is encountered in the HTML source code. (Note that images created with the Image() constructor are not included in the `images` array). You can then refer to images using `docu-ment.images[i]`, and obtain the number of images in the document using `document.images.length`.

Some remarks about the `Image` object properties:

- `complete` stores a Boolean value (`true` means that the Navigator has completed its attempt to load the image).

- `prototype` allows you to add properties to an existing `Image` object.

- `border`, `hspace`, `name`, and `vspace` have no meaning for images created with the `Image()` constructor.

## Examples

To see how you may wish to implement IMG with animation, do Exercise 7.11.

---

**EXERCISE 7.11**    USING IMAGE FOR ANIMATION.

1. Type (or copy and paste) the code shown in Listing 7.25 and save it.

2. Load the file to your browser. You should get a window similar to Figure 7.14.

3. Modify the code in Listing 7.25: add a Pause button. When the user clicks on it, the animation pauses; when she clicks again, it continues.

---

Here is a brief explanation of some opaque statements in Listing 7.25:

- The images reside in the `Images` subdirectory of the directory where the HTML file resides. The images are named consecutively in files `IMAGEI.GIF`, where *I* goes from `firstImage` to lastImage.

- In line 10 we create an `imageArray` that will hold the images. In lines 11 through 16 we populate the array. This is done by first creating a new image with the constructor function `Image()` and then assigning the appropriate image to the array element. The result is a series of images loaded into cache.

- The `animate()` function (lines 18 through 24) does the animation by assigning a new image to the `document`'s `form`, called `animation` (lines 19 and 20); when the last image has been reached, we reset the `imageIndex` to zero and start all over (lines 22–23).

- The `slowDown()` and `speedUp()` functions (lines 26 to 33) add or subtract 10 msec to the delay variable.

- In lines 39 to 41 we set up the IMG object and call it animation. We then use the built-in function setTimeout() with two parameters, the animate() function and the desired delay.

- The Slower and Faster buttons slowDown() and speedUp() the animation. This is done in lines 43 to 48.

**LISTING 7.25** Using Image for animation.

```
1    <HTML>
2    <HEAD>
3    <SCRIPT LANGUAGE = "JavaScript">
4    delay = 100
5    imageIndex = 1
6    firstImage = 2
7    lastImage = 5
8
9    // Load images to cache
10   imageArray = new Array()
11   for(i = firstImage; i <= lastImage; i++)
12   {
13    imageArray[i-firstImage] = new Image()
14    imageArray[i-firstImage].src =
15    "Images\\image" + i + ".gif"
16   }
17
18   function animate() {
19    document.animation.src =
20    imageArray[imageIndex].src
21    imageIndex++
22    if(imageIndex > lastImage - firstImage)
23    imageIndex = 0
24   }
25
26   function slowDown() {
27    delay += 10
28   }
29
30   function speedUp() {
31    delay -= 10
32    if(delay < 0) delay = 0
33   }
34
35   </SCRIPT>
36   </HEAD>
37
```

```
38   <BODY BGCOLOR = "lightblue">
39   <IMG NAME = "animation"
40    SRC = "Images\image2.gif"
41    onLoad = "setTimeout('animate()', delay)">
42   <FORM>
43   <INPUT TYPE = "button"
44    Value = "Slower"
45    onClick = "slowDown()">
46   <INPUT TYPE = "button"
47    Value = "Faster"
48    onClick = "speedUp()">
49   </FORM>
50   </BODY>
51   </HTML>
```

A word about the animation images: These were obtained from
http://tiger.census.gov/. This is where the U.S. Census Tiger maps are
stored. You can go there, build a collection of map images for any feature and
area in the United States that you wish, store it in a directory, and let the user
flip through these.

#  link and links array

## Purpose
Use this object to identify text or an image as a hyperlink. When the user
clicks the hyperlink, the link's reference is loaded to a window.

## Syntax

```
<A HREF = URL
 [NAME = "anchorObjectName"]
 [TARGET = "windowName"]
 [onClick = "onClickEventHandler"]
 [onMouseOver = "onMouseOverEventHandler"]
 [onMouseOut = "onMouseOutEventHandler"]>
 linkText
</A>
```

where:
   HREF =            URL is the URL or location of the link's destination.

**FIGURE 7.14** Using Image for animation.

| | |
|---|---|
| NAME = | "*anchorObjectName*" gives the hypertext tag. |
| TARGET = | "*windowName*" is the name of the window that the link is loaded into. |
| onClick = | "*onClickEventHandler*" is the event that is triggered when the user clicks the mouse on the link area in the HTML page. |
| onMouseOver = | "*onMouseOverEventHandler*" is the event that is triggered when the user moves the mouse (with no mouse-button pressed) over the link area in the HTML page. |

| | |
|---|---|
| onMouseOut = | "*onMouseOutEventHandler*" is the event that is triggered when the user moves the mouse (with no mouse-button pressed) out of the link area in the HTML page. |
| linkText | is the text that appears underlined and that invokes the link when clicked. |

| | |
|---|---|
| **Property of** | document |
| **Properties** | hash, host, hostname, length (property of links), pathname, port, protocol, search, target |
| **Methods** | None |
| **Event handlers** | onClick, onMouseOver, onMouseOut |
| **See also** | **Objects:** anchor<br>**Methods:** link()<br>**Operators:** void |

## Access

Elements in the links array are read only.

## Discussion

When working with link objects, keep the following in mind:

- The links array contains Area objects that are created with <AREA HREF ="...">.

- If you use the NAME attribute of the link object, then the link object is also an anchor object. The link will thus have an entry in the anchors array.

- A link object is also a location object.

- A link can be defined by using the link() method.

- You can trace where the link came from by examining the link's destination referrer property.

The TARGET attribute can refer to one of the following:

- an existing window object

- a frame name

- one of the literals _top, _parent, _self, or _blank
- an appropriate JavaScript expression

You access link properties with statements like this:

```
document.links[i].propertyName
```

where

- links is the links array
- *i* is an integer representing the index of the link you wish to refer to
- *propertyName* is one of the link object's properties

The links array is built when the document loads; as <A HREF = ...> tags are read, they are added as elements to the array in the order they are encountered in the HTML source code. You refer to a link in the document by using the syntax

```
document.links[i]
```

where *i* is the link's index in the links array.

You can determine the number of links in a document with a statement like this:

```
numberOfLinks = document.links.length
```

The links array contains Area objects that are created with <AREA HREF = "...">.

You can use the link object to execute a JavaScript function rather than a link to a hypertext reference. For example, to navigate via JavaScript, the statement

```
<A HREF = "javascript:history.back()">Back</A>
```

will take the user back one step in the history when she clicks on the Back hypertext.

Use this approach also when you want to

- Execute JavaScript code when the image an clicked
- Use a link instead of a button to execute JavaScript code

If you want a link object to do nothing, use the syntax

```
<A HREF = "javascript:void(0)">Some text</A>
```

For example:

```
<A HREF = "javascript:void(0)">
 <IMG SRC = "Images\\babe.jpg"
 ...
</A>
```

## Examples

To gain experience in working with link, do Exercise 7.12.

---

**EXERCISE 7.12**   USING THE LINK OBJECT AND THE LINKS ARRAY.

1. Type (or copy and paste) the code shown in Listing 7.26 and save it.

2. Load the file to your browser. You should get a window similar to Figure 7.15.

3. Note that as you pass the mouse over the Go... link, the alert window (Figure 7.16) appears, telling you the names of links in your file. To actually go to the link of your choice, press the Esc key on your keyboard and then, without moving the mouse, click on the Go... link.

4. Modify the code in Listing 7.26 to remove the annoying effect of having to press the Esc key and still get information about the links in the document. Hint: One way to do it is to write the linkArray string to a new window.

---

Let us see what the code in Listing 7.26 does. In line 5 we define a global variable that stores a destination; the variable is later used to react to a user's action (clicking on Go...). In lines 6 to 12 we define the showLinks() function. The function goes through all of the links in the document and adds the link information to the linkArray string (lines 9 and 10). Finally, it displays the string in an alert window.

In lines 19 through 35 we define radio buttons that the user can select. Clicking on a button assigns a URL to the variable destination. In lines 37 through 40 we define the Go... link, and assign the showLinks() function to its onMouseOver event handler. In line 41 we use the link to take some action (going back one step in the history object).

**LISTING 7.26** Using the `link` object and the `links` array.

```
1    <HTML>
2    <HEAD>
3    <TITLE>link and links</TITLE>
4    <SCRIPT LANGUAGE = "JavaScript">
5    var destination = "http://www.netscape.com/"
6    function showLinks()
7    {
8     linkArray = "The links in this document:\r"
9     for (var i = 0; i < document.links.length; i++)
10    linkArray += document.links[i] + "\r"
11    alert(linkArray)
12   }
13   </SCRIPT>
14   </HEAD>
15   <BODY>
16   <FORM NAME = "Destinations">
17   <B>Choose a destination:</B>
18   <BR>
19   <INPUT TYPE = "radio"
20    NAME = "url"
21    VALUE = "netscapeHomePage"
22    onClick =
23    "destination = 'http://www.netscape.com/'">
24   Netscape home page <BR>
25   <INPUT TYPE = "radio"
26    NAME = "url"
27    VALUE = "myHomePage"
28    onClick =
29    "destination = 'http://turtle.gis.umn.edu/'">
30   Turtle's home page<BR>
31   <INPUT TYPE = "radio"
32    NAME = "url"
33    VALUE = "netSearch"
34    onClick = "destination = 'http://home.netscape.com/home/
         internet-search.html'">
35    Net search
36   <P>
37   <A HREF = ""
38    onClick = "this.href=destination"
39    onMouseOver = "showLinks()">
40   <B>Go...</B></A> or
41   <A HREF="javascript:history.go(-1)">
42   Click here to go back</A>
43   one step
44   </FORM>
45   </BODY>
46   </HTML>
```

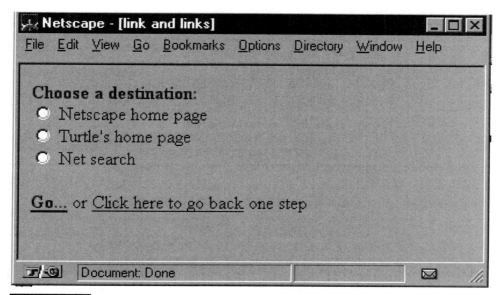

**FIGURE 7.15** Using the link object and the links array.

#  location

## Purpose

Use this object to obtain information about the current URL.

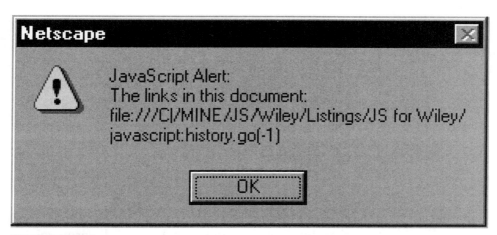

**FIGURE 7.16** Display of the links in a links array.

# Syntax

```
[windowVariable.]location[.propertyName]
```

where

| | |
|---|---|
| *windowVariable* | is a variable that stores a window object or one of the synonyms _top or _parent. |
| *propertyName* | is one of the location object's properties. |

| | |
|---|---|
| **Property of** | window |
| **Properties** | hash, host, href, port, protocol, search |
| **Methods** | reload(), replace() |
| **Event handlers** | None |
| **See also** | **Objects:** history<br>**Properties:** URL |

# Access
Read and write.

# Discussion
If you do not specify *propertyName* while using the object, you are in effect referring to the complete URL. Thus, for example, the statements:

```
[windowVariable.]location
```

and

```
[windowVariable.]location.href
```

are equivalent.

A complete URL is made up of the following components:

```
protocol//hostname:port pathname search hash
```

where

- *protocol*  is the communication protocol (file:, http:, ftp:, and so on). Note that the colon (:) is an integral part of the protocol.

- *hostname* is the host and domain name, or IP address, of a network host; for example: `turtle.gis.umn.edu,` or `128.101.73.24.`

- *port* is the communications port that the server uses for communications. The port (for example 80) determines some communication parameters. For example, to use server administration facilities you will need to communicate with the server via a port different from that of regular visitors. If you do not specify a port, it defaults to 80.

- *pathname* points the URL to a specific directory.

- *search* is query information you enter in the URL (query information begins with a question mark, "?").

- *hash* is an anchor name fragment (the part that begins with the hash mark #).

You can access the location by using the properties:

- `href` is the `location` object's complete URL.

- `host` is the `hostname: port` part of the URL.

To access the `location` object of windows other than the current, you need to add the window reference to the dot path of the object; for example,

`location.propertyName`

refers to the *propertyName* of the `location` object in the current window, while

`aWindow.location.propertyName`

refers to the `location` object in `aWindow`, which is a `window` object.

In anticipation of future releases of JavaScript, do not use `location` as a property; use the `document's URL` property instead.

You can use the following syntax to work with the `location` methods:

`[windowReference.]location.methodName(arguments)`

Be aware that the `location` object is different from the `location` property of a document object. There are different Internet protocols, and they are accesses by specifying different URL types. The common ones are listed in Table 7.1.

**TABLE 7.1** URL protocols.

| Protocol | URL | Examples |
|---|---|---|
| about: | Navigator information | about:plugins |
| | | about:cache |
| file: | File | file://directory/filename.html |
| ftp: | FTP | ftp://ftp.turtle.gis.umn.edu/pub |
| gopher: | Gopher | gopher://umn.edu/ |
| http: | World Wide Web | http://turtle.gis.umn.edu |
| javascript: | JavaScript code | javascript:history.back() |
| mailto: | MailTo | mailto:yc@turtle.gis.umn.edu |
| news: | Usenet | news://news.tc.umn.edu |

## Examples

Type some of the examples given in Table 7.1 in the Location text box in Navigator. In particular, try about:plugins, about:cache, and about:.

 # Math

## Purpose

Use this object to access mathematical methods (such as sine, cosine) and some mathematical constants (such as $\pi$).

## Syntax

    Math.propertyName

or

    Math.methodName(arguments)

where

    *propertyName*    is one of the Math object's properties.

| | |
|---|---|
| *methodName* | is one of the Math object's methods. |

| | |
|---|---|
| **Property of** | None |
| **Properties** | E, LN2, LN10, LOG2E, LOG10E, PI, SQRT1_2, SQRT2 |
| **Methods** | abs(), atan2(), acos(), asin(), atan(), ceil(), cos(), exp(), floor(), log(), max(), min(), pow(), random(), round(), sin(), sqrt(), tan() |
| **Event handlers** | None |
| **See also** | |

## Access

Read only.

## Discussion

Math constants possess the precision of real numbers in JavaScript. Note the insistence on capital M in using the Math object: it is necessary. The reason has to do more with Java than JavaScript. The following explanation will make sense to you if you know Java. Recall that in JavaScript you can create and manipulate objects, but not classes. Math happens to be a Java class that is implemented in JavaScript. All of Math's methods and variables are declared static. This means that the methods and variables belong to the class, not to objects of type Math. Because Java and JavaScript are case sensitive, you must capitalize the M in Math.

## Examples

Listing 7.27 shows two typical ways of using the Math object. In line 1, we simply access the sin() method; in lines 2–6 we access the constant PI and the methods abs() and max(), all without having to use the notation Math.*propertyName* or Math.*methodName*(*arguments*), because we take advantage of the JavaScript with.

**LISTING 7.27** Working with the Math object.

```
1    aSin = Math.sin(60)
2    with (Math) {
3      a = 2 * PI * r
4      b = abs(b)
5      c = max(a, b)
6    }
```

 # mimeTypes

## Purpose

Use this array object to access the MIME types that are supported by the client.

## Syntax

```
navigator.mimeTypes[i].propertyName
```

where

| | |
|---|---|
| *i* | is the index of the MIME-Type element in the mimeTypes array (see below). |
| *propertyName* | is one of the properties of the mimeTypes array. |

| | |
|---|---|
| **Property of** | navigator |
| **Properties** | description, enabledPlugin, suffixes, type |
| **Methods** | None |
| **Event handlers** | None |
| **See also** | **Objects:** Plugin, navigator |

## Access

Read only.

## Discussion

Often you need to know the kind of MIME (Multipart Internet Mail Extension) type that the client supports. You do that using the mimeTypes object. Netscape Navigator stores the MIME types that the client supports in the mimeTypes array. Each element of the array is a mimeType object, which has properties for its type, description, file extensions, and enabled plug-ins.

mimeTypes properties are:

- type—the name of the MIME type
- description—the type description
- enabledPlugin—the plug-in object that handles the MIME type
- suffixes—a string of file suffixes recognizable by the MIME type

# Examples

Exercise 7.13 shows how to obtain information about all of the installed MIME types for a particular client. You can use such an approach to determine which MIME types are installed on a client, and then modify your displayed HTML document accordingly.

**EXERCISE 7.13**   USING MIMETYPES.

1. Type (or copy and paste) the code shown in Listing 7.28 and save it.

2. Load the file to your browser. Click on the Show installed MIME types... button (Figure 7.17). You should get a response as shown in Figure 7.18.

3. How many different mimeTypes does your browser recognize? What is the average number of file extensions (suffixes) recognized by a mimeType?

**LISTING 7.28** Using mimeTypes.

```
1    <HTML>
2    <HEAD>
3    <TITLE>Installed MIME Types</TITLE>
4
5    <SCRIPT LANGUAGE = "JavaScript">
6    function showMimes()
7    {
8      document.writeln("<OL>")
9      for (i = 0; i < navigator.mimeTypes.length; i++)
10     {
11     document.writeln(
12     "<LI>Type: ", navigator.mimeTypes[i].type,
13     "<UL><LI>Description: ",
14     navigator.mimeTypes[i].description,
15     "<LI>Suffixes: ", navigator.mimeTypes[i].suffixes,
16     "</UL>")
17     }
18     document.writeln("</OL>")
19   }
20   </SCRIPT>
21   </HEAD>
22
23   <BODY>
24   <H3>Installed MIME Types</H3>
25   <FORM>
26   <INPUT TYPE = "button"
27          VALUE = "Show installed MIME types..."
28          onClick = "showMimes()">
29   </FORM>
30   </BODY>
31   </HTML>
```

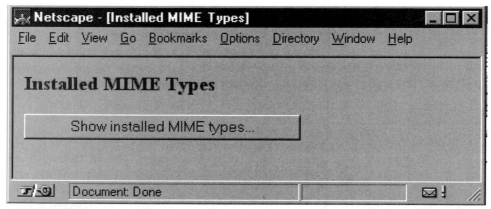

**FIGURE 7.17** Using mimeTypes.

#  navigator

## Purpose

Use this object to obtain information about the version of Netscape's Navigator in use.

## Syntax

navigator.*propertyName*

where

propertyName is one of the navigator object's properties.

---

| | |
|---|---|
| **Property of** | None |
| **Properties** | appCodeName, appName, appVersion, mimeTypes, plugins, userAgent |
| **Methods** | javaEnabled() |
| **Event handlers** | None |
| **See also** | **Objects:** link, anchor<br>**Arrays:** plugins, mimeTypes |

---

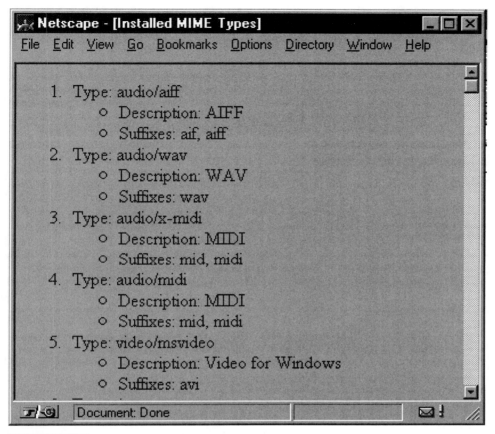

**FIGURE 7.18** Installed MIME types.

## Access

Read only.

## Discussion

With this object, you can determine the various properties of the client Navigator. This allows you to tailor your HTML page and JavaScript code to various clients.

## Examples

To examine all of the `navigator` properties, as recognized by your version of Navigator, do Exercise 7.14.

1. Type (or copy and paste) the code shown in Listing 7.29 and save it.

2. Load the file to your browser. Click on the Show navigator properties... button (Figure 7.19). You should get a response as shown in Figure
   7.20.

3. Modify Listing 7.29 to list the navigator.plugins.

We have discussed the inspectProperties() function before (Exercise
3.1 in Chapter 3). To repeat, the for loop inside the function (lines 11 to 15)
cycles through all of theObject's properties.

**LISTING 7.29** Using the navigator object.

```
1    <HTML>
2    <HEAD>
3    <TITLE>Navigator Properties</TITLE>
4
5    <SCRIPT LANGUAGE = "JavaScript">
6    function inspectProperties(theObject, theObjectName)
7    {
8    var theProperties = ""
9
10     for (var i in theObject)
11     {
12     theProperties += theObjectName + "." + i +
13     " = " + theObject[i] + "\n"
14     }
15     alert(theProperties)
16    }
17    </SCRIPT>
18    </HEAD>
19
20    <BODY>
21    <H3>Navigator Properties</H3>
22    <FORM>
23    <INPUT TYPE = "button"
24     VALUE = "Show navigator properties..."
25     onClick = "inspectProperties(navigator, 'navigator')">
26    </FORM>
27    </BODY>
28    </HTML>
```

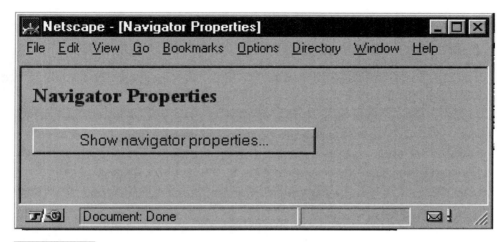

**FIGURE 7.19** Using the navigator object.

#  Option

## Purpose

Use it in conjunction with <SELECT> to change the text options of a select list.

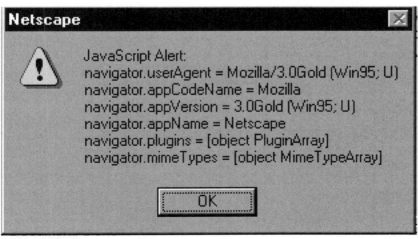

**FIGURE 7.20** Properties of the navigator object.

## Syntax

```
optionName = new Option([optionText, optionValue, defaultSelected,
selected])
```

where

| | |
|---|---|
| *optionName* = | new Option is either the name of a new object or a property of an existing object. |
| *optionText* = | is the text to display in the select list. |
| *optionValue* = | is a value that is returned to the server when the option is selected and the form in which the option resides is submitted. |
| *defaultSelected* = | specifies whether the option is initially selected (true or false). |
| *selected* = | is the current selection state of the option (true or false). |

For further details, see the select object.

| | |
|---|---|
| **Property of** | select |
| **Properties** | defaultSelected, index, selected, value |
| **Methods** | None |
| **Event handlers** | None |
| **See also** | **Objects:** select<br>**Arrays:** plugins, mimeTypes |

## Access

Read and write.

## Discussion

You can use the Option() constructor to create options for <SELECT> (see the select object). To add the new option to an existing select object, use the following:

```
selectName.options[i] = optionName
```

where

* *selectName* is the name of the select object

- `options` is the options array
- *i* is the index of the option
- *optionName* is your choice of option name

In working with the `Option` object, keep the following in mind:

- Options created with the `Option()` constructor are objects.
- These objects have the same properties as elements of the `options` array (see discussion in `select` and `options` array).
- To make sure that options are recognized after you add them to a `select` object, refresh the document by issuing `history.go(0)`. Be aware that when the document reloads, variable values are lost; to preserve such values between loads, you should save them in cookies.

## Examples

See the `select` object.

 # password

## Purpose

Use this object to display a text field. When the user enters text, it is hidden with asterisks (*).

## Syntax

```
<INPUT
 TYPE = "password"
 NAME = "passwordName"
 [VALUE = "textValue"]
 SIZE = integer>
```

where

```
NAME =      "passwordName" is the password object's name.
VALUE =     "textValue" is the initial value of the object.
```

| | |
|---|---|
| SIZE = | `integer` is the number of characters the object can have without scrolling. |

| | |
|---|---|
| **Property of** | `form` |
| **Properties** | `defaultValue, name, type, value` |
| **Methods** | `focus(), blur(), select()` |
| **Event handlers** | None |
| **See also** | **Objects:** `form`, `text` |

## Access
Neither read nor write (see below).

## Discussion
The `password` object's methods and properties are accessed in one of the following ways.

```
passwordName.propertyName

passwordName.methodName(arguments)

formName.elements[i].propertyName

formName.elements[i].methodName(arguments)
```

where

- *passwordName* is the value of the NAME attribute of the `password` object

- *propertyName* is one of the object's properties

- *methodName* is one of the object's methods

- *formName* is the value of the NAME attribute of the `form` object to which the `password` object belongs

- *i* is an integer index of the `password` object's entry in the `elements` array of the `form` to which the `password` object belongs

- *arguments* are the appropriate method's arguments

There is not much you can do with the password object from inside a JavaScript. If you set up the default value, you could display it, as Listing 7.30 demonstrates. To work with a password, the server needs to get it, and then use CGI to process it.

## Examples

Listing 7.30 demonstrates one way in which you can use the password object. If you set the default value in your document, you can view it. If the user changes the password, there not much you can do with JavaScript. The focus() and select() methods ensure that whatever happens, the field becomes focused (the cursor appears in it) and the text in it is selected.

**LISTING 7.30** Using the password object.

```
1    <HTML>
2    <HEAD>
3    <TITLE>Using Password</TITLE>
4
5    <SCRIPT LANGUAGE = "JavaScript">
6    function checkPassword(userPassword)
7    {
8     alert("default: "+userPassword.defaultValue)
9     userPassword.focus()
10    userPassword.select()
11   }
12   </SCRIPT>
13   </HEAD>
14
15   <BODY>
16   <H3>Using Password</H3>
17   <FORM NAME = "aForm">
18   <B>Password:</B>
19   <INPUT TYPE = "password"
20    NAME = "userPassword"
21    VALUE = "abc"
22    SIZE=25>
23   <SCRIPT LANGUAGE = "JavaScript">
24   checkPassword(document.aForm.userPassword)
25   </SCRIPT>
26   </FORM>
27   </BODY>
28   </HTML>
```

# ↳ Plugin and embeds array

## Purpose

Use this object to generate output from a plug-in application. Use the `plugins` array to determine the installed plug-ins.

## Syntax

```
<EMBED
 SRC = source
 NAME = "appletName"
 HEIGHT = heightInPixels
 WIDTH = widthInPixels>
 [<PARAM NAME = "parameterName"
VALUE = "parameterValue">]
                     [ ... <PARAM>]
</EMBED>
```

where

| | |
|---|---|
| SRC = | *source* is the URL containing the source content. |
| NAME = | "*appletName*" is the name of the embedded object in the document. |
| HEIGHT = | *heightInPixels* is the applet's height in pixels within the browser window. |
| WIDTH = | *widthInPixels* is the applet's width in pixels within the browser window. |
| <PARAM> | defines a parameter for the embedded object. |
| NAME = | "*parameterName*" is the name of the parameter. |
| VALUE = | "*parameterValue*" is a parameter value. |

| | |
|---|---|
| **Property of** | `document` |
| **Properties** | `length` (property of the `embeds` array) |
| **Methods** | None |
| **Event handlers** | None |
| **See also** | **Objects:** `applet`, `mimeTypes` |

## Access
Read only.

## Discussion
Use the `embeds` array to reference plug-ins in your code. Each `<EMBED>` tag adds a `plugin` object, and an entry in the `embeds` array is added as these objects are encountered. Use the `embeds` array with statements like this:

```
document.embeds[i]
```

where `i` is the integer index of the `plugin` object.

## Examples
See `plugins` array, Exercise 7.15, Listing 7.31, Figure 7.21, and Figure 7.22.

#  plugins array

## Purpose
Use this array to find out what plug-in applications are installed in the client's browser.

## Syntax

```
navigator.plugins["pluginName"]
```

```
navigator.plugins[i]
```

where

| | |
|---|---|
| *pluginName* | is the name of the plug-in. |
| *i* | is an integer index of the plug-in in the `plugins` array. |

| | |
|---|---|
| **Property of** | `navigator` |
| **Properties** | `description, filename, length, name)` |
| **Methods** | None |
| **Event handlers** | None |
| **See also** | **Objects:** `mimeTypes, navigator, Plugin` |

## Access

Read only.

## Discussion

Do not confuse the `plugins` array and the `plugin` object. They are different! If your HTML page includes plug-in dependent components (such as images), use this array to determine what plug-ins are installed, and then display these components conditionally. Similar to `mimeTypes`, `plugins` is an array of plug-in applications that are currently installed on the client. To determine if a particular plug-in is installed, use statements like this:

```
installedPlugin = navigator.plugins["pluginName"]
```

where *pluginName* is a plug-in name you wish to test for (for example, *Shockwave* or *QuickTime*).

The `plug-ins` properties store:

- The description of the plug-in (as supplied by the plug-in itself) in `description`
- The name of the disk plug-in file in `filename`
- The number of installed plug-ins in `length`
- The plug-in name in `name`

## Examples

**EXERCISE 7.15**   USING PLUGINS.

1. Type (or copy and paste) the code shown in Listing 7.31 and save it.
2. Load the file to your browser. Click on the `Show installed plug-ins...` button (Figure 7.21). You should get a response as shown in Figure 7.22.
3. How many different plug-ins does your browser recognize? In which directory do most of the plug-in files reside?

**LISTING 7.31** Using the `plugins` array.

```
1    <HTML>
2    <HEAD>
3    <TITLE>Installed Plug-ins</TITLE>
```

```
4
5    <SCRIPT LANGUAGE = "JavaScript">
6    function showPlugins()
7    {
8     document.writeln("<OL>")
9     for (i = 0; i < navigator.plugins.length; i++)
10    {
11    document.writeln(
12    "<LI>Name: ", navigator.plugins[i].name,
13    "<UL><LI>File name: ",
14    navigator.plugins[i].filename,
15    "<LI>Description: ",
16    navigator.plugins[i].description,
17    "</UL>")
18    }
19    document.writeln("</OL>")
20    }
21    </SCRIPT>
22    </HEAD>
23
24    <BODY>
25    <H3>Installed Plug-ins</H3>
26    <FORM>
27    <INPUT TYPE = "button"
28     VALUE = "Show installed plug-ins..."
29     onClick = "showPlugins()">
30    </FORM>
31    </BODY>
32    </HTML>
```

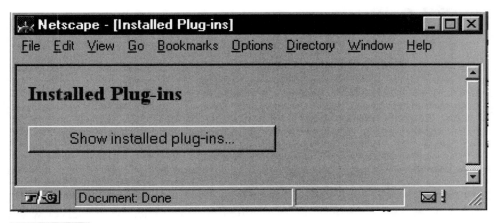

**FIGURE 7.21** Using the plugins array.

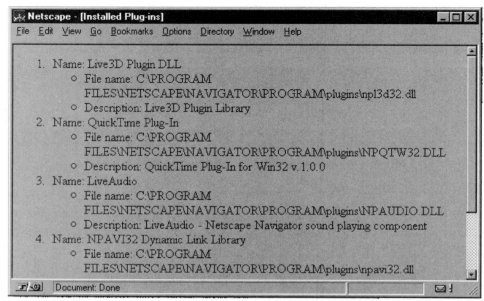

**FIGURE 7.22** Installed plug-ins.

 # radio

## Purpose

Use this object to allow the user to choose a single item from a list.

## Syntax

```
<INPUT
  TYPE = "radio"
  NAME = "radioName"
  VALUE = "radioValue"
  [CHECKED]
  [onClick = "eventHandler"]>
  radioLabel
```

where

| | |
|---|---|
| NAME = | "*radioName*" is the name of the radio object. |
| VALUE = | "*radioValue*" is a value that is returned to the server when the radio button is selected and the form is submitted. |

| | |
|---|---|
| CHECKED | indicates that the radio button is selected. |
| onClick = | "*eventHandler*" is the event handler that is executed when onClick occurs. |
| *radioLabel* | is the label to display beside the radio button. |

| | |
|---|---|
| **Property of** | form |
| **Properties** | check, defaultChecked, length, name, type, value |
| **Methods** | click() |
| **Event handlers** | onClick |
| **See also** | **Objects:** checkbox, form, select |

## Access
Read and write.

## Discussion
Use one of the following formats to access the radio object's properties and methods:

- *radioName[i].propertyName*
- *radioName[i].methodName(arguments)*
- *formName*.elements[*j*].*propertyName*
- *formName*.elements[*j*].*methodName(arguments)*

where

- *radioName* is the value of the NAME attribute of the radio object
- *i* is an integer index of a particular button in the radio object
- *propertyName* is one of the radio object's properties
- *arguments* are the arguments of the radio object's method
- *formName* is the value of the NAME attribute of the form to which the radio object belongs
- *j* is the integer index of the radio button on the form

The syntax for creating a radio objects shows how you create a single radio button that belongs to the radio object named radioName. You can associate more than one radio button with a single radio object. This is done by repeating the syntax with a different VALUE and identical NAME for the radio object. For example, to create a radio object with two radio buttons use the following:

```
<INPUT      TYPE = "radio"
            NAME = "aRadioObject"
            VALUE = "first radio">
<INPUT      TYPE = "radio"
            NAME = "aRadioObject"
            VALUE = "second radio">
```

The code above will automatically create an array of radio buttons called aRadioObject. Thus, you can access a radio button from two arrays: aRadioObject array, which has an entry for each button that belongs to the radio object aRadioObject, and the elements array. Because a form can contain a variety of elements, the index of a radio button in the elements array may not be the same as its index in aRadioObject. Here is an example:

```
<FORM       NAME = "aForm">
<INPUT      TYPE = "button"
            NAME = "aButton">
<INPUT      TYPE = "radio"
            NAME = "aRadioObject"
            VALUE = "first radio">
<INPUT      TYPE = "radio"
            NAME = "aRadioObject"
            VALUE = "second radio">
</FORM>
```

You can access the VALUE attribute of the second radio button like this:

```
aForm.elements[2].value
```

or

```
aRadioObject[1].value
```

## Examples

**EXERCISE 7.16** USING THE RADIO OBJECT.

1. Type (or copy and paste) the code shown in Listing 7.32 and save it.
2. Load the file to your browser. Click on the Which one... button (Figure 7.23). You should get a response as shown in Figure 7.24.

The function showCheckedButton() in Listing 7.16 takes a form for an argument. It then cycles through the buttons, using the radio object's length property. When a checked button is identified, we break out of the for loop and show the user the value of the checked button.

**LISTING 7.32** Using the radio object.

```
1    <HTML>
2    <HEAD>
3    <TITLE>Radio Object</TITLE>
4    </HEAD>
5    <SCRIPT LANGUAGE = "JavaScript">
6    function showCheckedButton(form)
7    {
8     for (var i = 0; form.r.length; i++)
9     if (form.r[i].checked)
10     break
11     alert(form.r[i].value + " is checked")
12    }
13   </SCRIPT>
14   <BODY>
15   <FORM>
16   <BR><INPUT TYPE = "radio"
17    NAME = "r"
18    VALUE = "Radio 1"
19    CHECKED> Radio 1
20   <BR><INPUT TYPE = "radio"
21    NAME = "r"
22    VALUE = "Radio 2"> Radio 2
23   <BR><INPUT TYPE = "radio"
24    NAME = "r"
25    VALUE = "Radio 3"> Radio 3
26   <BR><INPUT TYPE = "button"
27    NAME = "aButton"
28    VALUE = "Which one..."
29    onClick = "showCheckedButton(this.form)">
30   </FORM>
31   </BODY>
32   </HTML>
```

 reset

## Purpose

Use this object when you need to reset all information on an HTML form to its default values.

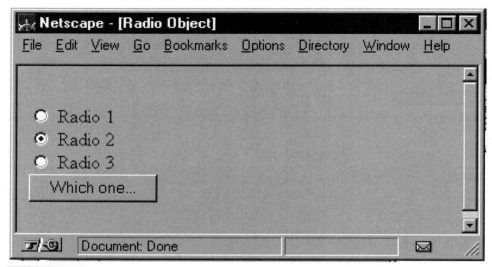

**FIGURE 7.23** Using the radio object.

## Syntax

```
<INPUT
 TYPE = "reset"
 NAME = "resetButtonName"
 VALUE = "resetButtonText"
 [onClick = "eventHandler"]>
```

where

NAME =      "resetButtonName" names the object.
VALUE =     "resetButtonText" gives the text to appear on the button face.
onClick =   "eventHandler" is the button event handler.

**FIGURE 7.24** The checked radio button.

| Property of | form |
|---|---|
| **Properties** | name, type, value |
| **Methods** | click() |
| **Event handlers** | onClick |
| **See also** | **Objects:** button, form, submit |

## Access

Read and write.

## Discussion

A reset object must be enclosed by the <FORM> </FORM> pair. Once clicked, you cannot cancel the form reset operation.

Use one of the following statement formats to access the object:

- *resetButtonName.resetPropertyName*

- *resetButtonName.resetMethodName(arguments)*

- *formName.elements[i].resetPropertyName*

- *formName.elements[i].resetMethodName(arguments)*

where

- *resetButtonName* is the value of the NAME attribute of the reset object

- *resetPropertyName* is one of the reset object's properties

- *resetMethodName* is one of the reset object's methods

- *arguments* is a list of arguments for the *resetMethodName*

- *formName* is the value of the NAME attribute of the form in which the reset button resides

- elements is the form object's elements array

- *i* is an integer index that specifies the index of the reset button object in the elements array

## Examples

To see how the reset button works, go through Exercise 7.17. The exercise is also designed to demonstrate how events are handled. In particular, as you go through the exercise, note what happens before the `confirm` window appears.

**EXERCISE 7.17**  USING THE `RESET` OBJECT.

1. Type (or copy and paste) the code shown in Listing 7.33 and save it.

2. Load the file to your browser. Click on the `Reset form...` button (Figure 7.25). Watch the values in the form entry areas. When do they go back to their default—before or after the confirm window appears?

3. How would you extend the exercise to allow the user to confirm before resetting the form's values to their default?

**LISTING 7.33**  Using the `reset` object.

```
1    <HTML>
2    <HEAD>
3    <TITLE>Reset</TITLE>
4    </HEAD>
5    <BODY>
6    <FORM NAME = "aForm">
7    <BR><B>Your name: </B>
8    <INPUT TYPE = "text"
9     NAME = "name"
10     VALUE = "James Dean"
11     SIZE = "20">
12    <P><B>Your occupation:</B>
13    <SELECT NAME = "occupation">
14    <OPTION SELECTED> Politician
15    <OPTION> Actor
16    <OPTION> JavaScripter
17    <OPTION> Irrelevant
18    <OPTION> Politician
19    <OPTION> Administrator
20    </SELECT>
21    <P>
22    <INPUT TYPE = "radio"
23     NAME = "gender"
24     VALUE = "Male"
25     CHECKED> Male
26    <INPUT TYPE = "radio"
27     NAME = "gender"
28     VALUE = "Female"> Female
29    <INPUT TYPE = "radio"
30     NAME = "gender"
31     VALUE = "noyb">None of your business
```

```
32   <P>
33   <INPUT TYPE = "reset"
34    VALUE = "Reset form..."
35    NAME = "resetForm"
36    onClick = "confirm('Are you sure?')">
37   </FORM>
38   </BODY>
39   </HTML>
```

# select and options array

## Purpose

Use this object to create a selection list or a scrolling list to allow the user to select a single value from the provided options.

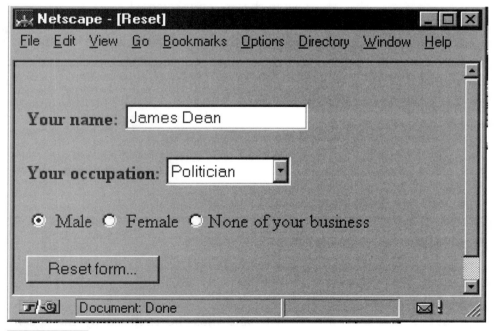

Using the reset object.

## Syntax

```
<SELECT
 NAME = "selectListName"
 [SIZE = numberOfOptionsToDisplay]
 [MULTIPLE]
 [onBlur = "onBlurEventHandler"]
 [onChange = "onChangeEventHandler"]
 [onFocus = "onFocusEventHandler"]>
 <OPTION VALUE = "valueReturnedToServer" [SELECTED]>
 optionText [ ... <OPTION> optionText ]
</SELECT>
```

where

| | |
|---|---|
| NAME = | "selectListName" is the name of the select object. |
| SIZE = | numberOfOptionsToDisplay integer determines the number of visible options. |
| MULTIPLE | specifies that the object is displayed as a scrolling list; otherwise it is displayed as a selection list. |
| OPTION | is an element in the selection list. |
| VALUE = | "valueReturnedToServer" is the value that is returned to the server when the option is selected. |
| SELECTED | sets the default to this option. |
| optionText | is the option's text of the option that is displayed in the list. |

| | |
|---|---|
| **Property of** | select (property of form), options (property of select) |
| **Properties** | select: length, options, text, type, selectedIndex<br>options: defaultSelected, index, length, name, prototype, selected, selectedIndex, text, value |
| **Methods** | blur(), focus() |
| **Event handlers** | onBlur, onChange |
| **See also** | **Objects:** form, radio |

## Access

Elements in the options array are read and write.

## Discussion

A select object is a form element, and must be enclosed by the <FORM> </FORM> pair.

Use one of the following statement formats to work with the select object:

- *selectListName.propertyName*
- *selectListName.methodName(arguments)*
- *formName.elements[i].propertyName*
- *formName.elements[i].methodName(arguments)*

where

- *selectListName* is the value assigned to the NAME attribute of the select object
- *propertyName* is one of the *select* object's properties
- *methodName* is one of the select object's methods
- *arguments* is the method's arguments
- *formName* is the value assigned to the NAME attribute of the form in which the select object resides
- elements is the elements array of the form
- *i* is the index of the select object in the elements array

## Working with the options **Array**

The options array contains an entry for each option of the select object. An option is identified with the <OPTION> tag, and options are added to the array in the order they are encountered in the HTML source code. You can change the text of options in a select object by assigning a value to the text property of options.

New options can be created via JavaScript with the Options() constructor like this:

```
optionName = new Option([optionText, optionValue, defaultSelected, selected])
```

or to add the new option to an existing select object, use the following syntax:

```
selectName.options[index]=optionName
```

where:

- *optionName* is either the name of a new object or a property of an existing object.

- *optionText* specifies the text to display in the selection list.

- *optionValue* specifies a value that is returned to the server when the option is selected and the form is submitted.

- defaultSelected specifies whether the option is initially selected (true or false).

- selected specifies the current selection state of the option (true or false).

- *selectName* is the name of an existing select object.

- *index* is an integer representing an option in a select object.

Each option created using the Option() constructor has the same properties as elements of the options array. To affect changes that you made with options, refresh the document by using history.go(0). Use this statement after you are done creating all the options you need. Keep in mind, however, that when the document reloads, variables are lost if not saved in cookies or form element values.

To delete an option from a select object, use the following syntax:

```
selectName.options[index] = null
```

where

- *selectName* is the name of an existing select object

- *index* is an integer representing an option in a select object.

Deleting options from the options array compresses the array and thus re-indexes its elements.

To access an option with the options array, use one of the following formats:

```
selectListName.options[i].propertyName
 formName.elements[j].options[i].propertyName
```

where

- *i* is the index of the option in the options array

- *j* is the index of the select object in the elements array

Recall that the `elements` array has an entry for each element (`text`, `radio`, `button`, etc.) in the `form`. Both the `select` object and the `options` array have a `length` property that stores the number of options in the `select` object. Thus, the following two statements are equivalent:

- *selectListName*.length

- selectListName.options.length

*selectListName*.options represents the full HTML statement for the *selectListName* object.

To change an `option`'s text, use the `text` property of the `options` array. To change the selection state of an option use the `selected` and `selectedIndex` properties. For example, the following sets a `select` object's `selectedIndex` property:

```
document.aForm.aSelectObject..selectedIndex = 1
```

`selected` is a Boolean value: true if an option is selected; false otherwise. For example, the statement

```
document.aForm.aSelectObject.options[i].selected = true
```

sets an option's `selected` property to `true`.

## Examples

Exercise 7.18 is intended to accomplish three things: First, to show you how to work with the `select` and `options` array; second, to allow you to figure out, precisely, when different events (`onBlur`, `onChange`, and `onFocus`) take effect; and third, to convince you that you should minimize the use of the `alert` and `confirm` windows in your interaction with a visitor, but use them profusely in your debugging work.

**EXERCISE 7.18** USING THE RESET OBJECT.

1. Type (or copy and paste) the code shown in Listing 7.34 and save it.

2. Load the file to your browser and click one the two lists (as shown in Figure 7.26), changing the selections every time you click.

3. Based on when the alert windows appear, figure out the precise sequence of events. When do the functions `onBlur`, `onFocus`, and `onChange` take effect? When you click on the object? When you click on another object (or another instance of the same object)?

The function showOptions() (lines 7 to 10 in Listing 7.34) uses the elements array of the form, along with the select index in the array, to display the HTML code that was used to generate the select object. One potential use of this feature is to gather information from select objects in one window, create a new window, and put the select objects in the new window using the options attribute of the select object.

In line 12 we create a form, and name it selectForm. In lines 14 through 23 we create a MULTIPLE select object, and in lines 25 to 33 we create a scrolling select object. When focus is on the select object named multipleSelection and the user clicks on another object, the onBlur event occurs, and the event is handled by showOptions().

When the select object named scrollingSelection receives a focus (the user clicks in it), the onFocus event occurs, and the event is handled by showOptions(). When the user changes an option item in the object, the alert window tells the user that the onChange event has occurred.

**LISTING 7.34** The select object and options array.

```
1    <HTML>
2    <HEAD>
3    <TITLE>Select Object</TITLE>
4    </HEAD>
5    <BODY>
6    <SCRIPT LANGUAGE = "JavaScript">
7    function showOptions(form, i)
8    {
9      alert(form.elements[i].options)
10   }
11   </SCRIPT>
12   <FORM NAME = "selectForm">
13   <P><H3>Multiple Selection</H3>
14   <SELECT NAME = "multipleSelection"
15     SIZE = 3
16     MULTIPLE
17     onBlur = "showOptions(this.form,0)">
18   <OPTION VALUE = "firstOption"
19   SELECTED> First option
20   <OPTION VALUE = "secondOption">Second option
21   <OPTION VALUE = "thirdOption"> Third option
22   <OPTION VALUE = "fourthOption"> Fourth option
23   </SELECT>
24   <P><H3>Scrolling Selection</H3>
25   <SELECT NAME = "scrollingSelection"
```

```
26    onFocus = "showOptions(this.form,1)"
27    onChange = "alert(onChange in scrollingSelection occured')">
28    <OPTION VALUE = "firstOption"
29    SELECTED> First option
30    <OPTION VALUE = "secondOption">Second option
31    <OPTION VALUE = "thirdOption"> Third option
32    <OPTION VALUE = "fourthOption"> Fourth option
33    </SELECT>
34    <SCRIPT LANGUAGE = "JavaScript">
35    </SCRIPT>
36    </FORM>
37    </BODY>
38    </HTML>
```

#  String

## Purpose

Use this object to work with strings.

## Syntax

You create a new string and access string properties and methods using the following syntax:

- var *stringName* = new String(["*stringText*"])

- *stringName.stringPropertyName*

- *stringName.stringMethodName(arguments)*

where

| | |
|---|---|
| *stringName* | is the name of a string variable. |
| *stringText* | is some text you wish to include in the initial string object. |
| *stringPropertyName* | is one of the string properties. |
| *stringMethodName* | is one of the string methods. |
| *arguments* | are the stringMethodName arguments. |

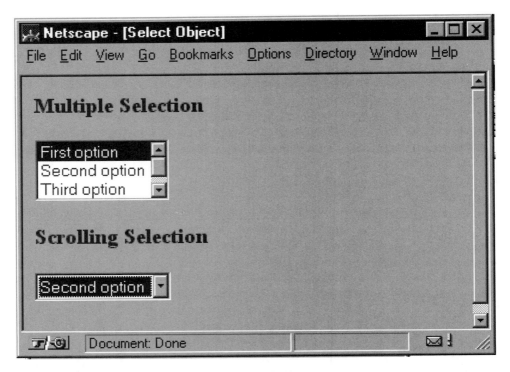

**FIGURE 7.26** The select object and options array.

| | |
|---|---|
| **Property of** | None |
| **Properties** | `length, prototype` |
| **Methods** | `anchor(), big(), blink(), bold(), charAt(), fixed(), font-color(), fontsize(), indexOf(), italics(), lastIndexOf(), link(), small(), split(), strike(), sub(), substring(), sup(), toLowerCase(), toUpperCase()` |
| **Event handlers** | None |
| **See also** | **Objects:** `text, textArea` |

## Access

Read and write.

## Discussion

Use the various string methods to manipulate strings.

# Examples

To see the effect of some of the string methods, do Exercise 7.19. You can then compare the original string to the output of the various methods. You may want to print, or save the HTML generated by the JavaScript in Listing 7.35 for future reference. A suggestion: When you plan on using JavaScript (or when using HTML) to build your HTML page, do not overdo it with strings. As in any advertisement war, the use of "eye-candy" is nothing short of an arms race. Your HTML page will be pleasing and easy on your visitor with no more than four colors (except for pictures) and three different fonts.

**EXERCISE 7.19**    WORKING WITH THE STRING OBJECT.

1. Type (or copy and paste) the code shown in Listing 7.35 and save it.

2. Load the file to your browser and observe the action of the various String methods on the string value (see Figure 7.27).

3. Combine the methods to: (a) make the third and fourth letters uppercase; (b) make the third character superscript and the fifth character subscript.

**LISTING 7.35** Working with the String object.

```
1    <HTML>
2    <HEAD>
3    <TITLE>Working with Strings</TITLE>
4    </HEAD>
5    <BODY>
6    <SCRIPT LANGUAGE = "JavaScript">
7    var aString = new String("abcdaBC")
8    var returnValue = 0
9    document.write("<UL>")
10   document.write("<LI>aStirng = " + aString)
11   document.write("<LI>aString.big() = " + aString.big())
12   document.write("<LI>aString.blink() = " + aString.blink())
13   document.write("<LI>aString.bold() = " + aString.bold())
14   document.write("<LI>aString.charAt(3) = " + aString.charAt(3))
15   document.write("<LI>aString.fixed() = " + aString.fixed())
16   document.write("<LI>aString.fontcolor('red') = " + aString.font-
color('red'))
17   document.write("<LI>aString.indexOf('c') = " +
aString.indexOf('c'))
18   document.write("<LI>aString.italics() = " + aString.italics())
19   document.write("<LI>aString.lastIndexOf('a') = " +
aString.lastIndexOf('a'))
20   document.write("<LI>aString.link() = " + aString.link())
```

```
21    document.write("<LI>aString.small() = " + aString.small())
22    document.write("<LI>aString.strike() = " + aString.strike())
23    document.write("<LI>aString.sub() = " + aString.sub())
24    document.write("<LI>aString.substring(1,3) = " + aString.sub-
string(1,3))
25    document.write("<LI>aString.sup() = " + aString.sup())
26    document.write("<LI>aString.toLowerCase() = " +
aString.toLowerCase())
27    document.write("<LI>aString.toUpperCase() = " +
aString.toUpperCase())
28    document.write("</UL>")
29    </SCRIPT>
30    </BODY>
31    </HTML>
```

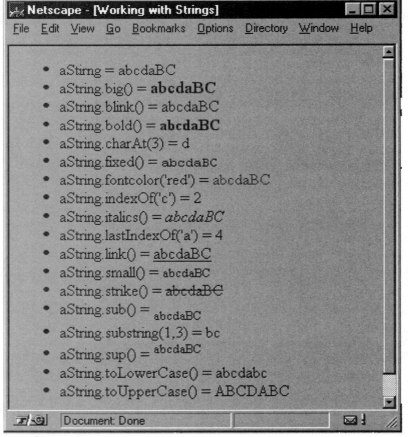

**FIGURE 7.27** Working with the String object.

 # submit

## Purpose

Use this object to submit form data to the server.

## Syntax

```
<INPUT
 TYPE = "submit"
 NAME = "submitButtonName"
 VALUE = "submitButtonText"
 [onClick = "submitEventHandler"]>
```

where:

| | |
|---|---|
| NAME = | "submitButtonName" is the submit button object's name. |
| VALUE = | "submitButtonText" is the text to appear on the face of the submit button in the HTML page. |
| onClick = | "submitEventHandler" is the event handler that is processed when the user clicks on the button. |

| | |
|---|---|
| **Property of** | form |
| **Properties** | name, type, value |
| **Methods** | click() |
| **Event handlers** | onClick |
| **See also** | **Objects:** button, form, reset<br>**Event handlers:** onSubmit<br>**Methods:** submit() |

## Access

Read and write.

## Discussion

Use one of the following statements to work with the object, its methods, or its properties:

• submitButtonName.submitPropertyName

- *submitButtonName*.*submitMethodName*(*submitMethodArguments*)

- *formName*.elements[*i*].*submitPropertyName*

- *formName*.elements[*i*].*submitMethodName*(*submitMethodArguments*)

where

- *submitButtonName* is the name of the submit object, as assigned to the VALUE attribute of the submit object.

- *submitPropertyName* is one of the submit object's properties.

- *submitMethodName* is one of the submit objet's methods.

- *submitMethodArguments* are the submitMethodName arguments (if any).

- *formName* is the value assigned to the VALUE attribute of the form object in which the submit button resides.

- elements is an array of elements in the form.

- *i* is the integer index of the submit button element in the elements array. Elements are added to the elements array in the order they are encountered during the HTML page loading.

A submit object must be enclosed by the <FORM> </FORM> tags. When the user clicks on the submit button, the data in the form are submitted to the URL that is specified in the ACTION attribute of the form to which the submit button belongs, and a new page (if so specified) or the current HTML page is reloaded into the client.

Once the user clicks on the submit button, the process of submitting the data to the URL cannot be stopped. To manipulate the process before submission, use the submit() method or the form's onSubmit event handler.

## Examples

Rather than deal with a vanilla type submit button, Exercise 7.21 shows you how to by pass the CGI headache when you want to get information from a user. Simply build a form, and have the submit button send the information to you. However, before submitting the information, you want to put it together so that it is legible. Go through the exercise; you will learn how to communicate with your user through forms: have the user submit information to you without relying on an Internet server facility.

1. Type (or copy and paste) the code shown in Listing 7.36 and save it.

2. Replace yourName@address in line 29 with your e-mail address.

3. Load the file to your browser, fill in the form (see Figure 7.28), and mail it to yourself.

4. Examine the e-mail and make sure that you are receiving the e-mail correctly.

5. If your e-mail receives attachments, you will receive two of them. What are they? To find out, add another text element to the form, then add it to the string you are mailing to yourself (you build this string in lines 15–19) and see how many attachments you get.

6. Move lines 33–35 to follow right after line 55 and mail the information to yourself again. Check the mail you got. Interesting, isn't it?

Let us discuss the code in Listing 7.36 briefly. In line 7 we begin the definition of the mailTheForm() function, with a form object as an argument (theForm). We collect the information stored in the document properties title and location in the variable info (with some formatting, such as tabs, indicated by "\t") in lines 11 to 13.

In line 15 we start inserting the information we wish to mail into the value of the hidden element named theInfo. This is an element of theForm. In line 17 we add the value stored in the firstName object's property value to theInfo. firstName is a text element (object) in theForm. We do the same with theForm's lastName element and then return.

In line 28 we start the form object definition, name it aForm, and attach a mailto action to it (line 29). The syntax ?subject=purchase order defines the subject of the mail message as purchase order. To see the submitted data formatted correctly as part of the e-mail message, we define the ENCTYPE attribute of aForm to be multipart/form-data. Because we want to do some processing of the form's data before submitting it, we call mailTheForm() with aForm (using this) as an argument through the onSubmit event handler.

In lines 33–35 we add a hidden object to aForm and name the object theInfo. We want to e-mail the data stored in the value property of this form's element. We then lay out the remaining form elements (see Figure 7.28), ending with the submit button.

When the user clicks on the Submit... button, the onSubmit event occurs, and is handled with the mailTheForm() function. After the function returns, the data is e-mailed.

You can use this approach to e-mail yourself data gathered from users and then process it. You have thus bypassed the use of server-side CGI to handle the data submitted by the form. You are still left with the task of processing the e-mail appropriately. This is not a JavaScript problem: you can save the message as a text file, and write a little program that reads the data in the file and processes it. For example, it is a (truly) simple matter to write a database program (in dBASE, FoxPro, etc.) that will parse the e-mail message text and add the data to your database automatically.

**LISTING 7.36** Working with submit and mailto.

```
1    <HTML>
2    <HEAD>
3    <TITLE>Working with Submit and MailTo</TITLE>
4
5    <SCRIPT LANGUAGE = "JavaScript">
6
7    function mailTheForm(theForm)
8    {
9     var info = ""
10
11    info += "\n\nDocument Title:\t" +
12    document.title + "\n"
13    info += "From:\t\t\t" + document.location + "\n"
14
15    theForm.theInfo.value = info + "\n" +
16    "First name:\t\t" +
17    theForm.firstName.value + "\n" +
18    "Last name:\t\t" +
19    theForm.lastName.value + "\n"
20
21    return true
22    }
23    </SCRIPT>
24    </HEAD>
25
26    <BODY>
27    <H3>Working with Submit and MailTo</H3>
28    <FORM NAME = "aForm"
29     ACTION = "mailto:yourName@address?subject=purchase order"
30     ENCTYPE = "multipart/form-data"
31     onSubmit = "mailTheForm(this)">
32
33    <INPUT TYPE = "hidden"
34     NAME = "theInfo"
```

```
35    VALUE = " ">
36   <TABLE>
37   <TR>
38    <TH ALIGN = right
39    VALIGN = top>Your first name:
40    <TD><INPUT TYPE = "text"
41    NAME = "firstName"
42    WIDTH = 25>
43   </TR>
44   <TR>
45    <TH ALIGN = right
46    VALIGN = top>Your last name:
47    <TD><INPUT TYPE = "text"
48    NAME = "lastName"
49    WIDTH = 25>
50   </TR>
51   <TR>
52    <TH>
53    <TD><INPUT TYPE = "submit"
54    VALUE = "Submit...">
55   </TR>
56   </TABLE>
57   </FORM>
58   </BODY>
59   </HTML>
```

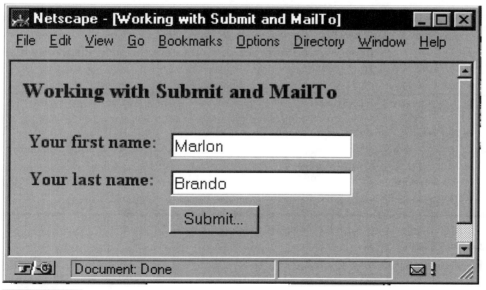

**FIGURE 7.28** Working with submit and mailto.

 text

## Purpose

Use this object to gather one-liner information from a user.

## Syntax

```
<INPUT
  TYPE = "text"
  NAME = "textObjectName"
  VALUE = "textObjectValue"
  SIZE = integer
  [onBlur = "onBlurEventHandler"]
  [onChange = "onChangeEventHandler"]
  [onFocus = "onFocusEventHandler"]
  [onSelect = "onSelectEventHandler"]>
```

where

| | |
|---|---|
| TYPE = | "text" identifies the object as a text object. |
| NAME = | "textObjectName" is the name of the object. |
| VALUE = | "textObjectValue" is the initial value of the object's value property. |
| SIZE = | integer is the number of characters the field displays without scrolling. |

| | |
|---|---|
| **Property of** | form |
| **Properties** | defaultValue, name, type, value |
| **Methods** | focus(), blur(), select() |
| **Event handlers** | onBlur, onChange, onFocus, onSelect |
| **See also** | **Objects:** form, password, string, textarea |

## Access

Read and write.

# Discussion

Because a text object is a form element, it must be enclosed within the `<FORM> </FORM>` tag. Use one of the following statement formats to work with this object:

- *textObjectName.textPropertyName*
- *textObjectName.textMethodName (textMethodArguments)*
- *formName.elements[i].textPropertyName*
- *formName.elements[i].textMethodName (textMethodArguments)*

where

- *textObjectName* is the value stored in the NAME attribute of the text element
- *textPropertyName* is one of the text object's properties
- *textMethodName* is one of the text object's methods
- *textMethodArguments* is the methods arguments (if any)
- *formName* is the value stored in the NAME attribute of the form in which the text object resides
- *elements* is the array of elements in the form
- *i* is an integer index of the text object in the elements array (elements are added to the elements array as they are encountered during page layout)

# Examples

Exercise 7.22 is designed to demonstrate the sequence in which the various text object events occur as you move in and out of a field and change data in it.

**EXERCISE 7.22** THE TEXT OBJECT AND ITS EVENT HANDLERS.

1. Type (or copy and paste) the code shown in Listing 7.37 and save it.
2. Load the file and enter a state code in lowercase and press the Tab key (Figure 7.29).
3. Based on the data that appear in the alert dialog window, which event occurs first: onChange or onBlur?

**LISTING 7.37** The text object and its event handlers.

```
1    <HTML>
2    <HEAD>
3    <TITLE> The text Object</TITLE>
4    <HEAD>
5
6    <BODY>
7    <H3> The text Object </H3>
8    <FORM NAME = "aForm">
9    <B>City: </B>
10   <INPUT TYPE = "text"
11          NAME = "city"
12          VALUE = "St. Paul"
13          SIZE="25"
14    onFocus = "this.select()">
15   <B>State: </B>
16   <INPUT TYPE = "text"
17    NAME = "state"
18    VALUE = "MN"
19    SIZE="3"
20    onChange =
21    'this.value = this.value.toUpperCase()'
22    onBlur =
23    'alert("State: " + this.value)'>
24   <P>Which occurs first: onChange or onBlur?
25   </FORM>
26   </BODY>
27   <HTML>
```

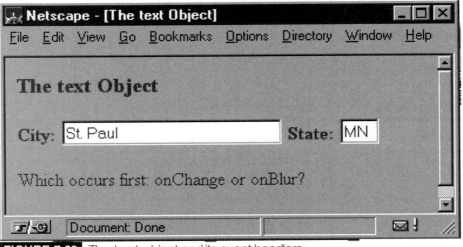

**FIGURE 7.29** The text object and its event handlers.

**270** Chapter 7

 # textarea

## Purpose

Use this object to allow the user to enter multi-line text in a form.

## Syntax

```
<TEXTAREA
 NAME = "textareaObjectName"
 ROWS = integer
 COLS = integer
 WRAP = "off | virtual | physical"
 [onBlur = "onBlurEventHandler"]
 [onChange = "onChangeEventHandler"]
 [onFocus = "onFocusEventHandler"]
 [onSelect = "onSelectEventHandler"]>
 defaultText
</TEXTAREA>
```

where

| | |
|---|---|
| NAME = | "textareaObjectName" is the object's name. |
| ROWS = | integer determines how many rows (in character units) are to be displayed. |
| COLS = | integer determines how many columns (in character units) are to be displayed. |
| WRAP = | "off | virtual | physical" determines what to do with the end of line: off, the default, means that text is transferred as is; virtual means that text is wrapped (a new line appears as the text reaches the right margin), but is transferred as is; and physical means that when the text is transferred, a new-line character is added where the text has wrapped in the display. |

| | |
|---|---|
| **Property of** | form |
| **Properties** | defaultValue, name, type, value |
| **Methods** | focus(), blur(), select() |
| **Event handlers** | onBlur, onChange, onFocus, onSelect |
| **See also** | **Objects:** form, password, string, text |

## Access

Read and write.

## Discussion

This object must appear as an element of a form, and must therefore be enclosed by the <FORM> </FORM> pair. Use one of the following statement formats to work with the textarea object:

- *textareaObjectName.textareaPropertyName*
- *textareaObjectName.textareaMethodName(textAreaMethodArguments)*
- *formName.elements[i].textareaPropertyName*
- *formName.elements[i].textareaMethodName(textAreaMethodArguments)*

where

- *textareaObjectName* is the value assigned to the NAME attribute of the textarea element in a form
- *textareaPropertyName* is one of the textarea object's properties
- *textareaMethodName* is one of the textarea object's methods
- *textAreaMethodArguments* are the method arguments (if any)
- *formName* is the value assigned to the NAME attribute of the form in which the textarea element resides, or to an element in the forms array of a document
- *i* is the integer index of the textarea element in the form's elements array (elements are added to the elements array as they are encountered during the HTML page layout)

You can update the textarea content in a form by setting the value property to some string. For example, the statement

```
this.value = "abcdef"
```

will reset the text shown in the textarea to abcdef, regardless of what is in there currently.

Keep in mind that the new-line character is different for different systems:

- New-line in UNIX is \n

- New-line in Macintosh is \n

- New-line in Windows is \r\n

## Examples

Exercise 7.23 is somewhat more elaborated than others. The reason is that one of the most frequent uses of JavaScript will probably be in communicating with the user; after all, what is the point of putting an elaborate form online without being able to gather the form data from the visitor? Furthermore, in communicating with the user, you may not wish to depend on your Internet provider and server-side processing; you may want to control your own destiny.

Exercise 7.23 is closely related to Exercise 7.21 (see also Listing 7.36 and Figure 7.28). There are some idiosyncrasies (introduced on purpose) in Listing 7.36, and you were asked in Exercise 7.21 to fix them. Here we have a fix. Do Exercise 7.23; the effort may pay off later.

**EXERCISE 7.23**    TEXTAREA **AND** MAILTO.

1. Type (or copy and paste) the code shown in Listing 7.38 and save it.

2. In line 83, change name@address to your e-mail address.

3. Load the file and enter some information on the form (shown in Figure 7.30).

4. Go to your mail and see if you got the information from the form, formatted as shown in Figure 7.31?

5. In line 62, change virtual to off and send yourself the same e-mail message again.

6. In line 62, change off to physical and send yourself the same e-mail again.

7. What are the differences in line formatting among the three e-mail messages you sent yourself?

8. What are the differences in line formatting in the textarea object using these three formats?

Here is an explanation of the code in Listing 7.38:

In lines to 44 to 80 we define the first form in the document, called dataForm. This form contains the elements that you see in Figure 7.30: two text objects (with the NAME attributes firstName and lastName); a textarea element with NAME attribute comments; and a three-button radio object named `checkGender`. The buttons designate `"Male"`, `"Female"`, and `"NOYB"` (None of Your Business).

Each of the radio buttons has an `onClick` event handler that calls `doGender()`. We shall see in a moment what `doGender()` does.

In lines 82 to 95 we construct the `submitForm` in the document. This form includes a single hidden input (lines 87 to 89), named `theData`. We shall send the e-mail content in the value of this field (we will see in a moment how). `submitForm` also includes the `submit` button (lines 92 to 93). When you click on it, the `onSubmit` event handler calls the `submitData()` function with the form as its argument.

This is what happens: The user enters data in the fields and clicks one of the radio buttons. When a radio button is clicked, `doGender()` (lines 10 to 20) is called. In `doGender()` we cycle through the `checkGender` radio buttons, one at a time, and see which one is checked (line 14). If we hit a checked button, we store the value of the index of the checked button in the global variable `genderIndex` (line 16). "Why?" You ask. Because we need to e-mail the gender information—You will see in a moment how.

In line 7 we construct the `gender` array with three entries.

Now that the user has entered the data, he/she is ready to submit it. When the user clicks the `Submit...` button, the `onSubmit` event handler in the `submitForm` occurs (line 86) and `submitData()` is called with the `submitForm` as its argument (the flow of execution goes from line 86 to line 22). In lines 24 to 25 we ask the user for the last time if he/she is sure that he/she wants to submit the data. This, incidentally, is how we get around the problem that you cannot stop the submit button from submitting (remember the problem presented to you in Exercise 7.21).

If the user confirms we fall to line 26, where we start building the data to submit. In line 27 we declare `theData` as a string variable and put nothing in it. Then, in lines 28 and 29 we put the HTML page title and the URL of where the document is coming from in `theData`. In lines 30 and 31 we add the first and last name data to `theData`. In line 32 we add the gender. We know which gender to send with the data because we have already set the `genderIndex` in `doGender`.

Finally, in line 34 we store `theData` and whatever is in the `textarea` element (named `comments`) in the `form.theData.value`. We return with `true`, and the data are sent.

If you are particularly ambitious, you can save the data that comes in with the e-mail message (as in Figure 7.31) to a text file, and write a little program in your favorite database system to update your database. This can be particularly easy because you control the format of the data, and can read it any way you want.

**LISTING 7.38** textarea and mailto.

```
1    <HTML>
2    <HEAD>
3    <title>textarea and mailto</title>
4
5    <SCRIPT LANGUAGE = "JavaScript">
6
7    gender = new Array("Male", "Female", "NOYB")
8    genderIndex = 0
9
10   function doGender(form)
11   {
12    for (var i = 0; form.checkGender.length; i++)
13    {
14    if (form.checkGender[i].checked)
15    {
16    genderIndex = i
17    break
18    }
19    }
20   }
21
22   function submitData(form)
23   {
24    if(!confirm("Are you sure?"))
25    return false
26    var data = document.dataForm
27    var theData = ""
28    theData += "Page title:\t\t" + document.title + "\n"
29    theData += "Data source:\t" + document.location + "\n\n"
30    theData += "First name:\t\t" + data.firstName.value + "\n"
31    theData += "Last name:\t\t" + data.lastName.value + "\n"
32    theData += "Gender:\t\t" + gender[genderIndex] + "\n\n"
33    theData += "Comments:\n"
34    form.theData.value = theData + data.comments.value
35    return true
36   }
37
38   </SCRIPT>
39   </HEAD>
40
41   <BODY>
42   <H3>textarea and mailto</H3>
43   <TABLE>
44   <FORM          NAME = "dataForm">
45   <TR>
46   <TH ALIGN = right>First name:
```

```
47    <TD><INPUT      TYPE = "text"
48                    NAME = "firstName"
49                    SIZE = 50>
50    </TR>
51    <TR>
52    <TH ALIGN = right>Last name:
53    <TD><INPUT      TYPE = "text"
54          NAME = "lastName"
55          SIZE = 50>
56    </TR>
57    <TR>
58    <TH ALIGN = right VALIGN = top>Comments:
59    <TD><TEXTAREA NAME = "comments"
60                    COLS = 50
61                    ROWS = 8
62                    WRAP = virtual>
63    </TEXTAREA>
64    </TR>
65    <TR>
66    <TH ALIGN = right>Gender:
67    <TD><INPUT      TYPE = "radio"
68                    NAME = "checkGender"
69                    VALUE = "Male"
70                    onClick = "doGender(form)">Male
71    <INPUT          TYPE = "radio"
72                    NAME = "checkGender"
73                    VALUE = "Female"
74                    onClick = "doGender(form)">Female
75    <INPUT          TYPE = "radio"
76                    NAME = "checkGender"
77                    VALUE = "NOYB"
78                    onClick = "doGender(form)">NOYB
79    </TR>
80    </FORM>
81
82    <FORM           NAME = "submitForm"
83                    ACTION = "mailto:name@address?subject=Here is a
                      message"
84                    METHOD = "post"
85                    ENCTYPE = "multipart/form-data"
86                    onSubmit = "return submitData(this)">
87    <INPUT          TYPE = "hidden"
88                    NAME = "theData"
89                    VALUE = "">
90    <TR>
91    <TD COLSPAN = 2 ALIGN = center>
92    <INPUT          TYPE = "submit"
93                    VALUE = "Submit...">
```

```
94       </TR>
95       </FORM>
96       </TABLE>
97     </BODY>
98   </HTML>
```

#  window

## Purpose

window is the top-level object in the object hierarchy. Use this object to access properties and methods of a variety of objects in the windows.

## Syntax

aWindow = window.open("URL", "windowName" [, "windowAttributes"])

where

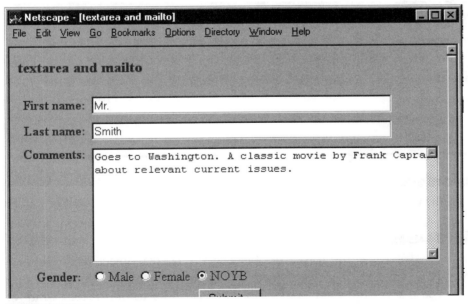

**FIGURE 7.30** textarea and mailto.

```
Page title:              textarea and mailto
Data source:             file:///C|/MINE/JS/Wiley/Listings/JS for
Wiley/try.html

First name:              Mr.
Last name:               Smith
Gender:                  NOYB

Comments:
Goes to Washington. A Classic movie by Frank Capra about rel-
evant current issues.
```

**FIGURE 7.31**  Form data (Figure 7.30) as received by e-mail.

| | |
|---|---|
| *aWindow* | is a window variable declared somewhere in the JavaScript code. |
| *window.open()* | is the method that creates the window. |
| *URL* | is the window URL. |
| *windowName* | is the value assigned to the TARGET attribute of a `<FORM>` tag or an `<A>` tag. |
| *windowAttributes* | determines window attributes (see Table 8.2) |

| | |
|---|---|
| **Property of** | None |
| **Properties** | defaultStatus, document, frame, frames, length, location, name, opener, parent, self, status, top, window |
| **Methods** | alert(), blur(), clearTimeout(), close(), confirm(), focus(), open(), prompt(), scroll(), setTimeout() |
| **Event handlers** | onBlur, onError, onFocus, onLoad, onUnload |
| **See also** | **Objects:** document, frame |

## Access
Read and write.

## Discussion
The window object is the top-level object in the client's object hierarchy (see Figure 3.1 in Chapter 3); a frame object is in fact a window object. Thus, although the self and window properties of a window object refer to the current window, they can be omitted in referencing the current window methods and properties.

There are two exceptions to this rule. When you wish to use the window object's methods `open()` or `close()` in an event handler, you must specify them thus: `window.open()` or `window.close()`. Without the window dot notation for these two functions, JavaScript will execute `document.open()` or `document.close()`.

Here are some ways to work with `window` objects:

- *window.windowPropertyName*
- *window.windowMethodName(windowMethodArguments)*
- *self.windowPropertyName*
- *self.windowMethodName(windowMethodArguments)*
- *top.windowPropertyName*
- *top.windowMethodName(windowMethodArguments)*
- *parent.windowPropertyName*
- *parent.windowMethodName(windowMethodArguments)*
- *aWindow.windowPropertyName*
- *aWindow.windowMethodName(windowMethodArguments)*
- *windowPropertyName*
- *windowMethodName(windowMethodArguments)*

where

- *aWindow* is a `window` object instance
- *windowPropertyName* is one of the `window` object's properties
- *windowMethodName* is one of the `window` object's methods
- *windowMethodArguments* are the method arguments (if any)

The `onLoad` and `onUnload` window event handlers are defined in either the `<BODY>` or `<FRAMESET>` tags.

Note that the `onBlur`, `onFocus`, `onLoad`, and `onUnload` event handlers must be called from within `<BODY>` or `<FRAMESET>` tags.

## Examples

Exercise 7.24 demonstrates how to work with `window` objects. The code is fairly simple (although it is tedious to figure out what it does). Follow the exercise and find out who is controlling whom, when `onLoad` and `onUnload` are executed, and so on.

1. Type (or copy and paste) the code shown in Listing 7.39 and save it as `ControllingWindow.HTML` (if you cannot save it by this long name, save it with another name).

2. Type (or copy and paste) the code shown in Listing 7.40 and save it as `ControlledWindow.HTML` (if you cannot save it by this long name, save it with another name).

3. Click on the various buttons and see what happens (see Figure 7.32 and Figure 7.33).

4. Modify the code in Listing 7.39 to install a button in the `ControlledWindow` from a button in the `ControllingWindow`.

**LISTING 7.39** Working with `window`: the `ControllingWindow.HTML`.

```
1    <HTML>
2    <HEAD>
3    <TITLE>Controlling Window</TITLE>
4    </HEAD>
5    <BODY BGCOLOR = "lightblue">
6    <H3>I'm the controlling window</H3>
7    <SCRIPT LANGUAGE = "JavaScript">
8    controlledWindow = open("ControlledWindow.HTML",
     "controlledWindow", "scrollbars = yes, width = 150, height = 150")
9    document.writeln("<B>From Controlling Window</B>")
10   </SCRIPT>
11   <FORM NAME = "controlWindowForm">
12   <P><INPUT TYPE = "button"
13    VALUE = "Open a window..."
14    onClick =
15    "aWindow = window.open('','aWindow', 'scrollbars = yes, width
     = 150, height = 150')">
16   <P><INPUT TYPE = "button"
17    VALUE = "Write to a window..."
18    onClick =
19    "aWindow.document.writeln('From Controlling
     Window');aWindow.document.close()">
20   <P><INPUT TYPE = "button"
21    VALUE = "Close a window..."
22    onClick = "aWindow.close()">
23   <P><INPUT TYPE = "button"
24    VALUE = "Close the controlled window..."
25    onClick = "controlledWindow.close()">
26   </FORM>
27   </BODY>
28   </HTML>
```

**LISTING 7.40** Working with window: the `ControlledWindow.HTML`.

```
1    <HTML>
2    <HEAD>
3    <TITLE>Controlled Window</TITLE>
4    </HEAD>
5    <BODY BGCOLOR = "white"
6     onLoad = "alert(window.name + '.onLoad')"
7     onUnload = "alert(window.name + '.onUnload')">
8    <B>I'm a controlled window. </B>
9    <P>I'm controlled by 'Controlling Window'
10   </BODY>
11   </HTML>
```

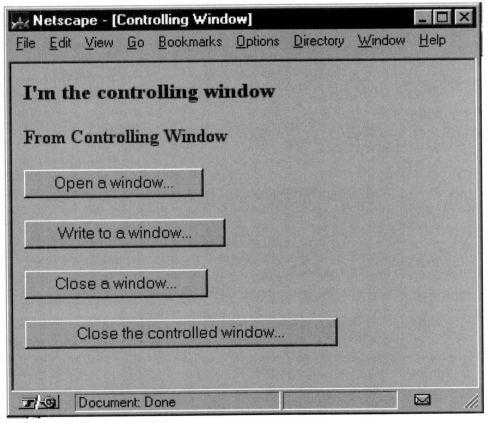

**FIGURE 7.32** Working with window: the `ControllingWindow.html`.

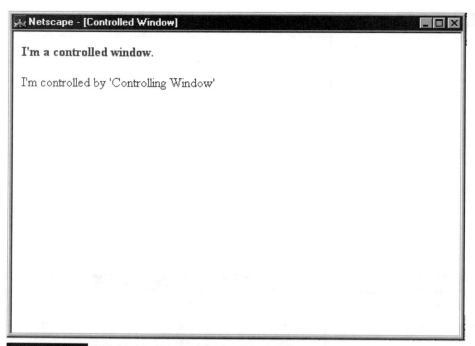

**FIGURE 7.33** Working with window: the ControlledWindow.html.

# METHODS AND FUNCTIONS REFERENCE

- ↳ Methods
- ↳ Functions
- ↳ Examples of forms
- ↳ Examples of data validation
- ↳ Random number generator
- ↳ Examples of animation

##  Introduction to Methods and Functions

Here we shall cover all of the JavaScript functions and methods in detail. Recall that in general, methods are functions that belong to objects, while functions are independent of objects. Parenthesis "( )" are appended to the names of methods and functions to emphasize what they are.

Recall that the notation [...] means that the arguments in the square brackets are optional, and that italics mean values that you choose. Values that must be typed as shown are not in italics.

# Chapter Format

Each method or function is discussed in more or less the same format:

- **Action**—a short sentence that describes what the method or function does, and often its return value.

- **Syntax**—the calling syntax, including arguments.

- **Arguments**—explanation of what the arguments are, their format, and their value ranges.

- **Method of**—the objects to which the method belongs. If None is specified, it is a function. Note that a method's behavior often depends on the object for which it is called.

- **See also**—some related methods or functions.

- **Discussion**—some special issues to pay attention to when using the method or function.

- **Examples**—one or more examples to clarify issues and demonstrate the method or function use; you can cut and paste the code in these examples (they are all on the enclosed CD).

## A Word about the Examples

I have tried to include examples that clarify some general issues and deal with some JavaScript language and specifications inconsistencies. Many of the examples also indicate some important programming tricks, and ways to avoid nasty bugs. The more examples you see, the more fluent you will become in JavaScript. Reading examples is like using a language you are learning and developing a vocabulary. Many of the examples include suggestions for further use and questions that you should try to explore; these questions are designed to clarify some sticky ideas.

## How to Read This Chapter

Read this chapter when you have nothing else to do, or if you regularly read—as many others do—in the bathroom. When you need to use a particular method or function, refer to it and review some of the details and examples. Remember that becoming a good JavaScript programmer entails developing a vocabulary. Part of the vocabulary is the methods and functions that are available for use with the language. So gloss over the chapter topics frequently to remind yourself what can and cannot be done with JavaScript. To get the most benefit from the material, when reading about a specific function, run the examples first, and then take a look at the code.

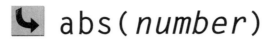 abs(*number*)

| | |
|---|---|
| **Action** | Returns the absolute value of a number. |
| **Syntax** | Math.abs(*number*) |
| **Arguments** | *number* is a number, an expression that evaluates to a number, or a property that is a number. |
| **Method of** | Math |
| **See also** | **Methods**: max(), min() |

## Discussion

The absolute value of a number returns:

- the positive value of the number if the number is negative
- zero if the number is zero
- the number if the number is positive

Thus, abs(0) returns 0, abs(-1) returns 1, and abs(1) returns 1.

## Examples

The expression

```
var absValue = Math.abs(5*(-1))
```

assigns the value 5 to absValue.

 acos(*number*)

| | |
|---|---|
| **Action** | Returns the arc cosine of a number in radians or NaN. |
| **Syntax** | Math.acos(*number*) |
| **Arguments** | *number* is a number, an expression that evaluates to a number, or a property that is a number, in the range of -1 to 1; otherwise, NaN is returned. |
| **Method of** | Math |
| **See also** | **Functions:** isNaN() |

**Methods:** `asin()`, `atan()`, `cos()`, `sin()`, `tan()`

**Properties:** `PI`

## Discussion

The return value is between 0 and `PI`. If the method's argument is less than -1 or greater than 1, the method returns `NaN` (not a number). Use `isNaN()` to test for errors.

The mathematical function arc cosine is the inverse of cosine—it returns the angle (usually in radians) of the cosine of a real number.

## Examples

Listing 8.1 demonstrates the use of `acos()`. Note the use of `isNaN()` in line 8 to test the return value of `acos()`. The results of Listing 8.1 are shown in Figure 8.1.

**LISTING 8.1** Using `acos()`.

```
1    <HTML>
2    <TITLE>acos()</TITLE>
3    <BODY>
4    <B>acos()</B>
5    <SCRIPT LANGUAGE = "JavaScript">
6    document.writeln("<BR> Math.acos(1) = " + Math.acos(1))
7    document.writeln("<BR>Math.acos(-1) = " + Math.acos(-1))
```

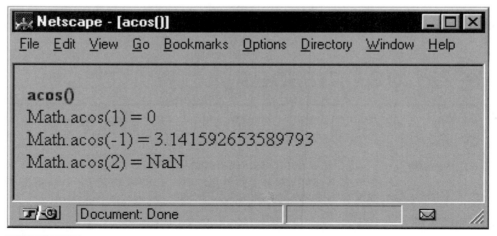

**FIGURE 8.1** Using `acos()`.

```
 8  if(isNaN(Math.acos(2)))
 9      document.writeln("<BR>Math.acos(2) = NaN")
10  else
11      document.writeln("<BR>Math.acos(2) = " + Math.acos(2))
12  </SCRIPT>
13  </BODY>
14  </HTML>
```

#  alert([*argument*])

| | |
|---|---|
| **Action** | Displays a JavaScript alert window with *argument* and an OK button. |
| **Syntax** | alert([*argument*]) |
| **Arguments** | *argument* can be: |
| | • a string literal, an expression that evaluate to a string, or a string value of a property of an existing object or |
| | • a numerical literal, an expression that evaluate to a number, or a numerical value of a property of an existing object. |
| **Method of** | window |
| **See also** | **Methods:** confirm(), prompt() |

## Discussion

In working with alert(), keep the following in mind:

- This window disrupts the user's interaction with Navigator, and often interferes with other applications. Use it sparingly, and mostly for debugging your JavaScript code.

- Use this window when no decision by the user is needed (e.g., use it for information, warning, etc.).

- You do not need to reference a window in a call to alert(). For example, both windowName.alert(Something) and alert(Something) work.

- If no *argument* is specified, the value undefined appears in the window.

## Examples

Listing 8.2 demonstrates one use of alert(). A source file commonf.js (given on the accompanying CD) is first identified. This file contains common

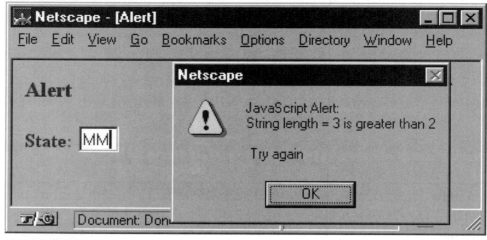

**FIGURE 8.2** Using alert().

functions—isValidLength() is one of them. The user is asked to enter some data in a text field (State). If the string length is greater than 2, the user is asked to try again. The test is done when the Return key is pressed—that is when the onBlur event handler calls validateStringLength(). Figure 8.2 shows what happens when the user enters three characters in the field.

**LISTING 8.2** Using alert().

```
1    <HTML>
2    <TITLE>Alert</TITLE>
3
4    <HEAD>
5    <SCRIPT LANGUAGE = "JavaScript" SRC = "commonf.js">
6    </SCRIPT>
7    <SCRIPT>
8    function validateSringLength(aString, maxLength)
9    {
10     if (!isValidLength(aString, maxLength))
11      alert("String length = " + aString.length +
12        " is greater than " + maxLength +
13        "\n\n Try again")
14
15     return true
16   }
17   </SCRIPT>
18   </HEAD>
19
20   <BODY>
```

```
21  <H3> Alert</H3>
22  <FORM>
23  <B>State:<B>
24  <INPUT    TYPE = "text"
25            NAME = "testLength"
26            SIZE = 3
27            onBlur = "validateSringLength(testLength.value,2)">
28  </FORM>
29  </BODY>
30  </HTML>
```

#  anchor(*anchorName Attribute*)

| | |
|---|---|
| **Action** | Creates an HTML anchor that is used as a hypertext target. |
| **Syntax** | aString.anchor(*anchorNameAttribute*) |
| **Arguments** | *anchorNameAttribute* is the value assigned to the NAME attribute of the <A> tag. |
| **Method of** | String |
| **See also** | **Objects:** anchor, anchors array |
| | **Methods:** link() |

## Discussion

Here are a couple of points to keep in mind using anchor():

- Use the function to create, display, and manipulate anchors in an HTML document via JavaScript.

- The *aString* string in the syntax is the text that is displayed for the *anchorNameAttribute*.

## Examples

Listing 8.3 demonstrates one way to use anchor(). The createAnchor() function creates a new window and puts an anchor in it. Line 11 is equivalent to

```
<A NAME = "JSanchor">This anchor was created via JavaScript</A>
```

**LISTING 8.3** Using `anchor()`.

```
1   <HTML>
2   <TITLE>Anchor</TITLE>
3
4   <HEAD>
5   <SCRIPT LANGUAGE = "JavaScript">
6   var aString = "This anchor was created via JavaScript"
7
8   function createAnchor()
9   {
10    aWindow=window.open("","aWindow")
11    aWindow.document.writeln(aString.anchor("JSanchor"))
12    aWindow.document.close()
13  }
14  </SCRIPT>
15
16  <BODY>
17  <H3> Anchor</H3>
18  <FORM>
19  <INPUT   TYPE = "button"
20           NAME = "makeAnchor"
21           VALUE = "Create anchor..."
22           onBlur = "createAnchor()">
23  </FORM>
24  </BODY>
25  </HTML>
```

#  asin(*number*)

| | |
|---|---|
| **Action** | Returns the arc sine (in radians) of a *number*. |
| **Syntax** | `Math.asin(number)` |
| **Arguments** | *number* is a number, an expression that evaluates to a number, or a property that is a number, in the range of -1 to 1; otherwise, `NaN` is returned. |
| **Method of** | `Math` |
| **See also** | **Functions:** `isNaN()` |
| | **Methods:** `acos()`, `atan()`, `cos()`, `sin()`, `tan()` |
| | **Properties:** `PI` |

## Discussion

The return value is between 0 and `PI`. If the method's argument is less than

-1 or greater than 1, the method returns NaN (not a number). Use isNaN() to test for errors.

The mathematical function arc sine is the inverse of sine—it returns the angle (usually in radians) of the sine of a real number.

## Examples

Listing 8.4 demonstrate the use of asin(). Note the use of isNaN() in line 8 to test the return value of asin(). The results of Listing 8.4 are shown in Figure 8.3.

**LISTING 8.4** Using asin().

```
 1  <HTML>
 2  <TITLE>asin()</TITLE>
 3  <BODY>
 4  <B>asin()</B>
 5  <SCRIPT LANGUAGE = "JavaScript">
 6  document.writeln("<BR> Math.asin(1) = " + Math.asin(1))
 7  document.writeln("<BR>Math.asin(-1) = " + Math.asin(-1))
 8  if(isNaN(Math.asin(2)))
 9     document.writeln("<BR>Math.asin(2) = NaN")
10  else
11     document.writeln("<BR>Math.asin(2) = " + Math.asin(2))
12  </SCRIPT>
13  </BODY>
14  </HTML>
```

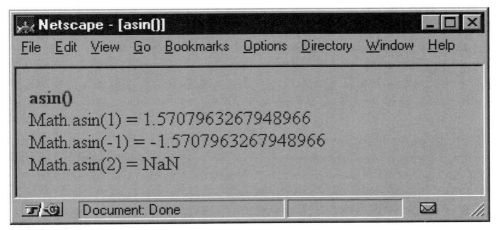

**FIGURE 8.3** Using asin().

# atan(*number*)

| | |
|---|---|
| **Action** | Returns the arc tangent (in radians) of a *number*. |
| **Syntax** | `Math.atan(number)` |
| **Arguments** | *number* is a number, an expression that evaluates to a number, or a property that is a number. |
| **Method of** | `Math` |
| **See also** | **Functions:** `isNaN()` |
| | **Methods:** `acos()`, `asin()`, `cos()`, `sin()`, `tan()` |
| | **Properties:** `PI` |

## Discussion

The return value is between `-PI/2` and `PI/2`.

The mathematical function arc tangent is the inverse of tangent—it returns the angle (usually in radians) of the tangent of a real number.

## Examples

Listing 8.5 demonstrate the use of `atan()`. Note the use of:

- `isNaN()` in line 8 to test the return value of `atan()`

- `E` notation to represent large numbers in lines 8, 9, and 11

The results of Listing 8.5 are shown in Figure 8.4.

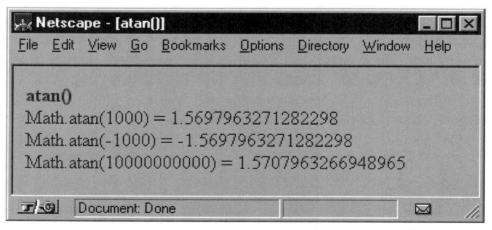

**FIGURE 8.4** Using `atan()`.

LISTING 8.5 Using atan().

```
 1  <HTML>
 2  <TITLE>atan()</TITLE>
 3  <BODY>
 4  <B>atan()</B>
 5  <SCRIPT LANGUAGE = "JavaScript">
 6  document.writeln("<BR> Math.atan(1000) = " + Math.atan(1000))
 7  document.writeln("<BR>Math.atan(-1000) = " + Math.atan(-1000))
 8  if(isNaN(Math.atan(1E10)))
 9     document.writeln("<BR>Math.atan(1E10) = NaN")
10  else
11     document.writeln("<BR>Math.atan(" + 1E10 + ") = " + Math.atan
       (1E10))
12  </SCRIPT>
13  </BODY>
14  </HTML>
```

#  atan2(*xCoordinate, yCoordinate*)

| | |
|---|---|
| **Action** | Returns the angle ($\theta$) of the polar coordinate ($r$, $\theta$) that corresponds to the specified Cartesian coordinates (*xCoordinate, yCoordinate*) |
| **Syntax** | *Math.atan2(xCoordinate, yCoordinate)* |
| **Arguments** | *xCoordinate* is a number, an expression that evaluates to a number, or a property that is a number that represent the x Cartesian coordinate. |
| | *yCoordinate* is a number, an expression that evaluates to a number, or a property that is a number that represent the *y* Cartesian coordinate. |
| **Method of** | Math |
| **See also** | **Functions:** isNaN() |
| | **Methods:** acos(), asin(), atan(), cos(), sin(), tan() |

## Discussion

A pair of numbers can represent a point on a Cartesian plane. The pair of numbers are called the *x* and *y* coordinates of the point. The distance of the point from the origin is the radius (*r*) value of the point, and the angle that a line through the origin and the point forms with the x-axis is called θ. Given *x,y* coordinates, atan2() returns θ. This function is useful in drawing and graphing.

The return value of atan() is between 0 and PI.

## Examples

Listing 8.6 demonstrate the use of atan2(). Note the use of:

- isNaN() in line 8 to test the return value of atan()
- E notation to represent large numbers in lines 8, 9, and 11

The results of Listing 8.6 are shown in Figure 8.5. Can you picture the location of the points specified in the calls to atan2() in Listing 8.6?

**LISTING 8.6** Using atan2().

```
1   <HTML>
2   <TITLE>atan2()</TITLE>
3   <BODY>
4   <B>atan2()</B>
5   <SCRIPT LANGUAGE = "JavaScript">
6   document.writeln("<BR> Math.atan2(1,1000) = " +
    Math.atan2(1,1000))
7   document.writeln("<BR>Math.atan2(1,-1000) = " + Math.atan2(1,-
    1000))
8   if(isNaN(Math.atan2(1,1E10)))
9     document.writeln("<BR>Math.atan2(1,1E10) = NaN")
```

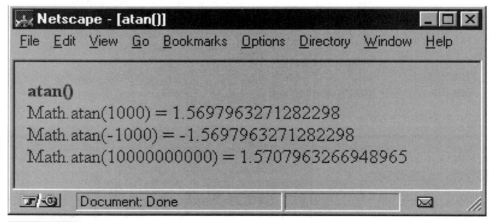

**FIGURE 8.5** Using atan2().

```
10 else
11   document.writeln("<BR>Math.atan2(1," + 1E10 + ") = " +
   Math.atan2(1,1E10))
12 </SCRIPT>
13 </BODY>
14 </HTML>
```

#  back( )

| | |
|---|---|
| **Action** | Loads the previous URL in the history list. |
| **Syntax** | `history.back( )` |
| **Arguments** | None |
| **Method of** | `history` |
| **See also** | **Methods:** `forward( )`, `go( )`. |

## Discussion

This function is equivalent to:

- Clicking on the Back button in the Navigator menubar
- Calling `history.go(-1)`

## Examples

The `<-Back` button in Listing 8.7 takes the user one URL back (where the Navigator was last time).

**LISTING 8.7** Using `back( )`.

```
1   <INPUT  TYPE = "button"
2       VALUE = "<- Back"
3       onClick = "history.back()">
```

# big( )

| | |
|---|---|
| **Action** | Emulates the action of the `<BIG>` HTML tag, enlarging the font of the display string. |

| | |
|---|---|
| **Syntax** | *aString*.big() |
| **Arguments** | None |
| **Method of** | String |
| **See also** | **Methods:** fontsize(), small(), and other String object methods. |

## Discussion

*aString* is a String object. Use the *aString*.big() function to format strings via JavaScript. The way the formatted string looks depends on the operating system on which the Internet browser is running.

## Examples

Listing 8.8 demonstrates the use of big() in an HTML document. It produces the same effect as

```
<BIG>Information != Knowledge</BIG>
```

**LISTING 8.8** Using big().

```
1   aString = new String("Information != Knowledge")
2   document.writeln(aString.big()
```

#  blink()

| | |
|---|---|
| **Action** | Emulates the action of the <BLINK> HTML tag, causing aString to blink. |
| **Syntax** | *aString*.blink() |
| **Arguments** | None |
| **Method of** | String |
| **See also** | **Methods:** bold(), italics(), strike() and other String object methods. |

## Discussion

*aString* is a String object. Use the *aString*.blink() function to make *aString* blink via JavaScript. The rate at which *aString* blinks depends on the user's computer, its operating system, and its current state. For example, low memory and numerous applications running at the same time slow down the blinking rate.

Blinking text can be annoying to your visitor; use it judiciously.

## Examples

Listing 8.9 demonstrates the use of blink() in an HTML document. It produces the same effect as

```
<BLINK>In fact, Information = 1/Knowledge</BLINK>
```

**LISTING 8.9** Using blink().

```
1  aString = new String("In fact, Information = 1/Knowledge")
2  document.writeln(aString.blink()
```

#  blur()

| | |
|---|---|
| **Action** | Removes focus from the object. |
| **Syntax** | objectName.blur() |
| **Arguments** | None |
| **Method of** | frame, password, select, text, textarea, window |
| **See also** | **Methods:** focus(), select() |

## Discussion

Use objectName.blur() to remove focus from a form element. objectName is the value assigned to the NAME attribute of one of the objects listed in **Method of,** or any legitimate reference to that object; for example, instead of writing

```
<FORM NAME = "aForm"> <INPUT TYPE = "text" NAME = "aText" ...
```

and then removing focus from the object with

```
aText.blur()
```

you could write

```
aForm.elements[0].blur()
```

to accomplish the same thing.

You can use `blur()` to removes focus from a `window` or a `frame`. Removing focus sends a window to the background in most windowing systems. For window and frame objects, use the following syntax:

- *frameReference*`.blur()` where *frameReference* is any legal `frame` reference

- *windowReference*`.blur()` where *windowReference* is any legal `window` reference

## Examples

Listing 8.10 demonstrates a specific use of `blur()`. Here, we are interested in allowing the user to switch between fields by a click on the button `Switch fields...` (see Figure 8.6). If you have a form with many fields, and you wish to allow the user to cycle through the fields with a click of the button, instead of having to hit the Tab key, or clicking the mouse in each field, use this approach.

Note the association of `blur()`, `focus()`, and `select()`. To gain a better understanding of what is going on, comment out a pair of functions at a time (for example, comment out lines 14 and 20), and run again. See what you get.

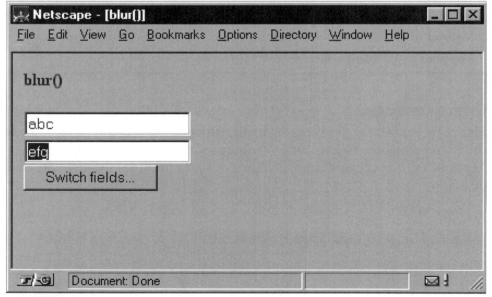

**FIGURE 8.6** Using `blur()`, `focus()`, and `select()`.

**LISTING 8.10** Using `blur()`, `focus()`, and `select()`.

```
1   <HTML>
2   <TITLE>blur()</TITLE>
3   <HEAD>
4   <SCRIPT LANGUAGE = "JavaScript">
5
6   var currentField = " "
7
8   function switchFields(aForm)
9   {
10    alert(currentField)
11    if (currentField == "text1")
12    {
13     aForm.text1.blur()
14     aForm.text2.focus()
15     aForm.text2.select()
16    }
17    else
18    {
19     aForm.text2.blur()
20     aForm.text1.focus()
21     aForm.text1.select()
22    }
23
24    return true
25  }
26  </SCRIPT>
27  </HEAD>
28
29  <BODY>
30  <B>blur()</B>
31  <P>
32  <FORM   NAME = "theForm">
33
34  <INPUT   TYPE = "text"
35       NAME = "text1"
36       onBlur = "currentField = 'text1'">
37  <BR>
38  <INPUT   TYPE = "text"
39          NAME = "text2"
40          onBlur = "currentField = 'text2'">
41  <BR>
42  <INPUT   TYPE = "button"
43          NAME = "button1"
44          VALUE = "Switch fields..."
45          onClick = "switchFields(theForm)">
46  </FORM>
```

```
47 </BODY>
48 </HTML>
```

# bold( )

| | |
|---|---|
| **Action** | Emulates the action of the `<B>` HTML tag, causing `aString` to show in boldface. |
| **Syntax** | `aString.bold()` |
| **Arguments** | None |
| **Method of** | `String` |
| **See also** | **Methods:** `blink()`, `italics()`, `strike()`, and other `String` object methods. |

## Discussion

*aString* is a `String` object. Use the *aString*.bold() function to change the typeface to bold via JavaScript.

## Examples

Listing 8.11 demonstrates the use of bold() in an HTML document. It produces the same effect as

```
<B>The more you know about one thing,
the fewer things you know about</B>
```

**LISTING 8.11** Using bold().

```
1  aString = new String("The more you know about one thing, the
   fewer things you know about")
2  document.writeln(aString.bold()
```

# ceil( *number* )

| | |
|---|---|
| **Action** | Returns the smallest integer greater than or equal to *number*. |
| **Syntax** | `Math.ceil(number)` |
| **Arguments** | *number* is a number, an expression that evaluates to a number, or a property that is a number. |

| | |
|---|---|
| **Method of** | Math |
| **See also** | **Methods:** floor() |

## Discussion

Use ceil() (ceil stands for ceiling) when you wish to round to whole numbers, upward—say, when you calculate a debt owed to you.

## Examples

The following statement will display 77:

```
document.write(Math.ceil(76.00001))
```

while this statement

```
document.write(Math.ceil(-76.00001))
```

will display -76.

#  charAt(*position*)

| | |
|---|---|
| **Action** | Returns the character at *position* in a string. |
| **Syntax** | *aString*.charAt(*position*) |
| **Arguments** | An integer literal, an object's property that holds an integer, or an expression that evaluates to an integer, signifying the desired position of a character in a string. The *position* must be between 0 and *aString*.length - 1. |
| **Method of** | String |
| **See also** | **Methods:** blink(), italics(), strike(), and other String object methods. |

## Discussion

*aString* is a String object. Use the *aString*.charAt(*position*) function to obtain a character at a specified *position* in *aString*. The first character is at position 0 and the last character is at position *aString*.length - 1. If *position* is outside this range, charAt() returns an empty string.

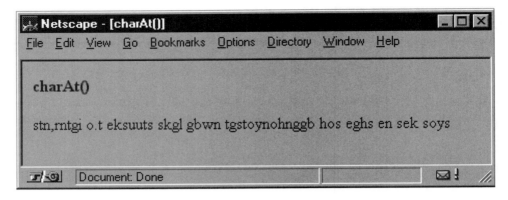

**FIGURE 8.7** Using charAt().

## Examples

Listing 8.12 demonstrates the use of charAt() in an HTML document. In line 8 we assign the string

```
The more things you know about, the less you know about one thing.
```

to aString, and in line 9, initiate position to 0. In line 12 we generate a random number between 0 and the number of characters in the string + 1 (= aString.length). We then take the floor() of this number, and thus assign to position a random number between 0 and aString.length - 1. We then display the randomly drawn character in line 13. The operations of lines 12 and 13 are repeated for the number of characters in aString. Run this example, and then click on the Navigator reload button many times to see what you get. One realization of these runs is shown in Figure 8.7.

**LISTING 8.12** Using charAt().

```
1   <HTML>
2   <TITLE>charAt()</TITLE>
3
4   <BODY>
5   <B>charAt()</B>
6   <P>
7   <SCRIPT LANGUAGE = "JavaScript">
8   var aString = new String("The more things you know about, the
    less you know about one thing.")
9   var position = 0
10  for (var i = 0; i < aString.length; i++)
```

```
11 {
12    position = Math.floor(aString.length * Math.random())
13    document.write(aString.charAt(position))
14 }
15 </SCRIPT>
16 </BODY>
17 </HTML>
```

#  clearTimeout(*idFrom _set Timeout*)

| | |
|---|---|
| **Action** | Cancels a time-out that was set with a previous call to setTimeout(). |
| **Syntax** | clearTimeout(*idFrom_setTimeout*) |
| **Arguments** | *idFrom_setTimeout* is an integer that was returned from the last call to setTimeout(). |
| **Method of** | frame, window |
| **See also** | **Methods:** setTimeout() |

## Discussion

Use clearTimeout() to cancel the action of setTimeout().

## Examples

Listing 8.13 demonstrates the dual interaction between setTimeout() and clearTimeout(). The example also demonstrates how to change a button's face (VALUE) via JavaScript. In line 5 we assign 1 to the toAlert global variable. This variable controls the switching between the alert and cancel-alert "modes." In lines 31 to 34 we set up the alertButton, and its initial VALUE (to Alert...). In line 34 we call displayAlert() when the button is clicked.

In displayAlert() we first increment toAlert by 1 (line 9), and then check to see if it is even (line 10). If it is, we change the alertButton button's value (note the use of the elements array) to Cancel alert, and then set the time-out to 3000 milliseconds (see setTimeout() for further details about this function). When the user returns from the alert window, we also change the alertButton's value (line 13).

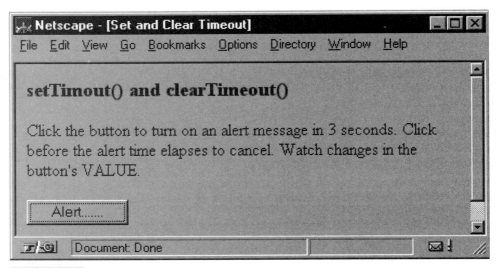

**FIGURE 8.8** Using `setTimeout()` and `clearTimeout()`.

If the `toAlert` switch is odd, we clear the time-out (line 17) and change the button's value to `Alert....` Figure 8.8 shows the window ready to accept the alert. When you click on it, the button's face should change to `Cancel alert`. Try it. As an exercise, move back and forth between `Alert` and `Cancel alert` a few times. Notice that sometimes you need to click on `Alert...` twice before activating `setTimeout()`. Why? Can you think of a way to fix the problem?

Use this approach in your work when you wish to set up a single button to do more than one task (changing a button's value in JavaScript), and when you wish to set aside periodic tasks (using the pair of time-out functions).

**LISTING 8.13** Using `setTimeout()` and `clearTimeout()`.

```
1   <HTML>
2   <HEAD><TITLE>Set and Clear Timeout</TITLE>
3   <SCRIPT LANGUAGE = "JavaScript">
4
5   var toAlert = 1
6
7   function displayAlert()
8   {
9     toAlert++
10    if ((toAlert % 2) == 0)
```

```
11   {
12     document.forms[0].elements[0].value = 'Cancel alert'
13     timerID = setTimeout('alert("3 seconds
   alert.");document.forms[0].elements[0].value = "Alert...
   "',3000)
14   }
15   else
16   {
17     clearTimeout(timerID)
18     document.forms[0].elements[0].value = 'Alert.......'
19   }
20 }
21 </SCRIPT>
22 </HEAD>
23
24 <BODY>
25 <H3>setTimout() and clearTimeout()</H3>
26 <FORM NAME = "timeout">
27 Click the button to turn on an alert message in 3
28 seconds. Click before the alert time elapses to cancel.
29 Watch changes in the button's VALUE.
30 <P>
31 <INPUT   TYPE = "button"
32          VALUE = "Alert...      "
33          NAME = "alertButton"
34          onClick = "displayAlert()">
35 </FORM>
36 </BODY>
37 </HTML>
```

#  click()

| | |
|---|---|
| **Action** | Simulates a mouse click on the calling event. |
| **Syntax** | *objectName*.click() or, for radio button, *objectName*[*i*].click() (see **Discussion** for further details). |
| **Arguments** | None |
| **Method of** | button, checkbox, radio, reset, submit |
| **See also** | |

## Discussion

In calling click(), *objectName* represents one of the following:

- For a `button`, `reset`, or `submit` object—the value of the NAME attribute of the object or an element in the `elements` array that refers to the object on a form.

- For a `radio` button—the value of the NAME attribute of the object or an element in the `elements` array; *i* is an integer representing a `radio` button in the radio object.

- For a `checkbox`—either the value of the NAME attribute of the `checkbox` object or an element in the `elements` array of a form in which the `checkbox` object resides.

The effect of `click()` varies according to the calling object as follows:

- For `button`, `reset`, and `submit`—simulates clicking on the object.

- For `radio`—selects a radio button.

- For `checkbox`—checks the calling `checkbox` and sets its value to on.

## Examples

Listing 8.14 demonstrates `click()` and a few other tricks. Here is what the program does:

- In lines 27 to 47 we create a form named `f`. It has one button (lines 31 to 33) and four radio buttons named `r` (see Figure 8.9) arranged to my order of preference (from total aversion to tolerable).

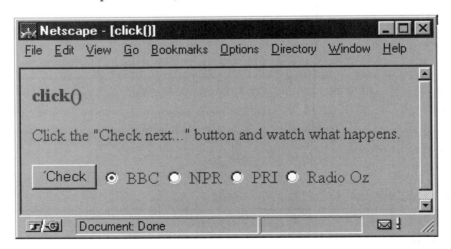

**FIGURE 8.9** Using `click()` and the checked property.

- Each time you click on the button, checkNext() is called. In checkNext() (lines 6 through 21) we cycle through all the radio buttons (line 8); if the last button is checked (line 10), we click() (check) the first button (line 12) and break out of the for loop (line 12).

- If any button other than the last is checked (lines 15 through 19), we click() on the next button (line 17), and break out of the loop (line 18).

Run this example on your own, and see what happens. This example is useful in cases where you wish to allow your user to navigate through fields in a form through button clicks, rather than moving the mouse to a field and clicking on it.

**LISTING 8.14** Using click() and the checked property.

```
1   <HTML>
2   <HEAD><TITLE>click()</TITLE>
3
4   <SCRIPT LANGUAGE = "JavaScript">
5
6   function checkNext()
7   {
8     for (i = 0; i < document.f.r.length; i++)
9     {
10      if (i == document.f.r.length - 1)
11      {
12        document.f.r[0].click()
13        break
14      }
15      if (document.f.r[i].checked == "1")
16      {
17        document.f.r[i+1].click()
18        break
19      }
20    }
21  }
22  </SCRIPT>
23  </HEAD>
24
25  <BODY>
26  <H3>click()</H3>
27  <FORM NAME = "f">
28  Click the "Check next..." button and watch
29  what happens.
30  <P>
31  <INPUT    TYPE = "button"
32            VALUE = 'Check next...'
```

```
33            onClick = "checkNext()">
34  <INPUT   TYPE = "radio"
35            NAME = "r"
36            VALUE = "Radio 1"
37            CHECKED> BBC
38  <INPUT   TYPE = "radio"
39            NAME = "r"
40            VALUE = "Radio 2"> NPR
41  <INPUT   TYPE = "radio"
42            NAME = "r"
43            VALUE = "Radio 3"> PRI
44  <INPUT   TYPE = "radio"
45            NAME = "r"
46            VALUE = "Radio 4"> Radio Oz
47  </FORM>
48  </BODY>
49  </HTML>
```

#  close()

| | |
|---|---|
| **Action** | For a document **object, closes an output stream and forces data sent to layout to display. For a** window **object, closes the window.** |
| **Syntax** | document.close(), windowReference.close() |
| **Arguments** | None |
| **Method of** | document, window |
| **See also** | **Methods:** open(), write(), writeln(). |

## Discussion

In the programming vernacular, a stream represents a flow of data. You put data in a stream's buffer, and the stream moves it somewhere. An input stream moves data from an input device (e.g., keyboard) to somewhere (to memory for example). An output stream moves data from somewhere (say memory) to an output device (e.g., screen). In JavaScript, an output "device" is usually the Navigator window. Data, however, are not written (or drawn) directly to the window, they are written to a document that resides inside a window. Thus, to see data on the screen, JavaScript uses output streams that direct data to a document. To see all of the data that are waiting in a stream's buffer, the stream's buffer must be flushed; in other words, the buffer's content must be emptied to the document. Thus, the effects of document.close() and window.close() are different.

`document.close()` pairs with `document.open()`. Here are the effects of `document.close()`:

- It closes a stream opened by `document.open()`.
- It forces the stream to be displayed.
- It stops the "meteor shower" in the Netscape icon.
- It displays `Document: Done` in the status bar.

The effects of `window.close()` are different from those of `document.close()`. If you want to close a window via an event handler, you must specify `window.close()` instead of simply using `close()`; otherwise, `document.close()` will be executed. `windowReference.close()` pairs with `windowReference.open()`.

When using `window.close()`, keep these points in mind:

- The object `windowReference` is any legitimate `window` reference (variable, `this`, `self`, etc.; see `window` object).
- The close method closes the `windowReference` window.
- You must call `close()` with `windowReference`; otherwise, JavaScript closes the current document.
- `close()` closes only windows opened by JavaScript using `open()`. If you attempt to close any other window, a `confirm()` is generated, which lets the user choose whether the window closes.
- If the `window` has only one `document` in its session history, then `close()` is allowed without `confirm()`.

## Examples

Listing 8.15 demonstrates the use of `open()` and `close()` for both the `window` and `document` objects. Let's see what the program does.

In line 6 we declare `aWindow` variable, which becomes a window reference in line 10 (by virtue of opening a `window` and assigning the object to it; remember the idea of dynamic binding discussed in Chapter 1? Here it is at work). The `Open...` button (see Figure 8.10) calls `openWinAndDoc()`, which in turn:

- opens a `window` (line 10; see also Figure 8.11)
- assigns a string literal to `aString` (lines 12 and 13)
- opens a `document` and writes `aString` to it (lines 15 and 16)

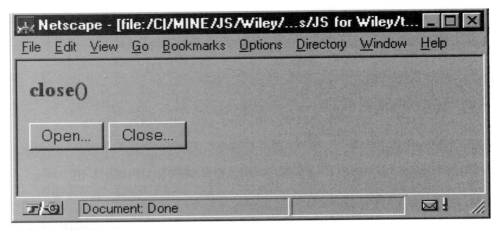

**FIGURE 8.10** Using open() and close().

- closes the document (line 17) and returns to the original window (line 18)

A click on the Close... button closes aWindow (line 32). Note that we specify aWindow.close() in the onClick event handler (line 32). If we just type close(), the current document, not aWindow, will be closed.

Use this example as a template for programmatically opening windows, writing to them, and communicating among windows.

Incidentally, the phrase written to the window (lines 12 and 13 in Listing 8.15) is the third in a sequence. The first was given in Listing 8.11, and the second in Listing 8.12.

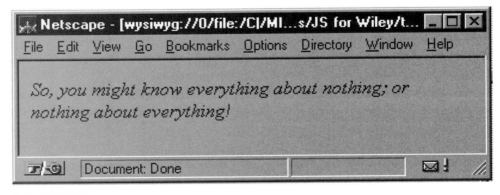

**FIGURE 8.11** Using open() and close().

**LISTING 8.15** Using open() and close().

```
1   <HTML>
2   <HEAD>
3   <SCRIPT LANGUAGE = "JavaScript">
4
5
6   var aWindow
7
8   function openWinAndDoc()
9   {
10    aWindow = window.open("","aWindow")
11
12    var aString = "So, you might know everything about nothing;"
13    aString += " or nothing about everything!"
14
15    aWindow.document.open()
16    aWindow.document.write("<I>" + aString + "<\I>")
17    aWindow.document.close()
18    return true
19  }
20
21  </SCRIPT>
22  </HEAD>
23
24  <BODY>
25  <H3>close()</H3>
26  <FORM>
27  <INPUT    TYPE = "button"
28            VALUE = "Open..."
29            onClick = 'openWinAndDoc()'>
30  <INPUT    TYPE = "button"
31            VALUE = "Close..."
32            onClick = 'aWindow.close()'>
33  </FORM>
34  </BODY>
35  </HTML>
```

# confirm([*argument*])

| | |
|---|---|
| **Action** | Displays a Confirm dialog window with a specified message, and OK and Cancel buttons. Returns true if the user clicks OK; false when he clicks Cancel. |
| **Syntax** | confirm(*argument*) |

| | |
|---|---|
| **Arguments** | *argument* can be: |
| | • a string literal, an expression that evaluates to a string, or a string value of a property of an existing object or |
| | • a numerical literal, an expression that evaluate to a number, or a numerical value of a property of an existing object |
| **Method of** | window |
| **See also** | **Methods:** alert(), prompt() |

## Discussion

When this method is called, the user is presented with the confirm dialog window and *argument* is presented to the user. Use this window to allow the user to make binary decisions (true or false). You can then act on the decision based on the method's return value.

If no argument is specified, the value undefined appears in the window.

## Examples

Listing 8.16 demonstrates the use of confirm() and undo. In lines 25 to 36 we create a form with a text and two button objects (see Figure 8.12). When the user clicks on the Clear... button, areYouSure() is called from line 32.

In areYouSure() (starting at line 8), we first store the string in the text field to the global variable lastString, and then ask the user if she is sure she wants to clear the string in aText (see Figure 8.12). If the answer is yes (that

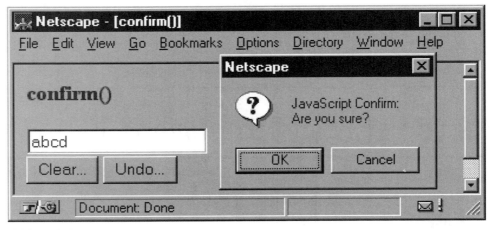

**FIGURE 8.12** Using confirm().

is, if the OK button is clicked), we empty aText. Otherwise, areYouSure() returns. If the user clicks on the Undo... button, the last change is undone by calling undo() from line 35. In undo() we simply reassign the last value of aText back to aText (line 17).

Use Listing 8.16 as a template to implement a confirm window, and also to allow the user to undo the last change.

**LISTING 8.16** Using confirm().

```
1    <HTML>
2    <HEAD>
3    <TITLE>confirm()</TITLE>
4    <SCRIPT LANGUAGE = "JavaScript">
5
6    var lastString = ""
7
8    function areYouSure(aForm)
9    {
10     lastString = aForm.aText.value
11     if (confirm("Are you sure?"))
12       aForm.aText.value = ""
13   }
14
15   function undo(aForm)
16   {
17     aForm.aText.value = lastString
18   }
19
20   </SCRIPT>
21   </HEAD>
22
23   <BODY>
24   <H3>confirm()</H3>
25   <FORM>
26   <INPUT    TYPE = "text"
27            NAME = "aText"
28            VALUE = "Initial value">
29   <BR>
30   <INPUT    TYPE = "button"
31            VALUE = "Clear..."
32            onClick = 'areYouSure(this.form)'>
33   <INPUT    TYPE = "button"
34            VALUE = "Undo..."
35            onClick = 'undo(this.form)'>
36   </FORM>
37   </BODY>
38   </HTML>
```

# cos(angle)

| | |
|---|---|
| **Action** | Returns the cosine of *angle* |
| **Syntax** | `Math.cos(angle)` |
| **Arguments** | *angle* in radians is a number, an expression that evaluates to a number, or a property that is a number. |
| **Method of** | `Math` |
| **See also** | **Methods:** `acos()`, `asin()`, `atan()`, `sin()`, `tan()` |
| | **Properties:** `PI` |

## Discussion

`cos()` returns the cosine value of *angle*. The value is between -1 and 1.

## Examples

Listing 8.17 and Figure 8.13 demonstrate the use of `cos()` and `sin()`. Notice two important points in this example:

- We use the keyword `with` (line 6) to set up an object context (the `Math` object, in this case). This saves typing and avoids common errors.

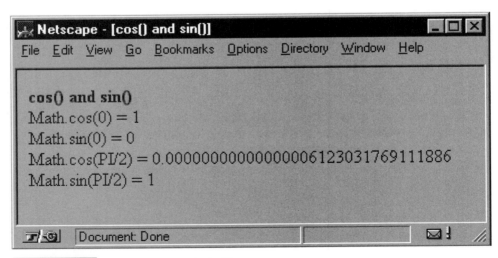

**FIGURE 8.13** Using `cos()` and `sin()`.

- The value of $\cos(PI/2)$ should be 0; yet the returned value is 0.00000000000000006123031769111886. This is because computers always have round-off errors. Keep in mind, then, that computations that should return zero often return a very small number. Thus, in Listing 8.17, the `if` statement in line 10 is evaluated to `false`, and it is the call to `writeln()` in line 13 that is executed, not the call in line 11.

The way to get around the "zero problem" is to set up a global variable in your code like this, for example:

```
zero = 10e-7
```

and then zero-test like this:

```
if (abs(someValue) < zero)
    document.writeln("We have zero, but no lift-off")
```

**LISTING 8.17** Using `cos()` and `sin()`.

```
1   <HTML>
2   <TITLE>cos() and sin()</TITLE>
3   <BODY>
4   <B>cos() and sin()</B>
5   <SCRIPT LANGUAGE = "JavaScript">
6   with (Math)
7   {
8     document.writeln("<BR> Math.cos(0) = " + cos(0))
9     document.writeln("<BR> Math.sin(0) = " + asin(0))
10    if (cos(PI/2) == 0)
11      document.writeln("<BR>Math.cos(PI/2) = 0")
12    else
13      document.writeln("<BR>Math.cos(PI/2) = " + cos(PI/2))
14    document.writeln("<BR>Math.sin(PI/2) = " + sin(PI/2))
15  }
16  </SCRIPT>
17  </BODY>
18  </HTML>
```

 # escape(*aString*)

| | |
|---|---|
| **Action** | Returns the ASCII encoding of a character in the ISO Latin-1 character set. |

| | |
|---|---|
| **Syntax** | `escape(aString)` |
| **Arguments** | `aString` is a string literal, an expression that evaluates to a string, or a property that is a number. |
| **Method of** | None |
| **See also** | **Functions:** `unescape()` |

## Discussion

If you pass `escape()` an alphanumeric character, the function returns the same character. There are other subtleties which are discussed in the example below.

## Examples

Listing 8.18 demonstrates the use of `escape()` and `unescape()`, and Figure 8.14 shows the results. Note the following:

- We build the syntax for `unescape()` in line 12 using ("%" + i), which automatically converts i to a string. (Why? Because "%" is a string.)

- We build the syntax to `escape()` in line 11 as (""+...) in order to convert whatever follows to a string.

- The call to `escape(...unescape(...))` in line 11 should produce the same result as `unescape()` in line 12. It does for some characters, but not for others; why? (Because some characters are non-printable; these are the so-called escape or control characters.)

Use this example to produce characters that you cannot otherwise print on an HTML page. For example, use

```
unescape("%"+99)
```

to produce the character™.

**LISTING 8.18** Using `escape()` and `unescape()`.

```
1   <HTML>
2   <TITLE>ISO Latin-1 ASCII Table</TITLE>
3   <BODY>
4   <B>ISO Latin-1 ASCII Table</B>
5   <P>
6   <SCRIPT LANGUAGE = "JavaScript">
7   document.write("<PRE>Value    unescape()    escape()</PRE?")
```

```
8   for (var i =0; i < 100; i++)
9   {
10    document.writeln("<PRE> " + i +
11    "        " + escape(""+unescape("%"+i)) +
12    "        " + unescape("%"+i) + "</PRE>")
13  }
14  </SCRIPT>
15  </BODY>
16  </HTML>
```

# ⤷ eval(*aString*)

**Action**          Evaluates a string as if it is a JavaScript expression(s) and

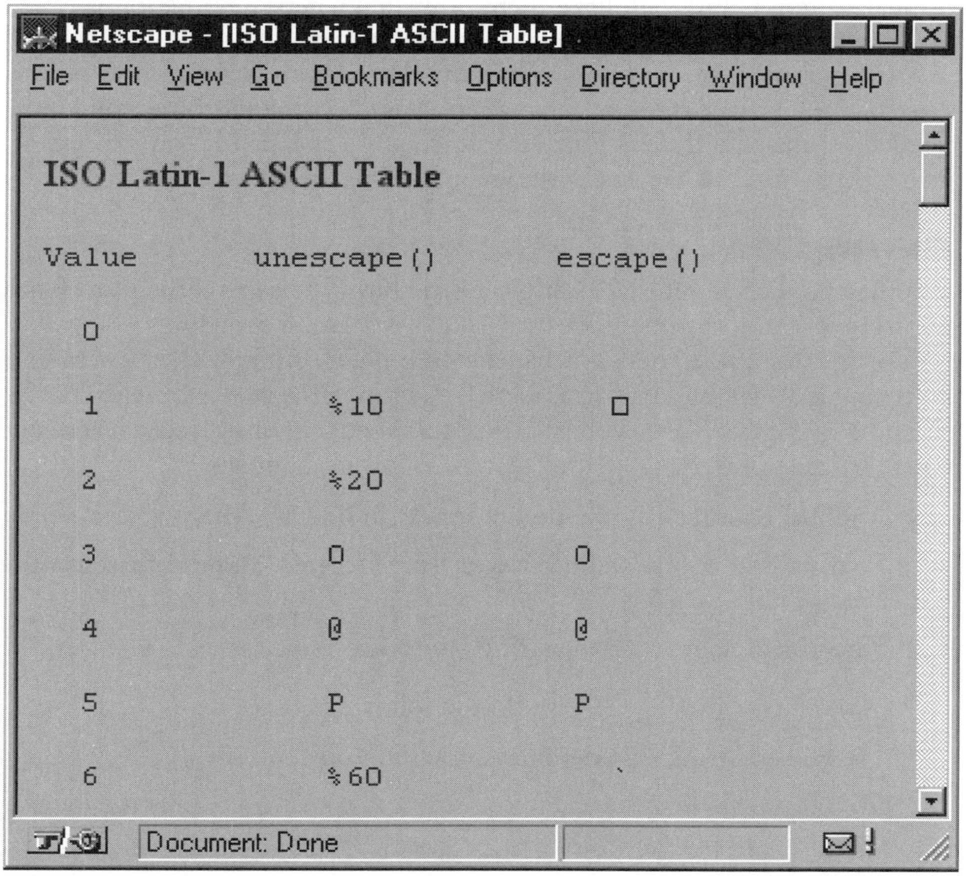

**FIGURE 8.14** Using escape() and unescape().

returns the value.

| | |
|---|---|
| **Syntax** | `eval(aString)` |
| **Arguments** | `aString` is a sequence of one or more JavaScript expressions or statements, identified to `eval()` as a string. The expressions can include variables and properties of existing objects. |
| **Method of** | `None` |
| **See also** | |

## Discussion

`eval()` is useful in cases where you wish to construct evaluation expressions using JavaScript, and then have them evaluated when the function is called. You can implement conditional evaluation this way.

For example, you may have different formulas to calculate the interest rate that you charge different customers. Based on the customer name, you need to evaluate different formulas, then build the evaluation expressions into strings, and call the string that matches the customer.

## Examples

You may ponder about this example a little bit. If it seems difficult to figure out, skip it, and just remember that `eval()` is a useful function.

For the ambitious, here is what the example (Listing 8.19) does. In lines 21 through 30 we build a form, named `f`. It contains two text fields, named `t1` and `t2` (Figure 8.15). When `t1` loses its focus (because you clicked anywhere outside of it, or tabbed to `t2`) the following happens:

- A global counter `i` is pre-iterated by 1 (in line 25, where it says ++i).

- A string that contains the value of `i` pre-iterated, and the current value of `i` is built.

- The object name (`t1`), the string, and `i` are passed to `setValue()`.

In setValue() (lines 8 - 11), we do the following:

- We build a string that denotes the calling object.

- We set the value of the calling object to the string `val` plus the index (`i` or `j`) post-iterated.

- This causes the `val + ij++` (line 10) to be displayed in the appropriate text field.

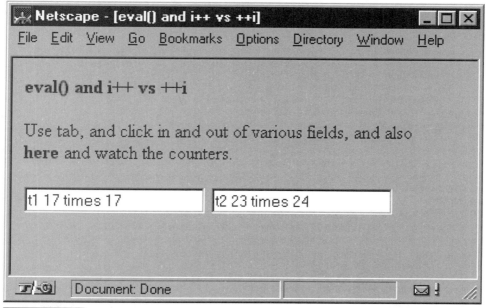

**FIGURE 8.15** Using `eval()` and the difference between i++ and ++i.

In line 28 we do the same thing we did in line 25, except that now we post- (not pre-) iterate j (we write `j++`).

To benefit from this example, run it, and then click in and out of fields, tab among fields, and so on. You will realize that in `t1`, the number of times the field has lost focus and the number of times `setValue()` is called are equal (in Figure 8.15, 17 times). In `t2`, these values differ by 1. Why? Because of the pre- and post-iteration. From this, you should be able to tell when, exactly, the pre- or post-iteration occurs (based on order of preference of JavaScript operators).

Keep your new understanding in mind; it will save you debugging time later. Another useful implementation of this example is to count (behind the scenes) the number of times a certain field in a form, or area in an image, is hit, and collect information about it. This may give you an idea about how to improve the friendliness of your JavaScript application.

Refer to Listing 8.21 and Figure 8.17 for another example of `eval()`.

**LISTING 8.19** Using `eval()` and the difference between i++ and ++i.

```
1   <HTML>
2   <TITLE>eval() and i++ vs ++i</TITLE>
3   <HEAD>
```

```
4   <SCRIPT LANGUAGE = "JavaScript">
5
6   var i = 0, j = 0
7
8   function setValue (obj, val, ij)
9   {
10    eval("document.f." + obj + ".value = val + ij++")
11  }
12  </SCRIPT>
13  </HEAD>
14
15  <BODY>
16  <B>eval() and i++ vs ++i</B>
17  <P>
18  Use tab, and click in and out of various fields,
19  and also <B>here</B> and watch the counters.
20  <P>
21  <FORM NAME = "f">
22  <INPUT    TYPE = "text"
23          NAME = "t1"
24          onBlur =
25                  'setValue(this.name,"t1 " + ++i + " times ",i)'>
26  <INPUT    TYPE = "text"
27          NAME = "t2"
28          onBlur =
29                  'setValue(this.name,"t2 " + j++ + " times ",j)'>
30  </FORM>
31  </BODY>
32  </HTML>
```

 # exp(x)

| | |
|---|---|
| **Action** | Returns $e^x$, where $e$ is Euler's constant, the base of the natural logarithm. |
| **Syntax** | `Math.exp(x)` |
| **Arguments** | $x$ is a number literal, an expression that evaluates to a number, or a value of a property of an existing object that represents a number. |
| **Method of** | `Math` |
| **See also** | **Methods:** `log()`, `pow()`. |

## Discussion

You can use this function as an inverse to `log()`.

## Examples

Listing 8.20 demonstrates the use of `exp()` and its inverse, `log()`. Figure 8.16 shows the results of loading Listing 8.20 to Navigator. Note the following:

- We use the `with` keyword to set the object context to `Math` (line 6).

- We use `E` to represent Euler's constant (line 9).

- When JavaScript encounters a large number (such as $e^{1000}$, line 12), it prints `Infinity`.

**LISTING 8.20** Using `exp()` and `log()`.

```
1  <HTML>
2  <TITLE>exp() and log()</TITLE>
```

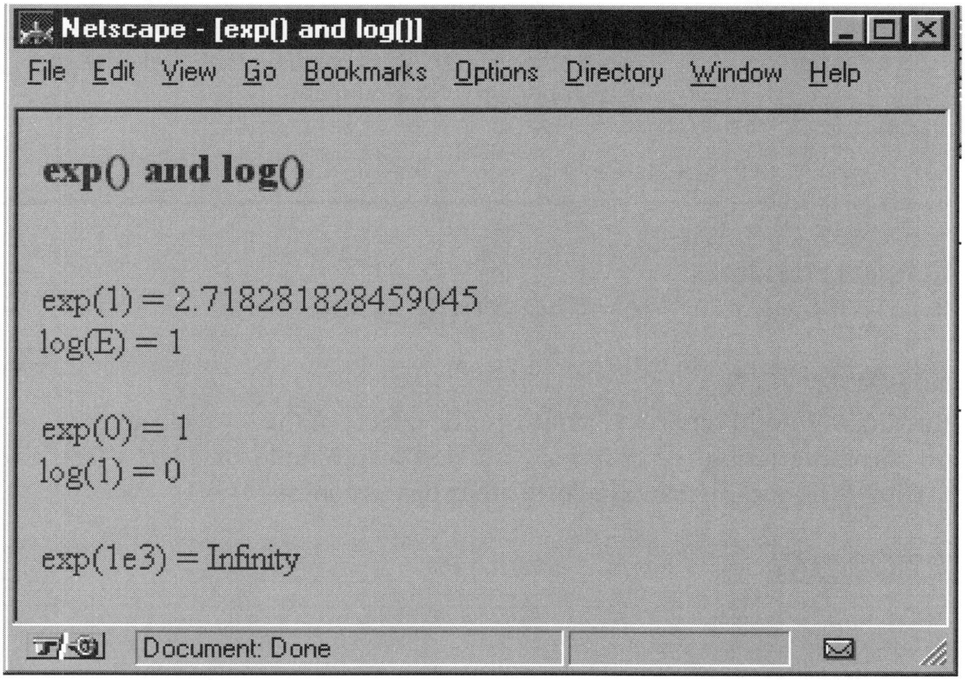

**Netscape - [exp[] and log[]]**

File  Edit  View  Go  Bookmarks  Options  Directory  Window  Help

### exp() and log()

exp(1) = 2.718281828459045
log(E) = 1

exp(0) = 1
log(1) = 0

exp(1e3) = Infinity

Document: Done

**FIGURE 8.16** Using `exp()` and `log()`.

```
3   <BODY>
4   <H3>exp() and log()</H3>
5   <SCRIPT LANGUAGE = "JavaScript">
6   with (Math)
7   {
8     document.write("<BR> exp(1) = " + exp(1))
9     document.write("<BR> log(E) = " + log(E))
10    document.write("<P> exp(0) = " + exp(0))
11    document.write("<BR> log(1) = " + log(1))
12    document.write("<P> exp(1e300) = " + exp(1e300))
13  }
14  </SCRIPT>
15  </BODY>
16  </HTML>
```

#  fixed()

| | |
|---|---|
| **Action** | Causes a string to be displayed in fixed-pitch font. |
| **Syntax** | `aString.fixed()` |
| **Arguments** | `aString` is a string literal, an expression that evaluates to a string, or a property that is a number. |
| **Method of** | `String` |
| **See also** | **Methods:** see `String` methods |

## Discussion

`fixed()` has the same effect as the HTML tag `<TT>`.

## Examples

Listing 8.21 and Figure 8.17 compare the effects of the `<TT>` tag and `fixed()` on the same string. As a bonus, I added an example of `eval()` (see also Listing 8.19 and Figure 8.15 for further discussion of `eval()`).

**LISTING 8.21** Using `fixed()` and `eval()`.

```
1   <HTML>
2   <TITLE>fixed()</TITLE>
3   <BODY>
4   <H3>fixed()</H3>
5   <TT> This is 4</TT> from TT tag<BR>
6   <SCRIPT LANGUAGE = "JavaScript">
```

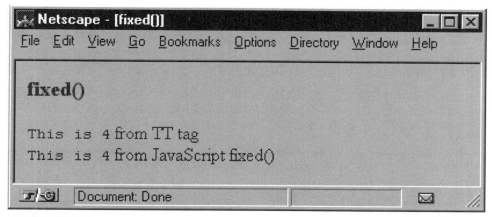

**FIGURE 8.17** Using fixed() and eval().

```
7   var expr = "2 * 2"
8   document.write(("This is " + eval(expr)).fixed() + " from
    JavaScript fixed()")
9   </SCRIPT>
10  </BODY>
11  </HTML>
```

#  floor(*number*)

| | |
|---|---|
| **Action** | Returns the greatest integer less than or equal to *number*. |
| **Syntax** | Math.floor(*number*) |
| **Arguments** | *number* is a number, an expression that evaluates to a number, or a property that is a number. |
| **Method of** | Math |
| **See also** | **Methods:** ceil() |

## Discussion

Use floor() when you wish to round to whole numbers, downward—say, when you calculate your income for tax purposes.

## Examples

The following statement will display 76;

```
document.write(Math.floor(76.999999))
```

while this statement

```
document.write(Math.floor(-76.999999))
```

will display -77.

#  focus()

| | |
|---|---|
| **Action** | Gives focus to a specified object. |
| **Syntax** | objectName.focus() |
| **Arguments** | None |
| **Method of** | frame, password, select, text, textarea, window |
| **See also** | **Methods:** blur(), select() |

## Discussion

Use *objectName*.focus() to give focus to an object. *objectName* is the value assigned to the NAME attribute of one of the objects listed in **Method of**, or any legitimate reference to that object; for example, instead of writing

```
<FORM NAME = "aForm"> <INPUT TYPE = "text" NAME = "aText" ...
```

and then giving focus to the object with

```
aText.focus()
```

you could write

```
aForm.elements[0].focus()
```

to accomplish the same thing.

Also, *frameReference*.focus() or *windowReference*.focus() gives focus to the specified frame or window. For a window object, focus() brings the window forward in most windowing systems.

## Examples

Listing 8.10 and Figure 8.6 demonstrate the interaction among blur(), focus(), and select(); see the example for blur().

#  fontcolor(*color*)

| | |
|---|---|
| **Action** | Emulates the action of the `<FONT COLOR = color>` HTML tag, endowing the display string with *color*. |
| **Syntax** | *aString*.fontcolor(*color*) |
| **Arguments** | *color* is either a literal color name or a hexadecimal value of color in RGB (see Appendix C). |
| **Method of** | String |
| **See also** | **Methods:** see other String object methods. |

## Discussion

Both the HTML syntax `<FONT COLOR = ...>` and the font color set by `font-color()` override the value of the `document.fgColor` property. The RGB color format is a triplet of hexadecimal values given as RRGGBB, where RR is the value of red, GG is green, and BB is blue. For example, the value of light-steel blue is `B0C4DE`, where `B0` is the value of red, `C4` the value of green, and `DE` the value blue. Appendix C lists the values of all color literals, along with their RGB color constants. You may use the RGB mix to create your own colors.

## Examples

Listing 8.22 demonstrates the use of `fontcolor()` in an HTML document, and Figure 8.18 shows the results of one run. The program generates a sequence of random characters, each colored with a random RGB color. There are several interesting ideas here, so let us discuss them in some detail. Because some of the functions in the listing are useful for other purposes, they are included in the file `commonf.js` (included in the accompanying CD); below, I discuss these individually.

- `randomInteger(n1, n2)`—This function (lines 6 to 17) takes two numbers, *n1* and *n2*—these can be integers (numbers with no decimal point) or real numbers (numbers that include a decimal point)—and returns a random integer between *n1* and *n2*. To return an integer, we add to `floor(n1)` a random number in the range of `floor(n2) - floor(n1)` (lines 13 and 14) and return the generated value (line 16). The function `randomInteger()` is included in the utility file `commonf.js`.

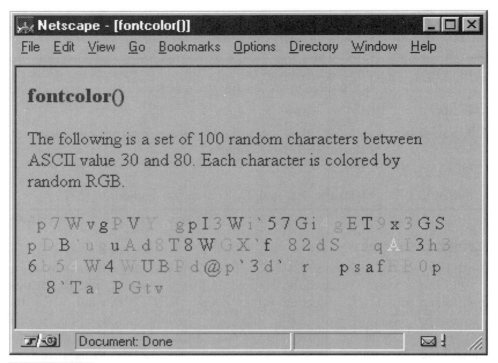

The image shows a Netscape browser window titled "Netscape - [fontcolor()]" with menu items: File, Edit, View, Go, Bookmarks, Options, Directory, Window, Help.

**fontcolor()**

The following is a set of 100 random characters between ASCII value 30 and 80. Each character is colored by random RGB.

p7WvgPVY gpI3Wi`57Gi gET9x3GS
pDB`u u Ad8T8WGX`f 82dS qAI3h3
6b54W4WUBPd@p`3d` r psaf 0p
8`Ta PGtv

Document: Done

**FIGURE 8.18** Using fontcolor() with random color generator.

- decimalToHexString(*decNumber*)—This function (lines 19 to 35) takes a *decNumber* between 0 and 255 decimal and returns its value as a two-character hexadecimal string. For example, the number 255 is returned as the string FF, while decimal 10 is returned as the string 0A. "Why do I need this function?" you may ask. Well, wait until you need to generate a hex number such as ABBCF0 as a string to specify an RGB color. Now here is what we do in this function: We convert *decNumber* to a hex string using toString() (see the reference to this function in this chapter) and then test to see how many digits we have in the string (line 25). If the generated hex string has one digit, we pre-pad it with "0" and assign the result to hexString (line 26). If the generated string has two characters (line 27), we just assign the string to hexString. If we get something else, we alert the user that there is an error (line 31) and return "error"; otherwise we return hexString. The function is included in the utility file commonf.js.

- makeRGB(*r*, *g*, *b*)—This function converts its arguments to the hex string that is required to specify an RGB color: *r* specifies the level of red; *g* specifies the level of green; and *b* specifies the level of blue (all in the range of 0 to 255 decimal). The function returns the necessary string. The function is included in the utility file `commonf.js`.

- In lines 63 to 71 we generate the random color (lines 65 to 68) and the random character `aChar` (line 69); and finally we write the character to the document (line 70).

- Note the use of `unescape()` in line 69 to generate a random character whose ASCII value is between 30 and 80.

As an exercise, change line 4 in Listing 8.22 to read

```
<SCRIPT LANGUAGE = "JavaScript" SRC = "commonf.js">
```

and delete lines 5 through 51 and run the code again. Before running, make sure that the file `commonf.js` is in the same directory from which you load Listing 8.22. You should see the same generic results (you will not see the same letters and characters). I will show you later—in the **Examples** for `random()`—how to generate a repeating sequence of pseudo-random numbers.

**LISTING 8.22** Using `fontcolor()` with random color generator.

```
1    <HTML>
2    <TITLE>fontcolor()</TITLE>
3    <HEAD>
4    <SCRIPT LANGUAGE = "JavaScript">
5
6    //Returns a random integer between
7    //the floor of n1 and floor of n2
8    function randomInteger(n1, n2)
9    {
10     var returnValue
11     with (Math)
12     {
13      returnValue = floor(n1) +
14        floor( (floor(n2) - floor(n1)) * random() )
15     }
16     return returnValue
17   }
18
19   //Converts decNumber to hex string
20   //decNumber must be between 0 and 255
21   function decimalToHexString(decNumber)
22   {
23     var hexString
```

```
24
25   if ((decNumber.toString(16)).length == 1)
26    hexString = "0" + decNumber.toString(16)
27   else if ((decNumber.toString(16)).length == 2)
28    hexString = decNumber.toString(16)
29   else
30   {
31    alert("Value of decimal number must be between 0 and 255")
32    return "error"
33   }
34   return hexString
35 }
36
37 function makeRGB(r, g, b)
38 {
39   var rr, bb, cc
40
41   rr = decimalToHexStringÆ
42   if (rr == "error")
43    return "error"
44   gg = decimalToHexString(g)
45   if (gg == "error")
46    return "error"
47   bb = decimalToHexString(b)
48   if (bb == "error")
49    return "error"
50   return rr + gg + bb
51 }
52 </SCRIPT>
53 </HEAD>
54
55 <BODY>
56 <H3>fontcolor()</H3>
57 The following is a set of 100 random characters
58 between ASCII value 30 and 80. Each character is
59 colored by random RGB.
60 <P>
61 <SCRIPT LANGUAGE = "JavaScript">
62 var r, g, b, rgb, aChar
63 for(var i = 0; i < 100; i++)
64 {
65   r = randomInteger(0,255)
66   g = randomInteger(0,255)
67   b = randomInteger(0,255)
68   rgb = makeRGB(r, g, b)
69   aChar = unescape("%"+randomInteger(30,80))
70   document.writeln(aChar.fontcolor(rgb))
```

```
71  }
72  </SCRIPT>
73  </BODY>
74  </HTML>
```

#  fontsize( *integer* )

| | |
|---|---|
| **Action** | Causes a string to be displayed in the font size specified in *integer*. |
| **Syntax** | aString.fontsize( *integer* ) |
| **Arguments** | *integer* is a literal integer, a string that represents an integer, an expression that evaluates to an integer, or a value of a property of an existing object that is an integer. The integer must range from 1 to 7. |
| **Method of** | String |
| **See also** | **Methods:** big( ), small( ) and other String object methods |

## Discussion

*aString* is a String object. Use fontsize( ) to format strings via JavaScript. The way the formatted string looks depends on the operating system on which the Internet browser is running. The effect of fontsize( ) is the same as that of the HTML tag <FONTSIZE = *integer*>.

If you call fontsize( ) with an argument as integer string, you can use the "+" and "-" signs to adjust the font size relative to the font size set in the <BASEFONT> HTML tag. For example

```
document.write(("No harm intended").fontsize("+2")
document.write(("So don't take jokes seriously").fontsize("-2")
```

will print No harm intended two sizes larger than the current font, and So don't take jokes seriously two sizes smaller than the current font.

## Examples

Listing 8.23 and Figure 8.19 demonstrate one potential use of fontsize( ).

**FIGURE 8.19** Using fontsize().

**LISTING 8.23** Using fontsize().

```
1  <HTML>
2  <TITLE>fontsize()</TITLE>
3
4  <BODY>
5  <H3>fontsize()</H3>
6  <SCRIPT LANGUAGE = "JavaScript">
7  document.write(("<CENTER>Angel hair").fontsize(1))
8  document.write("<BR>" + ("spaghetti").fontsize(3))
9  document.write("<BR>" + ("Fetucinni").fontsize(5))
10 document.write("<BR>" + ("Manicotti").fontsize(7))
11 </SCRIPT>
12 </BODY>
13 </HTML>
```

#  forward()

| | |
|---|---|
| **Action** | Loads the next URL in the history list. |
| **Syntax** | history.forward() |
| **Arguments** | None |

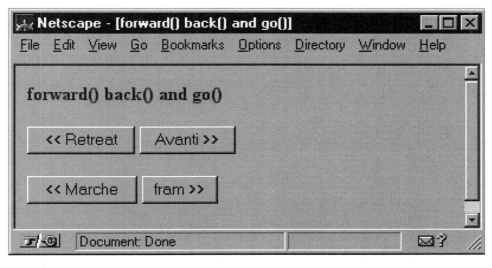

**FIGURE 8.20** Using `back()`, `forward()`, and `go()`.

| | |
|---|---|
| **Method of** | `history` |
| **See also** | **Methods:** `back()`, `go()`. |

## Discussion

`forward()` emulates the action of the `Forward` button in Navigator. Its action is equivalent to `history.go(1)`.

## Examples

Listing 8.24 and Figure 8.20 demonstrate the use of the navigation functions `back()`, `forward()`, and `go()`. The words that appear on the buttons are in English, Italian, French, and Swedish (there is no confusion with the direction of the arrows!).

**LISTING 8.24** Using `back()`, `forward()`, and `go()`.

```
1   <HTML>
2   <TITLE>forward() back() and go()</TITLE>
3   <BODY>
4   <B>forward() back() and go()</B>
5   <P>
6   <FORM>
7   <INPUT TYPE = "button" VALUE = "<< Retreat"
```

```
8    onClick = "history.back()">
9  <INPUT TYPE = "button" VALUE = "Avanti >>"
10   onClick = "history.forward()">
11 <P><INPUT TYPE = "button" VALUE = "<< Marche"
12   onClick = "history.go(-1)">
13 <INPUT TYPE = "button" VALUE = "fram >>"
14   onClick = "history.go(2)">
15 </FORM>
16 </BODY>
17 </HTML>
```

#  getDate()

| | |
|---|---|
| **Action** | Returns the day of the month for the date stored in the `dateObjectName` **date object** |
| **Syntax** | `dateObjectName.getDate()` |
| **Arguments** | None |
| **Method of** | `Date` |
| **See also** | **Methods:** `setDate()` |

## Discussion

`dateObjectName` is either the name of a `Date` object or a date property of an existing object. `getDate()` returns an integer between 1 and 31. For example, if `theDate` stores the date 1/2/2000, then `theDate.getDate()` returns 2.

## Examples

Listing 8.25 and Figure 8.21 demonstrate the use of the following `Date` functions (in order of appearance): `getDay()`, `getMonth()`, `getDate()`, `getYear()`, `getHours()`, `getMinutes()`, and `getSeconds()`. Also demonstrated are the `Date` constructor `new Date()` (line 20), and the construction of arrays. Note the use of `eval()` in line 25.

**LISTING 8.25** Using `Date` methods.

```
1   <HTML>
2   <HEAD><TITLE>Date Methods</TITLE>
3
4   <SCRIPT LANGUAGE = "JavaScript">
5   weekDay = new Array("Sunday", "Monday", "Tuesday",
```

```
 6      "Wednesday", "Thursday", "Friday", "Saturday")
 7   month = new Array("Jan.", "Feb.", "Mar.", "Apr.",
 8      "May", "June", "July", "Aug.", "Sep.", "Oct.",
 9      "Nov.", "Dec")
10   </SCRIPT>
11   </HEAD>
12
13   <BODY>
14   <B>Date Methods</B>
15   <P>
16   According to your system clock, this window
17   was loaded at:
18   <P>
19   <SCRIPT LANGUAGE = "JavaScript">
20   today = new Date()
21   document.write(weekDay[today.getDay()] + ", ")
22   document.write(month[today.getMonth()] + " ")
23   document.write(today.getDate()+ " ")
24   document.write("In the year" +
25      eval(1900 + today.getYear()))
26   document.write("<BR>at" + today.getHours() + ":")
27   document.write(today.getMinutes() + ":")
28   document.write(today.getSeconds())
29   </SCRIPT>
30   </BODY>
31   </HTML>
```

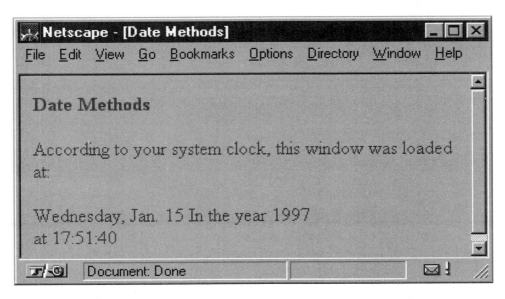

**FIGURE 8.21** Using Date methods.

# getDay()

| | |
|---|---|
| **Action** | Returns the day of the week stored in the `dateObjectName` date object. |
| **Syntax** | `dateObjectName.getDay()` |
| **Arguments** | None |
| **Method of** | `Date` |
| **See also** | See `Date` methods |

## Discussion

`dateObjectName` is either the name of a `Date` object or a date property of an existing object. `getDay()` returns an integer day of the week between 0 (Sunday) and 6 (Saturday).

### Examples

Listing 8.25 and Figure 8.21 demonstrate the use of the following Date functions (in order of appearance): `getDay()`, `getMonth()`, `getDate()`, `getYear()`, `getHours()`, `getMinutes()`, and `getSeconds()`. Also demonstrated are the `Date` constructor `new Date()` (line 20), and the construction of arrays.

# getHours()

| | |
|---|---|
| **Action** | Returns the hour for the day of the date stored in the `dateObjectName` date object |
| **Syntax** | `dateObjectName.getHours()` |
| **Arguments** | None |
| **Method of** | `Date` |
| **See also** | See `Date` methods |

## Discussion

`dateObjectName` is either the name of a `Date` object or a date property of an existing object. `getHours()` returns an integer value between 0 and 23.

## Examples

Listing 8.25 and Figure 8.21 demonstrate the use of the following Date functions (in order of appearance): getDay(), getMonth(), getDate(), getYear(), getHours(), getMinutes(), and getSeconds(). Also demonstrated are the Date constructor new Date() (line 20), and the construction of arrays.

 # getMinutes()

| | |
|---|---|
| **Action** | Returns the minutes stored in the dateObjectName date object. |
| **Syntax** | *dateObjectName*.getMinutes() |
| **Arguments** | None |
| **Method of** | Date |
| **See also** | See Date methods |

## Discussion

dateObjectName is either the name of a Date object or a date property of an existing object. getMinutes() returns an integer value between 0 and 59.

## Examples

Listing 8.25 and Figure 8.21 demonstrate the use of the following Date functions (in order of appearance): getDay(), getMonth(), getDate(), getYear(), getHours(), getMinutes(), and getSeconds(). Also demonstrated are the Date constructor new Date() (line 20), and the construction of arrays.

 # getMonth()

| | |
|---|---|
| **Action** | Returns the month stored in the dateObjectName date object. |
| **Syntax** | *dateObjectName*.getMonth() |
| **Arguments** | None |
| **Method of** | Date |
| **See also** | See Date methods |

## Discussion

*dateObjectName* is either the name of a Date object or a date property of an existing object. getMonth() returns an integer value between 0 (January) and 11 (December).

## Examples

Listing 8.25 and Figure 8.21 demonstrate the use of the following Date functions (in order of appearance): getDay(), getMonth(), getDate(), getYear(), getHours(), getMinutes(), and getSeconds(). Also demonstrated are the Date constructor new Date() (line 20), and the construction of arrays.

 # getSeconds()

| | |
|---|---|
| **Action** | Returns the seconds stored in the *dateObjectName* date object. |
| **Syntax** | *dateObjectName*.getSeconds() |
| **Arguments** | None |
| **Method of** | Date |
| **See also** | See Date methods |

## Discussion

*dateObjectName* is either the name of a Date object or a date property of an existing object. getSeconds() returns an integer value between 0 and 59.

## Examples

Listing 8.25 and Figure 8.21 demonstrate the use of the following Date functions (in order of appearance): getDay(), getMonth(), getDate(), getYear(), getHours(), getMinutes(), and getSeconds(). Also demonstrated are the Date constructor new Date() (line 20), and the construction of arrays.

 # getTime()

| | |
|---|---|
| **Action** | Returns the numeric value corresponding to the time stored in the *dateObjectName* date object. |

| | |
|---|---|
| **Syntax** | *dateObjectName*.getTime() |
| **Arguments** | None |
| **Method of** | Date |
| **See also** | See Date methods |

## Discussion

*dateObjectName* is either the name of a Date object or a date property of an existing object. getTime() returns the number of milliseconds since 1 January 1970 00:00:00. Use this method for date arithmetic and value assignment to variables, properties, and objects (where appropriate).

## Examples

See Listing 8.26.

**LISTING 8.26** Using getTime() and setTime().

```
1   aDate = new Date("August 18, 2000")
2   newDate = new Date() //initializes newDate as a Date object and
    stores the current system date and time in newDate
3   newDate.setTime(aDate.getTime())
```

#  getTimezoneOffset()

| | |
|---|---|
| **Action** | Returns the time zone offset in minutes for the locale recognized by the operating system. |
| **Syntax** | *dateObjectName*.getTimezoneOffset() |
| **Arguments** | None |
| **Method of** | Date |
| **See also** | See Date methods |

## Discussion

*dateObjectName* is either the name of a Date object or a date property of an existing object. getTimezoneOffset() returns the difference between the system's time zone and GMT. Daylight savings time is taken into account.

Use getTimezoneOffset() to standardize time calculations when needed.

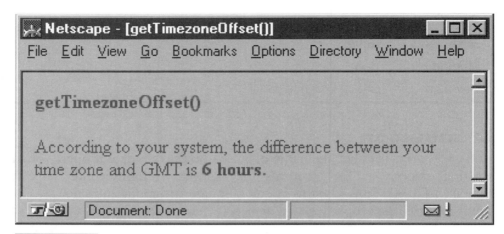

**FIGURE 8.22** Using getTimezoneOffset().

## Examples

Listing 8.27 and Figure 8.22 demonstrate a simple use of getTimezoneOffset().

**LISTING 8.27** Using getTimezoneOffset().

```
1   <HTML>
2   <TITLE>getTimezoneOffset()</TITLE>
3
4   <BODY>
5   <B>getTimezoneOffset()</B>
6   <P>
7   According to your system, the difference
8   between your time zone and GMT is <B>
9   <SCRIPT LANGUAGE = "JavaScript">
10  today = new Date()
11  document.write(today.getTimezoneOffset()/60)
12  </SCRIPT>
13  hours. </B>
14  </BODY>
15  </HTML>
```

 # getYear( )

| | |
|---|---|
| **Action** | Returns the year stored in the *dateObjectName* date object. |
| **Syntax** | *dateObjectName*.getYear() |

| | |
|---|---|
| **Arguments** | None |
| **Method of** | Date |
| **See also** | See Date methods |

## Discussion

*dateObjectName* is either the name of a Date object or a date property of an existing object. getYear() returns an integer value that represents the difference between the current year and 1900 (for 1998 it returns 98). If you wish to deal with dates for the year 2000 and beyond, specify four digits for the year in your date object. For example

```
future = new Date (2001, 01, 02)
aYear = future.getYear()
```

stores 2001 in aYear, while

```
present = new Date (1997, 01, 02)
aYear = present.getYear()
```

stores 97 in aYear. This was confusing to me when I first realized it!

## Examples

Listing 8.25 and Figure 8.21 demonstrate the use of the following Date functions (in order of appearance): getDay(), getMonth(), getDate(), getYear(), getHours(), getMinutes(), and getSeconds(). Also demonstrated are the Date constructor new Date() (line 20), and the construction of arrays.

 # go(*relativePosition* | "*url*")

| | |
|---|---|
| **Action** | Loads a URL from the history list. |
| **Syntax** | history.go(*relativePosition* | "*url*") |
| **Arguments** | *relativePosition* is an integer, an expression that evaluates to an integer, or an integer value of a property of an existing object. |
| | *url* is a string, an expression that evaluates to a string, or a |

string value of a property of an existing object that represents all or part of a URL in the history list.

| | |
|---|---|
| **Method of** | history |
| **See also** | **Methods:** back(), forward() |
| | **Objects:** location |

## Discussion

*relativePosition* can be a positive or a negative integer; it specifies how many locations to jump forwards or backwards, respectively. go(0) reloads the current page. *url* is a string that specifies all or part of a URL in the history list. Matching is case sensitive. The first URL in the history list that matches *url* is loaded. See the **Discussion** section of the location object in Chapter 7.

## Examples

Listing 8.24 and Figure 8.20 also demonstrate the use of the navigation functions back() and forward().

#  indexOf(*searchForString* [, *startFrom*])

| | |
|---|---|
| **Action** | Returns the index within the calling string object of the first occurrence of the specified value, starting the search at *startFrom*. |
| **Syntax** | *aString*.indexOf(*searchForString* [, *startFrom*]) |
| **Arguments** | *searchForString* is the string to search for; it can be a String object, a string literal, an expression that evaluates to a string, or a string value of a property of an existing object. |
| | *startFrom* determines the index in *aString* from which to start the search; it can be an integer literal, an expression that evaluates to an integer, or an integer value of a property of an existing object. It should be in the range 0 to aString.length - 1. |
| **Method of** | String |
| **See also** | **Methods:** charAt(), lastIndexOf() |

# Discussion

`indexOf()` is, in a sense, the inverse of `lastIndexOf()`. Here are some points to remember when using `indexOf()`:

- Characters in `aString` are indexed from 0 (leftmost) to `aString.length - 1` (rightmost).

- If you omit the *startFrom* argument, the search starts from position 0.

- If *searchForString* is not found, `indexOf()` returns `-1`.

- If you send wrong argument values (say, `startFrom = -1`), the method returns an `undefined` value.

# Examples

One of the problems with `aString.indexOf()` is that it returns an `undefined` value if you send it wrong argument values (say, `startFrom = -10`). Listing 8.28 shows you one potential solution. This example also deals with a variable number of arguments in a function call. Let's see what is going on.

In lines 5 through 25 we define our own `indexOf()`. Because it does not belong to any object, it is a function, and must take `aString` (a `String` object) as one of its arguments. It also needs the string to search for in the second argument (`searchString`), and potentially a starting index for the search (`startFrom`). So we have the following syntax for `indexOf()`:

```
indexOf(aString, searchString[, startFrom])
```

In lines 7 to 23 we deal with the function's arguments:

- If `indexOf()` is called with no arguments, we tell the user that he must specify a string to search, and the function returns `-1` (lines 7–11).

- If `indexOf()` is called with only one argument, we tell the user to specify the string to search for and return `-1` (lines 12–16).

- If `indexOf()` is called with only two arguments, we set `startFrom` to zero (lines 17–18).

- If `startFrom` is not in the appropriate range, we alert the user and return `-1` (lines 19–23).

Finally, if all goes well, we call `aString.indexOf()`. The results of search examples are shown in Figure 8.23. To see why you may want to use this function, modify lines 42, 44, 46, and 48 to call `aString.indexOf()` instead of `indexOf()` and observe the differences in behavior.

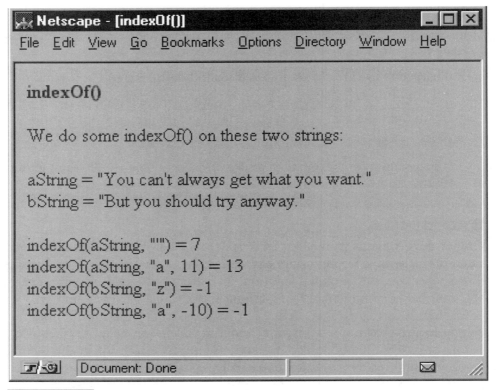

**FIGURE 8.23** Using `indexOf()` and modified `indexOf()`.

One more point about Listing 8.28: Take a look at line 41; we must use the pair \' to search for the single-quote character in bString.

For defensive programming, use this function, instead of *aString*.indexOf(). This function is included with the file commonf.js; you can use this file as the value for the SRC attribute in the <SCRIPT> tag.

**LISTING 8.28** Using `indexOf()` and modified `indexOf()`.

```
1   <HTML>
2   <HEAD>
3   <TITLE>indexOf()</TITLE>
4   <SCRIPT LANGUAGE = "JavaScript">
5   function indexOf(aString, searchString, startFrom)
6   {
7     if (indexOf.arguments.length < 1)
8     {
9       alert("from indexOf: specify the string to search")
10      return -1
```

```
11    }
12    if (indexOf.arguments.length < 2)
13    {
14     alert("from indexOf: specify a string to search")
15     return -1
16    }
17    if (indexOf.arguments.length < 3)
18     startFrom = 0
19    if (!((startFrom >= 0) && (startFrom < aString.length)))
20    {
21     alert("Wrong string index")
22     return -1
23    }
24     return aString.indexOf(searchString, startFrom)
25 }
26
27
28 </SCRIPT>
29 </HEAD>
30
31 <BODY>
32 <B>indexOf()</B>
33 <P>
34 We do some indexOf() on these two strings:
35 <P>
36 <SCRIPT LANGUAGE = "JavaScript">
37 var aString = "You can't always get what you want."
38 var bString = "But you should try anyway."
39 document.write('aString = "' + aString + '"')
40 document.write('<BR>bString = "' + bString + '"')
41 document.write('<P>indexOf(aString, "\'") = ' +
42    indexOf(aString,"'"))
43 document.write('<BR>indexOf(aString, "a", 11) = ' +
44    indexOf(aString, "a", 11))
45 document.write('<BR>indexOf(bString, "z") = ' +
46    indexOf(bString, "z"))
47 document.write('<BR>indexOf(bString, "a", -10) = ' +
48    indexOf(bString,"a",-10))
49 </SCRIPT>
50 </BODY>
51 </HTML>
```

 # isNaN(*aValue*)

| | |
|---|---|
| **Action** | Returns true if its argument is not a number, false otherwise. |
| **Syntax** | On UNIX: isNaN(*aValue*) |

On other operating systems: isNaN(parseFloat(*aValue*))
or isNaN(parseInt(*aValue*))

| | |
|---|---|
| **Arguments** | *aValue* is any value you wish to test for. |
| **Method of** | None |
| **See also** | **Methods:** parseFloat(), parseInt() |

## Discussion

Because isNaN() does not work as expected on systems other than UNIX, you can call parseInt() and parseFloat() with *aValue*. These return NaN if *aValue* is not a number, and isNaN() will then respond appropriately.

## Examples

Listing 8.29 and Figure 8.24 demonstrate the use of isNaN(). The code is self-explanatory. To see how isNaN() works on your system, remove the // from the beginning of line 11 and reload the list.

**LISTING 8.29** Using isNaN().

```
1    <HTML>
2    <TITLE>isNaN()</TITLE>
3
4    <BODY>
5    <B>isNaN()</B>
6    <P>
```

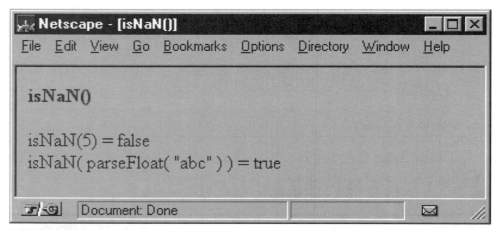

**FIGURE 8.24** Using isNaN().

```
7   <SCRIPT LANGUAGE = "JavaScript">
8   document.write("isNaN(5) = " + isNaN(5))
9   document.write('<BR>isNaN( parseFloat( "abc" ) ) = ' +
10    isNaN(parseFloat("abc")))
11  //document.write('<BR>isNaN( "abc" ) = ' + isNaN("abc"))
12  </SCRIPT>
13  </BODY>
14  </HTML>
```

#  italics()

| | |
|---|---|
| **Action** | Emulates the action of the <I> HTML tag, causing aString to show in italics. |
| **Syntax** | *aString*.italics() |
| **Arguments** | None |
| **Method of** | String |
| **See also** | **Methods:** blink(), bold(), strike() and other String object methods |

## Discussion

*aString* is a String object. Use the *aString*.italics() function to change the typeface to italics via JavaScript.

## Examples

Listing 8.30 and Figure 8.25 demonstrate a good use of italics().

**LISTING 8.30** Using italics().

```
1   <HTML>
2   <TITLE>italics()</TITLE>
3   <BODY>
4   <B>italics()</B>
5   <P><CENTER>
6   <SCRIPT LANGUAGE = "JavaScript">
7   aString = new String("Roses are red <BR> Violets are blue <BR><B>
    I'm </B>funny <BR> and so are <B>you</B>")
8   document.write(aString.italics())
9   </SCRIPT></CENTER>
10  </BODY>
11  </HTML>
```

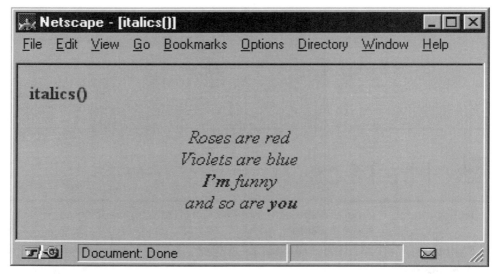

**FIGURE 8.25** Using `italics()`.

#  javaEnabled()

| | |
|---|---|
| **Action** | Returns `true` if Java is enabled, `false` otherwise. |
| **Syntax** | `navigator.javaEnabled()` |
| **Arguments** | None |
| **Method of** | `navigator` |
| **See also** | **Objects:** `navigator` |
| | **Properties:** `appName`, `appCodeName`, `userAgent` |

## Discussion

In Netscape's Navigator the user enables or disables Java by clicking on `Options | Network Preferences...` and then under the `Languages` tab, checking the `Enable Java` checkbox. Use this method if you wish to run a Java applet in your HTML page conditionally.

## Examples

Listing 8.31 and Figure 8.26 demonstrate the use of `javaEnabled()` with a real Java applet. Both the listing and the applet are provided on the CD so that

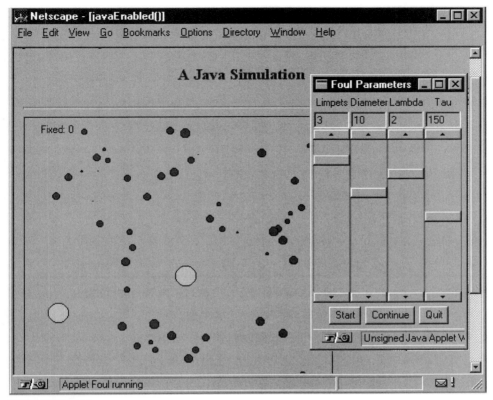

**FIGURE 8.26** Using javaEnabled() with <APPLET> and link().

you can fully test your own code. In line 7 we test to verify that Java is enabled in the client Navigator; if it is not, we alert the user. Otherwise, we go ahead and construct the HTML code that loads the applet (lines 13 to 17). The Foul.class file must reside in the directory from which Listing 8.31 is loaded.

Note the use of link() in lines 14 and 17 (see the link() reference).

**LISTING 8.31** Using javaEnabled() with <APPLET> and link().

```
1    <HTML>
2    <TITLE>javaEnabled()</TITLE>
3    <BODY>
4    <B>javaEnabled()</B>
5    <P><CENTER><H3>A Java Simulation</H3></CENTER>
6    <SCRIPT LANGUAGE = "JavaScript">
7    if (!navigator.javaEnabled())
8    {
9      alert("Enable Java to see an interesting thing and then
```

```
     reload")
10 }
11 else
12 {
13    document.write('<hr><applet code = "Foul.class" width=350
   height=350></applet><hr>')
14    document.write('<BR>' + "The source.".link("Foul.java"))
15    aString = "For more information"
16    hrefAttribute = "http://turtle.gis.umn.edu"
17    document.write('<BR>' + aString.link(hrefAttribute))
18 }
19 </SCRIPT>
20 </BODY>
21 </HTML>
```

#  join()

| | |
|---|---|
| **Action** | Joins all elements of an array into a single string. |
| **Syntax** | `anArray.join([separator])` |
| **Arguments** | `separator` is a string literal, an expression that evaluates to a string, a string value of a property of an existing object, or a control character. It separates string elements in the resulting string; if omitted, a comma (",") is used by default. |
| **Method of** | `Array` |
| **See also** | **Methods:** `reverse()`, `sort()` |

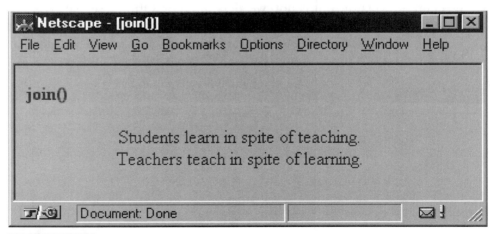

**FIGURE 8.27** Using `join()`.

## Discussion

You might use `join()` when you need to communicate an array (say, via e-mail) or prepare data for automatic update of database. You can use tabs (`"\t"`), new-line (`"\n"`), and other characters as separators.

## Examples

Listing 8.32 and Figure 8.27 demonstrate the use of `join()`.

**LISTING 8.32** Using `join()`.

```
1   <HTML>
2   <TITLE>join()</TITLE>
3   <BODY>
4   <B>join()</B>
5   <P><CENTER>
6   <SCRIPT LANGUAGE = "JavaScript">
7   aArray = new Array("Students", "learn", "in spite of", "teach-
    ing.")
8   bArray = new Array("Teachers", "teach", "in spite of", "learn-
    ing.")
9   document.write(aArray.join(" ") + "<BR>" + bArray.join(" "))
10  </SCRIPT></CENTER>
11  </BODY>
12  </HTML>
```

 # lastIndexOf(*searchFor String*[, *startFrom*])

| | |
|---|---|
| **Action** | Returns the index within the calling string object of the last occurrence of the specified value, starting the search at *startFrom* and going backwards. |
| **Syntax** | *aString*.lastIndexOf(*searchForString* [, *startFrom*]) |
| **Arguments** | *searchForString* is the string to search for; it can be a String object, a string literal, an expression that evaluates to a string, or a string value of a property of an existing object. |
| | *startFrom* determines the index in *aString* from which to start the search; it can be an integer literal, an expression that evaluates to an integer, or an integer value of a property of an existing object. It must be in the range 0 to aString.length - 1. |

| **Method of** | String |
| **See also** | **Methods:** charAt(), indexOf() |

## Discussion

lastIndexOf() is, in a sense, the inverse of indexOf(). Here are some points to remember when using lastIndexOf():

- Characters in *aString* are indexed from 0 (leftmost) to *aString*.length - 1 (rightmost).
- If you omit the *startFrom* argument, the search starts from position *aString*.length - 1.
- If *searchForString* is not found, lastIndexOf() returns -1.
- If you send wrong argument values (say, startFrom = -1), the method returns an undefined value.

## Examples

One of the problems with *aString*.lastIndexOf() is that it returns an undefined value if you send it wrong argument values (say, startFrom = -10). Listing 8.33 shows one potential solution and Figure 8.28 demonstrates some results. My implementation of lastIndexOf() is almost identical to indexOf(). Thus, instead of including the code, I include the commonf.js source file (line 4) where lastIndexOf() resides. The file commonf.js is included with the accompanying CD. For an explanation of the results, see **Examples** for indexOf() earlier in this chapter. For defensive programming, use this function instead of *aString*.lastIndexOf(). To implement it, use SRC = "commonf.js" in the <SCRIPT> tag (line 4).

Incidentally, notice the use of the font manipulation tags <BIG>, <SMALL>, and <B> to emphasize a point (line 15 and Figure 8.28).

**LISTING 8.33** Using lastIndexOf() and modified lastIndexOf().

```
1   <HTML>
2   <TITLE>indexOf()</TITLE>
3   <HEAD>
4   <SCRIPT LANGUAGE = "JavaScript" SRC = "commonf.js">
5   </SCRIPT>
6   </HEAD>
7
8   <BODY>
9   <B>lastIndexOf()</B>
```

```
10 <P>
11 We do some lastIndexOf() on these two strings:
12 <P>
13 <SCRIPT LANGUAGE = "JavaScript">
14 var aString = "All good things are:"
15 var bString = "<BIG>immoral</BIG>, <SMALL>illegal</SMALL>, or
   <BIG><B>fattening</B></BIG>."
16 document.write('aString = "' + aString + '"')
17 document.write('<BR>bString = "' + bString + '"')
18 document.write('<P>lastIndexOf(aString, "l") = ' +
19   indexOf(aString, "l"))
20 document.write('<BR>indexOf(aString, "o", 11) = ' +
21   indexOf(aString, "o", 11))
22 document.write('<BR>lastIndexOf(bString, "m") = ' +
23   indexOf(bString, "m"))
24 document.write('<BR>lastIndexOf(bString, "m", -10) = ' +
25   indexOf(bString,"m",-10))
26 </SCRIPT>
27 </BODY>
28 </HTML>
```

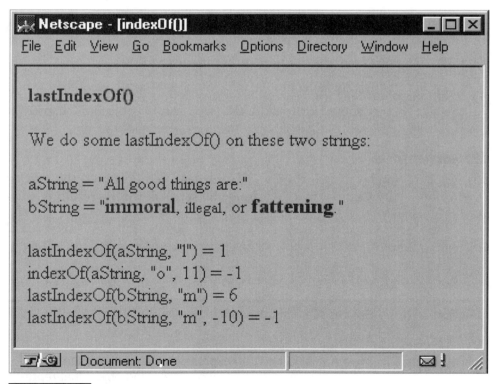

**FIGURE 8.28** Using lastIndexOf() and modified lastIndexOf().

Methods and Functions Reference

# link(*hrefAttribute*)

| | |
|---|---|
| **Action** | Creates an HTML hypertext. |
| **Syntax** | *aString*.link(*hrefAttribute*) |
| **Arguments** | *aString* is a string literal, an expression that evaluates to a string, or a string value of a property of an existing object. *hrefAttribute* is a string literal, an expression that evaluates to a string, or a string value of a property of an existing object. |
| **Method of** | String |
| **See also** | **Methods:** anchor() |
| | **Objects:** location |

## Discussion

Note the following:

- Use link() with write() or writeln() to create and display links via JavaScript.

- *aString* represents the literal text that the user to sees.

- *hrefAttribute* is equivalent to the value of the HREF attribute of the <A> tag.

- hrefAttribute should be a valid URL (see location object in Chapter 7).

## Examples

Listing 8.31 (under JavaEnabled(), **Examples**) demonstrates the use of link(). To see it in action, run the listing and scroll down the resulting window (Figure 8.26).

 # log(*x*)

| | |
|---|---|
| **Action** | Returns the natural logarithm (base *e*) of *x*. |
| **Syntax** | Math.log(*x*) |
| **Arguments** | *x* is a number literal, an expression that evaluates to a number, or a value of a property of an existing object that represents a number. |

| | |
|---|---|
| **Method of** | `Math` |
| **See also** | **Methods:** `exp()`, `pow()`. |

## Discussion

You can use this function as an inverse to `exp()`.

## Examples

See Listing 8.20 and Figure 8.16 and the example for `exp()`.

 # max(*x1*, *x2*)

| | |
|---|---|
| **Action** | Returns the larger of two numbers. |
| **Syntax** | `Math.max(x1, x2)` |
| **Arguments** | *x1* and *x2* are number literals, expressions that evaluate to a number, or values of a property of an existing object that represents a number. |
| **Method of** | `Math` |
| **See also** | **Methods:** `min()` |

## Discussion

See example.

## Examples

The statement

```
document.write(Math.max(2*10,10))
```

returns 20.

 # min(*x1*, *x2*)

| | |
|---|---|
| **Action** | Returns the smaller of two numbers. |
| **Syntax** | `Math.max(x1, x2)` |

| | |
|---|---|
| **Arguments** | *x1* and *x2* are number literals, expressions that evaluate to a number, or values of a property of an existing object that represents a number. |
| **Method of** | `Math` |
| **See also** | **Methods:** `max()` |

## Discussion

See example.

## Examples

The statement

```
document.write(Math.min(2*10,10))
```

returns 10.

#  open([*mimeType*])

| | |
|---|---|
| **Action** | Opens a stream to collect the output of `write()` or `writeln()` methods. |
| **Syntax** | `document.open([mimeType])` |
| **Arguments** | *mimeType* (see **Discussion**) |
| **Method of** | `document` |
| **See also** | **Methods:** `close()`, `write()`, `writeln()` |
| | **Objects:** `document` |

## Discussion

The *mimeType* documents that are currently recognized by Navigator are given in Table 8.1. The effect of *mimeType* in `open()` depends on the `mimeType`.

In working with it, keep in mind that `open()` prepares the document for input; once you are done with output to the document—using `write()` or `writeln()`, for example—you must `close()` the document for the output to be displayed (i.e., for the stream to be flushed to the appropriate destination).

**TABLE 8.1**  mimeType documents. Except for `plugIn`, `open()` opens all streams to layout.

| mimeType | Comments |
| --- | --- |
| text/HTML | A document that contains ASCII text with HTML formatting. |
| text/plain | A document that contains ASCII text with end-of-line characters to delimit displayed lines. |
| image/gif | A document with encoded bytes constituting a GIF header and pixel data. |
| image/jpeg | A document with encoded bytes constituting a JPEG header and pixel data. |
| image/x-bitmap | A document with encoded bytes constituting a bitmap header and pixel data. |
| plugIn | A plug-in document such as `x-world/vrml` or `application/x-direct`. `open()` opens the stream to the specified plug-in; if the plug-in is open, its content is cleared. |

## Examples

See the entry for `close()`, and Listing 8.15 and Figure 8.10, for a demonstration and discussion of the use of `open()` and `close()` for both the `window` and `document` objects.

#  open([*URL, windowName*[, *windowFeatures*]])

| | |
| --- | --- |
| **Action** | Opens a new browser window. |
| **Syntax** | [*aWindow* =][window].open(*URL, windowName*[, *windowFeatures*]) |
| **Arguments** | *aWindow* is the variable name of a new window you wish to open. |
| | *URL* is the URL to open in the window. |
| | *windowName* is the window name (the value assigned to) in the TARGET attribute of a <FORM> or <A> tag. |

*windowFeatures* is a string listing the window features (see **Discussion**).

**Method of**    `window`

**See also**    **Methods:** `close()`

                **Objects:** `window`

## Discussion

`open()` emulates the action of the `File | New Web Browser` menu. The method's call and arguments behave as follows:

- If you call `open()` in event handlers, you must specify `window.open()`, not `open()`; otherwise, the `document's` `open()` method is invoked.

- If *URL* is omitted, an empty window is opened; otherwise, the specified *URL* is opened in the window.

- The *windowName* can contain only alphanumeric characters (the integer symbols 0–9, letters) and the underscore character ("_").

- *windowFeatures* is a comma-separated list (without spaces) that can contain one or more of the features as explained in Table 8.2.

- *windowFeatures* options are set to true if they are specified without a value, or if their value is set to yes, or 1. Thus, `open ("", "aWindow", "toolbar")`, `open ("", "aWindow", "toolbar=1")`, and `open ("","aWindow", "toolbar=yes")` all set the `toolbar` option to true.

- If you open a window without a name and no *windowFeatures* are specified, all features are set to 1.

- If you specify a single *windowFeatures*, all others automatically become 0.

## Examples

See the entry for `close()`, and Listing 8.15 and Figure 8.10, for a demonstration and discussion of `open()` and `close()` for both the `window` and `document` objects.

**TABLE 8.2** window.open() window features.

| Feature | Comments |
|---|---|
| toolbar[=yes\|no]\|[=1\|0] | Creates standard Navigator toolbar |
| location[=yes\|no]\|[=1\|0] | Creates location entry field |
| directories[=yes\|no]\|[=1\|0] | Creates standard Navigator directories button |
| status[=yes\|no]\|[=1\|0] | Creates status bar at the bottom of the window |
| menubar[=yes\|no]\|[=1\|0] | Creates menu at the top of the window |
| scrollbars[=yes\|no]\|[=1\|0] | Creates scrollbars when necessary |
| resizable[=yes\|no]\|[=1\|0] | Makes the window resizable |
| width=*pixels* | Initial window width in pixels specified as integer |
| height=*pixels* | Initial window height in pixels specified as integer |

#  parse(*aDate*)

| | |
|---|---|
| **Action** | Returns the number of milliseconds that have elapsed from January 1, 1970 00:00:00 (local time) to *aDate*. |
| **Syntax** | Date.parse(aDate) |
| **Arguments** | aDate is a string representing a date or a string value of a property of an existing object. |
| **Method of** | Date |
| **See also** | **Methods:** UTC |

## Discussion

Use parse() to manipulate dates, do some date computations, set a date value based on string values, and so on (see **Examples** below).

When using parse(), keep the following in mind:

- parse() is a static method of Date (meaning that it belongs to Date, but not to instances of Date); thus, you must call the method as Date.parse(), **not** as dateObject.parse().

- parse() accepts the IETF standard date syntax (for example, Sun, 1 Jan 2001 13:33:33 GMT).

- parse() can handle the continental U.S. time zone abbreviations (EST, CST, MST, PST).

- For local time, use a time zone offset; for example, "Sun, 1 Jan 2001 13:33:34 GMT+0333" means that you are 3 hours and 33 minutes west of the Greenwich meridian.

- If you do not specify a time zone, the local time zone is assumed.

- GMT and UTC are equivalent.

## Examples

Listing 8.34 and Figure 8.29 demonstrate the use of parse() and setTime(). Two important points about working with dates are demonstrated in Listing 8.34:

- To setTime(), you should provide an argument that represents a date. This is done with Date.parse() which parses the string Aug 9, 2995 and converts it to a date object (line 9).

- As with Math functions and properties, parse() is a method of the class Date, not of an object of type Date. Thus, you call parse() with the syntax Date.parse() (case is important here).

**LISTING 8.34** Using parse() and setTime().

```
1   <HTML>
2   <TITLE>parse()</TITLE>
3   <BODY>
4   <H3>parse()</H3>
5   <SCRIPT LANGUAGE = "JavaScript">
6   today = new Date()
7   document.writeln("today = " + today + "<BR><BR>")
8   today.setTime(Date.parse("Aug 9, 1995"))
9   document.write('today.setTime(Date.parse("Aug 9, 1995")) = '
10    + '<BR>' + today)
11  </SCRIPT>
12  </BODY>
13  </HTML>
```

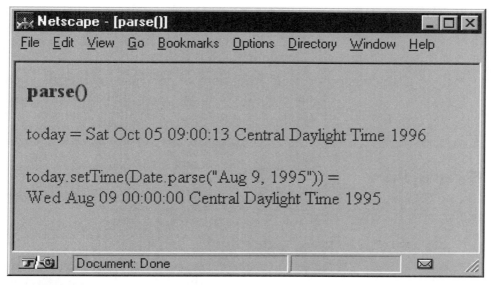

```
Netscape - [parse()]                              _ □ ×
File   Edit   View   Go   Bookmarks   Options   Directory   Window   Help

parse()

today = Sat Oct 05 09:00:13 Central Daylight Time 1996

today.setTime(Date.parse("Aug 9, 1995")) =
Wed Aug 09 00:00:00 Central Daylight Time 1995


            Document: Done                                    ✉
```

**FIGURE 8.29** Using setTime().

 # parseFloat(*aString*)

| | |
|---|---|
| **Action** | Converts *aString* to a floating-point number. |
| **Syntax** | parseFloat(*aString*) |
| **Arguments** | *aString* is a literal string, an expression that evaluates to a string, or a string value of a property of an existing object. |
| **Method of** | None |
| **See also** | **Functions:** isNaN(), parseInt() |

## Discussion

For parseFloat() to interpret a string as a floating number correctly, *aString* should include the following characters only:

- The digits 0 through 9
- A decimal point
- The character e or E (denoting scientific notation)
- The sign "+" or "-"

If *aString* contains characters other than the above, parseFloat() returns the following:

- If the first character is illegal, then NaN is returned.
- If a character other than the first in *aString* is illegal, then parseFloat() parses the string up to the illegal character, and returns the interpreted substring as a float; the remaining characters in *aString* are ignored.

## Examples

Listing 8.35 and Figure 8.30 demonstrate the use of parseFloat(). In particular, note the following:

- The string F123 returns NaN (line 8).
- For aString = "01", the expression aString + e2 evaluates to the string 1e2, which is 100 in scientific notation (line 10).
- Because 0.5 + "A21" evaluates to the string 0.5A21, parseFloat() returns .5 (line 11).

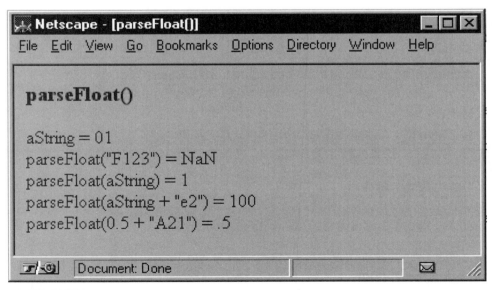

**FIGURE 8.30** Using parseFloat().

LISTING 8.35 Using parseFloat().

```
1   <HTML>
2   <TITLE>parseFloat()</TITLE>
3   <BODY>
4   <H3>parseFloat()</H3>
5   <SCRIPT LANGUAGE = "JavaScript">
6   var aString = "01"
7   document.writeln('aString = ' + aString + '<BR>')
8   document.writeln('parseFloat("F123") = ' + parseFloat("F123") +
    '<BR>')
9   document.writeln('parseFloat(aString) = ' + parseFloat(aString) +
    '<BR>')
10  document.writeln('parseFloat(aString + "e2") = ' +
    parseFloat(aString + "e2") + '<BR>')
11  document.writeln('parseFloat(0.5 + "A21") = ' + parseFloat(0.5) +
    '<BR>')
12  </SCRIPT>
13  </BODY>
14  </HTML>
```

#  parseInt(*aString[, radix]*)

| | |
|---|---|
| **Action** | Converts aString to an integer of the specified radix. |
| **Syntax** | parseInt(*aString[, radix]*) |
| **Arguments** | *aString* is a literal string, an expression that evaluates to a string, or a string value of a property of an existing object. |
| | *radix* is an integer that specifies the base of the returned integer. |
| **Method of** | None |
| **See also** | **Functions:** isNaN(), parseFloat() |

## Discussion

Radix is the basis for a number system—it determines how many different unique digits are recognized as the base for all other numbers. For example, in octal (radix 8), only 8 unique digits are recognized: 0 to 7. In hex, 16 different digits are recognized: 0 to 9, and A, B, C, D, E, F. By convention, for any radix greater than 10, the eleventh digit is A, the twelfth is B, and so on.

For parseInt() to interpret a string as a floating number correctly, *aString* should include the following characters only:

- The digits 0 through 9
- The signs "+" or "-"
- Any character that belongs to the radix, if the radix is specified. In addition, parseInt() will interpret *aString* as follows:
- If *aString* begins with 0x or 0X and the radix is not specified, then the string is parsed in base 16 (hexadecimal).
- If *aString* begins with 0 (zero) and the radix is not specified, then the string is parsed in base 8 (octal).
- If *aString* begins with a digit other than 0 (zero) and the radix is not specified, then the string is parsed as an integer in base 10 (decimal).

If *aString* contains characters other than the above, parseInt() returns the following:

- If the first character is illegal, then NaN is returned (there is a problem here; see **Examples** below).
- If a character other than the first in *aString* is illegal, then parseInt() parses the string up to the illegal character, and returns the interpreted substring as an integer; the remaining characters in *aString* are ignored.

## Examples

Listing 8.36 and Figure 8.31 demonstrate the use of parseInt(). In particular, note the following:

- The string F123 returns NaN (line 8).
- F123 in base 16 returns 61731 decimal, as it should (line 9).
- 011 in octal is 9 in decimal (line 10).
- 0A in octal is NaN, but JavaScript returns 0—this is counter to what you would expect (line 11).
- 0.5 + ... returns NaN, as you would expect (line 13).

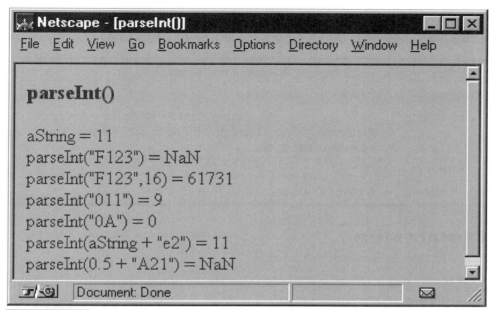

**FIGURE 8.31** Using parseInt().

**LISTING 8.36** Using parseInt().

```
1  <HTML>
2  <TITLE>parseFloat()</TITLE>
3  <BODY>
4  <H3>parseFloat()</H3>
5  <SCRIPT LANGUAGE = "JavaScript">
6  var aString = "11"
7  document.writeln('aString = ' + aString + '<BR>')
8  document.writeln('parseInt("F123") = ' + parseInt("F123") +
   '<BR>')
9  document.writeln('parseInt("F123",16) = ' + parseInt("F123",16) +
   '<BR>')
10 document.writeln('parseInt("011") = ' + parseInt("011") + '<BR>')
11 document.writeln('parseInt("0A") = ' + parseInt("0A") + '<BR>')
12 document.writeln('parseInt(aString + "e2") = ' + parseInt(aString
   + "e2") + '<BR>')
13 document.writeln('parseInt(0.5 + "A21") = ' + parseInt(0.5) +
   '<BR>')
14 </SCRIPT>
15 </BODY>
16 </HTML>
```

#  pow(*base, exponent*)

| | |
|---|---|
| **Action** | Returns base to the exponent **power** |
| **Syntax** | pow(*base, exponent*) |
| **Arguments** | *base* and *exponent* are any number literal, an expression that evaluates to a number, or a numerical value of a property of an existing object. |
| **Method of** | Math |
| **See also** | **Methods:** exponent(), log() |

## Discussion

pow() has the following peculiarities:

- If the result of raising the base to the exponent power is a complex number, pow() returns zero.
- If the number is too large, pow() returns Infinity.
- If the number is too small, pow() returns Infinity (although you might expect it to return -Infinity).

## Examples

Listing 8.37 and Figure 8.32 demonstrate the use of pow(), and the points raised in the **Discussion** above.

**LISTING 8.37** Using pow().

```
1   <HTML>
2   <TITLE>pow()</TITLE>
3   <BODY>
4   <H3>pow()</H3>
5   <SCRIPT LANGUAGE = "JavaScript">
6   var base = "11", exponent = 100000000
7   document.writeln('Math.pow(base, exponent) = ' + Math.pow(base,
    exponent) + '<BR>')
8   document.writeln('Math.pow(-base, exponent) = ' + Math.pow(-base,
    exponent) + '<BR>')
9   document.writeln('Math.pow(base,-exponent) = ' + Math.pow(base,-
    exponent) + '<BR>')
10  </SCRIPT>
11  </BODY>
12  </HTML>
```

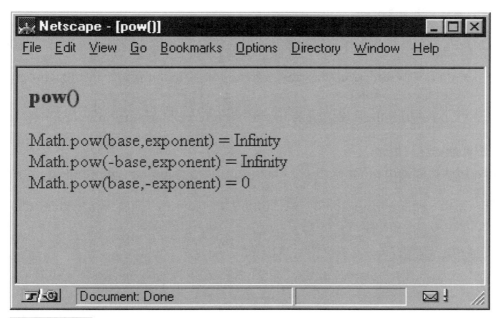

**FIGURE 8.32** Using pow().

 # prompt([*argument*][, *defaultArgument*])

| | |
|---|---|
| **Action** | Displays a Prompt dialog window with *argument* and an input field showing *defaultArgument*. |
| **Syntax** | prompt([*argument*][, *defaultArgument*]) |
| **Arguments** | *argument* and *defaultArgument* can both be: |
| | • string literals, expressions that evaluate to strings, or string values of a property of an existing object, or |
| | • numerical literals, expressions that evaluate to numbers, or numerical values of a property of an existing object. |
| **Method of** | window |
| **See also** | **Methods:** alert(), confirm() |

## Discussion

Use `prompt()` to display a dialog window and obtain an input from the user. When working with `prompt()`, keep these points in mind:

- If you do not specify a value for the function's arguments, the window displays the value `undefined`.
- You do not need to specify a window reference when you call `prompt()`.

## Examples

Listing 8.38 demonstrates the effect of using various combinations of arguments to `prompt()`, `alert()`, and `confirm()`. Figure 8.33 shows the result of the first statement in line 6 of Listing 8.38; note the `undefined` values that appear in the dialog window.

**LISTING 8.38** Using `prompt()`, `alert()`, and `confirm()`.

```
1   <HTML>
2   <TITLE>prompt(), alert(), and confirm()</TITLE>
3   <BODY>
4   <H3>prompt(), alert(), and confirm()</H3>
5   <SCRIPT LANGUAGE = "JavaScript">
6   prompt(); prompt(Math.sin(10)); prompt(Math.sin(10),
    Math.sin(10));
7   alert() ; alert(Math.sin(10))
8   confirm(); confirm(Math.sin(10))
9   </SCRIPT>
10  </BODY>
11  </HTML>
```

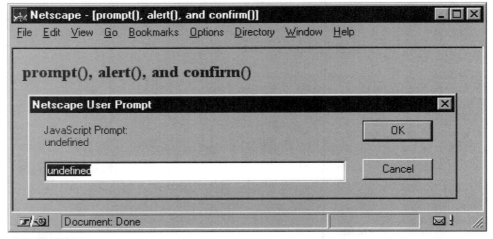

**FIGURE 8.33** Using `prompt()`, `alert()`, and `confirm()`.

 # random()

| | |
|---|---|
| **Action** | Returns a pseudo-random number between 0 and 1. |
| **Syntax** | random() |
| **Arguments** | None |
| **Method of** | Math |
| **See also** | |

## Discussion

A pseudo-random number is—for most practical purposes—a random number. It is called "pseudo-random" because a sequence of such numbers can be repeated exactly (if one starts the sequence generation from the same "seed"), and because after a long enough sequence, the numbers will start repeating themselves cyclically.

## Examples

Listing 8.39 demonstrates how to generate sequences of random numbers. In the example, we wish to generate a sequence of 10 random numbers between 10.5 and 11.5; so we call randomNumber() (from line 23) and compare its results to random() (see Figure 8.34).

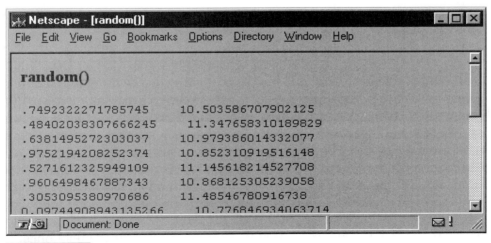

**FIGURE 8.34** Using random().

The function `randomNumber()` is defined in lines 5 through 13; it returns a random number between `n1` and `n2`. For convenience, it is also listed in the `commonf.js file` (on the accompanying CD) and you can include it in your code by adding the attribute `SRC = "commonf.js"` to your `<SCRIPT>` tag.

**LISTING 8.39** Using `random()`.

```
1  <HTML>
2  <HEAD><TITLE>random()</TITLE>
3
4  <SCRIPT LANGUAGE = "JavaScript">
5  function randomNumber(n1, n2)
6  {
7    var returnValue
8    with (Math)
9    {
10     returnValue = n1 + (n2 - n1) * random()
11   }
12   return returnValue
13 }
14 </SCRIPT>
15 </HEAD>
16
17 <BODY>
18 <H3>random()</H3>
19 <SCRIPT LANGUAGE = "JavaScript">
20 for (var i = 0; i < 10; i++)
21 {
22   document.write("<PRE>" + Math.random() +
23    "   " + randomNumber(10.5,11.5))
24 }
25 </SCRIPT>
26 </BODY>
27 </HTML>
```

I want to take a moment and introduce you to your own random number generator, `ran1()`. "Why?" you might ask. Well, you may be interested in generating a sequence of random numbers, and then repeating that sequence exactly at some other time. For example, you may be interested in using a random number–based encryption of data that is submitted to you via e-mail (this way you do not have to rely on server-side services). Or you may run a simulation of a process, relying on a sequence of random numbers, and want to be able to repeat the simulation exactly (e.g., on different computers), or let other users regenerate and test your simulation. Again, you will need to generate the same sequence of pseudo-random numbers more than once.

The function `ran1()` (in Listing 8.40) does just that. I translated the function to JavaScript from C. `ran1()` is based on the C function `ran1()` as given in Press, *et al. Numerical Recipes in C* (Cambridge University Press, 1988); I have even retained their original function and variable names. `ran1()` is based on the so-called three linear congruential generators. This random number generator is not likely to produce cycles in your sequence of randomly generated numbers. I am not going to go into the details here—all I want to do is explain how to use this portable random number generator.

`ran1()` starts with a "seed." You use `seed()` to initialize `ran1()` once per sequence. The seed can be any negative number. Once you seed `ran1()`, you

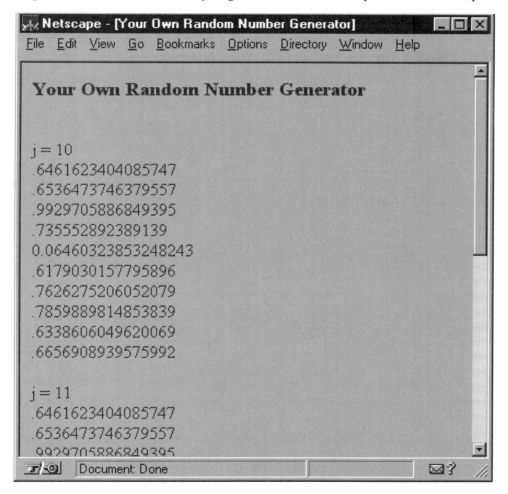

**FIGURE 8.35** Your own random number generator—`ran1()`.

can call it as many times as you wish to get the identical sequence of random numbers. In lines 67 to 75 we generate a sequence of 10 random numbers; each sequence is seeded with -10 (line 70). The results are shown in Figure 8.35.

ran1() returns a random number between 0 and 1. You can use the ideas in randomInteger() and randomNumber() (listed in commonf.js on the accompanying CD) to generate integer random numbers or any random numbers within a specified range. ran1() is included in commonf.js; to use it in your code, just add the attribute SRC = "commonf.js" to your <SCRIPT> tag, and be sure to have commonf.js in the same folder (directory) from which your code is invoked.

**LISTING 8.40** Your own random number generator—ran1().

```
1   <HTML>
2   <HEAD><TITLE>Your Own Random Number Generator</TITLE>
3
4   <SCRIPT LANGUAGE = "JavaScript">
5   var M1 = 259200
6   var IA1 = 7141
7   var IC1 = 54773
8   var M2 = 134456
9   var IA2 = 8121
10  var IC2 = 28411
11  var M3 = 243000
12  var IA3 = 4561
13  var IC3 = 51349
14
15  var idum = -1
16  var ix1, ix2, ix3
17  var iff = 0
18  var  r = new Array(98)
19
20  function seed(aNumber)
21  {
22    if (aNumber < 0)
23      idum = aNumber
24    else
25      alert("Seed with any negative number")
26  }
27
28  function ran1()
29  {
30    var temp, j
```

```
31
32   if (idum < 0 || iff == 0)
33   {
34    iff = 1
35    ix1 = (IC1 - idum) % M1
36    ix1 = (IA1 * ix1 + IC1) % M1
37    ix2 = ix1 % M2
38    ix1 = (IA1 * ix1 + IC1) % M1
39    ix3 = ix1 % M3
40    for (j = 1; j <= 97; j++)
41    {
42      ix1 = (IA1 * ix1 + IC1) % M1
43      ix2 = (IA2 * ix2 + IC2) % M2
44      r[j] = (ix1 + ix2 * (1/M2)) * (1/M1)
45    }
46    idum = 1
47   }
48   ix1 = (IA1 * ix1 + IC1) % M1
49   ix2 = (IA2 * ix2 + IC2) % M2
50   ix3 = (IA3 * ix3 + IC3) % M3
51   j = 1 + ((97 * ix3)/M3)
52   if (j > 97 || j < 1)
53   {
54    alert("from ran1: We have a problem")
55    return -1
56   }
57   temp = r[Math.floor(j)]
58   r[j] = (ix1 + ix2 * (1/M2)) * (1/M1)
59   return temp
60 }
61 </SCRIPT>
62 </HEAD>
63
64 <BODY>
65 <H3>Your Own Random Number Generator</H3>
66 <SCRIPT LANGUAGE = "JavaScript">
67 for (var j = 10; j < 13; j++)
68 {
69   document.write("<BR>" + "j = " + j + "<BR>")
70   seed(-10)
71   for (var i = 0; i < 10; i++)
72   {
73    document.write(ran1()+ "<BR>")
74   }
75 }
76 </SCRIPT>
77 </BODY>
78 </HTML>
```

# reload([*true*])

| | |
|---|---|
| **Action** | Forces a reload of the window's current document. |
| **Syntax** | *aLocation*.reload([true]) |
| **Arguments** | true forces an unconditional HTTP GET of the document from the server. |
| **Method of** | Location |
| **See also** | **Method:** replace() |

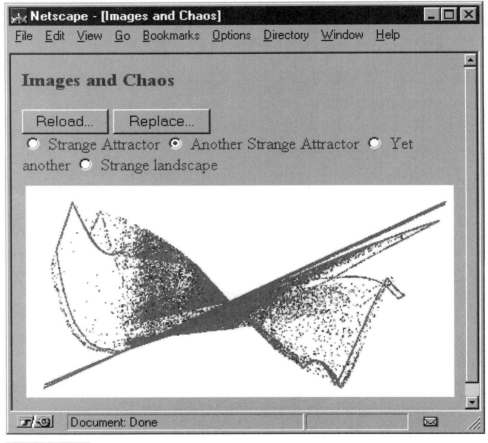

**FIGURE 8.36** reload(), replace(), and images and chaos.

## Discussion

Keep the following in mind when using `reload()`:

- Do not use the optional `true` argument unless you believe that disk and memory caches are off or broken, or the server has a new version of the document.

- `reload()` loads the document specified by the URL in the `aLocation.href` property.

- The method follows the defaults set in the Navigator's `Option | Network Preferences` menu and the `Cache` tab, where the user chooses to verify the document `Once per session`, `Every Time`, or `Never`.

- `reload()` reloads from the cache, unless the user has specified `Every Time` and the document has changed on the server since it was last loaded and saved in the cache.

- When calling `reload()`, specify its full hierarchical relations as in `aWindow.aLocation.reload()`, not as in `aLocation.reload()`. In the latter case, the document's URL is recognized, not the window's.

## Examples

Listing 8.41 and Figure 8.36 demonstrate the use of `reload()`. Run the listing, and see what it does. You can use the demonstrated approach to develop a Web slide presentations.

**LISTING 8.41** `reload()`, `replace()`, and images and chaos.

```
1   <HTML>
2   <TITLE>Images and Chaos</TITLE>
3   <HEAD>
4   <SCRIPT LANGUAGE = "JavaScript">
5   function loadImage(theImage)
6   {
7     document.images[0].src = theImage
8   }
9   </SCRIPT>
10  </HEAD>
11
12  <BODY>
13  <H3>Images and Chaos</H3>
14  <FORM NAME = "aForm">
15    <P><INPUT  TYPE = "button"
16              VALUE = "Reload..."
```

```
17                onClick = "window.location.reload()">
18   <INPUT       TYPE = "button"
19                VALUE = "Replace..."
20                onClick =
     "window.location.replace('images\\StrangeAttractor1.jpg')">
21   <BR><INPUT TYPE = "radio"
22                NAME = "imageChoice" VALUE="image1"
23                CHECKED
24                onClick =
     "loadImage('images\\StrangeAttractor1.jpg')">
25                Strange Attractor
26   <INPUT       TYPE = "radio"
27                NAME = "imageChoice"
28                VALUE = "image2"
29                onClick =
     "loadImage('images\\StrangeAttractor2.jpg')">
30                Another Strange Attractor
31   <INPUT       TYPE = "radio"
32                NAME = "imageChoice"
33                VALUE = "image3"
34                onClick =
     "loadImage('images\\StrangeAttractor3.jpg')">
35                Yet another
36   <INPUT       TYPE = "radio"
37                NAME = "imageChoice"
38                VALUE = "image4"
39                onClick = "loadImage('images\\sinai.jpg')">
40                Strange landscape
41   <BR><IMG     NAME = "strange"
42                SRC = "images\\StrangeAttractor1.jpg"
43                ALIGN = "left" VSPACE="10">
44   </FORM>
45   </BODY>
46   </HTML>
```

Incidentally, in case you are interested, the strange attractors are a mathematical phenomena and were produced by mathematical equations that model evolution of competitors, predators, and prey species. The landscape is from the Sinai peninsula.

#  replace(*URL*)

| | |
|---|---|
| **Action** | Replaces the current URL entry and loads the *URL*. |
| **Syntax** | *aLocation*.replace(*URL*) |

| Arguments | *URL* is a string literal, an expression that evaluates to a string, or a string value of a property of an existing object; all must be evaluated to a correct URL (refer to the **Discussion** section of the `location` object in Chapter 7 for details about the URL syntax). |
|---|---|
| **Method of** | `Location` |
| **See also** | **Methods:** `reload()` |

## Discussion

When working with `replace()`, keep the following in mind:

- `replace()` replaces the current URL with the specified *URL* entry. Thus, a call to `go(-1)` will not go to the previous URL.

- When calling `replace()`, specify its full hierarchical relations as in `aWindow.aLocation.replace()`, not as in `aLocation.replace()`. In the latter case, the document's URL is recognized, not the window's.

## Examples

Listing 8.41 demonstrates the use of `replace()` (line 20). Run the example and click on the `Replace...` button and then on the Navigator's `Back` button. What is the effect?

#  reset()

| **Action** | Simulates a mouse click on a reset button for the calling form. |
|---|---|
| **Syntax** | *aForm*.`reset()` |
| **Arguments** | None |
| **Method of** | `Form` |
| **See also** | **Event Handlers:** `onReset` |
| | **Object:** `Reset` |

## Discussion

`reset()` restores all of the form elements' default values.

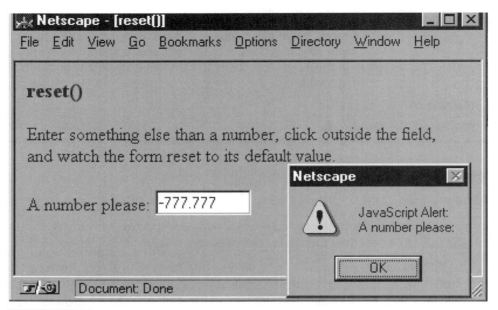

**FIGURE 8.37** Using reset().

## Examples

Listing 8.42 and Figure 8.37 demonstrate the use of reset(). In particular note the following:

- In line 7 we test for the conversion of theObject.value to a float; we use isNaN() to test if the conversion went wrong.

- If the conversion fails, we call reset(), which simulates a click on a Reset button; then, through the onReset event handler, the alert window tells us to enter a number (line 23).

**LISTING 8.42** Using reset().

```
1    <HTML>
2    <HEAD><TITLE>reset()</TITLE>
3
4    <SCRIPT LANGUAGE = "JavaScript">
5    function verifyInput(theObject)
6    {
7      if (isNaN(parseFloat(theObject.value)))
8      {
9        document.aForm.reset()
```

```
10    return false
11    }
12    return true
13 }
14 </SCRIPT>
15 </HEAD>
16
17 <BODY>
18 <H3>reset()</H3>
19 Enter something else than a number, click
20 outside the field, and watch
21 the form reset to its default value.
22 <FORM NAME = "aForm"
23    onReset = "alert('A number please:')">
24 A number please:
25 <INPUT   TYPE = "text"
26          NAME = "aNumber"
27          SIZE="10"
28          VALUE = "-777.777"
29          onChange = verifyInput(this)><P>
30 </FORM>
31 </BODY>
32 </HTML>
```

#  reverse()

| | |
|---|---|
| **Action** | Reverses order of elements of an array (last becomes first, first becomes last). |
| **Syntax** | *anArray*.reverse() |
| **Arguments** | None |
| **Method of** | Array |
| **See also** | **Methods:** join(), sort() |

## Examples

Listing 8.43 demonstrates the use of reverse(), and then some. There are some—what might seem on first sight—idiosyncrasies. So let us see what is actually happening:

- In line 7 we create a new array, aArray, with four elements.

- In line 8 we "copy" aArray to bArray, and in line 9 we copy aArray to cArray.

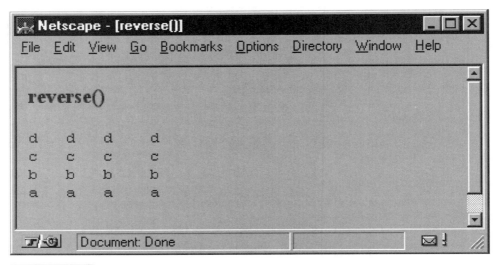

**FIGURE 8.38** Using reverse().

- In lines 10 and 11 we create a new array, dArray, and copy aArray to it.
- Then in line 12 we reverse aArray.

What would you expect? Normally, you would expect that bArray is reversed, and perhaps even aArray. Because we have copied aArray to cArray and to dArray before the reverse, you would expect the original aArray to be preserved in cArray and dArray; not so! Even though we reverse aArray after we have copied it to cArray and to dArray, all arrays, aArray through dArray, are reversed (see lines 13–16 and Figure 8.38).

Before I explain to you what happens, comment out line 12 and reload the file. You should get a window similar to Figure 8.39.

**LISTING 8.43** Using reverse().

```
1   <HTML>
2   <TITLE>reverse()</TITLE>
3   <BODY>
4   <H3>reverse()</H3>
5   <PRE>
6   <SCRIPT LANGUAGE = "JavaScript">
7   aArray = new Array("a", "b", "c", "d")
8   bArray = aArray
9   cArray = aArray
```

```
10 dArray = new Array()
11 dArray = aArray
12 bArray = aArray.reverse()
13 for (var i = 0; i < aArray.length; i++)
14    document.write(aArray[i] + "   " +
15      bArray[i] + "   " + cArray[i] +
16      "   " + dArray[i] + "<BR>")
17 </SCRIPT>
18 </PRE>
19 </BODY>
20 </HTML>
```

What really has happened is that in this case, the Array objects are copied by reference. This means that when you copy an object, you are really copying the *address* (in memory) of the object data to the new object. So when you change data in that address, any reference to data in that address (your copied object) will display the changed data. In other words, objects do not contain data; they contain a memory address of where the data is found. For simple variables that are not objects, (e.g., numbers) the code

```
var a = 1, b, c; b = a; c = a; a = 2
```

will result in a = 2, b = 1, and c = 1. In other words, a, b, and c hold values, not addresses of values.

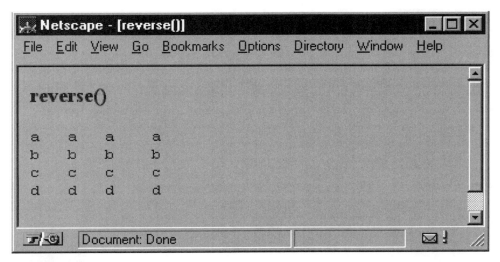

**FIGURE 8.39** reverse() does not always work as you might expect.

 # round(x)

| | |
|---|---|
| **Action** | Returns the value of $x$ rounded to the nearest integer. |
| **Syntax** | `Math.round(x)` |
| **Arguments** | $x$ is a number literal, an expression that evaluates to a number, or a numerical property of an existing object. |
| **Method of** | `Math` |
| **See also** | **Methods:** `ceil()`, `floor()` |

## Discussion

For $n$ integer and $y$ between 0 and 1, $n + y$ is rounded according to these rules:

- If $y >= 0.5$ then the rounding is to $n + 1$.
- If $y < 0.5$ then the rounding is to $n$.

## Examples

Listing 8.44 demonstrates the use of `round()`; it is self-explanatory. The results are shown in Figure 8.40.

**LISTING 8.44** Using `round()`.

```
1   <HTML>
2   <TITLE>round()</TITLE>
```

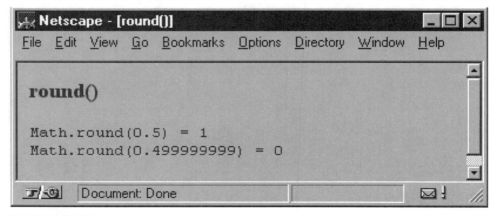

**FIGURE 8.40** Using `round()`.

```
 3  <BODY>
 4  <H3>round()</H3>
 5  <PRE>
 6  <SCRIPT LANGUAGE = "JavaScript">
 7  document.write("Math.round(0.5) = " + Math.round(0.5) + "<BR>")
 8  document.write("Math.round(0.499999999) = " +
    Math.round(0.499999999))
 9  </SCRIPT>
10  </PRE>
11  </BODY>
12  </HTML>
```

#  scroll(*x,y*)

| | |
|---|---|
| **Action** | Scrolls a window to its *x,y* coordinate. |
| **Syntax** | `aWindow.scroll(x,y)` |
| **Arguments** | *x* and *y* are integers representing the *x,y* pixel coordinates in *aWindow* coordinate system. |
| **Method of** | `window` |
| **See also** | **Objects:** `window` |

## Discussion

In using `scroll()`, keep the following in mind:

- 0,0 is the top left corner of the window.

- JavaScript does not keep track of the window coordinate system, and thus x,y must be hard-coded.

## Examples

The following example is designed to demonstrate two things:

- Using `scroll()`

- Defensive programming

As far as using `scroll` is concerned, here is what is going on:

- `scrollset.html` sets up two frames, the `scrolling` frame and the `scrolled` frame (see Listing 8.45).

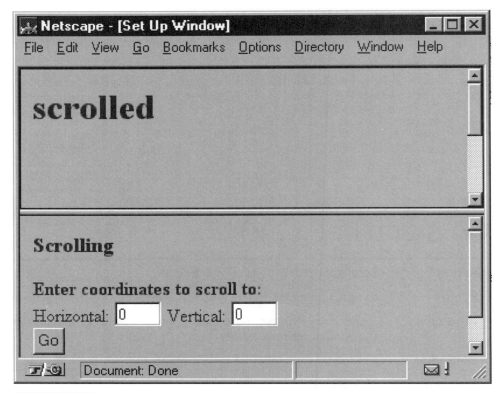

**FIGURE 8.41** Using scroll().

- scrolling.html is the frame that is scrolling scrolled frame (see Listing 8.46).

- scrolled.html is the frame that is scrolled (I'll get back to the code in it in a moment) (see Listing 8.47).

To run the code, load scrollset.html, press a few times on the Cancel that appears in the confirm dialog window, and then press OK. You should see something like Figure 8.41. Enter some numbers in the text boxes and press Go. The joke should appear.

**LISTING 8.45** Using scroll(): scrollset.html.

```
1   <HTML>
2   <HEAD>
3   <TITLE>Set Up Window </TITLE>
4   </HEAD>
5     <FRAMESET  ROWS="50%,50%">
```

```
6    <FRAME     SRC = scrolled.html
7               NAME = "scrolled">
8    <FRAME     SRC = scrolling.html
9               NAME = "scrolling">
10   </FRAMESET>
11   </HTML>
```

**LISTING 8.46** Using `scroll()`: `scrolling.html`.

```
1    <HTML>
2    <TITLE>Scrolling</TITLE>
3    <HEAD>
4    <SCRIPT LANGUAGE = "JavaScript">
5    function scrollWindow(form)
6    {
7      var x = parseInt(form.x.value)
8      var y = parseInt(form.y.value)
9      parent.scrolled.scroll(x, y)
10   }
11   </SCRIPT>
12   </HEAD>
13
14   <BODY>
15   <H3>Scrolling</H3>
16   <FORM   NAME = "myForm">
17   <P><B>Enter coordinates to scroll to:</B>
18   <BR>Horizontal:
19   <INPUT     TYPE = "text"
20             NAME = x
21             VALUE = "0"
22             SIZE=4>
23   Vertical:
24   <INPUT     TYPE = "text"
25             NAME = y
26             VALUE = "0"
27             SIZE=4>
28   <BR><INPUT    TYPE = "button"
29                VALUE = "Go"
30                onClick = "scrollWindow(document.myForm)">
31   </FORM>
32   </BODY>
33   </HTML>
```

**LISTING 8.47** Using `scroll()`: `scrolled.html`.

```
1    <HTML>
2    <BODY>
3    <A NAME = "scrolled"><H1>scrolled</H1></A>
```

Methods and Functions Reference

```
4  <P>
5  <SCRIPT LANGUAGE = "JavaScript">
6  for (var i = 0; i = 10; i++)
7  {
8    if (confirm("i = " + i + " Break" ))
9      break
10   else
11     document.write("<BR> ")
12 }
13 </SCRIPT>
14 It takes <I>one</I> psychiatrist to change a light bulb;
15 <BR> but the light bulb has to want to <B>change</B> first.
16 </HTML>
```

Now why do you think I added the `for` loop (lines 6 to 12) in Listing 8.47? The reason is that I wanted to add some empty lines in the document so that you could scroll down to the `joke` (using Courier for the font here is a joke itself); that is, I wanted to make the window "long" enough so that scrolling will operate. "Then why the `confirm` dialog window in lines 8 and 9?" you might ask. Well, there is a code error somewhere. Because I am terrible at proofreading, I could not find the error (it is not a syntax error). So I added the confirm dialog window to see what happened (can you find the error?). Use this technique to debug your work.

#  select()

| | |
|---|---|
| **Action** | Selects the input area of the specified *anObject* object |
| **Syntax** | *anObject*.select() |
| **Arguments** | None |
| **Method of** | password, text, textarea |
| **See also** | **Methods:** blur(), focus() |

## Discussion

select() is used to highlight the input area of a form element.

The method's owning objects (password, text, textarea) must be one of the following:

• The value of the NAME attribute of the appropriate object

• An element in the `elements` array of the form in which *anObject* resides

## Examples
See Listing 8.10 under `blur()` in this chapter.

 # setDate(*dayOfTheMonth*)

| | |
|---|---|
| **Action** | Sets the day of the month for a specified date. |
| **Syntax** | *aDate*.setDate(*dayOfTheMonth*) |
| **Arguments** | *dayOfTheMonth* is an integer literal, an expression that evaluates to an integer, or an integer value of a property of an existing object; it must be between 1 and 31. |
| **Method of** | Date |
| **See also** | **Methods:** getDate() |

## Discussion
If you specify `dayOfTheMonth` > 31, then the `data` may be incremented appropriately (see example below).

## Examples
Listing 8.48 demonstrates some of the subtleties that are associated with `setDate()`; in particular, note the following:

• If *dayOfTheMonth* is 55 (line 9), then the current date is updated appropriately—25 days are added to the current month, and Daylight Savings Time is calculated.

• If *dayOfTheMonth* is 85 (line 11), then again the date is calculated correctly.

• If *dayOfTheMonth* forces a year increment on the current date (line 13), then the year is incremented, but the date is not calculated correctly.

Figure 8.42 demonstrates the results of running Listing 8.48; your system may misbehave differently. The upshot is that you should specify *dayOfTheMonth* in the appropriate range.

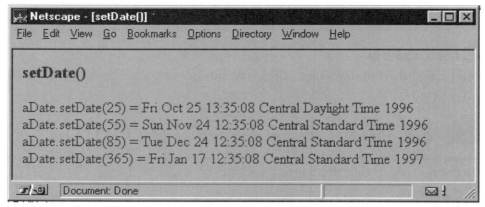

**FIGURE 8.42** Using setDate().

**LISTING 8.48** Using setDate().

```
 1  <HTML>
 2  <TITLE>setDate()</TITLE>
 3
 4  <BODY>
 5  <H3>setDate()</H3><P>
 6  <SCRIPT LANGUAGE = "JavaScript">
 7  aDate = new Date(); aDate.setDate(25)
 8  document.write("aDate.setDate(25) = " + aDate)
 9  aDate = new Date(); aDate.setDate(55)
10  document.write("<BR>aDate.setDate(55) = " + aDate)
11  aDate = new Date(); aDate.setDate(85)
12  document.write("<BR>aDate.setDate(85) = " + aDate)
13  aDate = new Date(); aDate.setDate(365)
14  document.write("<BR>aDate.setDate(365) = " + aDate)
15  </SCRIPT>
16  </BODY>
17  </HTML>
```

 # setHours(*hourOfTheDay*)

| | |
|---|---|
| **Action** | Sets the hour of the day for a specified date. |
| **Syntax** | *aDate*.setHours(*hourOfTheDay*) |
| **Arguments** | *hourOfTheDay* is an integer literal, an expression that evaluates to an integer, or an integer value of a property of an existing object; it must be between 0 and 23. |
| **Method of** | Date |

## Discussion

If you specify *hourOfTheDay* > 23, then the results are unpredictable.

## Examples

Listing 8.49 demonstrates some of the subtleties that are associated with setHours(); in particular, note the following:

- If *hourOfTheDay* is 23 (line 9), then the current date is updated appropriately—the hour of the current date is updated to 23.

- If *hourOfTheDay* is 46 (line 11), then again the date is calculated correctly.

- If *hourOfTheDay* forces a month increment on the current date (line 13), then the result is unpredictable.

- And so it goes for higher increments.

Figure 8.43 demonstrates the results from running Listing 8.49; your system may misbehave differently. The upshot is that you should specify hourOfTheDay in the appropriate range.

**LISTING 8.49** Using setHours().

```
1   <HTML>
2   <TITLE>setHours()</TITLE>
3
4   <BODY>
5   <H3>setHours()</H3><P>
6   <SCRIPT LANGUAGE = "JavaScript">
7   aDate = new Date();
8   document.write("aDate = " + aDate)
9   aDate.setHours(23)
10  document.write("<BR>aDate.setHours(23) = " + aDate)
11  aDate = new Date(); aDate.setHours(46)
12  document.write("<BR>aDate.setHours(46) = " + aDate)
13  aDate = new Date(); aDate.setHours(31*24)
14  document.write("<BR>aDate.setHours(31*24) = " + aDate)
15  aDate = new Date(); aDate.setHours(365*24)
16  document.write("<BR>aDate.setHours(365*24) = " + aDate)
17  </SCRIPT>
18  </BODY>
19  </HTML>
```

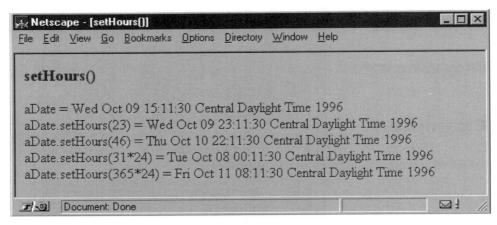

**FIGURE 8.43** Using setHours().

 # setMinutes(*minuteOfThe Hour*)

| | |
|---|---|
| **Action** | Sets minutes of the hour for a specified date |
| **Syntax** | *aDate*.setMinutes(*minuteOfTheHour*) |
| **Arguments** | *minuteOfTheHour* is an integer literal, an expression that evaluates to an integer, or an integer value of a property of an existing object; it must be between 0 and 59. |
| **Method of** | Date |
| **See also** | **Methods:** getMinutes() |

## Discussion

If you specify *minuteOfTheHour* > 59, then the results are unpredictable.

## Examples

Listing 8.50 demonstrates some of the subtleties that are associated with setMinutes(); in particular, note the following:

- If *minuteOfTheHour* is 50 (line 9), then the current date is updated appropriately—the minute of the current date is updated to 50 (Figure 8.44).

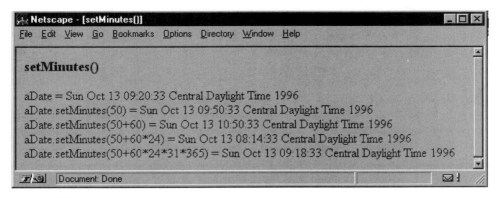

FIGURE 8.44 Using setMinutes().

- If *minuteOfTheHour* is 110 (line 11), then again the date is calculated correctly.

- If *minuteOfTheHour* forces a day increment on the current date (line 13), then the result is unpredictable.

- And so it goes for higher increments.

Figure 8.44 demonstrates the results from running Listing 8.50; your system may misbehave differently. The upshot is that you should specify *minuteOfTheHour* in the appropriate range.

**LISTING 8.50** Using setMinutes().

```
1   <HTML>
2   <TITLE>setMinutes()</TITLE>
3
4   <BODY>
5   <H3>setMinutes()</H3><P>
6   <SCRIPT LANGUAGE = "JavaScript">
7   aDate = new Date();
8   document.write("aDate = " + aDate)
9   aDate.setMinutes(50)
10  document.write("<BR>aDate.setMinutes(50) = " + aDate)
11  aDate = new Date(); aDate.setMinutes(50+60)
12  document.write("<BR>aDate.setMinutes(50+60) = " + aDate)
13  aDate = new Date(); aDate.setMinutes(50+60*24)
14  document.write("<BR>aDate.setMinutes(50+60*24) = " + aDate)
15  aDate = new Date(); aDate.setMinutes(50+60*24*31*365)
16  document.write("<BR>aDate.setMinutes(50+60*24*31*365) = " + aDate)
```

```
17 </SCRIPT>
18 </BODY>
19 </HTML>
```

 # setMonth(*monthOfThe Year*)

| | |
|---|---|
| **Action** | Sets month of the year for a specified date. |
| **Syntax** | *aDate*.setMinutes(*monthOfTheYear*) |
| **Arguments** | *monthOfTheYear* is an integer literal, an expression that evaluates to an integer, or an integer value of a property of an existing object; it must be between 0 (January) and 11 (December). |
| **Method of** | Date |
| **See also** | **Methods:** getMonth() |

## Discussion

If you specify *monthOfTheYear* > 11, then the results may be unpredictable.

## Examples

Listing 8.51 demonstrates some of the subtleties that are associated with setMonth(); in particular, note the following:

- If *monthOfTheYear* is 11 (line 9), then the current date is updated appropriately—the month of the current year is updated to Dec (Figure 8.45).

- If *monthOfTheYear* is 11 + 11 (line 11), then again the date is calculated correctly.

- If *monthOfTheYear* forces a year increment on the current date (line 13), then the result is still correct.

- For higher increments, the results may become unpredictable.

Figure 8.45 demonstrates the results from running Listing 8.51; your system may behave differently. The upshot is then that you should specify *monthOfTheYear* in the appropriate range.

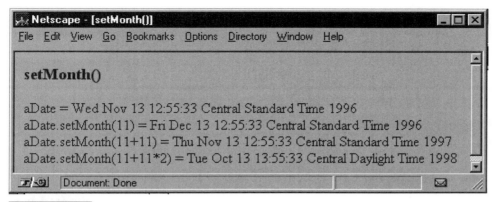

FIGURE 8.45 Using setMonth().

LISTING 8.51 Using setMonth().

```
1   <HTML>
2   <TITLE>setMonth()</TITLE>
3
4   <BODY>
5   <H3>setMonth()</H3><P>
6   <SCRIPT LANGUAGE = "JavaScript">
7   aDate = new Date();
8   document.write("aDate = " + aDate)
9   aDate.setMonth(11)
10  document.write("<BR>aDate.setMonth(11) = " + aDate)
11  aDate = new Date(); aDate.setMonth(11+11)
12  document.write("<BR>aDate.setMonth(11+11) = " + aDate)
13  aDate = new Date(); aDate.setMonth(11+11*2)
14  document.write("<BR>aDate.setMonth(11+11*2) = " + aDate)
15  </SCRIPT>
16  </BODY>
17  </HTML>
```

 # setSeconds(*secondOfThe Minute*)

| | |
|---|---|
| **Action** | Sets seconds of the hour for a specified date. |
| **Syntax** | *aDate*.setSeconds(*secondOfTheMinute*) |
| **Arguments** | *secondOfTheMinute* is an integer literal, an expression that |

evaluates to an integer, or an integer value of a property of an existing object; it must be between 0 and 59.

**Method of**     Date

**See also**     **Methods:** getSeconds()

## Discussion

If you specify *secondOfTheMinute*> 59, then the results may be unpredictable.

## Examples

Listing 8.52 demonstrates some of the subtleties that are associated with setSeconds(); in particular, note the following:

- If *secondOfTheMinute* is 50 (line 9), then the second of the current minute is updated correctly (Figure 8.46).

- If *secondOfTheMinute* is 50 + 60 (line 11), then again the minute is calculated correctly.

- If *secondOfTheMinute* forces an increment of more than 1 minute (line 13), then the result is incorrect.

- And so it goes for higher increments.

Figure 8.46 demonstrates the results from running Listing 8.52; your system may behave differently. The upshot is that you should specify *secondOfTheMinute* in the appropriate range.

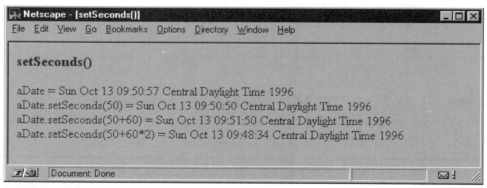

**FIGURE 8.46**  Using setSeconds().

LISTING 8.52 Using setSeconds().

```
1   <HTML>
2   <TITLE>setSeconds()</TITLE>
3
4   <BODY>
5   <H3>setSeconds()</H3><P>
6   <SCRIPT LANGUAGE = "JavaScript">
7   aDate = new Date();
8   document.write("aDate = " + aDate)
9   aDate.setSeconds(50)
10  document.write("<BR>aDate.setSeconds(50) = " + aDate)
11  aDate = new Date(); aDate.setSeconds(50+60)
12  document.write("<BR>aDate.setSeconds(50+60) = " + aDate)
13  aDate = new Date(); aDate.setSeconds(50+60*2)
14  document.write("<BR>aDate.setSeconds(50+60*2) = " + aDate)
15  </SCRIPT>
16  </BODY>
17  </HTML>
```

#  setTime(*milliseconds SinceEpoch*)

| | |
|---|---|
| **Action** | Assigns a date to a Date object. |
| **Syntax** | *aDate*.setTime(*millisecondsSinceEpoch*) |
| **Arguments** | *millisecondsSinceEpoch* is an integer literal, an expression that evaluates to an integer, or an integer value of a property of an existing object. It represents the number of milliseconds that have elapsed since 1 January 1970 00:00:00 (the so-called epoch). |
| **Method of** | Date |
| **See also** | **Methods:** getTime() |

## Discussion

Use setTime() to do date arithmetic: for example, assigning date to another Date object, adding and subtracting time from dates, and so on.

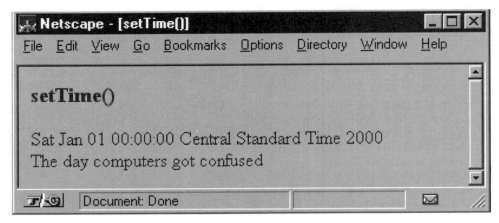

FIGURE 8.47 Using setTime().

aDate is either the name of a Date object or a Date property of an existing object.

## Examples

Listing 8.53 and Figure 8.47 demonstrate the use of setTime(). Note that to assign anotherDate to aDate, we must first getTime().

LISTING 8.53 Using setTime().

```
1   <HTML>
2   <TITLE>setTime()</TITLE>
3
4   <BODY>
5   <H3>setTime()</H3><P>
6   <SCRIPT LANGUAGE = "JavaScript">
7   aDate = new Date();
8   anotherDate = new Date("January 1, 2000")
9   aDate.setTime(anotherDate.getTime())
10  document.write(aDate)
11  document.write("<BR>The day computers got confused")
12  </SCRIPT>
13  </BODY>
14  </HTML>
```

# setTimeout(*expression, milliseconds*)

| | |
|---|---|
| **Action** | Evaluates the *expression* after the specified number of *milliseconds* have elapsed and returns a timeoutID. |
| **Syntax** | *timeoutID* = setTimeout(*expression, milliseconds*) |
| **Arguments** | *expression* is a literal string that represents an expression, an expression that evaluates to a string that represents an expression, or a string value of a property of an existing object that evaluates to an expression. |
| | *milliseconds* is a numeric literal, a numeric string, an expression that evaluates to a number, or a numeric value of a property of an existing object. |
| **Method of** | frame, window |
| **See also** | **Methods:** clearTimeout() |

## Discussion

setTimeout() evaluates an expression after a specified amount of time only once. Use *timeoutID* as an identifier to clearTimeout() if you wish to cancel the effect of setTimeout().

## Examples

See clearTimeout() and Listing 8.13 and Figure 8.8 for an example of setTimeout() and clearTimeout().

 # setYear(*yearInteger*)

| | |
|---|---|
| **Action** | Sets the year portion of a specified date |
| **Syntax** | *aDate*.setYear(*yearInteger*) |
| **Arguments** | *yearInteger* is an integer literal, an expression that evaluates to an integer, or an integer value of a property of an existing object; it must be greater than or equal to 1970. |

| **Method of** | Date |
|---|---|
| **See also** | **Methods:** getYear() |

## Discussion

If you specify *yearInteger* < 1970, the results may be unpredictable.

## Examples

Listing 8.54 and Figure 8.48 demonstrate the use of setYear(). It so happens that this works on my computer. There is no guarantee it will work on yours, or in the future.

**LISTING 8.54** Using setYear().

```
1   <HTML>
2   <TITLE>setYear()</TITLE>
3
4   <BODY>
5   <H3>setYear()</H3><P>
6   <SCRIPT LANGUAGE = "JavaScript">
7   aDate = new Date();
8   anotherDate = new Date("January 1, 1200")
9   aDate.setYear(anotherDate.getYear())
10  document.write(aDate)
11  document.write("<BR>A distant mirror")
12  </SCRIPT>
13  </BODY>
14  </HTML>
```

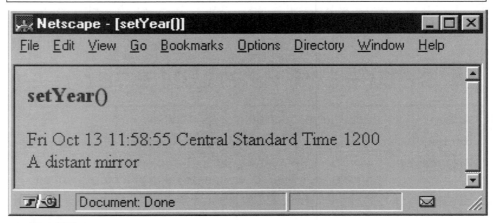

**FIGURE 8.48** Using setYear().

# sin(*angle*)

| | |
|---|---|
| **Action** | Returns the sine of angle. |
| **Syntax** | Math.sin(*angle*) |
| **Arguments** | *angle* in radians is a number, an expression that evaluates to a number, or a property that is a number. |
| **Method of** | Math |
| **See also** | **Methods:** acos(), asin(), cos(), atan(), tan() |
| | **Properties:** PI |

## Discussion

sin() returns the sine value of *angle*. The value is between -1 and 1.

## Examples

See Listing 8.17 and Figure 8.13 in the discussion of cos().

 # small()

| | |
|---|---|
| **Action** | Emulates the action of the <SMALL> HTML tag, decreasing the font size of the displayed string. |
| **Syntax** | *aString*.small() |
| **Arguments** | None |
| **Method of** | String |
| **See also** | **Methods:** big(), fontsize() and other String object methods |

## Discussion

*aString* is a String object. Use the *aString*.small() function to format strings via JavaScript. The way the formatted string looks depends on the operating system on which the Internet browser is running.

## Examples

Listing 8.55 demonstrates the use of `small()` in an HTML document. It produces the same effect as

```
<SMALL>Information == Knowledge</SMALL>
```

**LISTING 8.55** Using `small()`.

```
aString = new String("Information == Knowledge")
document.writeln(aString.small()
```

# sort([sortOrder Function])

| | |
|---|---|
| **Action** | Sorts elements of an array. |
| **Syntax** | *anArray*.sort([*sortOrderFunction*]) |
| **Arguments** | *sortOrderFunction* specifies a function that defines the sort order; if omitted, the array is sorted lexicographically. |
| **Method of** | Array |
| **See also** | **Methods:** join(), reverse() |

## Discussion

In using `sort()`, keep the following in mind:

- *anArray* is the name of an Array object or an Array object that is a property of an existing object.

- If *sortOrderFunction* is not specified, the sorting order is lexicographic (i.e., A<a, B<a,. . .).

- Lexicographic sort means sorting in dictionary order according to the string conversion of each of the array's element.

- If some elements are not strings, they are first converted to strings and then sorted.

When comparing two array elements, a and b, sortOrderFunction works as follows:

- If *sortOrderFunction(a,b)* returns a negative value, then sorting order is b[i], a[j], where the array indices are i < j.

- If *sortOrderFunction(a,b)* returns a zero, then sorting order of a and b remains unchanged with respect to each other, but both are sorted with respect to the remaining array elements.

- If *sortOrderFunction(a,b)* returns a positive value, then sorting order is a[i], b[j], where the array indices are i < j.

This means that *sortOrderFunction* must take on a generic form like that shown in Listing 8.56.

**LISTING 8.56** Generic form of a sortOrderFunction().

```
1   function sortOrderFunction(a, b)
2   {
3     if (a < b)
4       return -1
5     if (a > b)
6       return 1
7     return 0
8   }
```

When numbers are sorted, *sortOrderFunction* take on the form shown in Listing 8.57.

**LISTING 8.57** Generic form of a sortOrderFunction() for numbers.

```
1   function sortOrderFunction(a, b)
2   {
3     return a - b
4   }
```

## Examples

Listing 8.58 and Figure 8.49 demonstrate the use of sort().

**LISTING 8.58** Using sort().

```
1   <HTML>
2   <TITLE>sort()</TITLE>
3
4   <BODY>
5   <H3>sort()</H3><P>
6   <I>Sort a joke and destroy it</I>:<P>
```

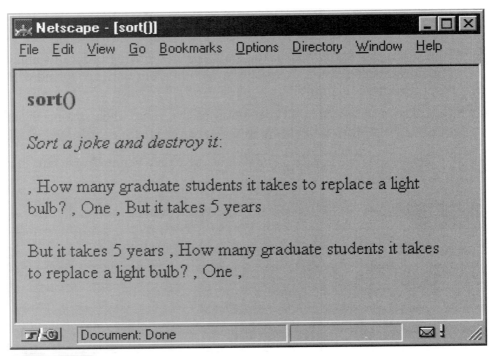

**FIGURE 8.49** Using sort().

```
7   <SCRIPT LANGUAGE = "JavaScript">
8   aArray = new Array()
9   aArray[1] = " How many graduate students does it take to replace
    a light bulb? "
10  aArray[2] = " One "
11  aArray[3] = " But it takes 5 years "
12  document.write(aArray)
13  document.write("<P>" + aArray.sort())
14  </SCRIPT>
15  </BODY>
16  </HTML>
```

#  split([*separator*])

| | |
|---|---|
| **Action** | Splits a String object into an array of strings by separating the string into substrings. |

**400**                    Chapter 8

| | |
|---|---|
| **Syntax** | *aString*.split([*separator*]) |
| **Arguments** | *separator* is a character, treated as a string, that is used as a criterion for splitting *aString*; if missing, split() returns the whole string. |
| **Method of** | String |
| **See also** | **Methods:** charAt(), indexOf(), lastIndexOf() |

## Discussion

*aString* is a string or a string value of a property of an existing object.

## Examples

Listing 8.59 and Figure 8.50 demonstrate the use of split().

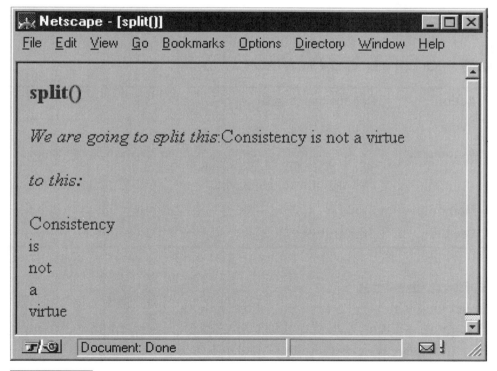

**FIGURE 8.50** Using split().

**LISTING 8.59** Using split().

```
1  <HTML>
2  <TITLE>split()</TITLE>
3
4  <BODY>
5  <H3>split()</H3><P>
6  <SCRIPT LANGUAGE = "JavaScript">
7  var aString = "Consistency is not a virtue"
8  document.write("<I>We are going to split this</I>:" + aString)
9  document.write("<P><I>to this:</I><P>")
10 var splitter = " "
11 var stringArray = aString.split(splitter)
12 for (var i = 0; i < stringArray.length; i++)
13 {
14    document.write(stringArray[i] + "<BR>")
15 }
16 </SCRIPT>
17 </BODY>
18 </HTML>
```

 # sqrt( *aNumber* )

| | |
|---|---|
| **Action** | Returns the square root of *aNumber*. |
| **Syntax** | Math.sqrt(*aNumber*) |
| **Arguments** | *aNumber* is a literal number, a numerical variable, an expression that evaluates to a number, or a numerical value of a property of an existing object. |
| **Method of** | Math |
| **See also** | **Property:** SQRT1_2 |

## Discussion

In working with sqrt(), keep the following in mind:

- If *aNumber* < 0, sqrt() returns NaN. Strictly speaking, this is incorrect—the square root of a negative number is a complex number.

- If *aNumber* is larger than the largest number JavaScript can handle, sqrt() returns Infinity.

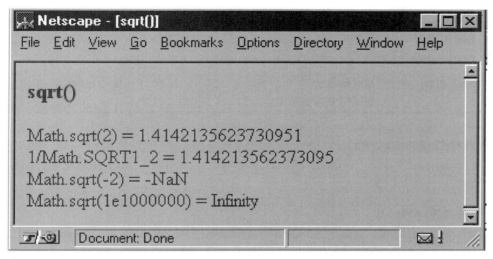

FIGURE 8.51 Using sqrt() and SQRT1_2.

## Examples

Listing 8.60 and Figure 8.51 demonstrate the use of sqrt() and SQRT1_2.

LISTING 8.60 Using sqrt() and SQRT1_2.

```
1   <HTML>
2   <TITLE>sqrt()</TITLE>
3
4   <BODY>
5   <H3>sqrt()</H3><P>
6   <SCRIPT LANGUAGE = "JavaScript">
7   document.write("Math.sqrt(2) = " + Math.sqrt(2))
8   document.write("<BR>1/Math.SQRT1_2 = " + 1/Math.SQRT1_2)
9   document.write("<BR>Math.sqrt(-2) = " + Math.sqrt(-2))
10  document.write("<BR>Math.sqrt(1e1000000) = " +
    Math.sqrt(1e1000000))
11  </SCRIPT>
12  </BODY>
13  </HTML>
```

 # strike()

| Action | Emulates the action of the <STRIKE> HTML tag, causing *aString* to show as struck out. |

| Syntax | *aString*.strike() |
|---|---|
| **Arguments** | None |
| **Method of** | String |
| **See also** | **Methods:** blink(), bold(), italics(), **and other** String object methods |

## Discussion

*aString* is a String object. Use the *aString*.strike() function to change typeface via JavaScript.

## Examples

Listing 8.61 and Figure 8.52 demonstrate the use of strike() in an HTML document to (hopefully) produce a desirable effect.

**LISTING 8.61** Using strike().

```
1    <HTML>
2    <TITLE>strike()</TITLE>
3
4    <BODY>
5    <H3>strike()</H3><P>
6    <SCRIPT LANGUAGE = "JavaScript">
7    aString = new String("It takes 3 lawyers to replace a light bulb:
     a prosecutor, a defense attorney, and a judge.")
8    document.writeln(aString.strike())
```

**FIGURE 8.52** Using strike().

```
 9  </SCRIPT>
10  </BODY>
11  </HTML>
```

 # sub()

| | |
|---|---|
| **Action** | Emulates the action of the `<SUB>` HTML tag, causing *aString* to show as a subscript. |
| **Syntax** | *aString*.sub() |
| **Arguments** | None |
| **Method of** | String |
| **See also** | **Methods:** sup() and other String object methods |

## Discussion

*aString* is a String object. Use the *aString*.sub() function to change type-face via JavaScript.

## Examples

Listing 8.62 and Figure 8.53 demonstrate the use of sub() and sup() in an HTML document to (hopefully) produce a desirable effect.

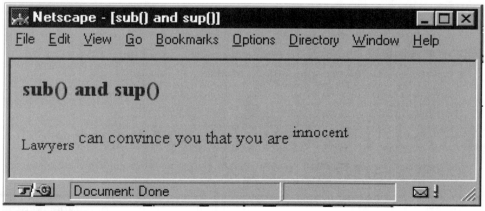

**FIGURE 8.53** Using sub() and sup().

LISTING 8.62 Using sub() and sup().

```
1   <HTML>
2   <TITLE>sub() and sup()</TITLE>
3
4   <BODY>
5   <H3>sub() and sup()</H3><P>
6   <SCRIPT LANGUAGE = "JavaScript">
7   aString = new String("can convince you that you are")
8   document.writeln("Lawyers ".sub() + aString + " innocent".sup())
9   </SCRIPT>
10  </BODY>
11 </HTML>
```

 # submit()

| | |
|---|---|
| **Action** | Submits a form. |
| **Syntax** | *aFrom*.submit() |
| **Arguments** | None |
| **Method of** | form |
| **See also** | **Objects:** submit |
| | **Event Handlers:** onSubmit |

## Discussion

*aForm* is a form object or anything that evaluates to a form object.

## Examples

See examples of the form and window objects in Chapter 7.

 # substring([*beginIndex*] [, *endIndex*])

| | |
|---|---|
| **Action** | Returns a String object that is a substring of another String object. |

| Syntax | substring([*beginIndex*][, *endIndex*]) |
|---|---|
| **Arguments** | *beginIndex* and *endIndex* are integer literals, integer variables, expressions that evaluate to integers, or an integer value of a property of an existing object. |
| **Method of** | String |
| **See also** | **Methods:** indexOf(), split() |

## Discussion

In working with substring(), keep the following in mind:

- If you do not specify any of the arguments, the whole string is returned (see line 10 in Listing 8.63 and Figure 8.54).

- If you specify a single argument, the substring from the index to the end of the string is returned; you can use this technique to split a string (see lines 12 and 13 in Listing 8.63 and Figure 8.54).

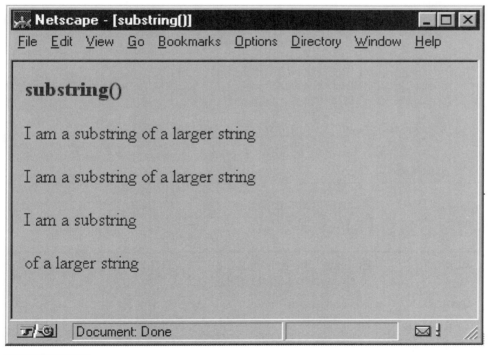

**FIGURE 8.54** Using substring() and indexOf().

## Examples

Listing 8.63 and Figure 8.54 demonstrate the use of substring(); in particular note the following:

- In line 8 we take the substring up to and including g; the expected substring is produced and then printed in line 11.

- No arguments to substring() produce the whole string (line 10).

- A single argument to substring() produce a substring from the specified position to the end of the string (line 12).

- Arguments outside the range produce an empty string (line 13).

**LISTING 8.63** Using substring() and indexOf().

```
1   <HTML>
2   <TITLE>substring()</TITLE>
3
4   <BODY>
5   <H3>substring()</H3><P>
6   <SCRIPT LANGUAGE = "JavaScript">
7   aString = new String("I am a substring of a larger string")
8   bString = aString.substring(0,aString.indexOf("g")+1)
9   document.writeln(aString)
10  document.writeln("<P>" + aString.substring())
11  document.writeln("<P>" + bString)
12  document.writeln("<P>" +
    aString.substring(aString.indexOf("g")+1))
13  document.writeln("<P>" + aString.substring(1000))
14  </SCRIPT>
15  </BODY>
16  </HTML>
```

#  sup()

| | |
|---|---|
| **Action** | Emulates the action of the <SUP> HTML tag, causing *aString* to show as a superscript. |
| **Syntax** | *aString*.sup() |
| **Arguments** | None |
| **Method of** | String |
| **See also** | **Methods:** sub() and other String object methods |

## Discussion

*aString* is a `String` object. Use the *aString*`.sup()` function to change typeface via JavaScript.

## Examples

Listing 8.62 and Figure 8.53 demonstrate the use of `sub()` and `sup()` in an HTML document to (hopefully) produce a desirable effect.

 # taint(*aProperty*)

| | |
|---|---|
| **Action** | Adds tainting to a property. |
| **Syntax** | `taint(aProperty)` |
| **Arguments** | `aProperty` is the name of the property to taint. |
| **Method of** | `None` |
| **See also** | **Methods:** `untaint()` |

## Discussion

See "Data Tainting" in Chapter 6.

## Examples

See "Data Tainting" in Chapter 6.

 # tan(*anAngle*)

| | |
|---|---|
| **Action** | Returns the tangent of an angle *anAngle*. |
| **Syntax** | `Math.tan(anAngle)` |
| **Arguments** | *anAngle* is a number, an expression that evaluates to a number, or a property that is a number; its units are in radians. |
| **Method of** | `Math` |
| **See also** | **Methods:** `atan()`, `sin()`, `cos()` |
| | **Properties:** `PI` |

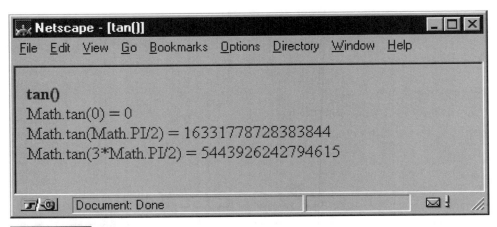

FIGURE 8.55 Using `tan()`.

## Discussion

The return values of `Math.tan()` should between `-Infinity` and `Infinity`; however, the call `Math.tan (Math.PI/2)` or `Math.tan (3*Math.PI/2)` return two large integers (see Figure 8.55). You should therefore not rely on the return values if they are very large.

The mathematical function tangent is the inverse of arc tangent.

## Examples

Listing 8.64 and Figure 8.55 demonstrate the use of `tan()`. Note the following:

- `tan(0)` returns `0`, as it should (line 6 and Figure 8.55).
- `tan(Math.PI/2)` should be `Infinity`; however, a large integer is returned (line 7 and Figure 8.55).
- `tan(3*Math.PI/2)` should be `-Infinity`; however, a large integer is returned (line 8 and Figure 8.55).

The upshot is that you are essentially left to your own devices to make sure that when the value of *anAngle* is $\pi/2$ or $3\pi/2$ the function behaves as it should.

**LISTING 8.64** Using `tan()`.

```
1   <HTML>
2   <TITLE>tan()</TITLE>
```

```
3   <BODY>
4   <B>tan()</B>
5   <SCRIPT LANGUAGE = "JavaScript">
6   document.writeln("<BR> Math.tan(0) = " + Math.tan(0))
7   document.writeln("<BR>Math.tan(Math.PI/2) = " +
    Math.tan(Math.PI/2))
8   document.writeln("<BR>Math.tan(3*Math.PI/2) = " +
    Math.tan(3*Math.PI/2))
9   </SCRIPT>
10  </BODY>
11  </HTML
```

#  toGMTString()

| | |
|---|---|
| **Action** | Converts a date to a string, using the Internet GMT conventions. |
| **Syntax** | *aDate*.toGMTString() |
| **Arguments** | None |
| **Method of** | Date |
| **See also** | **Methods:** toLocaleString() |

## Discussion

aDate is a date object. The exact format of the returned string is platform dependent.

## Examples

Listing 8.65 and Figure 8.56 demonstrate the use of toGMTString().

**LISTING 8.65** Using toGMTString().

```
1   <HTML>
2   <TITLE>toGMTString()</TITLE>
3   <BODY>
4   <B>toGMTString()</B><P>
5   <SCRIPT LANGUAGE = "JavaScript">
6   aDate = new Date()
7   document.write(aDate.toGMTString())
8   </SCRIPT>
9   </BODY>
10  </HTML>
```

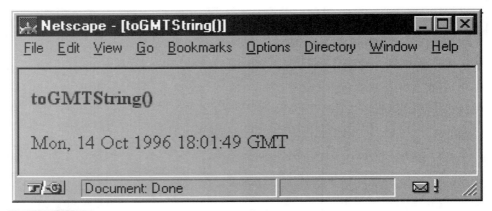

**FIGURE 8.56** Using `toGMTString()`.

#  toLocaleString()

| | |
|---|---|
| **Action** | Converts a date to a string, using the conventions of the system's locale. |
| **Syntax** | *aDate*.toLocaleString() |
| **Arguments** | None |
| **Method of** | Date |
| **See also** | **Methods:** toGMTString() |

## Discussion

*aDate* is a date object. The exact format of the returned string is platform and locale dependent. For example, Europeans like to write 31/1/96, while Americans write 1/31/96.

## Examples

Listing 8.66 and Figure 8.57 demonstrate the use of `toLocaleString()`.

**LISTING 8.66** Using `toLocaleString()`.

```
1   <HTML>
2   <TITLE>toLocaleString ()</TITLE>
3   <BODY>
```

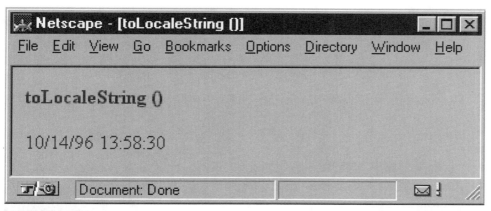

**FIGURE 8.57** Using toLocaleString().

```
4   <B>toLocaleString ()</B><P>
5   <SCRIPT LANGUAGE = "JavaScript">
6   aDate = new Date()
7   document.write(aDate.toLocaleString ())
8   </SCRIPT>
9   </BODY>
10  </HTML>
```

#  toLowerCase()

| | |
|---|---|
| **Action** | Returns *aString* converted to lowercase. |
| **Syntax** | *aString*.toLowerCase() |
| **Arguments** | None |
| **Method of** | String |
| **See also** | **Methods:** toUpperCase() |

## Discussion

aString is a String object. Use toLowerCase() to convert a whole string to lowercase.

## Examples

Listing 8.67 and Figure 8.58 demonstrate the use of toLowerCase() and toUpperCase().

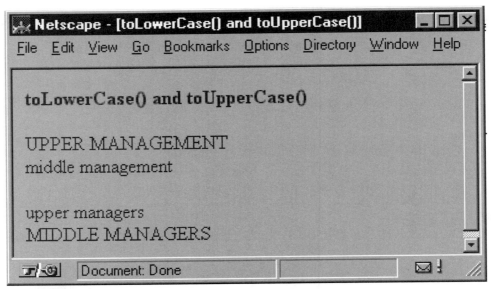

**FIGURE 8.58** Using toLowerCase() and toUpperCase().

**LISTING 8.67** Using toLowerCase() and toUpperCase().

```
1   <HTML>
2   <TITLE>toLowerCase() and toUpperCase()</TITLE>
3   <BODY>
4   <B>toLowerCase() and toUpperCase()</B><P>
5   <SCRIPT LANGUAGE = "JavaScript">
6   document.write("Upper Management".toUpperCase())
7   document.write("<BR>MIDDLE MANAGEMENT".toLowerCase())
8   document.write("<P>Upper Managers".toLowerCase())
9   document.write("<BR>Middle Managers".toUpperCase())
10  </SCRIPT>
11  </BODY>
12  </HTML>
```

# ↳ toString([*radix*])

| | |
|---|---|
| **Action** | Converts an object to a string. |
| **Syntax** | *anObject*.toString([*radix*]) |
| **Arguments** | *radix* is the base used to represent numeric values. |

| **Method of** | All objects |
| **See also** | **Objects:** String |

## Discussion

Use toString() when:

- You need to represent an object name as a text value
- You need to reference an object in a string concatenation
- You need to convert an object into a string

When working with toString(), keep the following in mind:

- If *anObject* has no string value, its toString() returns [object type].
- When *anObject* is an array, toString() returns a single string, containing all of the array's elements, separated by commas.
- When *anObject* is a function, toString() decompiles the function back into a source string formatted according to some pre-established format.

## Examples

Listing 8.68 and Figure 8.59 demonstrate the use of toString() and some of the points discussed above. In particular note:

- When you click on aButton, the effect of toString() (line 19) is to reveal the whole <...> HTML statement (Figure 8.60).
- The weakDays (in case you wonder, there is no spelling error here) array is transformed into a string (lines 22 and 23 and Figure 8.59).
- document.toString() does not behave as expected, and returns nothing (lines 24 and 25 and Figure 8.59).
- aForm.toString() behaves as expected (lines 26 and 27).
- aButton.toString(), instead of returning the expected [object Button], returns the button itself (lines 28 and 29 and Figure 8.59).
- aFunction.toString() returns the code for the whole function in a single string (lines 30 and 31 and Figure 8.59).

You can recreate buttons on an HTML page with the technique illustrated in lines 28 to 29.

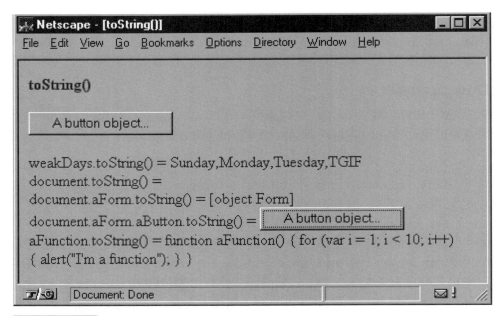

**FIGURE 8.59** Using toString().

**LISTING 8.68** Using toString().

```
1   <HTML>
2   <TITLE>toString()</TITLE>
3   <HEAD>
4   <SCRIPT LANGUAGE = "JavaScript">
5   function aFunction()
6   {
7     for (var i = 1; i < 10; i++)
8       alert("I'm a function")
9   }
10  </SCRIPT>
11  </HEAD>
12
13  <BODY>
14  <B>toString()</B><P>
15  <FORM    name = "aForm">
16  <INPUT   TYPE = "button"
17          NAME = "aButton"
18          VALUE = "A button object..."
19          onClick = 'alert(this.toString())'>
20  <P>
21  <SCRIPT LANGUAGE = "JavaScript">
```

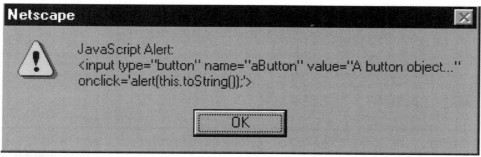

**FIGURE 8.60**  Using toString() to reveal a <...>.

```
22 var weakDays = new Array("Sunday", "Monday", "Tuesday", "TGIF")
23 document.write("weakDays.toString() = " + weakDays.toString())
24 document.write("<BR>document.toString() = " +
25    document.toString())
26 document.write("<BR>document.aForm.toString() = " +
27    document.aForm.toString())
28 document.write("<BR>document.aForm.aButton.toString() = " +
29    document.aForm.aButton.toString())
30 document.write("<BR>aFunction.toString() = " +
31    aFunction.toString())
32 </SCRIPT>
33 </BODY>
34 </HTML>
```

# ↳ toUpperCase( )

| | |
|---|---|
| **Action** | Returns *aString* converted to uppercase. |
| **Syntax** | *aString*.toUpperCase() |
| **Arguments** | None |
| **Method of** | String |
| **See also** | **Methods:** toLowerCase() |

## Discussion

aString is a String object. Use toUpperCase() to convert a whole string to uppercase.

## Examples

Listing 8.67 and Figure 8.58 demonstrate the use of `toLowerCase()` and `toUpperCase()`.

 # unescape( )

| | |
|---|---|
| **Action** | Returns the ASCII string of a specified value according to the ISO Latin-1 character set. |
| **Syntax** | unescape(*aString*) |
| **Arguments** | *aString* is a string literal, an expression that evaluates to a string, or a property that is a number. |
| **Method of** | None |
| **See also** | **Functions:** escape( ) |

## Discussion

`aString` can take one of the following forms:

- %decimalInteger, where decimalInteger is a number between 0 and 255

- hexNumber, where hexNumber is a number between 0x0 and 0xFF

## Examples

Listing 8.18 demonstrates the use of `escape()` and `unescape()` and Figure 8.14 shows the results. Refer to `escape()`'s example.

 # untaint(*aProperty*)

| | |
|---|---|
| **Action** | Removes tainting to a property. |
| **Syntax** | untaint(*aProperty*) |
| **Arguments** | *aProperty* is the name of the property to taint. |
| **Method of** | None |
| **See also** | **Methods:** taint( ) |

## Discussion

See "Data Tainting" in Chapter 6.

## Examples

See "Data Tainting" in Chapter 6.

#  UTC()

| | |
|---|---|
| **Action** | Returns the Universal Coordinate Time, in milliseconds, that passed since January 1, 1970 00:00:00. |
| **Syntax** | Date.UTC(*year, month, day*[, *hours*][, *minutes*][, *seconds*]) |
| **Arguments** | *year* is a year after 1900. |
| | *month* is an integer designating the month of the year between 0 (January) and 11 (December). |
| | *day* is an integer designating a day of the month between 1 and 31. |
| | *hours* is an integer designating the hour of the day between 0 and 23. |
| | *minutes* is an integer designating the minute of the hour between 0 and 59. |
| | *seconds* is an integer designating the seconds of the minute between 0 and 59. |
| **Method of** | Date |
| **See also** | **Methods:** parse() |

## Discussion

UTC() is a static method of Date, and you must use the Date.UTC() syntax.

## Examples

Listing 8.69 and Figure 8.61 demonstrate the use of Date.UTC(). Note that in spite of the fact that some parameters are outside the required ranges, Date.UTC() may return correct results.

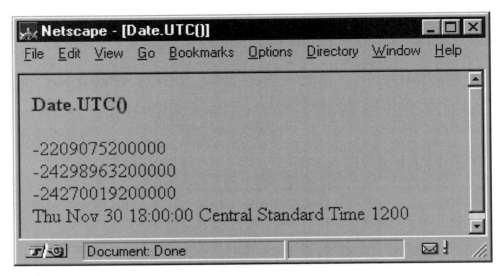

**FIGURE 8.61** Using Date.UTC().

**LISTING 8.69** Using Date.UTC().

```
1   <HTML>
2   <TITLE>UTC()</TITLE>
3   <BODY>
4   <B>UTC()</B><P>
5   <P>
6   <SCRIPT LANGUAGE = "JavaScript">
7   document.write(Date.UTC())
8   document.write("<BR>" + Date.UTC(1200))
9   document.write("<BR>" + Date.UTC(1200, 11))
10  aDate = new Date(Date.UTC(1200, 11, 1))
11  document.write("<BR>" + aDate)
12  </SCRIPT>
13  </BODY>
14  </HTML>
```

# ↳ write()

| | |
|---|---|
| **Action** | Writes one or more HTML expressions to a document in the specified window. |
| **Syntax** | document.write(*expression1*[, *expression2*],...[, *expressionN*]) |

| | |
|---|---|
| **Arguments** | *expression1...expressionN* are JavaScript expressions or properties of existing objects. |
| **Method of** | document |
| **See also** | **Methods:** close(), open(), writeln() |

## Discussion

In working with write(), keep the following in mind:

- You can use write() to build an HTML page.

- Expressions can be numerical, string, or logical.

- write() and writeln() are similar, except that writeln(), under some conditions, adds an new-line character at the end of the output.

- If you use write() in an event handler, it is executed after the document to which the write() belongs closes; thus, the write() implicitly opens a new document of mimeType text/html if you do not issue a document.open() in the event handler.

## Examples

write() is used profusely throughout this chapter; pick any example.

 # writeln()

| | |
|---|---|
| **Action** | Writes one or more HTML expressions to a document in the specified window. |
| **Syntax** | document.writeln(*expression1*[, *expression2*],...[, *expressionN*]) |
| **Arguments** | *expression1...expressionN* are JavaScript expressions or properties of existing objects. |
| **Method of** | document |
| **See also** | **Methods:** close(), open(), write() |

## Discussion

In working with writeln(), keep the following in mind:

- HTML ignores the new-line character, except within certain tags such as <PRE>.

- You can use writeln() to build an HTML page.

- Expressions can be numerical, string, or logical.

- write() and writeln() are similar, except that writeln(), under some circumstances, adds an new-line character at the end of the output.

- If you use writeln() in an event handler, it is executed after the document to which the writeln() belongs closes; thus, the writeln() implicitly opens a new document of mimeType text/html if you do not issue a document.open() in the event handler.

## Examples

Because the new-line character is ignored except in certain cases, many of the examples throughout this chapter use write() with <BR> or <P> as an argument.

# PROPERTIES REFERENCE

⮱ Dicussion of each of the available JavaScript properties

⮱ Examples for each of these properties

⮱ Examples demonstrating debugging techniques and specific applications

#  Introduction

Each of the JavaScript provided properties is discussed in detail. The presentations adhere to the following template structure:

| | |
|---|---|
| **Stores** | Briefly states the value this property stores. |
| **Syntax** | The syntax you use to work with this property. |
| **Access** | Whether the property is read, or read and write. A property is defined as read and write if its value can be changed via JavaScript in at least in one case. Be aware that some properties are read only when they belong to one object, and read and write when they belong to another object. |
| **Property of** | A list of the objects that have a property of this name. |
| **See also** | Some related objects, properties, or methods. |

After the list above, each property's presentation has corresponding:

- **Discussion.** Details pertinent to the property, such as elaboration on the syntax, the property's behavior under various circumstances, and so on.

- **Examples.** Examples that demonstrate the use of the property.

## How to Read This Chapter

Keep in mind that the material in this chapter is for reference. This means that the presentation, in most cases, is rigid and dry. To make it more entertaining, I have buried jokes in some of the examples (and in the text here and there). When you do your work and use a property that does not behave as expected, or when you want to learn about the potential uses of a property, read its relevant section here.

When you get to an example, you should first run it and examine its behavior. Then, take a look at the code and see what it does.

Learning JavaScript is like learning a language: Vocabulary develops with use but needs occasional review. I suggest you review this chapter every now and then, even if you are an experienced user. This will remind you what can be done with JavaScript, its objects, their methods and their properties.

 # action

| | |
|---|---|
| **Stores** | The destination URL for submitted form data |
| **Syntax** | *formName*.action |
| **Access** | Read and write |
| **Property of** | form |
| **See also** | **Objects:** submit |
| | **Event handlers:** onSubmit |

## Discussion

In the syntax above, *formName* is the value assigned to the NAME attribute of the <FORM> tag.

Here are some points to remember when using the `action` property:

- It holds the value assigned to the `ACTION` attribute of the `<FORM>` tag.

- See discussion of the `location` object in Chapter 7.

- Currently there is discussion about implementing a way for clients to submit files to a server. How this will affect your ability to receive information from a visitor of your page without having to rely on intermediate server processing is not clear. To learn more about these efforts, see http://www.ics.uci.edu/pub/ietf/html/rfc1867.txt.

## Examples

Listing 9.1 and Figure 9.1 demonstrate the use of `action`. Here is a quick explanation of the code:

- In lines 6 to 15 we set a message to be e-mailed. The message includes the values of `document.title` and `document.location` properties, and a supposedly smart quotation.

- In line 32 we define the action: `mailto` in this case. To send the message to yourself, change `name@address` to your e-mail address; if you want the message subject to be different, change `Not again?!` to something else.

- The message is actually sent in the value of the `hidden` object named `theInfo`—we assign the message `value` to the value of `theInfo` in lines 12 and 13.

Here is an interesting challenge:

- Construct an array of e-mail addresses of your friends.

- Construct the `mailto...` string in line 22 with the array elements.

- Send a single message to all of your friends, looping through the array elements.

This is a challenging assignment. Once you do it, you can blast a single message by a click of a button to as many people as you wish. Some hints: You will need to construct all of aForm (lines 21 to 31) using JavaScript; you can simulate a click on the `submit` button in the sending loop. Can you think of interesting applications?

**LISTING 9.1** Using action, hidden, mailto, and submit.

```
1    <HTML>
2    <HEAD>
3    <TITLE>action</TITLE>
4
5    <SCRIPT LANGUAGE = "JavaScript">
6    function mailIt(theForm)
7    {
8      var info = ""
9      info += "\n\nDocument Title:\t" +
10     document.title + "\n"
11     info += "From:\t\t\t" + document.location + "\n"
12     theForm.theInfo.value = info + "\n" +
13      "Success precedes Work in dictionaries only"
14     return true
15   }
16   </SCRIPT>
17   </HEAD>
18
19   <BODY>
20   <H3>Action... said the director</H3>
21   <FORM  NAME = "aForm"
22       ACTION = "mailto:name@address?subject=Not again?!"
23       ENCTYPE = "multipart/form-data"
24       onSubmit = "mailIt(this)">
25
26   <INPUT  TYPE = "hidden"
27       NAME = "theInfo"
28       VALUE = " ">
29   <INPUT TYPE = "submit"
30   VALUE = "Submit...">
31         </FORM>
32   </BODY>
33   </HTML>
```

#  alinkColor

| | |
|---|---|
| **Stores** | The color of an active link |
| **Syntax** | document.alinkColor |
| **Access** | Read and write |
| **Property of** | document |
| **See also** | **Objects:** link |
| | **Properties:** linkColor, vlinkColor |

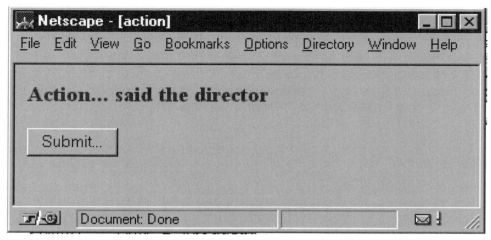

**FIGURE 9.1** Using `action`, `hidden`, `mailto`, and `submit`.

## Discussion

Here are some details to remember when working with the `alinkColor` property:

- A link is defined as active as long as the mouse button is pressed on it.

- `alinkColor` holds the value assigned to the `ALINK` attribute of the `<BODY>` tag.

- Once an HTML source file has been loaded, you cannot change the value of this property; thus, your assignment to `alinkColor` will work if it appears within the `<HEAD>` ... `</HEAD>` tags.

- Color can be expressed as the hexadecimal value of the mix of red, green, and blue using the syntax RRGGBB, where RR is the amount of red, GG is the amount of green, and BB is the amount of blue in the mix; RR, GG, and BB range from 00 to FF.

- Color can also be expressed as one of the string literals in Appendix C.

## Examples

Listing 9.2 and Figure 9.2 demonstrate the use of `alinkColor`. The code is self-explanatory.

**LISTING 9.2** Using `alinkColor`.

```
1    <HTML>
2    <HEAD>
3    <TITLE>alinkColor</TITLE>
4    <SCRIPT LANGAUGE = "JavaScript">
5    document.alinkColor = "00FF00"
6    </SCRIPT>
7    </HEAD>
8
9    <BODY>
10   <H3>alinkColor</H3>
11   <A HREF = "http://turtle.gis.umn.edu">
12   link color is green when mouse is down on it</A>
13   </BODY>
14   </HTML>
```

# anchors

| | |
|---|---|
| **Stores** | An array of anchor objects |
| **Syntax** | document.anchors |
| **Access** | Read only |
| **Property of** | document |
| **See also** | **Objects:** anchor |

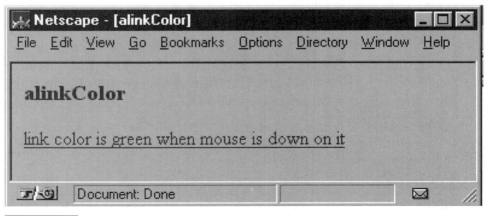

**FIGURE 9.2** Using `alinkColor`.

## Discussion

The anchors property behaves (roughly) as follows:

- Elements (anchor objects) are added to the anchors array as they are encountered in the HTML source code.

- Each document has its own anchors array.

- The anchors array is discussed in detail in the reference to the anchor object (Chapter 7).

## Examples

Listing 9.3 and Figure 9.3 demonstrate the use of anchors. The code is self-explanatory.

**LISTING 9.3** Using anchors.

```
1    <HTML>
2    <HEAD>
3    <TITLE>anchors</TITLE>
4    </HEAD>
5    <BODY>
6    <H3>anchors</H3>
7    <A HREF = "http://turtle.gis.umn.edu"
8       NAME = 'anAnchor'
9       onMouseOver = 'alert(document.anchors)'>
10   mouse over this will display the anchor</A>
11   </BODY>
12   </HTML>
```

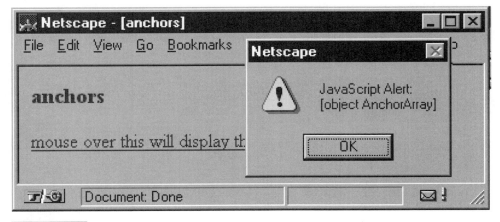

**FIGURE 9.3** Using anchors.

# appCodeName

| | |
|---|---|
| **Stores** | The code name of the browser |
| **Syntax** | `navigator.appCodeName` |
| **Access** | Read only |
| **Property of** | `navigator` |
| **See also** | **Properties:** `appName`, `appVersion`, `userAgent` |

## Discussion

Use this property to test for the browser your visitor is running. You can then execute part of your JavaScript conditionally.

## Examples

Listing 9.4 and Figure 9.4 demonstrate the use of `appCodeName`. There is an error in the listing; can you find it?

**LISTING 9.4** Using `appCodeName`.

```
1    <HTML>
2    <TITLE>appCodeName</TITLE>
3
4    <BODY>
5    <B>appCodeName</B>
6    <P>
7    <SCRIPT LANGUAGE = "JavaScript">
8    var app = 'mozilla'
9    if (app == 'Mozilla')
10   document.write('navigator.appCodeName is = "' +
11   navigator.appCodeName + '"')
12   else
13   document.write('Sorry, to take full benefit of this page you
     should be running Netscape Navigator')
14   </SCRIPT>
15   </BODY>
16   </HTML>
```

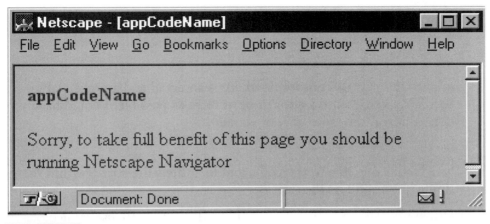

**FIGURE 9.4** Using appCodeName.

#  appName

| | |
|---|---|
| **Stores** | A string specifying the code name of the browser |
| **Syntax** | navigator.appName |
| **Access** | Read only |
| **Property of** | navigator |
| **See also** | **Properties:** appVersion, appCodeName, userAgent |

## Discussion

Use this property when you need to know the name of the browser application that the visitor of your page is using. You can then execute JavaScript and HTML code conditionally.

## Examples

Listing 9.5 and Figure 9.5 demonstrate the use of appName to verify that the visitor is running Netscape; if she is not, she is bumped back() one step in her history. Try running this example and see what happens.

Here are a couple of things to note about the code:

- The `if` statement in line 9:

```
if((an=navigator.appName)!="netscape")
```

might seem a little contorted—there is an equal and a not-equal in there. Why? Because I want to be as terse as possible. I could have done this (on the same line, of course):

```
'an=navigator.appName;if(an!=...'
```

which adds one line to the code, and lengthens the string within the single quotes in line 9.

- When using JavaScript code in an HTML tag (line 9), use semicolons to separate statements, and braces (`"{...}"`) everywhere possible whether needed or not. For example, although the statements `if (x == y) do_something` and `if (x == y) { do_something }` are both correct, you should include the braces when JavaScript code is embedded in a string.

**LISTING 9.5** Using `appName` and `back()`.

```
1    <HTML>
2    <HEAD>
3    <TITLE>appName and back()</TITLE>
4    <SCRIPT LANGUAGE = "JavaScript">
5    var an = ""
6    </SCRIPT>
7    </HEAD>
8
9    <BODY onLoad =
'if((an=navigator.appName)!="netscape"){alert("Sorry, you are using
"+an+"\nThis page is designed for Netscape users");history.back()}'>
10   <H3>appName and back()</H3>
11   <BIG>Congratulations</BIG>, you're in!
12   </BODY>
13   </HTML>
```

Oh, and one more thing, I forgot to tell you that there is an error in the code in Listing 9.5. Did you find it? If not, the clue is: JavaScript is case sensitive (in line 9 I meant `Navigator`, **not** `navigator`).

**FIGURE 9.5** Using appName and back().

 # appVersion

| | |
|---|---|
| **Stores** | The version information for the Navigator |
| **Syntax** | navigator.appVersion |
| **Access** | Read only |
| **Property of** | navigator |
| **See also** | **Properties:** appCodeName, appName, userAgent |

## Discussion

Use this property when you need to know what version of the application the user is using. You can then execute JavaScript and HTML code conditionally.

The value stored in appVersion has the following format:

```
releaseNumber(platform; country)
```

where

- releaseNumber is the version number of the Navigator (for example, read 2.0b4 as Navigator 2.0, beta 4).

- `platform` is the operating system on which the Navigator is running (e.g., Win16, Win32, Win95, MacOS, and so on).

- `country` is either I (international release), or U (U.S. release). These differ in their encryption features.

## Examples

Listing 9.6 and Figure 9.6 demonstrate the use of `appName` and `appVersion`.

**LISTING 9.6** appVersion and appName.

```
1    <HTML>
2    <HEAD>
3    <TITLE>appVersion and appName</TITLE>
4    <SCRIPT LANGUAGE = "JavaScript">
5    var an = navigator.appName
6    var av = navigator.appVersion
7    </SCRIPT>
8    </HEAD>
9    <BODY onLoad = 'alert("You are running "+an+"\nVersion "+av)'>
10   <H3>appVersion and appName</H3>
11   <BIG>Congratulations</BIG>, you're in; no errors this time.
12   </BODY>
13   </HTML>
```

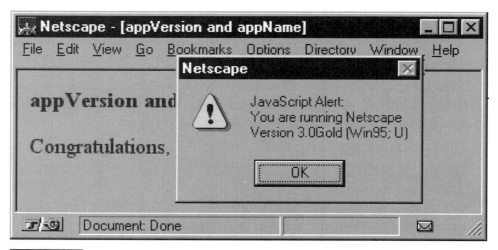

**FIGURE 9.6** appVersion and appName.

# arguments

| | |
|---|---|
| **Stores** | `Function` object's arguments in an array |
| **Syntax** | *functionObjectName*`.arguments[`*index*`]` |
| **Access** | Read only |
| **Property of** | `Function` |
| **See also** | **Keyword:** `function` |

## Discussion

In the syntax above:

- *functionObjectName* is the name of a `Function` object.

- *index* is an integer index designating the desired argument of the function.

Keep the following in mind:

- If you use `arguments` inside the code (braces) of a `Function` in order to see the function's arguments, use the keyword `this` instead of *functionObjectName*.

- You can use this property to deal with functions that get a variable number of arguments.

## Examples

Listing 9.7 and Figure 9.7 demonstrate the use of `arguments`. The code is (almost) self-explanatory. For further elaboration, see examples for `indexOf()` in Chapter 8.

**LISTING 9.7** Using `arguments`.

```
1    <HTML>
2    <HEAD>
3    <TITLE>arguments</TITLE>
4    <SCRIPT LANGUAGE = "JavaScript">
5    function seeArguments(arg1,arg2)
6    {
7      alert(seeArguments.arguments[0]+",  "+seeArguments.arguments[1])
```

```
8       return true
9     }
10    </SCRIPT>
11    </HEAD>
12
13    <BODY>
14    <H3>arguments</H3>
15    <FORM>
16    <INPUT   TYPE = "button"
17          VALUE = "See my"
18          NAME = "name"
19          onClick = "seeArguments(this.value, this.name);">
20    </BODY>
21    </HTML>
```

#  bgColor

| | |
|---|---|
| **Stores** | The HTML page background color |
| **Syntax** | `document.bgColor` |
| **Access** | Read and write |
| **Property of** | `document` |
| **See also** | **Properties:** `alinkColor`, `fgColor`, `linkColor`, `vlinkColor` |

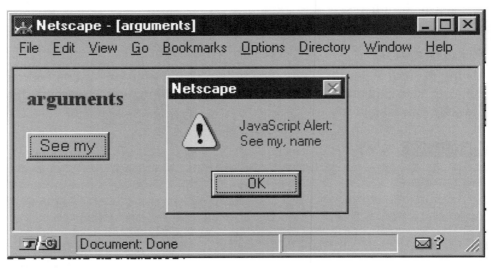

**FIGURE 9.7** Using arguments.

## Discussion

When working with bgColor, keep the following in mind:

- You can specify the bgColor as a string literal (Appendix C) or a hexadecimal RGB mix.

- If you specify bgColor as an RGB mix, follow the format RRGGBB where RR, GG, and BB are the mix levels of red, green, and blue. Each color ranges in value from 00 to FF (hexadecimal). For example, FF0000 is pure red.

- The value stored in bgColor is the value assigned to the BGCOLOR attribute of the <BODY> tag.

- The default value of bgColor is set by the user through the Options | General Preferences | Color | Background.

## Examples

Listing 9.8 and Figure 9.8 demonstrate the use of both bgColor and fgColor. Note the following:

- In line 4 we indicate commonf.js as a source file. This file is provided on the accompanying CD, and includes a number of useful functions and constants. In particular, commonf.js includes the array colors which lists the literal names of all of the colors listed in Appendix C (probably more than what you need).

- In lines 7 to 10 we set bgColor based on the index of the selected item in the select list.

- In lines 12 to 15 we do the same for the fgColor.

- In lines 27 to 30 we build the HTML options for the bgColor select object based on the list of color literals stored in the colors array and store the code in the string bgSelectList.

- In line 31 we insert the list of selected colors in the select object named bgSelectList.

- The last two actions are repeated for the fgSelectList in lines 39 to 43.

This JavaScript does not work as expected; try it and find out why!

**LISTING 9.8** Using `bgColor` and `fgColor`.

```
1    <HTML>
2    <HEAD>
3    <TITLE>bgColor and fgColor</TITLE>
4    <SCRIPT SRC = "commonf.js" LANGUAGE = "JavaScript">
5    </SCRIPT>
6    <SCRIPT LANGUAGE = "JavaScript">
7    function setBackgroundColor(selectObj)
8    {
9       document.bgColor = colors[selectObj.selectedIndex]
10   }
11
12   function setForegroundColor(selectObj)
13   {
14      document.fgColor = colors[selectObj.selectedIndex]
15   }
16   </SCRIPT>
17   </HEAD>
18
19   <BODY>
20   <H3>bgColor and fgColor</H3>
21   <FORM NAME = "aForm">
22   <B>Choose a background color:</B>
23   <SELECT NAME = "bgColor"
24        onChange = 'setBackgroundColor(this)'>
25   <SCRIPT LANGUAGE = "JavaScript">
26   var bgSelectList = "<OPTION SELECTED>" + colors[0]
27   for (var i = 1; i < colors.length; i++)
28   {
29      bgSelectList += "<OPTION>" + colors[i]
30   }
31   document.write(bgSelectList)
32   </SCRIPT>
33   </SELECT>
34   <P><B>Choose a foreground color:</B>
35   <SELECT NAME = "fgColor"
36        onChange = 'setForegroundColor(this)'>
37   <SCRIPT LANGUAGE = "JavaScript">
38   var fgSelectList = "<OPTION SELECTED>" + colors[0]
39   for (var i = 1; i < colors.length; i++)
40   {
41      fgSelectList += "<OPTION>" + colors[i]
42   }
43   document.write(fgSelectList)
44   </SCRIPT>
45   </SELECT>
46   </FORM>
47   </BODY>
48   </HTML>
```

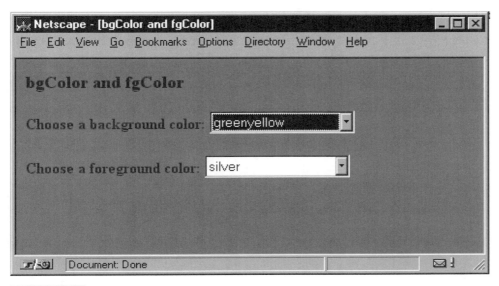

**FIGURE 9.8** Using bgColor and fgColor.

 # border

| | |
|---|---|
| **Stores** | The width, in pixels, of an image border |
| **Syntax** | *objectName*.border |
| **Access** | Read only |
| **Property of** | Image |
| **See also** | **Properties:** height, hspace, vspace, width |

## Discussion

Keep these points in mind when working with border:

- *objectName* is either the name of an Image object or an element in the images array.

- border reflects the value of the BORDER attribute of the <IMG> tag.

- If an image was created via the Image() constructor, the value of border is 0.

## Examples

Listing 9.9 and Figure 9.9 demonstrate the use of border. The code is self-explanatory:

**LISTING 9.9** Using border, align, height, vspace, and width.

```
1    <HTML>
2    <HEAD>
3    <TITLE>Border: Soar</TITLE>
4    <SCRIPT LANGUAGE = "JavaScript">
5    function soar(oh)
6    {
7       alert('Image border = ' + oh.border)
8    }
9    </SCRIPT>
10   </HEAD>
11
12   <BODY>
13   <B>border: <BIG>Soar</BIG></B>
14   <FORM NAME = "aForm">
15   <IMG NAME = "ohSoar"
16      SRC = "images\\eagle1.jpg"
17      WIDTH = 300
18      HEIGHT = 250
19      ALIGN = "left"
20      VSPACE="10"
21      BORDER = 10
22      onLoad = 'soar(this)'>
23   </FORM>
24   </BODY>
25   </HTML>
```

 # checked

| | |
|---|---|
| **Stores** | A Boolean value specifying the selection state of a checkbox or radio object |
| **Syntax** | *checkBoxName*.checked or *radioName[index]*.checked |
| **Access** | Read and write |
| **Property of** | checkbox, radio |
| **See also** | **Properties:** defaultChecked |

**FIGURE 9.9** Using `border`, `align`, `height`, `vspace`, and `width`.

## Discussion

In the syntax above:

- *checkboxName* indicates the value of the `NAME` attribute of a `checkbox` object or an element in the `elements` array.

- *radioName* indicates the value of the `NAME` attribute of a radio object.

- *index* is an integer that represents a radio button in a radio object.

In working with `checked`, keep the following in mind:

- The value of `checked` is true for a selected `radio` button in a `radio` object; otherwise it is false.

- The value of `checked` is true for a selected button in a `checkbox` object; otherwise it is false.

- The display of the checkbox or radio button updates as soon as you set `checked`.

## Examples

Listing 9.10 and Figure 9.10 demonstrate the use of `checked` and a few other things:

- In `who()` (line 5), we cycle through the buttons. If the `noyb` button is not `checked`, we tell the user that her choice is not allowed.

- No matter which button is checked, `who()` checks `noyb`.

- Note one way to test for a true condition in JavaScript (line 10).

- Note how to refer to the last element of an array (line 16).

See also Listing 9.14 and Figure 9.15.

**LISTING 9.10** Using `checked` and NOYB.

```
1    <HTML>
2    <HEAD>
3    <TITLE>checked and NOYB</TITLE>
4    <SCRIPT LANGUAGE = "JavaScript">
5    function who()
6    {
7      for (var i = 0; i < document.aForm.gender.length; i++)
8      {
9       if ( (document.aForm.gender[i].value != "noyb") &&
10        (document.aForm.gender[i].checked == "1") )
11       {
12         alert("Sorry, the only choice is NOYB")
13         break
14       }
15      }
16      document.aForm.gender[document.aForm.gender.length-1].checked
         = "1"
17      return true
18    }
19    </SCRIPT>
```

```
20    </HEAD>
21    <BODY>
22    <H3> checked and NOYB</H3>
23    <FORM NAME = "aForm">
24    <BR><B>Your name: </B>
25    <INPUT   TYPE = "text"
26          NAME = "name"
27          VALUE = "James Dean"
28          SIZE = "20">
29    <P>
30    <INPUT   TYPE = "radio"
31          NAME = "gender"
32          VALUE = "Male"
33          onClick = 'who()'> Male
34    <INPUT   TYPE = "radio"
35          NAME = "gender"
36          VALUE = "Female"
37          onClick = 'who()'> Female
38    <INPUT   TYPE = "radio"
39          NAME = "gender"
40          VALUE = "noyb"
41          CHECKED
42          onClick = 'who()'>NOYB
43    </FORM>
44    </BODY>
45    </HTML>
```

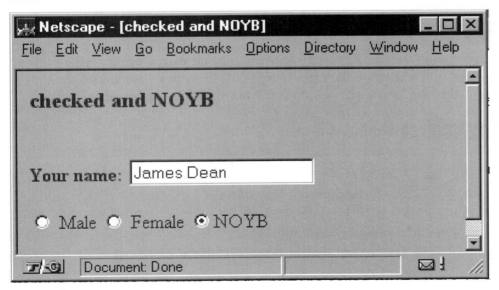

**FIGURE 9.10** Using checked and NOYB.

 complete

| | |
|---|---|
| **Stores** | `true` if Navigator has completed its attempt to load an image; otherwise `false` |
| **Syntax** | *imageName*`.complete` |
| **Access** | Read only |
| **Property of** | `Image` |
| **See also** | **Properties:** `lowsrc, src` |

## Discussion

In the syntax above, *imageName* is either the name of an `Image` object or an element in the `images` array.

Use `complete` when you need to know if an image has finished loading. In certain activities, Navigator does not wait to finish loading an image before continuing with loading a document. This is done for the sake of speed (it is usually slower to load an image than to load text). You may wish to wait in your code until an image has finished loading. For example, you can use an image for a button's face, and you do not want the button activated until the image is loaded.

## Examples

In Listing 9.11 and Figure 9.11 we are playing with soaring a little more in order to demonstrate the use of `complete`. To get it to work, load the file (or reload it), and click on the `Finished?` button while the image is loading.

**LISTING 9.11** Using `complete`.

```
1    <HTML>
2    <HEAD>
3    <TITLE>Border: Squeezed Soar</TITLE>
4    <SCRIPT LANGUAGE = "JavaScript">
5    function imageLoaded(oh)
6    {
7      if (document.images[0].complete != "1")
8          alert('Oh no!')
9      else
10         alert('Oh yeah')
```

```
11    }
12    </SCRIPT>
13    </HEAD>
14
15    <BODY>
16    <B>Border: squeezed <BIG>Soar</BIG></B>
17    <FORM NAME = "aForm">
18    <INPUT   TYPE = "button"
19          VALUE = "Finished?"
20          onClick = "imageLoaded()">
21    <IMG NAME = "ohSoar"
22       SRC = "images\\eagle1.jpg"
23       WIDTH = 350 HEIGHT = 150
24       ALIGN = "left"
25       VSPACE="10"
26       BORDER = 10>
27    </FORM>
28    </BODY>
29    </HTML>
```

 # cookie

| | |
|---|---|
| **Stores** | A string stored in the `cookies.txt` file |
| **Syntax** | `document.cookie` |
| **Access** | Read and write |
| **Property of** | `document` |
| **See also** | **Objects:** `hidden`, `String` |
| | **Methods:** see `String` methods |

## Discussion

A cookie is a string stored in the `cookies.txt` file. You can use `cookie` along with `String` methods to store and retrieve information in `cookies.txt`. For further details, refer to http://www.netscape.com/newsref/std/cookie_spec.html or http://www.ids.net/~oops/tech/ref1.html.

For security reasons, `cookies.txt` is the only file that JavaScript can read from and write to on the client's machine. The cookie mechanism allows "persistent communication" with the client; i.e., you can store information

**FIGURE 9.11** Using `complete`.

in `cookies.txt`, and the information will be available to your JavaScript code next time the user loads your URL.

The information written to `cookies.txt` is tagged with the domain and pathname that stored that information. You can then process only the information that belongs to you (that is, to your domain and pathname that wrote the information) in `cookies.txt`. The information for each cookie begins with the cookie name and ends with a semicolon. Thus, `cookies.txt` may look like this:

```
cookieName1=data1;cookieName2=data2;...;cookieNameN=dataN
```

Although not difficult, the subject of cookies is cumbersome and unpleasant to deal with. Unfortunately it must remain so for security reasons. If you decide to pursue this topic further, take a look at the example below. The file `commonf.js` contains some cookie manipulation routines. These were inserted, as is, from Bill Dortch's (of hIdaho Design) code (bdortch@netw.com). The functions are updated periodically. For the latest version, visit http://www.hidaho.com/cookies/cookie.txt.

## Examples

To see how `cookie` can be manipulated:

1. Type (or copy and paste) the code in Listing 9.12 and save it as `cookies.html`.

2. Type (or copy and paste) Listing 9.13 and save it as `SeeCookie.html`. If you cannot save long filenames, save it with a name of your choice, also replacing `SeeCookie.html` in line 30 of Listing 9.12 with the new name.

3. Load `cookies.html`, enter some text in the text box, and click on the `Set...` button (Figure 9.12).

4. Click on the `See...` button; you should see something like Figure 9.13.

Here is what the code does:

- In line 4 of Listing 9.12 we include `commonf.js`. The file contains `cookie` manipulation routines (courtesy of Bill Dortch, at bdortch@netw.com and included by permission), and is included in the enclosed CD.

- In lines 8 to 23 we define `submitCookie()`. This function verifies that there are data to be submitted in the text filed (shown in Figure 9.12).

- If there is text, then the expiration date `expdate` is set to 24 hours from now and the `cookie` and its `expdate` are written to `cookies.txt` using `SetCookie()` as shown in line 14. `SetCookie()` resides in `commonf.js`.

- If no text was entered in the text field (Figure 9.12), the user is alerted (line 19).

- When the user clicks on the `See...` button, `showCookie()` is invoked from line 48.

- In `showCookie()` (defined in lines 25 to 31) we `GetCookie()` (line 27) and then display it in another window (in line 30) as shown in Figure 9.13.

- In Listing 9.13 we simply `GetCookie()` and then show it (line 13).

- Part of what the saved cookie may look like in cookies.txt is shown in Figure 9.14; note the contorted way data are written (it is hard, but not impossible, to decipher the jokes in cookies.txt).

**LISTING 9.12** Using cookie—cookies.html.

```
1    <HTML>
2    <HEAD>
3    <TITLE>cookie</title>
4    <SCRIPT SRC = "commonf.js" LANGUAGE = "JavaScript">
5    </SCRIPT>
6    <SCRIPT LANGUAGE = "JavaScript">
7
8    function submitCookie()
9    {
10     if (document.cookieForm.cookieData.value.length != 0)
11     {
12      var expdate = new Date ()
13      expdate.setTime(expdate.getTime() + (24 * 60 * 60 * 1000))
14      SetCookie('CookieName', document.cookieForm.cookieData.value,
         expdate)
15      return false
16     }
17     else
18     {
19      alert('Enter some data to store in cookies.txt')
20      return false
21     }
22     return true
23    }
24
25    function showCookie()
26    {
27     if (GetCookie('CookieName') == null)
28      alert('Click on Set... before See...')
29     else
30      window.open('SeeCookie.html', '_top')
31    }
32    </SCRIPT>
33    <BODY>
34    <H3>cookie</H3>
35    Enter some information, click on <B>Set...,</B>
36    and then on <B>See...</B> to see the result.
37    <FORM  NAME = "cookieForm"
38      onSubmit = "submitCookie()">
39    Data to store in cookie:
```

```
40    <INPUT   TYPE = "text"
41         NAME = "cookieData"
42         SIZE=50>
43    <P>
44    <INPUT   TYPE = "submit"
45         VALUE = "Set...">
46    <INPUT   TYPE = "button"
47         VALUE = "See..."
48         onClick = "showCookie()">
49    </FORM>
50    </BODY>
51    </HTML>
```

**LISTING 9.13** Using cookie—SeeCookie.html.

```
1     <HTML>
2     <HEAD>
3     <TITLE>See the cookie</TITLE>
4     <SCRIPT SRC = "commonf.js">
5     </SCRIPT>
6     </HEAD>
7
8     <BODY>
9     <H3>See the cookie</H3>
10    Here is the data that were stored in COOKIES.TXT:
11    <P>
12    <SCRIPT LANGUAGE = "JavaScript">
13      document.write(GetCookie('CookieName'))
14    </SCRIPT>
15    </BODY>
16    </HTML>
```

# defaultChecked

| | |
|---|---|
| **Stores** | A Boolean value indicating the default selection state of a checkbox or radio button |
| **Syntax** | *checkboxName*.defaultChecked |
| | *radioName*[*index*].defaultChecked |
| **Access** | Read and write |
| **Property of** | checkbox, radio |
| **See also** | **Property:** checked |

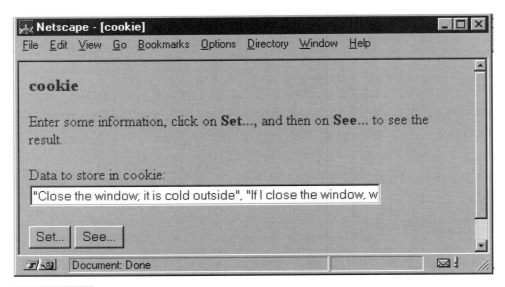

**FIGURE 9.12** Using cookie—cookies.html.

## Discussion

The defaultChecked syntax is interpreted as follows:

- *checkboxName* is either the value assigned to the NAME attribute of a checkbox object or an element in the elements array.

- *radioName* is the value of the value assigned to the NAME attribute of a radio object.

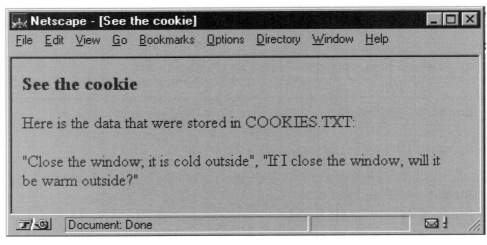

**FIGURE 9.13** Using cookie—SeeCookie.html.

```
# Netscape HTTP Cookie File

# http://www.netscape.com/newsref/std/cookie_spec.html

# This is a generated file!  Do not edit.

                846083211   CookieName
%22Close%20the%20window%3B%20it%20is%20cold%20outside%22%2C%20%22I
f%20I%20close%20the%20window%2C%20will%20it%20be%20warm%20out-
side%3F%22
defaultChecked
```

**FIGURE 9.14** A `cookies.txt` file.

- *index* is the integer index of the button in the `radio` object.

`defaultChecked` behaves as follows:

- If the object's button (`checkbox` or `radio`) is selected by default, the value of `defaultChecked` is true; otherwise, it is false.
- If the `CHECKED` attribute is indicated within an `<INPUT>` tag, then `defaultChecked` is initially set to true.
- Setting `defaultChecked` overrides the `CHECKED` attribute.
- `defaultChecked` does not update the display of its object (a `checkbox` or a `radio` button).
- To update the display of a `checkbox` or `radio` button object, use the `checked` property.

## Examples

Listing 9.14 and Figure 9.15 demonstrate the use of `defaultChecked` and `checked` (see also Listing 9.10 and Figure 9.10). The example also shows how you can force a radio button to be checked.

**LISTING 9.14** `defaultChecked`, `checked`, and campaign contributions.

```
1   <HTML>
2   <HEAD>
3   <TITLE>defaultChecked, checked, and campaign laws</TITLE>
4   <SCRIPT LANGUAGE = "JavaScript">
```

```
5     function defaultReset()
6     {
7       for (var i =0; i< document.aForm.tf.length; i++)
8         if (document.aForm.tf[i].defaultChecked == true)
9         {
10          alert("Sorry, it is true!")
11          document.aForm.tf[i].checked = true
12        }
13    }
14    </SCRIPT>
15    </HEAD>
16
17    <BODY>
18    <H3>defaultChecked, checked, and campaign laws</H3>
19    I would like to see campaign laws changed
20    <FORM NAME = "aForm">
21    <INPUT  TYPE = "radio"
22          NAME = "tf"
23          VALUE = "True"
24          CHECKED
25          onClick = 'defaultReset()'> True
26    <INPUT  TYPE = "radio"
27          NAME = "tf"
28          VALUE = "False"
29          onClick = 'defaultReset()'> False
30    <INPUT  TYPE = "radio"
31          NAME = "tf"
32          VALUE = "NotSure"
33          onClick = 'defaultReset()'>I'm not sure
34    </FORM>
35    </BODY>
36    </HTML>
```

 # defaultSelected

| | |
|---|---|
| **Stores** | A Boolean value indicating the default selection state of an option in a `select` object |
| **Syntax** | *selectName*.options[*index*].defaultSelected |
| | or |
| | *optionName*.defaultSelected |
| **Access** | Read and write |
| **Property of** | *options* array |
| **See also** | **Properties:** index, selected, selectedIndex |

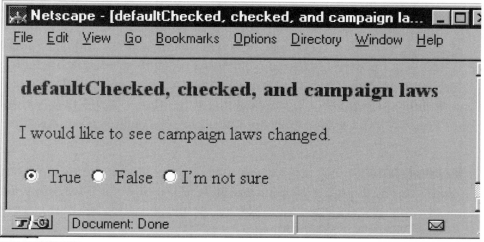

**FIGURE 9.15**  defaultChecked, checked, and campaign contributions.

## Discussion

The syntax of defaultSelected is interpreted as follows:

- *selectName* is either the value assigned to the NAME attribute of a select object or an element in the elements array.
- *index* is an integer representing an option in a select object.
- *optionName* is the name of a Select object option created using the Option() constructor.

defaultSelected behaves as follows:

- The defaultSelected value is set to true if an option is selected by default; otherwise, it is set to false.
- The initial value of defaultSelected is set to true for the option for which the SELECTED attribute is used within the <OPTION> tag.
- Setting defaultSelected overrides the SELECTED attribute.
- Setting the value of defaultSelected does not update the display of the select object.
- To update the display of the select object, set the selected or selectedIndex properties.

- If you want to use defaultSelected for more than one option at a time, use the MULTIPLE attribute of the select object.

- Using the MULTIPLE attribute of the select object causes defaultSelected to clear any previous default selections, including defaults set with the SELECTED attribute.

- If you use the MULTIPLE attribute of the select object, the defaultSelected value does not affect previous default selections.

## Examples

Listing 9.15 and Figure 9.16 demonstrate the use of defaultSelected and selected. Run it and learn about these properties.

Here is what the code does:

- In lines 21 to 29 we define the truth form with a bribe (a select object)!

- In line 24 the True option is defaultSelected!

- Any time an option is changed, restoreTheTruth() is executed (line 23).

- In restoreTheTruth() we either tell the user what a rational number is (lines 7 and 8) or that her choice was wrong (lines 9 and 10).

- In lines 11 to 13 we restore True.

**LISTING 9.15** defaultSelected and selected.

```
1    <HTML>
2    <TITLE>defaultSelected, selected, and Irrational Numbers</TITLE>
3    <HEAD>
4    <SCRIPT LANGUAGE = "JavaScript">
5    function restoreTheTruth
6    {
7      if (theTruth.options[3].selected == true)
8        alert("A number that cannot be expressed as a ratio of two
integers")
9      else
10       alert("You chose the wrong answer")
11     for (var i = 0; i < theTruth.length; i++)
12       if (theTruth.options[i].defaultSelected == true)
13           theTruth.options[i].selected = true
14   }
15   </SCRIPT>
```

```
16    </HEAD>
17
18    <BODY>
19    <H3>defaultSelected, selected, and Irrational numbers</H3>
20    The square root of 2 is an irrational number!
21    <FORM  NAME = "truth">
22    <SELECT NAME = "bribe"
23         onChange = 'restoreTheTruth(this)'>
24     <OPTION SELECTED> True
25     <OPTION> False
26     <OPTION> I'm not sure
27     <OPTION> What is an irrational number?
28    </SELECT>
29    </FORM>
30    </BODY>
31    </HTML>
```

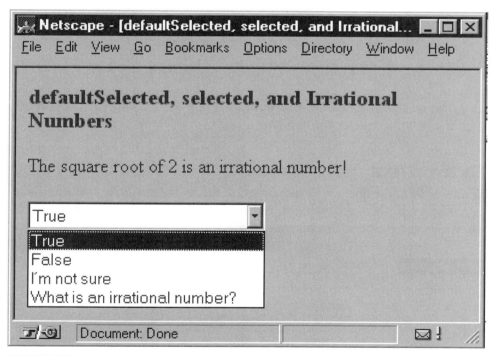

**FIGURE 9.16**  defaultSelected and selected.

# defaultStatus

| | |
|---|---|
| **Stores** | The default message displayed in the status bar at the bottom of the Navigator window |
| **Syntax** | *windowReference*.defaultStatus |
| **Access** | Read and write |
| **Property of** | window |
| **See also** | **Property:** status |

## Discussion

For explanation of windowReference, see **Discussion** of the window object in Chapter 7.

defaultStatus behaves as follows:

- It is displayed when no other string is specified for the status bar.

- the status property overrides (has a higher priority over) the defaultStatus.

- You must return true if you want to set the defaultStatus property via the onMouseOver event handler.

## Examples

Listing 9.16 and Figure 9.17 demonstrate the use of defaultStatus and status. The example is self-evident. As you use the example, note in particular when the status line at the bottom of the window changes.

**LISTING 9.16** defaultStatus and status.

```
1    <HTML>
2    <TITLE>defaultStatus, status</TITLE>
3    <HEAD>
4    <SCRIPT LANGUAGE = "JavaScript">
5    function statusOfTruth()
6    {
7      window.defaultStatus = "Click any link to the answer"
8      window.status = "Naturally"
9    }
```

```
10    </SCRIPT>
11    </HEAD>
12
13    <BODY>
14    <H3>defaultStatus and status</H3>
15    Who is on first base.
16    <P>
17    <A HREF = "9-1.html"
18       onMouseOver = "statusOfTruth(); return true">Yes
19    </A>
20    or
21    <A HREF = "9-16.html"
22       onMouseOver = "statusOfTruth(); return true">No
23    </A>
24    </BODY>
25    </HTML>
```

 # defaultValue

| | |
|---|---|
| **Stores** | A string indicating the default value of its object |
| **Syntax** | *objectName*.defaultValue |
| **Access** | Read and write |
| **Property of** | password, text, textarea |
| **See also** | **Properties:** value |

## Discussion

In the syntax above, *objectName* can take one of the following values:

- The value of the NAME attribute of a password object, or a password object that is an element in the elements array

- The value of the NAME attribute of a text object, or a text object that is an element in the elements array

- The value of the NAME attribute of a textarea object, or a textarea object that is an element in the elements array

The initial value of defaultValue depends on the object that owns the property and is set as follows:

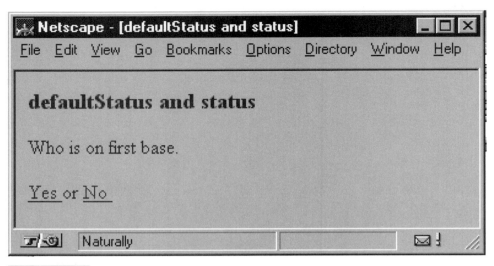

**FIGURE 9.17** defaultStatus and status.

- For `password` objects, it initially is `null` (for security reasons), regardless of the value of the `VALUE` attribute.
- For `text` objects, it initially reflects the value of the `VALUE` attribute.
- For `textarea` objects, it initially reflects the value specified between the `<TEXTAREA>` and `</TEXTAREA>` tags.

Setting `defaultValue` programatically behaves as follows:

- It overrides the initial setting.
- For the password object, it causes JavaScript to return the current value.
- It does not update the display of the object that owns it. To update the display of the relevant object, set its `value` property.

## Examples

Listing 9.17 and Figure 9.18 demonstrate the use of `defaultValue`. The result of running the code is the message window shown in Figure 9.19.

**LISTING 9.17** Using `defaultValue`.

```
1    <HTML>
2    <TITLE>defaultValue</TITLE>
3    <HEAD>
```

```
4     <SCRIPT LANGUAGE = "JavaScript">
5     function dv()
6     {
7       msgWindow = window.open("")
8       msgWindow.document.write("<B>Default Values for:</B><P>")
9       msgWindow.document.write("password = " +
10      document.f.p.defaultValue + "<BR>")
11      msgWindow.document.write("text = " +
12      document.f.t.defaultValue + "<BR>")
13      msgWindow.document.write("textarea = " +
14      document.f.a.defaultValue + "<BR>")
15      msgWindow.document.close()
16    }
17    </SCRIPT>
18    </HEAD>
19
20    <BODY>
21    <H3>defaultValue</H3>
22    <FORM   NAME = "f">
23    <INPUT   TYPE = "password"
24        NAME = "p"
25        VALUE = "password default value"><BR>
26    <INPUT   TYPE = "text"
27        NAME = "t"
28        VALUE = "text default value"><BR>
29    <INPUT   TYPE = "textarea"
30        NAME = "a"
31        VALUE = "textarea default value"><BR>
32    <INPUT   TYPE = "button"
33        VALUE = "Reveal the truth"
34        onClick = 'dv()'>
35    </BODY>
36    </HTML>
```

 # description

| | |
|---|---|
| **Stores** | Description of the type of the mimeTypes object or description of an item in the plugins array |
| **Syntax** | navigator.*aName*[*anIdentifier*] |
| **Access** | Read only |
| **Property of** | mimeTypes, plugins array |
| **See also** | **Objects:** mimeTypes, plugins |

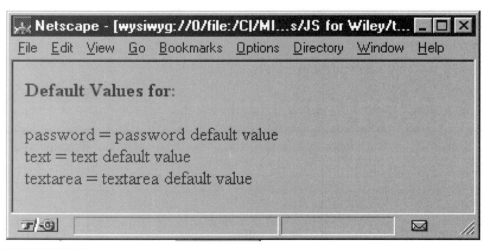

**FIGURE 9.18** Using `defaultValue`.

## Discussion

In the syntax above, *aName* and *anIdentifier* can take one of the following values:

**FIGURE 9.19** Seeing `defaultValue`.

- `navigator.mimeTypes[`*`index`*`].description`
- `navigator.mimeTypes[`*`mimeTypeName`*`].description`
- `navigator.plugins[`*`index`*`].description`
- `navigator.plugins[`*`pluginName`*`].description`

For further details, refer to the discussion of the `mimeTypes` object and `plugins` array in Chapters 6 and 7.

## Examples

See Exercise 7.13, Listing 9.21, Figure 9.23, and the discussion of `mimeTypes` and `Plugins` in Chapters 7 and 8.

 E

| | |
|---|---|
| **Stores** | Euler's constant and the base of natural logarithms |
| **Syntax** | `Math.E` |
| **Access** | Read only |
| **Property of** | `Math` |
| **See also** | **Properties:** `PI` |

## Discussion

The approximate value of E is shown in Figure 9.20.

## Examples

Listing 9.18 and Figure 9.20 conspire to reveal the value of all of the `Math` object's constants.

**LISTING 9.18** `Math` constants.

```
1    <HTML>
2    <TITLE>Math Constants</TITLE>
3    <BODY>
4    <H3>Math Constants</H3>
5    <SCRIPT LANGUAGE = "JavaScript">
6    with (Math)
```

```
7    {
8       document.write("E = ", E)
9       document.write("<BR>LN2 = ", LN2)
10      document.write("<BR>LN10 = ", LN10)
11      document.write("<BR>LOG2E = ", LOG10E)
12      document.write("<BR>LOG10E = ", LOG10E)
13      document.write("<BR>PI = ", PI)
14      document.write("<BR>SQRT1_2 = ", SQRT1_2)
15      document.write("<BR>SQRT2 = ", SQRT2)
16    }
17    </SCRIPT>
18    </BODY>
19    </HTML>
```

#  elements

| | |
|---|---|
| **Stores** | An array of objects corresponding to form elements |
| **Syntax** | *formName*.elements[*index*] |
| **Access** | Read and write |
| **Property of** | form |
| **See also** | **Objects:** button, checkbox, password, radio, select, text, textarea |

## Discussion

In the elements syntax:

- *formName* is either the name of a form or an element in the forms array.

- *index* is an integer representing an object on a form.

Elements (buttons, checkboxes, radios, texts, textareas) are added to elements in the order they appear in the HTML source code. Because elements is an array object, it has a length property. For further details, see the discussion of the elements array in Chapter 7.

## Examples

See the example for the elements array in Chapter 7.

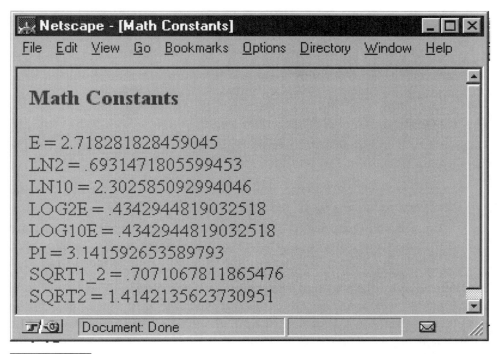

Netscape - [Math Constants]

File  Edit  View  Go  Bookmarks  Options  Directory  Window  Help

# Math Constants

E = 2.718281828459045
LN2 = .6931471805599453
LN10 = 2.302585092994046
LOG2E = .4342944819032518
LOG10E = .4342944819032518
PI = 3.141592653589793
SQRT1_2 = .7071067811865476
SQRT2 = 1.4142135623730951

Document: Done

**FIGURE 9.20**  Math constants.

#  enabledPlugin

| | |
|---|---|
| **Stores** | A reference to the `Plugin` object for the plug-in that handles a specified MIME type, or NULL if no plug-in handles the specified MIME type |
| **Syntax** | *mimeTypesObjectName*.`enabledPlugin` |
| **Access** | Read only |
| **Property of** | `mimeTypes` |
| **See also** | **Objects:** `plugins` |

## Discussion

This property might be confusing, and the example below is intended to clarify its purpose. Also, recall that:

• The `mimeTypes` object is an array of all MIME types supported by the client. Each element of the array is a `mimeType` object.

- The `plugins` object is an array of all plug-ins currently installed on the client. Each element of the array is a `plugin` object. One of the `plugins` object's properties is the array of `mimeTypes` objects for the MIME types supported by that plug-in.

All of this is confusing to me. So I ran the example below.

## Examples

Listing 9.19 is intended to clarify the role of `enabledPlugin`. In particular, note the following:

- In line 9 we declare an `obj` variable; this variable stores the object name that is stored in `enabledPlugin` (line 13).
- If there is an object stored in `enabledPlugin` (line 14), we go ahead and print the values stored in the `mimeTypes`'s properties `type` (line 17), `enabledPlugin` (line 19), `description` (line 20), and `suffixes` (line 21).

"Why do you have to first use the assignment statement in line 13 and then print `obj.name` in line 19? Couldn't you just write the `navigator.mimeTypes[i].enabledPlugin` in line 19?" you might ask. The answer is because, otherwise, the response from the write statement (beginning in line 16) would be `[object Plugin]`, but not the object name! To see this, replace `obj.name` in line 19 with `navigator.mimeTypes[i].enabledPlugin` and run the listing again.

Here are a few more points to notice:

- A single `enabledPlugin` can reference more than one `mimeTypes type`. For example, `Live Audio` references both `audio/x-midi` and `audio/midi` (see Figure 9.21).
- An `enabledPlugin` might not have a `type`. For example, `Netscape Default Plugin` holds the * type, which is not an object (Figure 9.21). To clarify this idea, remove the `if` statement in line 14 and run the listing again. What happened?
- Your display of available MIME types might differ from mine (Figure 9.21).

**LISTING 9.19** Using the `mimeTypes` properties `description`, `enabledPlugin`, `mimeTypes`, `suffixes`, and `type`.

```
1    <HTML>
2    <TITLE>Installed MIME Types</TITLE>
```

```
3     <HEAD>
4     <H3>Installed MIME Types</H3>
5
6     <SCRIPT LANGUAGE = "JavaScript">
7     function showMimes()
8     {
9       var obj = ""
10      document.writeln("<OL>")
11      for (i = 0; i < navigator.mimeTypes.length; i++)
12      {
13       obj = navigator.mimeTypes[i].enabledPlugin
14       if (obj != null)
15       {
16         document.write(
17           "<LI>Type: ", navigator.mimeTypes[i].type,
18           "<UL><LI>enabledPlugin: ",
19           obj.name,
20           "<LI>Description: ", navigator.mimeTypes[i].description,
21           "<LI>Suffixes: ", navigator.mimeTypes[i].suffixes,
22    "</UL>")
23        }
24      }
25      document.writeln("</OL>")
26    }
27    </SCRIPT>
28    </HEAD>
29
30    <BODY>
31    <FORM>
32    <INPUT  TYPE = "button"
33        VALUE = "Show installed MIME types..."
34        onClick = "showMimes()">
35    </FORM>
36    </BODY>
37    </HTML>
```

 # encoding

| | |
|---|---|
| **Stores** | A string specifying the MIME encoding of a form |
| **Syntax** | *formName*.encoding |
| **Access** | Read and write |
| **Property of** | form |
| **See also** | **Objects:** mimeTypes |
| | **Properties:** action, method, target |

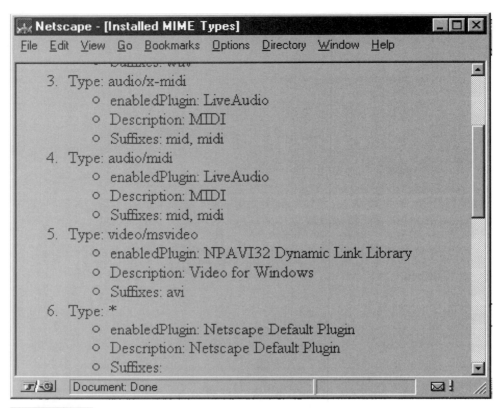

**FIGURE 9.21** Using the mimeTypes properties description, enabledPlugin, mimeTypes, suffixes, and type.

## Discussion

In the syntax above, *formName* refers to one of the following:

- The name of a form
- An element in the forms array

encoding initially reflects the value stored in the ENCTYPE attribute of the <FORM> tag. Setting encoding overrides the ENCTYPE attribute. Refer to http://www.ics.uci.edu/pub/ietf/html/rfc1867.txt for more information.

## Examples

Listing 9.20 and Figure 9.22 demonstrate the use of encoding. The example is self-explanatory.

**LISTING 9.20** Using encoding.

```
1    <HTML>
2    <TITLE>encoding</TITLE>
3    <HEAD>
4    <SCRIPT LANGUAGE = "JavaScript">
5    function showEncoding()
6    {
7       alert(document.forms[0].encoding)
8    }
9    </SCRIPT>
10   </HEAD>
11
12   <BODY>
13   <H3>encoding</H3>
14   <FORM  ENCTYPE = "multipart/form-data">
15   <INPUT  TYPE = "button"
16        VALUE = "This form's encoding is..."
17        onClick = "showEncoding()">
18   </FORM>
19   </BODY>
20   </HTML>
```

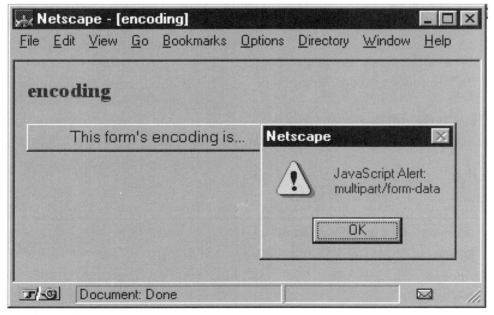

**FIGURE 9.22** Using encoding.

 # fgColor

| | |
|---|---|
| **Stores** | The HTML page foreground color |
| **Syntax** | *objectName*.fgColor |
| **Access** | Read and write |
| **Property of** | document |
| **See also** | **Properties:** bgColor, alinkColor, linkColor, vlinkColor |

## Discussion

When working with fgColor, keep the following in mind:

- You can specify the fgColor as a string literal (see Appendix C) or a hexadecimal RGB mix.
- If you specify fgColor as an RGB mix, follow the format RRGGBB, where RR, GG, and BB are the mix levels of red, green, and blue. Each color ranges in value from 00 to FF (hexadecimal). For example, FF0000 is pure red.
- The value stored in fgColor is the value assigned to the FGCOLOR attribute of the <BODY> tag.
- The default value of fgColor is set by the user via the Options | General Preferences... | colors | Text.
- You can set fgColor at any time.

## Examples

Listing 9.8 and Figure 9.8 demonstrate the use of both bgColor and fgColor.

 # filename

| | |
|---|---|
| **Stores** | A plug-in's filename |
| **Syntax** | navigator.plugins[*index*].filename |
| **Access** | Read only |
| **Property of** | plugins |
| **See also** | **Object:** mimeTypes |

## Discussion

In the syntax above, *index* can be specified in one of two ways:

- Integer, which reflects the index of the specific plug-in in the plugins array

- Plug-in name, specified as a string, as in navigator.plugins ["Shockwave"].filename

## Examples

Listing 9.21 and Figure 9.23 demonstrate how to access the plugins properties description, filename, length, and name. Your display of available plugins might differ from mine (Figure 9.23).

**LISTING 9.21** Using the plugins properties description, filename, length, and name.

```
1    <HTML>
2    <TITLE>Installed plugins</TITLE>
3    <HEAD>
4    <SCRIPT LANGUAGE = "JavaScript">
5    function showPlugins()
6    {
7      document.writeln("<OL>")
8      for (i = 0; i < navigator.plugins.length; i++)
9      {
10      document.write(
11        "<LI>name: ", navigator.plugins[i].name,
12        "<UL><LI>filename: ",
13        navigator.plugins[i].filename,
14        "<LI>description: ", navigator.plugins[i].description,
15   "</UL>")
16      }
17      document.writeln("</OL>")
18    }
19    </SCRIPT>
20    </HEAD>
21
22    <BODY>
23    <H3>Installed plugins</H3>
24    <FORM>
25    <INPUT  TYPE = "button"
26        VALUE = "Show installed plug-ins..."
27        onClick = "showPlugins()">
28    </FORM>
29    </BODY>
30    </HTML>
```

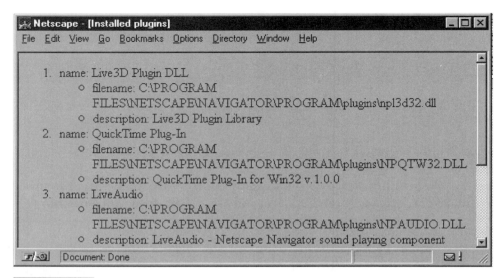

**FIGURE 9.23** Using the `plugins` properties `description`, `filename`, `length`, and `name`.

 # forms

| | |
|---|---|
| **Stores** | An array of `form` objects |
| **Syntax** | `document.forms[index]` |
| **Access** | Read only |
| **Property of** | `document` |
| **See also** | **Objects:** `form` |

## Discussion

Here are a few points to keep in mind:

- `index` in the syntax above can be an integer in the range 0 to `forms.length` −1, or a string specifying the `form` name as in `document.forms["aForm"]`, where `aForm` is the value assigned to the NAME attribute of the `<FORM>` tag.

- Each entry in the `forms` array corresponds to one `<FORM>` tag in a document. Array elements are ordered according to their order in the source HTML document.

See the discussion of the `form` object in Chapter 7 for further details.

## Examples

Listing 9.22 and Figure 9.24 demonstrate the use of the `forms` array and the `name` property of the `form` object. Note in particular the two ways to index the `forms` array:

- with the form name (line 8)
- with the form index (line 11)

**LISTING 9.22** Using `forms` and the `name` properties.

```
1    <HTML>
2    <TITLE>forms</TITLE>
3    <HEAD>
4    <SCRIPT LANGUAGE = "JavaScript">
5    function showForms()
6    {
7      formsArray = "forms[\"aForm\"].name = " +
8      document.forms["aForm"].name
9      for (var i = 1; i < document.forms.length; i++)
10      formsArray += "\n forms[" + i + "].name = " +
11     document.forms[i].name
12     alert(formsArray)
13   }
14   </SCRIPT>
15   </HEAD>
16
17   <BODY>
18   <H3>forms</H3>
19   <FORM  NAME = "aForm">
20   <INPUT  TYPE = "button"
21       VALUE = "Show forms..."
22       onClick = "showForms()">
23   </FORM>
24   <FORM  NAME = "bForm">
25   <INPUT  TYPE = "button"
26       VALUE = "Show forms..."
27       onClick = "showForms()">
28   </FORM>
29   </BODY>
30   </HTML>
```

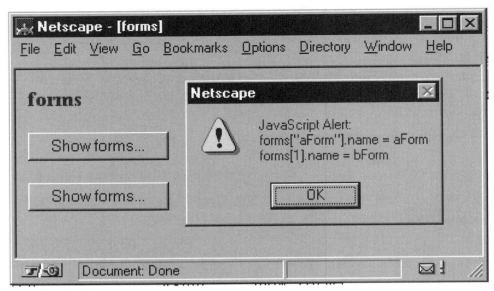

**FIGURE 9.24** Using `forms` and the `name` properties.

#  frames

| | |
|---|---|
| **Stores** | An array of objects corresponding to child frames (`<FRAME>` tag) |
| **Syntax** | *objectReference*.`frames[`*index*`]` |
| **Access** | Read only |
| **Property of** | `frame, window` |
| **See also** | **Object:** `form` |

## Discussion

In the property's syntax:

- *objectReference* can be a `window` or a `frame` reference.

- *index* is either an integer in the range 0 to `frames.length` – 1 or a string representing the value assigned to the `NAME` property in the `<FRAME>` tag.

Refer to the discussion of the `frame` object and the `frames` array in Chapter 7.

## Examples

Refer to the discussion of the `frame` object and the `frames` array in Chapter 7.

 # hash

| | |
|---|---|
| **Stores** | A string beginning with a hash mark (#) that specifies an anchor name in the URL |
| **Syntax** | `links[index].hash` or `objectName.hash` |
| **Access** | Read and write |
| **Property of** | `area`, `link`, `location` |
| **See also** | **Properties:** `host`, `hostname`, `href`, `pathname`, `port`, `protocol`, `search` |

## Discussion

In the syntax above `objectName` is:

- a reference to any valid area or `location` objects
- the value assigned to the `NAME` attribute of the `<AREA>` HTML tag (see `Area` in Chapter 7).

Keep the following in mind when working with `hash`:

- This property specifies a portion of the URL (see discussion of the `location` object in Chapter 7 for further details).
- It is safer to set the `href` property to change a `location` than to use `hash`.
- See http://www.cis.ohio-state.edu/htbin/rfc/rfc1738.html for detailed information about `hash`.

## Examples

Listings 7.8 to 7.10 and Figure 7.6 demonstrate the use of `hash`.

 height

| | |
|---|---|
| **Stores** | A string specifying the height of an image either in pixels or as a percentage of the window |
| **Syntax** | *anImage*.height |
| **Access** | Read only |
| **Property of** | Image |
| **See also** | **Properties:** border, hspace, vspace, width |

## Discussion

In the property syntax above, *anImage* is either the name of an Image object or an element in the images array.

## Examples

Listing 9.23 and Figure 9.25 demonstrate the use of onLoad and the Image properties height, width, hspace, and vspace.

**LISTING 9.23** The Image properties height, width, hspace, and vspace.

```
1    <HTML>
2    <TITLE>Image properties are tight</TITLE>
3    <HEAD>
4    <SCRIPT LANGUAGE = "JavaScript">
5    function imageProperties(theImage)
6    {
7      alert(' height = ' + theImage.height+
8      '\n width = ' + theImage.width +
9      '\n hspace = ' + theImage.hspace +
10     '\n vspace = ' + theImage.vspace)
11   }
12   </SCRIPT>
13   </HEAD>
14
15   <BODY>
16   <H3>Image properties are tight</H3>
17   <FORM  NAME = "aForm">
18   <IMG  NAME = "ohSoar"
19        SRC = "images\\eagle1.jpg"
20        HEIGHT = 150
```

```
21        HSPACE = 25
22        WIDTH = 350
23        ALIGN = "left"
24        VSPACE="10"
25        BORDER = 10
26        onLoad = 'imageProperties(this)'>
27     </FORM>
28     </BODY>
29     </HTML>
```

# ↳ host

| | |
|---|---|
| **Stores** | The hostname:port portion of a specified URL |
| **Syntax** | links[*index*].host, location.host or *areaObjectName*.host |
| **Access** | Read and write |
| **Property of** | Area, links, location |
| **See also** | **Properties:** URL |

**FIGURE 9.25** The Image properties height, width, hspace, and vspace.

## Discussion

In the syntax above:

- *index* is an index integer of a link in the `links` array.

- *areaObjectName* is the value of the `NAME` attribute of an `Area` object.

When working with `host`, keep the following in mind:

- `host` stores the `hostname` and `port` properties of a URL, separated by a colon.

- If the `port` is null, `host` is the same as the `hostname` property.

- It is safer to set the `href` property to change a `location` than to change the value of `host`.

- An error message is displayed if the specified `host` cannot be found in the current `location`.

- Refer to http://www.cis.ohio-state.edu/htbin/rfc/rfc1738.HTML for further information.

- The complete syntax of `URL` is described in the discussion of the `location` object in Chapter 7.

## Examples

Listing 9.24 and Figure 9.26 demonstrate the use of `host` and other `links` properties. The string `aString` collects the information (lines 8 to 15). In line 16 we display the information about the `links` properties.

**LISTING 9.24** The `links` array and its `hash`, `host`, `hostname`, `href`, `pathname`, `port`, `protocol`, and `search` properties.

```
1    <HTML>
2    <TITLE>Area links and Location Properties</TITLE>
3    <HEAD>
4    <SCRIPT LANGUAGE = "JavaScript">
5
6    function seeProperties()
7    {
8    var aString = "\n hash = " + window.document.links[0].hash
9      aString += "\n host = " + window.document.links[0].host
10     aString += "\n hostname = " + window.document.links[0].hostname
11     aString += "\n href = " + window.document.links[0].href
12     aString += "\n pathname = " + window.document.links[0].pathname
```

```
13      aString += "\n port = " + window.document.links[0].port
14      aString += "\n protocol = " + window.document.links[0].proto-
col
15      aString += "\n search = " + window.document.links[0].search
16      alert(aString)
17    }
18    </SCRIPT>
19    </HEAD>
20
21    <BODY>
22    <H3>Area links and Location Properties</H3>
23    <a href = "http://turtle.gis.umn.edu/index.html">Turtle</a>
24    <FORM>
25    <INPUT  TYPE = 'button'
26        VALUE = 'See URL...'
27        onClick = 'seeProperties()'>
28    </FORM>
29    </BODY>
30    </HTML>
```

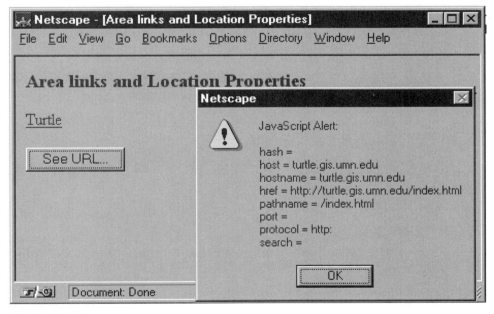

**FIGURE 9.26**  The links array and its hash, host, hostname, href, pathname, port, protocol, and search properties.

# hostname

| | |
|---|---|
| **Stores** | The host and domain name, or IP address, of a network host |
| **Syntax** | `links[index].hostname` or `objectName.hostname` |
| **Access** | Read and write |
| **Property of** | *Area, location, links* |
| **See also** | **Properties:** hash, host, href, pathname, port, protocol, search |

## Discussion

In the syntax above, `objectName` specifies:

- any legitimate `location` object or
- the value of the `NAME` attribute of an `Area` object

When working with `hostname`, keep the following in mind:

- Use this property to obtain the host name part of a URL string.
- To extract other substrings of a URL, use the properties `href`, `hash`, `host`, `pathname`, `port`, `protocol`, and `search`; use `href` to extract the entire URL.
- Visit http://www.cis.ohio-state.edu/htbin/rfc/rfc1738.html for further details.
- The complete syntax of `URL` is described in the discussion of the `location` object in Chapter 7.

## Examples

Listing 9.24 and Figure 9.26 demonstrate the use of `hostname` and other `links` properties.

 # href

| | |
|---|---|
| **Stores** | A URL |
| **Syntax** | `links[index].href` or *objectName*`.href` |
| **Access** | Read and write |
| **Property of** | `Area, location, links` |
| **See also** | **Properties:** `hash, host, hostname, pathname, port, protocol, search` |

## Discussion

In the syntax above, *objectName* specifies:

- any legitimate `location` object or
- the value of the `NAME` attribute of an `Area` object

When working with `href`, keep the following in mind:

- Use this property to obtain the entire URL string.
- To extract a substring of a URL, use the properties `href`, `hash`, `host`, `pathname`, `port`, `protocol`, and `search`.
- The statements `window.location.href = "..."` and `window.location = "..."` are equivalent.
- Visit http://www.cis.ohio-state.edu/htbin/rfc/rfc1738.html for further details.
- The complete syntax of `URL` is described in the discussion of the `location` object in Chapter 7.

## Examples

Listing 9.24 and Figure 9.26 demonstrate the use of `href` and other `links` properties.

 # hspace

| | |
|---|---|
| **Stores** | The margin in pixels between the left and right edges of an image and the surrounding text |
| **Syntax** | `imageObjectName.hspace or document.images[index].hspace` |
| **Access** | Read only |
| **Property of** | `Image` |
| **See also** | **Properties:** `border`, `height`, `vspace`, `width` |

## Discussion

Here are points to remember when using `hspace`:

- It reflects the value assigned to the `HSPACE` attribute of the `<IMG>` tag.
- For images created with the `Image()` constructor, the value of the hspace property is 0.

## Examples

See Listing 9.23 and Figure 9.25.

 # index

| | |
|---|---|
| **Stores** | An integer representing the index of an option in a select object or the index of an option in the `Option` object |
| **Syntax** | `optionObjectName.index or`<br>`selectObjectName.options[i].index` |
| **Access** | Read and write |
| **Property of** | `Option`, `options` array |
| **See also** | **Properties:** `defaultSelected`, `selected`, `selectedIndex` |

## Discussion

In the property syntax above:

- `optionObjectName` is the name of a `Select` object option created using the `Option()` constructor.

- *selectObjectName* is either the value of the `NAME` attribute of a `select` object or an element in the `elements` array.

- *i* is an integer representing an option in a `select` object.

## Examples

Listing 9.25 shows how to work with `Option()`, `index`, and `selectedIndex`. The ability to use the `Option()` constructor and build a list of options on the fly is powerful. You can modify an HTML page based on interactions with the user. The example is therefore elaborate, but I hope you find it useful. To understand the code, run it before reading the explanation below.

Listing 9.25 includes two functions. The `buildOptions()` function (lines 4 to 26) works as follows:

- It has three arrays: `dArray` (holds data for Democrats), `rArray` (holds data for Republicans), and `pArray` (for politics). These arrays are defined in lines 6–8.

- Based on the calling form (stored in `theForm` argument—see line 4), we set `pArray` to either `dArray` or `rArray` (lines 9 to 12).

- Next, we create the options array `opArray` (line 13), and populate it with `Option` objects (lines 14 to 15).

- The arguments to `Option()` (line 15) are `pArray[i]`, which holds a data item (for either Democrats or Republicans), and the `option value`, which is constructed to hold the values `optionValue1`, `optionValue2`, ... This allows us to create as many `Option` objects as we wish.

- In lines 16 to 23 we insert the data in `opArray[i]` (each element is an `Option` object) to the `options` array of the `Select` object named `politics`.

- When we are done building the options, we reload the document (line 25).

Next, we define `tellTruth()` in lines 28 to 39, which simply shows us the values of the `selectedIndex` and `index` properties (in this case they should be equal) in an alert dialog window.

In lines 48 through 63 we insert the `Republicans` and `Democrats` forms in the `document`. Each form contains a `Select` object (the `Democrats` form uses the `MULTIPLE` attribute).

When you first load the listing you do not see any options yet (Figure 9.27). A click on the `Republican...` button responds with `buildOptions()` (line 54); so does a click on the `Democrat...` button (line 62). These clicks build the `Select` options (Figure 9.28). Now when a `Democrat` or a `Republican` changes any of the options, `tellTruth()` informs her (or him, respectively) about the `Select` object `name`, and the `Option` object properties `index`, `selectedIndex`, and `value` (Figure 9.29).

When a `Democrat` or a `Republican` presses the appropriate button, the dialog window appears with the values for the option clicked.

**LISTING 9.25** Working with `Option()`, `index`, `name`, `selectedIndex` and `value`.

```
1    <HTML><TITLE>new Option()</TITLE>
2    <HEAD>
3    <SCRIPT>
4    function buildOptions(theForm)
5    {
6      dArray = new Array("Yes", "No", "Maybe", "Ask the
         Republicans")
7      rArray = new Array("Yes", "No", "Maybe", "Ask the Democrats")
8      pArray = new Array()
9      if (theForm.name == "Democrats")
10      pArray = dArray
11     else
12      pArray = rArray
13     opArray = new Array(4)
14     for (var i = 0; i < 4; i++)
15      opArray[i] = new Option(pArray[i],"optionValue" + i)
16     for (var i=0; i < 4; i++)
17     {
18      eval("theForm.politics.options[i] = opArray[i]")
19      if (i == 0)
20      {
21         theForm.politics.options[i].selected = true
22      }
23     }
24
25     history.go(0)
26   }
27
28   function tellTruth(theForm)
29   {
30     var i = theForm.politics.selectedIndex
31     var aString = " selectedIndex = " + i
```

```
32    aString += "\n index = " +
33    theForm.politics.options[i].index
34    aString += "\n name = " +
35    theForm.politics.name
36    aString += "\n value = " +
37    theForm.politics.options[i].value
38    alert(aString)
39    }
40    </SCRIPT>
41    </HEAD>
42
43
44    <H3>new Option()</H3>
45    Are there ideological differences between the major political
      parties?
46    <BR>Click on the appropriate button to see the possible answers
47    <FORM    NAME = "Republicans">
48    <SELECT   NAME = "politics"
49        onChange = 'tellTruth(this.form)'>
50    </SELECT>
51    <INPUT   TYPE = "button"
52        VALUE = "Republican..."
53        onClick = "buildOptions(this.form)">
54    </FORM>
55    <FORM    NAME = "Democrats">
56    <SELECT   NAME = "politics" multiple
57        onChange = 'tellTruth(this.form)'>
58    </SELECT>
59    <INPUT   TYPE = "button"
60        VALUE = "Democrat..."
61        onClick = "buildOptions(this.form)">
62    </FORM>
63    </HTML>
```

#  lastModified

| | |
|---|---|
| **Stores** | A string representing the date that a document was last modified |
| **Syntax** | document.lastModified |
| **Access** | Read only |
| **Property of** | document |
| **See also** | **Properties:** status |

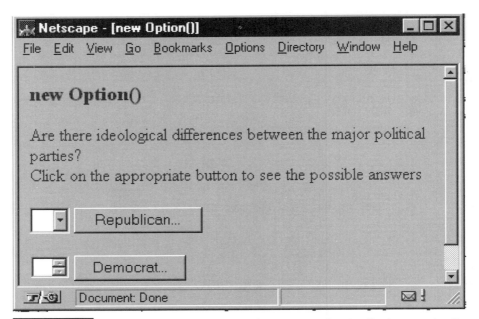

**FIGURE 9.27** Working with Option(), index, name, selectedIndex, and value.

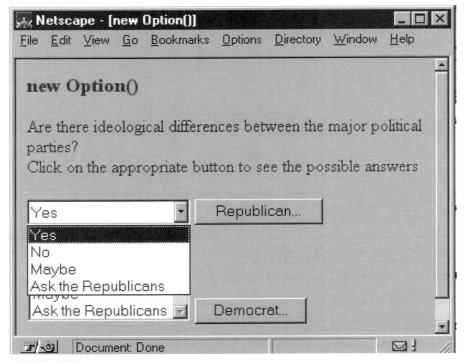

**FIGURE 9.28** Working with Option(), index, name, selectedIndex, and value.

**FIGURE 9.29** Working with Option(), index, name, selectedIndex, and value.

## Discussion

Use this property to time-stamp your HTML documents.

## Examples

This

```
<SCRIPT LANGUAGE = "JavaScript">
document.write("Last modified: " + document.lastModified)
</SCRIPT>
```

will write

```
Last modified: 03/26/96 14:24:22
```

in your document. See also the last-modified example in Chapter 1.

#  length

| | |
|---|---|
| **Stores** | The number of elements in an array or an object that owns this property |
| **Syntax** | *objectName*.length |
| **Access** | Read and write |
| **Property of** | **Objects:** Array, frame, history, Plugin, radio, select, string, window |
| | **Arrays:** anchors, elements, forms, frames, images, links, options |
| **See also** | **Objects:** Array |

## Discussion

In the syntax above, *objectName* stands for any of the objects or arrays that own this property. You can use the length property to truncate a length, but not to extend it.

## Examples

Listing 9.26 and Figure 9.30 demonstrate one use of length. We define two arrays in lines 9 and 10—for politicians and for parties—and then print them (lines 11 and 12). In line 14 we truncate C; Figure 9.30 shows the results.

**LISTING 9.26** Using length.

```
1    <HTML>
2    <TITLE>length</TITLE>
3
4    <BODY>
5    <H3>length</H3>
6    <PRE>
7    <U>Politician</U>    <U>Party</U>
8    <SCRIPT>
9    politicians = new Array("A    ", "B    ", "C    ")
10   parties = new Array("Democratic", "Republican", "Independent ")
11   for (var i = 0; i < politicians.length; i++)
12     document.write("<BR>" + politicians[i] + "  " + parties[i])
13   document.write("<BR> <BR> We truncated " + politicians[2])
14   politicians.length = 2
15   for (var i = 0; i < parties.length; i++)
16     document.write("<BR>" + politicians[i] + "  " + parties[i])
17   </SCRIPT></PRE>
18   </BODY>
19   </HTML>
```

# ↳ linkColor

| | |
|---|---|
| **Stores** | The color of the document hyperlinks |
| **Syntax** | document.linkColor |
| **Access** | Read and write |
| **Property of** | document |
| **See also** | **Properties:** vlinkColor |

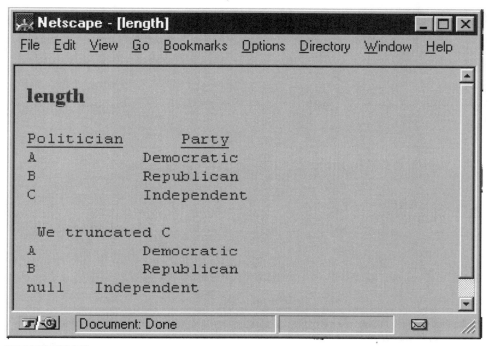

**FIGURE 9.30** Using length.

## Discussion

You can specify the linkColor in one or two ways:

- As a string literal (see Appendix C)
- As an RGB mix, following the format RRGGBB, where RR, GG, and BB are the mix levels of red, green, and blue. Each color ranges in value from 00 to FF (hexadecimal). For example, 00FF00 is pure green.

In working with linkColor, keep the following in mind:

- Its value reflects the LINK attribute of the <BODY> tag.
- Its default is set by the user through the menu sequence Options | General Preferences... | Colors | Links.

## Examples

Listing 9.27 and Figure 9.31 demonstrate the use of linkColor. The example is self-explanatory.

**LISTING 9.27** Using linkColor.

```
1       <HTML>
2       <HEAD>
3       <TITLE>linkColor</TITLE>
4       <SCRIPT LANGUAGE = "JavaScript">
5       document.linkColor = "FF0000"
6       </SCRIPT>
7
8       <BODY>
9       <H3>linkColor</H3>
10      <A HREF = "http://turtle.gis.umn.edu">
11      link color is red when active </A>
12      </BODY>
13      </HTML>
```

# ↳ links

| | |
|---|---|
| **Stores** | An array of objects corresponding to link objects in the document |
| **Syntax** | document.links.length or document.links[*index*] |
| **Access** | Read and write |
| **Property of** | document |
| **See also** | **Objects:** link |

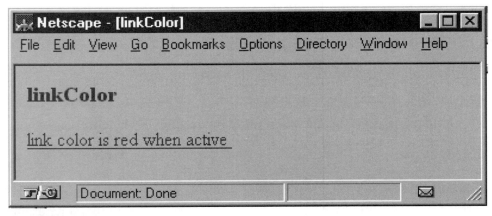

**FIGURE 9.31** Using linkColor.

## Discussion

In the syntax above, *index* is the index of a `link` in the `links` array. The array is constructed during document loading, and `link` objects are added as elements to the array in the order they appear in the HTML source code. See the discussion of the `link` object in Chapter 7 for further details.

## Examples

See the examples for the `link` object in Chapter 7.

 # LN2

| | |
|---|---|
| **Stores** | The natural logarithm of 2 |
| **Syntax** | `Math.LN2` |
| **Access** | Read only |
| **Property of** | `Math` |
| **See also** | **Properties:** `LN10` |

## Discussion

The approximate value of `LN2` is shown in Figure 9.20.

## Examples

Listing 9.18 and Figure 9.20 show all of the `Math` object's constants.

 # LN10

| | |
|---|---|
| **Stores** | The natural logarithm of 10 |
| **Syntax** | `Math.LN10` |
| **Access** | Read only |
| **Property of** | `Math` |
| **See also** | **Properties:** `LN2` |

## Discussion

The approximate value of `LN10` is shown in Figure 9.20.

## Examples

Listing 9.18 and Figure 9.20 show all of the `Math` object's constants.

#  location

| | |
|---|---|
| **Stores** | Information about the current URL |
| **Syntax** | `[windowReference.]location` |
| **Access** | Read and write |
| **Property of** | `window` |
| **See also** | **Objects:** `URL` |

## Discussion

See discussion of the `location` object in Chapter 7.

## Examples

See examples for the `location` object in Chapter 7.

#  LOG2E

| | |
|---|---|
| **Stores** | The base 2 logarithm of $e$ |
| **Syntax** | `Math.LOG2E` |
| **Access** | Read only |
| **Property of** | `Math` |
| **See also** | **Properties:** `LOG10E` |

## Discussion

The approximate value of `LOG2E` is shown in Figure 9.20.

## Examples

Listing 9.18 and Figure 9.20 show all of the Math object's constants.

 # LOG10E

| | |
|---|---|
| **Stores** | The base 10 logarithm of *e* |
| **Syntax** | Math.LOG10E |
| **Access** | Read only |
| **Property of** | Math |
| **See also** | **Properties:** LOG2E |

## Discussion

The approximate value of LOG10E is shown in Figure 9.20.

## Examples

Listing 9.18 and Figure 9.20 show all of the Math object's constants.

 # lowsrc

| | |
|---|---|
| **Stores** | The URL of a low-resolution version of an image to be displayed in a document |
| **Syntax** | *imageObjectName*.lowsrc |
| **Access** | Read and write |
| **Property of** | Image |
| **See also** | **Properties:** complete, src |

## Discussion

In the syntax above, *imageObjectName* indicates:

- a name of an Image object or
- an element in the images array

Note some other points about this property:

- Its initial value reflects the value assigned to the LOWSRC attribute of the <IMG> tag.

- To save time during Internet transactions, Navigator loads the low-resolution image first, and then replaces it with the high-resolution image specified by the value assigned to the SRC attribute of the <IMG> tag or by the src property of Image.

## Examples

Listing 9.28 and Figure 9.32 demonstrate the use of src and lowsrc. Assume, for the moment, that crabs are low resolution and trout are high resolution. Then:

- In lines 12–32 we construct the form imageProblem.

- In it we install two radio objects.

- onClick for each radio object calls lowResHighRes() with the arguments' order switched (lines 19 and 24).

- lowResHighRes() simply assigns values to the lowsrc and src properties of images[0] (lines 7 and 8).

- The effect of clicking on the radio buttons is then to switch between the two images.

Click on the various radio buttons and reload the file several times until you understand what happens.

**LISTING 9.28** Using src and lowsrc.

```
1     <HTML>
2     <HEAD>
3     <TITLE> lowsrc and src</TITLE>
4     <SCRIPT LANGUAGE = 'JavaScript'>
5     function lowResHighRes(lowRes, highRes)
6     {
7        document.images[0].lowsrc = lowRes
8        document.images[0].src = highRes
9     }
10    </SCRIPT>
11    <BODY>
12    <FORM NAME = "imageProblem">
```

```
13    <B>Switch radio to switch images:</B>
14    <BR>
15    <INPUT   TYPE = "radio"
16          NAME = "lowHig"
17          VALUE = "LowToHigh"
18          CHECKED
19          onClick =
"lowResHighRes('images\\crab.jpg','images\\trout.jpg')">
20          Low to High
21    <INPUT   TYPE = "radio"
22          NAME = "lowHig"
23          VALUE = "HighToLow"
24          onClick =
"lowResHighRes('images\\trout.jpg','images\\crab.jpg')">
25          High to Low
26    <BR>
27    <IMG    NAME = "babe"
28          SRC = "images\\crab.jpg"
29          LOWSRC = "images\\trout.jpg"
30          ALIGN = "left"
31          VSPACE = "10">
32    </FORM>
33    </BODY>
34    </HTML>
```

**FIGURE 9.32**  Using src and lowsrc.

 method

| | |
|---|---|
| **Stores** | A string specifying how form field input information is sent to the server |
| **Syntax** | *formName*.method |
| **Access** | Read and write |
| **Property of** | form |
| **See also** | **Properties:** action |

## Discussion

In the syntax above, *formName* is:

- the value assigned to the NAME property of the <FORM> tag or

- an element in the forms array

In working with method, keep the following in mind:

- The value of method reflects the value of the METHOD attribute of the <FORM> tag.

- method should evaluate to either get or post.

Certain values of method may require specific values for other form properties; refer to http://www.ics.uci.edu/pub/ietf/html/rfc1867.txt for further information.

## Examples

See Listings 7.12 and 7.38 in Chapter 7.

 name

| | |
|---|---|
| **Stores** | The name of an object |
| **Syntax** | *objectReference*.name |
| **Access** | Read only for the objects designated with a star (*), and read and write for the remaining objects (see below) |

| **Property of** | **Objects:** Applet*, button, checkbox, frame, FileUpload*, hidden, Image*, password, Plugin*, radio, reset, select, submit, text, textarea, window* |
| --- | --- |
| | **Arrays:** options, plugins |
| **See also** | **Properties:** value, text |

## Discussion

In the syntax above, `objectReference` can designate any of the following:

- The value assigned to the NAME attribute of any of the objects to which this property belongs or an element—that owns this property—in the elements array

- A frame reference (see the discussion of the `frame` object in Chapter 7)

- `radioName[index]`, where `radioName` is the value assigned to the NAME attribute of a radio object and `index` is the integer index of the specified radio button in the radio object

- `selectName`.options, where `selectName` is either the value assigned to the NAME attribute of a select object or an element in the elements array

- `windowReference` or `windowReference`.frames, where `windowReference` must be an appropriate reference to a window (see discussion of the window object in Chapter 7)

- `fileUploadName`, which is either the value assigned to the NAME attribute of a FileUpload object or an element in the elements array

- `imageName`, which is either the value assigned to the NAME attribute of an Image object or an element in the images array

- navigator.plugins[`index`], where `index` represents the index of a plug-in

- navigator.plugins[`pluginName`]

Also, bear in mind that:

- For images created with the Image() constructor, the value of name is null.

- For all objects for which the name property is read and write, its initial value represents the value assigned to the NAME attribute of the relevant object.

- The name of all radio buttons is the same as the name of the radio object.

- When two or more objects on the same form have identical names, then an array of this name is created automatically, with the elements entered in the array according to source order; for example, if two elements in a form carry the name `aName`, then an array `aName` is created with two elements.

## Examples

Almost any example that includes form elements demonstrates the use of `name`. Many of these examples can be found in Chapter 7.

 # opener

| | |
|---|---|
| **Stores** | The reference to the window of the calling document when a window is opened using the `open()` method |
| **Syntax** | `window.opener` |
| **Access** | Read and write |
| **Property of** | `window` |
| **See also** | **Methods:** `close()`, `open()` |

## Discussion

Keep these in mind:

- The opener property is evaluated from the destination window.

- The value of `opener` does not change even when the opened window executes a document unload (it is persistent).

## Examples

In Listing 9.29 we open a `newWin` from the window titled `opener` (line 8). We then insert a button in the opened window, and tell `onClick` to close the opener (line 9). Be sure to use `document.close()` (line 10); otherwise the stream built in `document.write()` (line 9) will not flush to the opened window's `document`.

When you click on the `Close opener...` button (Figure 9.33), the opener window will be closed, but not before a confirm dialog window asks you if you are sure.

**LISTING 9.29** Using `opener`.

```
1     <HTML>
2     <HEAD>
3     <TITLE> opener</TITLE>
4
5     <BODY>
6     <H3>opener</H3>
7     <SCRIPT LANGUAGE = 'JavaScript'>
8     newWin = window.open("")
9     newWin.document.write('<FORM><INPUT TYPE="button" VALUE="Close
opener..." onClick="opener.close()"></FORM>')
10    newWin.document.close()
11    </SCRIPT>
12    </BODY>
13</HTML>
```

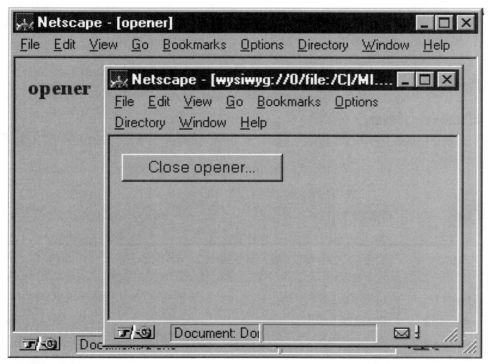

**FIGURE 9.33** Using opener.

 options

| | |
|---|---|
| **Stores** | An array corresponding to `options` in a `select` object |
| **Syntax** | `selectListName.options[i].propertyName` |
| | or |
| | `formName.elements[j].options[i].propertyName` |
| **Access** | Read and write |
| **Property of** | `select` object, `elements` array |
| **See also** | **Objects:** `select` |
| | **Arrays:** `elements` |

## Discussion

In the syntax above

- *i* is the index of the `option` in the `options` array.
- *j* is the index of the `select` objects in the `elements` array.

The `options` array is discussed in details with the `select` object in Chapter 7.

## Examples

See examples for the `select` objects in Chapter 7, and Listing 9.25 and Figure 9.28.

 parent

| | |
|---|---|
| **Stores** | The `window` or `frame` whose `frameset` contains the current `frame` |
| **Syntax** | `parent.something` |
| **Access** | Read only |
| **Property of** | `frame`, `window` |
| **See also** | **Objects:** `frame`, `window` |

## Discussion

In the syntax above, *something* stands for one of the following:

- *propertyName*—When parent refers to a window, then *propertyName* is one of the following properties: defaultStatus, status, length, or name. When parent refers to a frame, then *propertyName* refers to one of the following properties: length, name, or parent.

- *methodName*—Refers to one of the window object methods.

- *frameName*—The value assigned to the NAME attribute in a <FRAME> tag.

- frames[*index*]—The *index* of the specified frame in the frames array, where *index* is an integer.

Use this property to refer to:

- the <FRAMESET> window of a frame

- sibling frames, using the syntax parent.*frameName* or parent .frames[*index*]

- grandparent frame or window when a frameset is embedded in a child frame

If the parent is a frame, then parent stores the value of the NAME attribute of the object; if the parent is a window, then parent stores a window object's internal name (that is, a name assigned by the Navigator, not by you).

## Examples

See discussion and examples for the frame object and frames array in Chapter 7.

#  pathname

| | |
|---|---|
| **Stores** | The path portion of the URL |
| **Syntax** | objectName.pathname or links[index].pathname |
| **Access** | Read and write |
| **Property of** | area, link, location |
| **See also** | **Properties:** hash, host, hostname, href, port, protocol, search |

## Discussion

In the syntax above, *objectName* can be one of the following:

- The value assigned to the NAME attribute of the Area object
- location

In working with pathname, keep the following in mind:

- pathname specifies a portion of the URL (see discussion of the location object in Chapter 7).
- It provides the details of how the specified resource can be accessed.
- To change location, use href, rather than assigning a new value to pathname.
- See http://www.cis.ohio-state.edu/htbin/rfc/rfc1738.html for further details.

## Examples

Listing 9.24 and Figure 9.26 demonstrate the use of pathname and other related properties.

 # PI

| | |
|---|---|
| **Stores** | The ratio of the circumference of a circle to its diameter |
| **Syntax** | Math.PI |
| **Access** | Read only |
| **Property of** | Math |
| **See also** | **Properties:** E |

## Discussion

The approximate value of PI is shown in Figure 9.20.

## Examples

Listing 9.18 and Figure 9.20 show all of the Math object's constants.

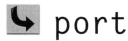 # port

| | |
|---|---|
| **Stores** | The communications port that the server uses |
| **Syntax** | *objectName*.port or links[*index*].port |
| **Access** | Read and write |
| **Property of** | area, link, location |
| **See also** | **Properties:** hash, host, hostname, href, pathname, protocol, search |

## Discussion

In the syntax above, *objectName* can be one of the following:

- The value assigned to the NAME attribute of the Area object

- location

In working with port, keep the following in mind:

- port specifies a portion of the URL (see discussion of the location object in Chapter 7).

- port represents a substring of host; the latter is a concatenation of hostname and port, separated by a colon.

- If port is not defined, host and hostname store the same value.

- To change location, use href, rather than assigning a new value to port.

- The default value for the server's port is 80.

- See http://www.cis.ohio-state.edu/htbin/rfc/rfc1738.html for further details.

## Examples
Listing 9.24 and Figure 9.26 demonstrate the use of port and other related properties.

 # protocol

| | |
|---|---|
| **Stores** | The beginning of the URL, up to and including the first colon |
| **Syntax** | *objectName*.protocol or links[*index*].protocol |
| **Access** | Read and write |
| **Property of** | area, link, location |
| **See also** | **Properties:** hash, host, hostname, href, pathname, port, search |

## Discussion
In the syntax above, *objectName* can be one of the following:

- The value assigned to the NAME attribute of the Area object
- location

In working with protocol, keep the following in mind:

- protocol specifies a portion of the URL (see discussion of the location object in Chapter 7).
- protocol indicates the access method of the URL (for example, http:, file:, ftp:, telnet:, javascript:).
- To change location, use href, rather than assigning a new value to port.
- See http://www.cis.ohio-state.edu/htbin/rfc/rfc1738.html for further details.

## Examples
Listing 9.24 and Figure 9.26 demonstrate the use of port and other related properties.

 # prototype

| | |
|---|---|
| **Stores** | A definition of a property that is shared by all objects of the specified type |
| **Syntax** | *objectType*.prototype.*propertyName* = *value* |
| **Access** | Read and write |
| **Property of** | Any object that has a constructor (objects that are created with the keyword new) |
| **See also** | **Properties:** value, name |

## Discussion

In the syntax above:

- *objectType* specifies the name of the constructor of the object type.

- *propertyName* is the name of the property that you wish to create.

- *value* is the initial value for all objects of the type *objectType* of the property that you have created.

All objects that have an explicit constructor can be created with a statements such as

```
objectName = new Constructor()
```

where *Constructor* is one of the following: Array, Date, Function, Image, option, String, or a user-defined object. prototype allows you to add properties to such objects explicitly.

This property is useful in case you create objects of the same class (Date, Array, etc.), and want to add the same properties to all of them.

## Examples

Listing 9.30 and Figure 9.34 demonstrate the use of prototype. Note the following:

- In addProperties() (lines 5 to 23) we create a new Date object, named today (line 8).

- Then we build a string that lists today's properties (lines 9 to 12) and display these properties (line 13).

- In lines 14 and 15 we add the PROPERTIES description and mood to the object.

- These two properties now also become properties of today, even though they were not declared as such explicitly.

- To verify that description and mood are indeed properties of today, we rebuild the theProperties string (lines 18 to 21) and then display it (line 22) as shown in Figure 9.34.

**LISTING 9.30** Using prototype.

```
1    <HTML>
2    <HEAD>
3    <TITLE>prototype</TITLE>
4    <SCRIPT LANGUAGE = "JavaScript">
5    function addProperties()
6    {
7      var theProperties = "Date properties before: \n"
8      today = new Date()
9      for (var i in today)
10     {
11       theProperties += i + "\n"
12     }
13     alert(theProperties)
14     Date.prototype.description = null
15     Date.prototype.mood = null
16     theProperties = "Date properties after: \n"
17     alert (today.length)
18     for (var i in today)
19     {
20       theProperties += i + "\n"
21     }
22     alert(theProperties)
23   }
24   </SCRIPT>
25   </HEAD>
26
27   <BODY>
28   <H1> prototype </H1>
29   <BODY>
30   <FORM>
31   <INPUT  TYPE = "button"
32        VALUE = "List Properties"
33        onClick = "addProperties()">
34   </FORM>
35   </BODY>
36   </HTML>
```

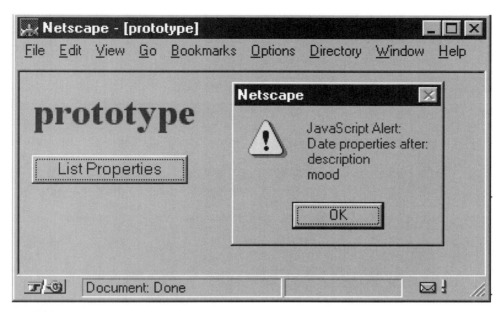

**FIGURE 9.34** Using prototype.

#  referrer

| | |
|---|---|
| **Stores** | The URL of the calling document when a user clicks a link object |
| **Syntax** | document.referrer |
| **Access** | Read only |
| **Property of** | document |
| **See also** | **Objects:** URL |

## Discussion

referrer is evaluated from the destination document.

## Examples

Listing 9.31 establishes the referrer document. From it, we call the referenced document (Listing 9.32). When you click on the link in referrer

(Figure 9.35), the referenced window comes up (Figure 9.36). Click on the Referrer... button to see how you got there.

```
1    <HTML>
2    <HEAD>
3    <TITLE>The referrer</TITLE>
4    <BODY>
5    <H1> The referrer </H1>
6    <BODY>
7    <A  HREF = "referenced.html">
8      Click here to bring up referenced
9    </A>
10   </BODY>
11   </HTML>
```

```
1    <HTML>
2    <HEAD>
3    <TITLE>The Referenced</TITLE>
4    <SCRIPT LANGUAGE = "JavaScript">
5    function who()
6    {
7      alert("I was referred to by " + document.referrer)
8    }
9    </SCRIPT>
10   </HEAD>
11
12   <BODY>
13   <H1> The Referenced </H1>
14   <BODY>
15   <FORM>
16   Click on Referrer... to see how I got here.<P>
17   <INPUT  TYPE = "button"
18         VALUE = "Referrer..."
19         onClick = "who()">
20   </FORM>
21   </BODY>
22   </HTML>
```

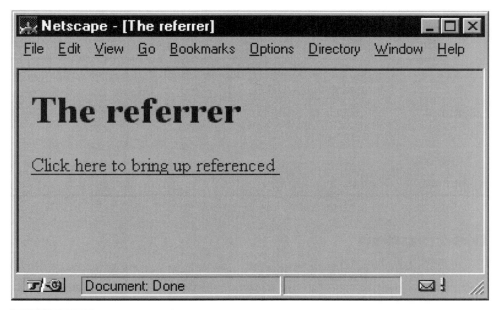

**FIGURE 9.35** The referrer.

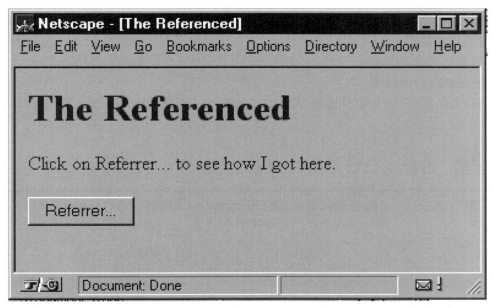

**FIGURE 9.36** The referenced.html.

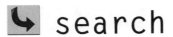 # search

| | |
|---|---|
| **Stores** | A string beginning with a question mark that specifies any query information in the URL |
| **Syntax** | `links[index].search` or `objectName.search` |
| **Access** | Read and write |
| **Property of** | `Area`, `link`, `location` |
| **See also** | **Objects:** `location` |

## Discussion

In the syntax above:

- *index* is an integer referring to the `link` object in the `links` array.

- *objectName* is the value assigned to the NAME attribute of an `Area`, a `link`, or a `location` object.

Although you can assign a value to `search` at any time, use `href` to change a `location`.

## Examples

See Listing 9.24 and Figure 9.26.

 # selected

| | |
|---|---|
| **Stores** | A Boolean value specifying the current selection state of an `option` in a `select` object. |
| **Syntax** | `optionName.selected` or `selectName.options[index].selected` |
| **Access** | Read and write |
| **Property of** | `Option` object, `options` array |
| **See also** | **Properties:** `defaultSelected`, `index`, `selectedIndex` |

## Discussion

In the syntax above:

- *optionName* is the name of a `Select` object option created using the `Option()` constructor.
- *selectName* is either the value assigned to the `NAME` attribute of `select` or an element in the `elements` array.
- *index* is the integer index of an option in a `select` object.

In working with `selected`, keep the following in mind:

- If an option is selected, the value of `selected` is true; otherwise, it is false.
- Setting `selected` for an option updates the option's display immediately.

`selected` is more flexible than `selectedIndex`. With it you can:

- Determine, for every option in a `MULTIPLE` `select` object, whether the option is selected or not.
- Set `selected` to true for each option without clearing the selection of other options.

## Examples

Listing 9.15 and Figure 9.16 demonstrate the use of `defaultSelected` and `selected`.

 # selectedIndex

| | |
|---|---|
| **Stores** | An integer specifying the index of the selected option in a select object |
| **Syntax** | *selectName*.options.selectedIndex **or** *selectName*.selectedIndex |
| **Access** | Read and write |
| **Property of** | select object, options array |
| **See also** | **Properties:** defaultSelected, index, selected |

## Discussion

In the syntax above, *selectName* is either the value assigned to the NAME attribute of a select object or an element in the elements array.

In working with selectedIndex, keep the following in mind:

- Options are indexed in the order in which they are defined, starting with an index of 0.
- Setting selectedIndex updates the option's display immediately.
- When multiple options are selected, selectedIndex specifies the value of the first selected option.
- Setting selectedIndex clears any other options that are selected in the select object.

## Examples

Examples are given in Listing 9.8 and Figure 9.8 and in Listing 9.25 and Figure 9.27, Figure 9.28, and Figure 9.29.

#  self

| | |
|---|---|
| **Stores** | Reference to the current window or current frame |
| **Syntax** | self.*something* |
| **Access** | Read only |
| **Property of** | frame, window |
| **See also** | **Properties:** window |

## Discussion

In the syntax above, *something* stands for

- a property of the appropriate object (window or frame) or
- a method of the window object

Also, keep the following in mind:

- When self refers to a window, the properties that can be used are defaultStatus, status, length, or name.

- When self refers to a `frame`, the properties that can be used are `length` and name.
- When self refers to a `window`, its value is the internal name assigned to the `window` object.
- When self refers to a `frame`, its value is the value assigned to the NAME attribute of the `<FRAME>` tag.

## Examples
See Listing 7.3 and Figure 7.3 in Chapter 7.

#  SQRT1_2

| | |
|---|---|
| **Stores** | The square root of $\frac{1}{2}$ |
| **Syntax** | `Math.SQRT1_2` |
| **Access** | Read only |
| **Property of** | `Math` |
| **See also** | **Properties:** `SQRT2` |

## Discussion
The approximate value of `SQRT1_2` is shown in Figure 9.20.

## Examples
Listing 9.18 and Figure 9.20 show all of the `Math` object's constants.

#  SQRT2

| | |
|---|---|
| **Stores** | The square root of 2 |
| **Syntax** | `Math.SQRT2` |
| **Access** | Read only |
| **Property of** | `Math` |
| **See also** | **Properties:** `SQRT1_2` |

## Discussion

The approximate value of SQRT2 is shown in Figure 9.20.

## Examples

Listing 9.18 and Figure 9.20 show all of the Math object's constants.

 # src

| | |
|---|---|
| **Stores** | The URL of an image to be displayed in a document |
| **Syntax** | *imageName*.src |
| **Access** | Read and write |
| **Property of** | Image |
| **See also** | **Properties:** complete, lowsrc |

## Discussion

In the syntax above, *imageName* is:

- the name of an Image object or
- an element in the images array

Keep the following in mind:

- The initial value of src stores the value of the SRC attribute of the <IMG> tag.
- Any time a new value is assigned to src, the current transfer of image data (if any) is aborted, and the new URL is loaded into the image area.
- If you do assign a new value to src, change the value of lowsrc first.
- The image loaded with src is scaled to the size of the image cell it is loaded into.

## Examples

See Listing 9.28 and Figure 9.32.

 # status

| | |
|---|---|
| **Stores** | A string of a priority or transient message in the status bar at the bottom of the window |
| **Syntax** | *windowReference*.status |
| **Access** | Read and write |
| **Property of** | window |
| **See also** | **Methods:** onMouseOver() |
| | **Properties:** defaultStatus |

## Discussion

In the syntax above, *windowReference* refers to a valid way of referring to a window.

When working with status, keep the following in mind:

- status and defaultStatus interact. When nothing is specified to be displayed in the status bar, the string stored in defaultStatus is displayed. When the status property is set (as in the case of setting status with onMouseOver), then the string stored in status in displayed.

- For change of status to take effect, return true to the event handler (such as onMouseOver) that sets it.

## Examples

Listing 9.16 and Figure 9.17 demonstrate the use of defaultStatus and status.

 # suffixes

| | |
|---|---|
| **Stores** | Filename extensions (suffixes) for a MIME type |
| **Syntax** | navigator.mimeTypes[*index*].suffixes |
| **Access** | Read only |
| **Property of** | mimeTypes |
| **See also** | **Properties:** type, description, enabledPlugin |

## Discussion

In the syntax above, *index* is an integer designating the index of a MIME type in the mimeTypes array.

For each MIME type, suffixes stores the (usually three-letter) designation of the filename extensions known to it. If more than one suffix corresponds to a MIME type, the suffixes are separated by commas. For example, the suffixes known to the image/jpeg MIME type may be jpeg, jpg, jpe, jfif, pjpeg, and pjp.

## Examples

See Listing 7.28 and Figures 7.17 and 7.18 in Chapter 7, and Listing 9.19 and Figure 9.21.

 # target

| | |
|---|---|
| **Stores** | For area, the name of the window that displays the content of a clicked area |
| | For form, the name of the window that responses go to after a form has been submitted |
| | For link, the name of the window that displays the content of a clicked hypertext link |
| **Syntax** | *objectName*.target or links[*index*].target |
| **Access** | Read and write |
| **Property of** | Area, form, and link objects; links array |
| **See also** | **Properties:** action, encoding, method |

## Discussion

In the syntax above, *objectName* stands for one of the following:

- The value assigned to the NAME attribute of an Area object
- The value assigned to the NAME attribute of a form object, or the index of the form in the forms array

In the syntax above, *index* represents an integer index of the link in the links array.

In working with target, keep the following in mind:

- You cannot assign the value of a JavaScript expression or variable to target.

- The initial value of target is the value assigned to the TARGET attribute of the <FORM> or <A> tags.

## Examples

See Listings 7.9 and 7.10 and Figures 7.6, 7.15, and 7.17 in Chapter 7.

 # text

| | |
|---|---|
| **Stores** | The text that follows an <OPTION> tag in a select object |
| **Syntax** | *optionName*.text or *selectName*.options[*index*].text |
| **Access** | Read and write |
| **Property of** | Option object, options array |
| **See also** | |

## Discussion

In the syntax above:

- *optionName* is the name assigned to an option when creating the option with the Option() constructor.

- *selectName* is either the value assigned to the NAME attribute of a select object or an element in the elements array.

- *index* is an integer index of an option in a select object.

In working with text, keep the following in mind:

- The initial value of text equals the text that follows an <OPTION> tag in a select object.

- When you change the value of text, the change is reflected in the text that the specified option displays.

## Examples

Listing 9.33 and Figure 9.37 demonstrate the use of text. Here is what we do:

- In line 24, we set up the campaignReform form.
- In it, we install the democracyRestored select object, with the various options (lines 27 to 30).
- On changing a democracyRestored choice, we call democracy(), and set up a different text for the options (lines 5 to 16).
- Run the listing and see what it does.

**LISTING 9.33** Using text with options.

```
1    <HTML>
2    <HEAD>
3    <TITLE>text</TITLE>
4    <SCRIPT LANGUAGE = "JavaScript">
5    function democracy()
6    {
7      for (var i = 0; i <
     document.campaignReform.democracyRestored.length; i++)
8      {
9       if
     (document.campaignReform.democracyRestored.options[i].selected
     == true)
10      {
11      document.campaignReform.democracyRestored.options[i].    text
     = "Absolutely"
12       return
     document.campaignReform.democracyRestored.options[i].text
13      }
14      }
15     return null
16   }
17   </SCRIPT>
18   </HEAD>
19
20   <BODY>
21   <H3>text</H3>
22   Would you like to see campaign reform enacted?
23   Click on the answer of your choice.
24   <FORM   NAME = "campaignReform">
25   <SELECT  NAME = "democracyRestored"
26        onChange = 'democracy()'>
```

```
27     <OPTION SELECTED> Yes
28     <OPTION> No
29     <OPTION> Ask me before elections
30     <OPTION> I really do not care!
31  </SELECT>
32  </FORM>
33  </BODY>
34  </HTML>
```

# ↳ title

| | |
|---|---|
| **Stores** | The title of a document |
| **Syntax** | document.title |
| **Access** | Read only |
| **Property of** | document |
| **See also** | **Objects:** location |

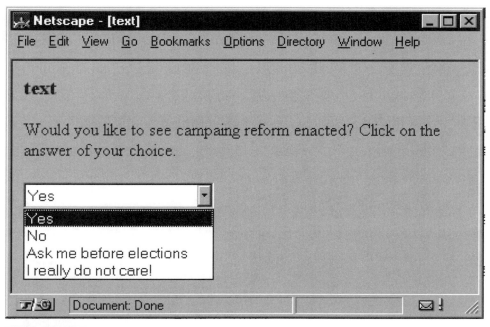

**FIGURE 9.37** Using text with options.

## Discussion

`title` stores the value enclosed by the `<TITLE>` and `</TITLE>` tags. If no title is assigned to the document, the property's value is null.

## Examples

Listing 9.34 and Figure 9.38 demonstrate the use of `title` and also how confusing context can be to humans (who understand context), and not to computers (who do not understand context).

**LISTING 9.34** Using `title`.

```
1    <HTML>
2    <HEAD>
3    <TITLE>My title is title</TITLE>
4    </HEAD>
5
6    <BODY>
7    <H3>My title is title</H3>
8    <SCRIPT LANGUAGE = "JavaScript">
9    document.write(document.title)
10   </SCRIPT>
11   </BODY>
12   </HTML>
```

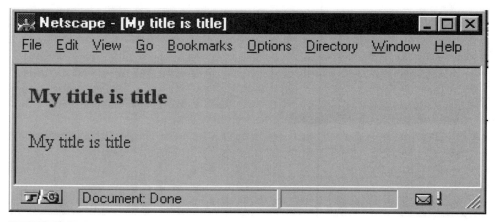

**FIGURE 9.38** Using `title`.

 # top

| | |
|---|---|
| **Stores** | A synonym for the topmost Navigator window |
| **Syntax** | `top.something` |
| **Access** | Read only |
| **Property of** | `window` |
| **See also** | **Properties:** `parent`, `self` |

## Discussion

In the syntax above, *something* stands for one of the following:

- *propertyName*—`defaultStatus`, `status`, or `length`
- *windowMethod( )*—one of the `window` object's methods
- *frameName*—the top frame
- `frames[`*index*`]`—an integer index of the desired frame

Keep these points in mind:

- `top` refers to the root `window`. Thus, if `top` created two windows, `child1` and `child2`, then to refer to `child2` from `child1`, you have to go through `top`: i.e., `top.child2`.
- The value of `top` is maintained internally.

## Examples

See Listing 9.12.

 # type

| | |
|---|---|
| **Stores** | The type of an object (see Discussion below) |
| **Syntax** | *objectName*`.type` or `mimeTypes[`*index*`].type` |
| **Access** | Read only |
| **Property of** | `button`, `checkbox`, `fileUpload`, `hidden`, `mimeType`, `password`, `radio`, `reset`, `select`, `submit`, `text`, `textarea` |
| **See also** | **Operator:** `typeof` |

## Discussion

In the syntax above:

- *objectName* specifies the value assigned to the NAME attribute of a form element object.

- *index* is an integer index of an element in the elements array.

- type stores a string specifying one of the following:

  - The type of the form element for those elements created with the tag <INPUT>, <SELECT>, or <TEXTAREA>.

  - The name of the MIME type for mimeTypes objects.

  - The value that type stores depends on the object—for all objects except Select, type holds the name of the object (for example, for a button, the value of the type property is button).

  - For the <SELECT ...> tag, the value of type is select-one.

  - For the <SELECT MULTIPLE ...> tag, the value of type is select-multiple.

## Examples

Listing 9.35 and Figure 9.39 demonstrate the use of type and name. Here is what is going on:

- In lines 15 to 18 we set up a button named to press and call whoAmI() when it is pressed.

- In lines 20 to 24 we set up select multiple objectives and call whoAmI() when one or more option of objectives (Win or Happ) is selected.

- In lines 26 to 28 we set up another select object, this time with no multiple, and call whoAmI() when an option of objective is changed.

- whoAmI(), defined in lines 5 to 8 simply alerts us to the object type and its name.

- Thus, when you change an objectives option, for example, you get an alert telling you "I am a select-multiple objectives" (Figure 9.39).

**LISTING 9.35** Using type and name.

```
1     <HTML>
2     <HEAD>
3     <TITLE>My type</TITLE>
4     <SCRIPT LANGUAGE = "JavaScript">
5     function whoAmI(theObject)
6     {
7         alert('I am a ' + theObject.type + ' ' + theObject.name)
8     }
9     </SCRIPT>
10    </HEAD>
11
12    <BODY>
13    <H3>My type</H3>
14    <FORM>
15    <INPUT    TYPE = 'button'
16              NAME = 'to press'
17              VALUE = 'What type of an object am I?'
18              onClick = 'whoAmI(this)'>
19    <P>
20    <SELECT   MULTIPLE
21              NAME = 'objectives'
22              onChange = 'whoAmI(this)'>
23       <OPTION> Win
24       <OPTION> Happy
25    </SELECT>
26    <SELECT   NAME = 'objective'
27              onChange = 'whoAmI(this)'>
28       <OPTION> Win
29       <OPTION> Happy
30    </SELECT>
31    </FORM>
32    </BODY>
33    </HTML>
```

# URL

| | |
|---|---|
| **Stores** | document's URL |
| **Syntax** | document.URL |
| **Access** | Read and write |
| **Property of** | document |
| **See also** | **Properties:** hash, host, hostname, href, pathname, port, protocol, search |

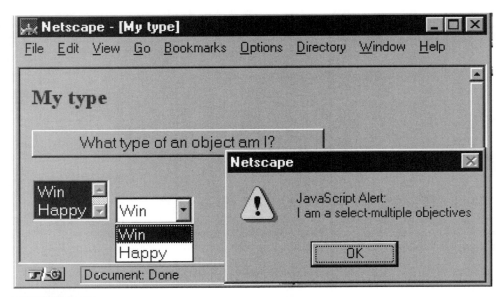

**FIGURE 9.39** Using type and name.

## Discussion

Use this property to retrieve and set the document's URL.

## Examples

Listing 9.36 and Figure 9.40 demonstrate the use of URL.

**LISTING 9.36** Using URL.

```
1    <HTML>
2    <TITLE>URL</TITLE>
3    <BODY>
4    <H3>URL</H3>
5    document.write(document.URL + '<BR>')
6    </SCRIPT>
7    </BODY>
8    </HTML>
```

 # userAgent

| Stores | The value of the user-agent header sent in the HTTP protocol from client to server |
|---|---|

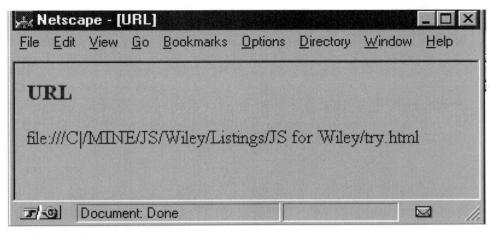

**FIGURE 9.40** Using URL.

| | |
|---|---|
| **Syntax** | `navigator.userAgent` |
| **Access** | Read only |
| **Property of** | `navigator` |
| **See also** | **Properties:** `appName`, `appVersion`, `appCodeName` |

## Discussion

Used by the server to identify the client.

## Examples

Listing 9.37 and Figure 9.41 demonstrate `userAgent`.

**LISTING 9.37** Using `userAgent`.

```
1    <HTML>
2    <HEAD>
3    <TITLE>userAgent</TITLE>
4    </HEAD>
5
6    <BODY>
7    <H3>userAgent</H3>
8    <SCRIPT LANGUAGE = "JavaScript">
9    document.write(navigator.userAgent + '<BR>')
10   </SCRIPT>
11   </BODY>
12   </HTML>
```

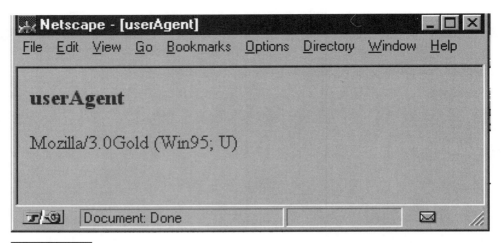

**FIGURE 9.41** Using userAgent.

#  value

| | |
|---|---|
| **Stores** | A string that is related to the VALUE attribute of its object |
| **Syntax** | *something*.value |
| **Access** | Read and write |
| **Property of** | **Objects:** button, checkbox, FileUpload, hidden, Option, password, radio, reset, submit, text, textarea |
| | **Arrays:** options |
| **See also** | **Properties:** text |

## Discussion

In the syntax above, *something* should be replaced by one of the following:

- *objectName*—standing for either the value assigned to the NAME attribute of a checkbox, FileUpload, hidden, password, text, textarea, button, reset, or submit object, or the desired element in the elements array

- *objectName*—designating the name of a Select object option created with the Option() constructor

- *radioName[index]*—where `radioName` is the value of the `NAME` attribute of a `radio` object.

- *selectName.options.[index]*—where *selectName* is either the value assigned to the `NAME` attribute of a `select` object or the desired element in the `elements` array. *index* is an integer representing a `radio` button in a radio object or an option in a `select` object.

Keep in mind that the name of the property is used to refer to an object, while its value is essentially the data that the object holds; these are two entirely different things.

The value of `value` depends on the object that owns it, according to the discussion below.

## hidden, text, and textarea objects

- Initially, `value` holds the string assigned to the `VALUE` attribute of the object.

- When a user or a program modifies the field, `value` changes accordingly.

- `value`'s data can be changed at any time.

- The display updates immediately when `value` is changed.


## password object

- Initially, `value` holds the string assigned to the `VALUE` attribute of the object.

- To hide its value, this string is displayed as asterisks in the `password` object field.

- The user can change the value in the field, the change will also be displayed as asterisks in the `password` object field.

- A JavaScript program can change the value in the field; the change will also be displayed as asterisks in the `password` object field.

- JavaScript returns the current string that `value` holds.

- JavaScript cannot access changes to the field made by the user (you will need to access the changed value through the server).

## button, reset, and submit **objects**

- Initially, value holds the string—if there is one—assigned to the VALUE attribute of the object.

- This string is displayed on the face of the button.

If a VALUE attribute is not specified with the HTML tag for the appropriate object, value is assigned a value based on the object:

- If the object is a button, value is empty and nothing is displayed on the face of the button

- If the object is reset, the string Reset is assigned to value and is also displayed on the face of the object

- If the object is submit, the string Submit Query is assigned to value and is also displayed on the face of the object.

## options **array**

- Initially, value holds the string assigned to the VALUE attribute of the object.

- JavaScript can change value at any time.

- value is not displayed on-screen, but is returned to the server if the option is selected.

Note that value, the selection state of the select object, and the option's text properties mean different things:

- The selected and selectedIndex properties determine which options are selected.

- The defaultSelected property determines the default selection state.

- The text property determines the text that is displayed in each option.

## checkbox **and** radio **objects**

- Initially, value holds the string—if there is one—assigned to the VALUE attribute of the object.

- If no string is assigned to the VALUE attribute of the object, then the string on is assigned to value.

- value is not displayed, but is returned to the server if the radio button or checkbox is selected.

- value can be set at any time.

Note that the string stored in value is different from the selection state of the checkbox or radio object, or the text that is displayed next to each checkbox or radio button:

- The selection state of the object is determined by the value of checked.

- The default selection of the object is determined by the value of defaultChecked.

- The text displayed by the object is determined by the string *text*, where *text* follows the appropriate object's tag as in

```
<INPUT TYPE = "checkbox"> text
<INPUT TYPE = "radio"> text
```

### Select **object options**

For Select object options created using the Option() constructor, value behaves as follows:

- Initially, value holds the string—if there is one—assigned to the VALUE attribute of the object.

- value is not displayed on-screen, but is returned to the server if the option is selected.

- You can change the string stored in value at any time.

### FileUpload **objects**

Use value to obtain the filename that the user typed into a FileUpload object.

For this object:

- value reflects the current value of a FileUpload object's field.

- It is read-only.

## Examples

Listing 9.38 and Figure 9.42 demonstrate how value works. Note the following:

- We set two objects on the form—a button and a checkbox (lines 24–32).
- onClick for each object calls valueName() (lines 27 and 32).
- In valueName() we display the values of value and name, change them, and display them again (lines 8–15).
- The change to the button object's value is displayed as soon as it is made.
- This example clarifies the difference between value, name, and text.

You can use this example as a template for debugging. In particular, you may need to change the appearance of form elements in response to user interactions. To examine which objects' properties on the form can change and when the changes occur, implement the approach in this example.

**LISTING 9.38** How value works.

```
1   <HTML>
2   <HEAD>
3   <TITLE>value</TITLE>
4   <SCRIPT LANGUAGE = "JavaScript">
5   function valueName(theObj)
6   {
7     var reveal
8     reveal = 'My name is "' + theObj.name + '"'
9     reveal += '\n My value is "' + theObj.value + '"'
10    alert(reveal)
11    theObj.name = 'new name'
12    theObj.value = 'New values'
13    reveal = 'My name is "' + theObj.name + '"'
14    reveal += '\n My value is "' + theObj.value + '"'
15    alert(reveal)
16    return true
17  }
18  </SCRIPT>
19  </HEAD>
20
21  <BODY>
22  <H3>value</H3>
23  <FORM>
24  <INPUT  TYPE = 'button'
25        NAME = 'no-name'
26        VALUE = 'Old values'
27        onClick = 'valueName(this)'>
```

```
28
29    <INPUT  TYPE = 'checkbox'
30        NAME = 'no-name'
31        VALUE = 'Old vales'
32        onClick = 'valueName(this)'>Change values
33    </FORM>
34    </BODY>
35    </HTML>
```

# 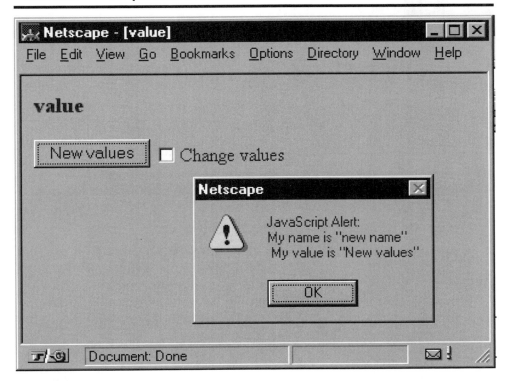 vlinkColor

| | |
|---|---|
| **Stores** | The color of links that have been visited at least once during a session |
| **Syntax** | document.vlinkColor |
| **Access** | Read only |
| **Property of** | document |
| **See also** | **Properties:** alinkColor, bgColor, fgColor, linkColor |

**FIGURE 9.42** How value works.

## Discussion

You can specify the `vlinkColor` in one of two ways:

- As a string literal (Appendix C).
- As an RGB mix, following the format RRGGBB, where RR, GG, and BB are the mix levels of red, green, and blue. Each color ranges in value from 00 to FF (hexadecimal). For example, `FF0000` is pure red.

In working with `vlinkColor`, keep the following in mind:

- Its value reflects the `VLINK` attribute of the `<BODY>` tag.
- Its value cannot be changed after the HTML page had been laid out.
- Its default is set by the user through the menu sequence `Options | General Preferences... | Colors | Followed links`.

## Examples

Listing 9.39 and Figure 9.43 demonstrate the use of vlinkColor.

**LISTING 9.39** Using `vlinkColor`.

```
1    <HTML>
2    <HEAD>
3    <TITLE>vlinkColor</TITLE>
4    <SCRIPT LANGUAGE = "JavaScript">
5    document.vlinkColor = "00FFFF"
6    </SCRIPT>
7    </HEAD>
8
9    <BODY>                                        Continued
```

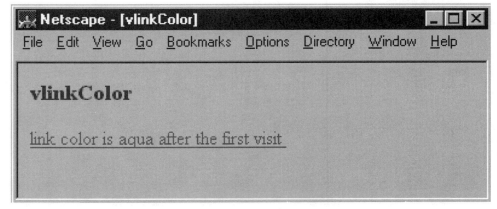

**FIGURE 9.43** Using vlinkColor.

```
10    <H3>vlinkColor</H3>
11    <A HREF = "http://turtle.gis.umn.edu">
12    link color is aqua after the first visit </A>
13    </BODY>
14    </HTML>
```

 # vspace

| | |
|---|---|
| **Stores** | The margin in pixels between the top and bottom edges of an image and the surrounding text |
| **Syntax** | *imageName*.vspace |
| **Access** | Read only |
| **Property of** | Image |
| **See also** | **Properties:** border, height, hspace, width |

## Discussion

In the syntax above, *imageName* stands for the name of an Image object or the desired element in the images array.

In working with vspace, keep the following in mind:

- The value of vspace reflects the value assigned to the VSPACE attribute of the <IMG> tag.
- The value of vspace is zero for images created with the Image() constructor.

## Examples

See Listing 9.9 and Figure 9.9.

 # width

| | |
|---|---|
| **Stores** | The width of an image either in pixels or as a percentage of the window width |
| **Syntax** | *imageName*.width |
| **Access** | Read only |
| **Property of** | Image |
| **See also** | **Properties:** border, height, hspace, vspace |

## Discussion

In the syntax above, *imageName* stands for the name of an `Image` object or the desired element in the `images` array.

In working with `width`, keep the following in mind:

- The value of `width` reflects the value assigned to the `WIDTH` attribute of the `<IMG>` tag.

- The value of `width` is the actual width of the image for images created with the `Image()` constructor.

## Examples

See Listing 9.9 and Figure 9.9.

 # window

| | |
|---|---|
| **Stores** | The current window or frame |
| **Syntax** | `window.something` |
| **Access** | Read only |
| **Property of** | `frame, window` |
| **See also** | |

## Discussion

In the syntax above, *something* stands for:

- `defaultStatus`, `status`, `length`, or `name` when the calling window is a `window` object

- `length` or `name` when the calling window is a `frame` object

- any method of the `window` object

The value of the `window` property depends on the object that owns it:

- For a `frame` object, it is `<object` *frameName*`>`, where *frameName* is the value assigned to the `NAME` attribute of the `<FRAME>` tag.

- For a `window` object, it is the window's name, maintained internally by the browser.

# Examples

Listing 9.40 and Figure 9.44 demonstrate the use of window. The code is self-explanatory.

**LISTING 9.40** The window property.

```
1    <HTML>
2    <HEAD>
3    <TITLE>window</TITLE>
4    <SCRIPT LANGUAGE = "JavaScript">
5    document.vlinkColor = "FF0000"
6    </SCRIPT>
7    </HEAD>
8
9    <BODY>
10   <H3>window</H3>
11   <FORM>
12   <INPUT  TYPE = 'button'
13        VALUE = 'window...'
14        onClick = 'alert(window)'>
15   </FORM>
16   </BODY>
17   </HTML>
```

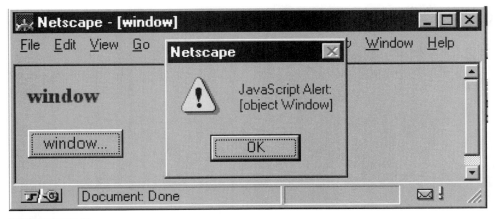

**FIGURE 9.44** The window property.

# EVENT HANDLERS REFERENCE

▷ Definitions and Discussions of event handlers

▷ Examples using event handlers

 # Introduction

In JavaScript, all event handlers begin with the letters on, followed by the event name. It is important to realize the difference between an event, an event handler, and an action of the event handler. For example, the statement

```
<BODY onUnload = 'aFunction()'>
```

should be interpreted as follows: When the document or form is unloaded (as when the user exits Navigator), an unload event occurs. The event handler is onUnload, and its action is implemented through aFunction().

In presenting event handlers, I followed a consistent format:

- Event name
- The action or actions that trigger the event
- The object or objects to which this event handler belongs
- Some related event handlers, methods, objects, or properties

- A discussion of issues relevant to the event handler
- An example

 # onAbort

| | |
|---|---|
| **Invoked when** | an abort event occurs |
| **Event handler of** | Image |
| **See also** | **Event handlers:** onClick |

## Discussion

An abort event occurs when the user aborts loading an image. Image abortion occurs, for example, when:

- the user clicks on the Stop button before loading of the image is finished
- the user clicks on a link in an HTML document before loading of the image is finished

Use this event handler when you want to make sure that your program exits gracefully (with no side effects) even if the user stops loading an image, or when you need to load the image fully before proceeding.

## Examples

Listing 10.1 and Figure 10.1 demonstrate the use of onAbort. In lines 7 to 9 we load the image named snake. If you click on the Navigator's Stop, Back, or Forward buttons fast enough, the alert window (Figure 10.1) will show up.

**LISTING 10.1** Using onAbort.

```
1    <HTML>
2    <HEAD>
3    <TITLE>onAbort</TITLE>
4    </HEAD>
5    <BODY>
6    <H3>onAbort</H3>
7    <IMG NAME = "snake"
8        SRC = "images\\snake.jpg"
9        onAbort = "alert('Don\'t you want to see me?')">
10   </BODY>
11   </HTML>
```

**FIGURE 10.1** Using onAbort.

 # onBlur

| | |
|---|---|
| **Invoked when** | an object loses focus |
| **Event handler of** | frame, select, text, textarea, window |
| **See also** | **Event handlers:** onBlur, onChange, onFocus |

## Discussion

A blur event occurs when one of the objects to which this event handler belongs loses focus. By definition:

- For frames, framesets, and windows, focus is lost when the window that contains them loses focus (when it is no longer the topmost window on the desktop).

- For `select`, `text`, and `textarea`, focus is lost when the user clicks anywhere outside the input area of the object.

Note the following:

- For `window`, `frame`, and `framesets`, the event handler should be included in the `<BODY>` tag.

- If `onBlur` appears both in the `<BODY>` and in the `<FRAME>` tag, `onBlur` in the `<FRAME>` tag overrides the one in the `<BODY>` tag of the document loaded into the frame.

- On windows platforms, `onBlur` in a `<FRAMESET>` tag has no effect.

## Examples

In Listing 10.2 we create a frameset file (`blur.html`) with four frames in it. Each frame uses the same source file, `onblur.html` (Listing 10.3). Load `blur.html`, click on the various frames, and see what happens (Figure 10.2). Note that `fgColor` does not work here.

**LISTING 10.2** Using `onBlur`—the `blur.html` file.

```
1    <HTML>
2    <HEAD>
3    <TITLE>onBlur</TITLE>
4    </HEAD>
5    <FRAMESET ROWS="50%,50%" COLS="40%,60%">
6    <FRAME SRC = onblur.html NAME = "northeast">
7    <FRAME SRC = onblur.html NAME = "northwest">
8    <FRAME SRC = onblur.html NAME = "southeast">
9    <FRAME SRC = onblur.html NAME = "southwest">
10   </FRAMESET>
11   </HTML>
```

**LISTING 10.3** Using `onBlur`—the `onblur.html` file.

```
1    <HTML>
2    <BODY  BGCOLOR = "lightyellow"
3         onBlur = "document.bgColor='lightyellow';
     document.fgColor='blue'"
4         onFocus = "document.bgColor='lightblue';
     document.fgColor='green'">
5    <H2> A Frame</H2>
6    </BODY>
7    </HTML>
```

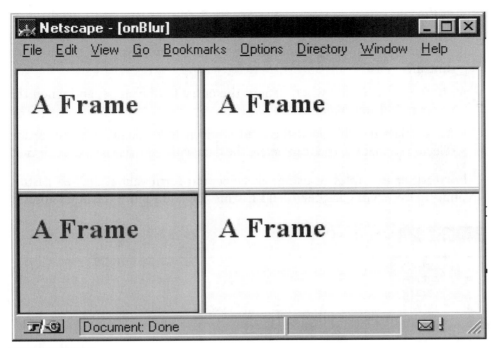

**FIGURE 10.2** Using onBlur.

#  onChange

| | |
|---|---|
| **Invoked when** | a change occurs to an object |
| **Event handler of** | select, text, textarea |
| **See also** | **Event handlers:** onBlur, onFocus |

## Discussion

By definition, a change event occurs when the object's (select, text, or textarea) field loses focus *and* its value has been modified. This event is often used for data validation: The user enters data in a field, and onChange calls your code to check the data, usually stored in the object's value property.

## Examples

Listing 10.4 and Figure 10.3 demonstrate the use of onChange along with focus() and select(). Here is what we do:

- In line 4 we include the JavaScript source file `commonf.js`. This file contains common functions, including `nInRange()`, which tests if the datum is a number; if it is, the function tests that the number is within a range (line 14).

- `nInRange()` is called when data in the entry field change, and when the `aText` field loses its focus.

- After validating the data, the field is given focus again, and the text is selected so that the user can delete the data without having to select it first.

For further examples of using `onChange` and form validation, see Listing 7.6 and Figure 7.6 in Chapter 7, and Listing 8.2 and Figure 8.2 in Chapter 8.

**LISTING 10.4** Using `onChange`.

```
1    <HTML>
2    <HEAD>
3    <TITLE>onChange</TITLE>
4    <SCRIPT LANGUAGE = "JavaScript" SRC = "commonf.js">
5    </SCRIPT>
6    </HEAD>
7    <BODY>
8    <H3>onChange</H3>
9    <FORM>
10   Enter a number:
11   <INPUT  TYPE = "text"
12        VALUE = ""
13        NAME = "aText"
14        onChange = "if(!nInRange(this.value, 0,
100)){this.focus();this.select()}">
15   </FORM>
16   </BODY>
17   </HTML>
```

 # onClick

| | |
|---|---|
| **Invoked when** | a form element is clicked on |
| **Event handler of** | button, checkbox, radio, link, reset, submit |
| **See also** | **Methods:** confirm() |

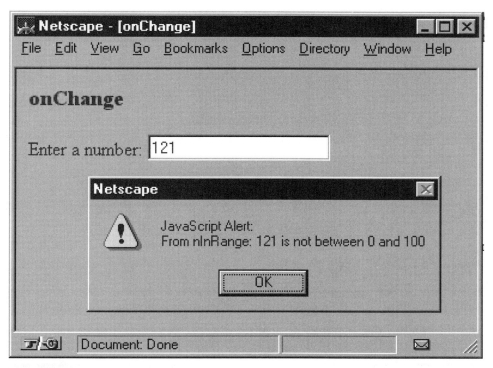

**FIGURE 10.3** Using onChange.

## Discussion

A click event occurs when the mouse pointer is in the object's area, and the mouse button is pressed. The event reacts slightly differently for the different objects it belongs to:

- For checkbox and link objects, and for radio, reset, and submit buttons, if the return value of the code triggered by the event handler is false, the clicked action can be canceled (simply return false).

- For button objects and for reset buttons in the Windows environment, returning false in reaction to onClick has no effect.

## Examples

Listing 10.5 and Figure 10.4 demonstrate the use of onClick. In line 7 we invoke the confirm dialog window. If the user clicks Cancel, nothing happens.

**LISTING 10.5** Using onClick.

```
1    <HTML>
2    <HEAD>
3    <TITLE>onClick</TITLE>
4    </HEAD>
5    <BODY>
6    <H3>onClick</H3>
7    <A   HREF = "http://turtle.gis.umn.edu/"
8       onClick = "return confirm('Load turtle?')">
9     Turtle
10   </A>
11   </BODY>
12   </HTML>
```

#  onError

| | |
|---|---|
| **Invoked when** | the loading of a document or image causes an error |
| **Event handler of** | Image, window |
| **See also** | **Event handlers:** onLoad |

## Discussion

An error event occurs when the invoking JavaScript code contains errors (syntax or run-time). Navigator errors do not trigger this event handler.

**FIGURE 10.4** Using onClick.

`onError` can be set to one of the following:

- **null**. If you set `window.onerror` to null, the `onError` event will be null, and all error dialogs that are normally invoked by your JavaScript code will be suppressed. Note the syntax here: use lowercase for `onerror`. This is so because windows are handled before HTML code can be interpreted. Thus, you must spell `onerror` all in lowercase and set it within a `<SCRIPT>` tag.

- **Name of the error-handling function**. This function takes three arguments: a string that appears in the message text, a URL, and the line number of the offending code. You must return `true` from the error-handling function if you want to suppress the standard JavaScript error dialog windows.

- **Any JavaScript variable**. Set the variable's value either to `null` or to a valid function reference.

- **Any JavaScript property**. Set the property's value either to `null` or to a valid function reference.

In your error-handling function you can deal with errors in one of the following ways:

- Have your error-handling function return `false`. In this case you can trace the errors, and JavaScript will use the standard dialog windows to report them.

- Have your error-handling function return `true`. In this case, the standard JavaScript dialog windows will be disabled, and you can use your own code to report the error.

- Set `onError` to `false`. In this case, all error reporting is turned off.

If you want to suppress all error reporting, use the following code in the HTML head section (`onerror` must be all lowercase here):

```
...<HEAD> ...
<SCRIPT LANGUAGE = "JavaScript>
  window.onerror = null
...
</SCRIPT>...
```

## Examples

In this example we are going to brew our own homemade error report. Let's see how:

- In line 4 of Listing 10.6 we assign the `onErrorHandling` function to `window.onerror` (note the lowercase for `onerror`).

- In lines 6 to 8 we build arrays for error messages, URLs of the error messages, and line numbers for the error messages.

- In lines 10 through 16 we define `onErrorHandling()`: It takes three arguments: `aMessage`, `aURL`, and `aLine` number. It then adds an element to each of the arrays defined in lines 6 to 8 and returns `true`. Note that since the index of the last element in an array is `length` $-1$, storing an element with the index `length` adds it to the end of the array and increase the array's length by 1.

- Because we want to use our own error reporting, we make `onErrorHandling()` return `true`.

- In lines 18 to 38 we build the error reporting in `report()`.

  - First, we open an `errorWindow` (where we are going to put the errors) in line 20.

  - Next, we build a table to arrange the error report neatly on the page (line 21).

  - Then we go through each element in the three arrays, and add them to the report with the appropriate HTML-table-generating-code (lines 24 to 35).

  - Finally, we close the table and the form (line 36) and close the document so that we can see the report.

- In line 42 there is a run-time error: a function that does not exist (`whoAmI`) is called.

- In line 50 there is a syntax error in the quotes.

To see how things work, click on the `Syntax...` button and then on the `Report errors...` button (Figure 10.5). This should produce the report shown in Figure 10.6. Note the slight inconsistency between the report line numbers and the true line numbers where the errors occur. This discrepancy can sometimes cause difficulties in debugging. Inexperienced programmers look for errors in the reported lines, never to find them. Always look for errors in the vicinity of the reported line. This is true not only for JavaScript, but also for many other debugging environments.

**LISTING 10.6** Using onError.

```
1    <HTML>
2    <HEAD><TITLE>onError</TITLE>
3    <SCRIPT>
4    window.onerror = onErrorHandling
5
6    messages = new Array()
7    urls = new Array()
8    lines = new Array()
9    function onErrorHandling(aMessage, aURL, aLine)
10
11   {
12     messages[messages.length] = aMessage
13     urls[urls.length] = aURL
14     lines[lines.length] = aLine
15     return true
16   }
17
18   function report()
19   {
20     errorWindow = window.open('','Errors')
21     errorWindow.document.write(
22        '<B>Error Report</B><P><FORM><TABLE>')
23
24     for (var i = 0; i < messages.length; i++)
25     {
26      errorWindow.document.write(
27         '<TR><TH><B>File:</B><TD> ' +
28         urls[i] + '</TR>')
29      errorWindow.document.write(
30         '<TR><TH><B>Line:</B><TD> ' +
31         lines[i] + '</TR>')
32      errorWindow.document.write(
33         '<TR><TH><B>Message:</B><TD> ' +
34         messages[i] + '</TR>')
35     }
36     errorWindow.document.write('</TABLE></FORM>')
37     errorWindow.document.close()
38   }
39   </SCRIPT>
40   </HEAD>
41
42   <BODY onLoad = "whoAmI()">
43   Click on the "Syntax..." button to produce a
44   syntax error. Click on the "Report errors..."
```

```
45    button to produce errors report.
46    <FORM>
47    <BR>
48    <INPUT   TYPE = "button"
49        VALUE = "Syntax..."
50      onClick = "alert('Wrong quotes)">
51
52    <P>
53    <INPUT   TYPE = "button"
54        VALUE = "Report errors..."
55        onClick = "report()">
56    </FORM>
57    </BODY>
58    </HTML>
```

#  onFocus

| | |
|---|---|
| **Invoked when** | the appropriate object (form element) receives a focus |
| **Event handler of** | frame, text, textarea, window |
| **See also** | **Event handlers:** onBlur, onSelect |

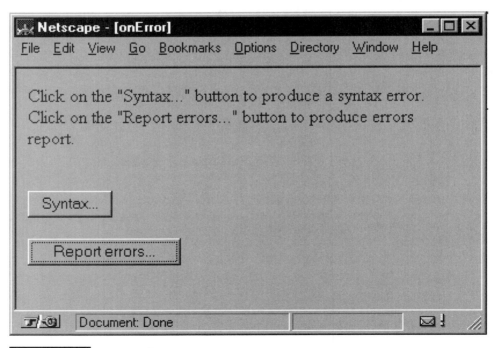

**FIGURE 10.5** Using onError.

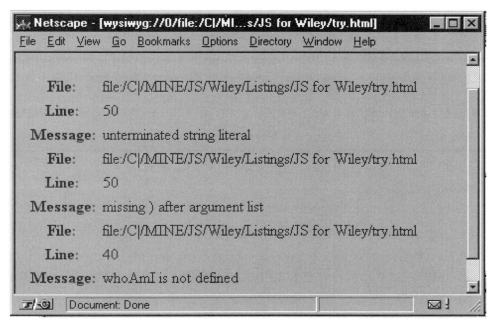

**FIGURE 10.6** Homemade JavaScript error report.

## Discussion

By definition, a focus event of a field (usually a form's element) occurs when either a tab or a mouse click activates the field (bring it into focus).

Note the following:

- `onFocus` and `onSelect` are two different events; `onSelect` occurs when text is selected in a field of a `text` object or a `textarea` object. Thus, if the user enters from another field by selecting text, first the `onFocus` event occurs and then `onSelect`.

- For `frame` objects, `onFocus` overrides an `onFocus` in the `<BODY>` tag of the relevant document.

- Do not use `alert()` with `onFocus`, because once you dismiss the alert dialog window, `onFocus` occurs again in the field that produced the alert in the first place, and so on, *ad nauseam*.

- On Windows platforms, `onFocus` in a `<FRAMESET>` tag has no effect.

## Examples

In Listing 10.3, change the `onBlur` event handlers with `onFocus` event handlers. Then experiment clicking on the various frames and see what happens.

 onLoad

| | |
|---|---|
| **Invoked when** | Navigator finishes loading a window or all frames in a frameset |
| **Event handler of** | Image, window |
| **See also** | **Event handlers:** onAbort, onError, onUnload |

## Discussion

In using onLoad, note the following:

- Use onLoad in either the <BODY> or the <FRAMESET> tags.
- If you use onLoad in a <BODY> tag of a <FRAME> and in the <FRAMESET> that owns the <FRAME>, the onLoad in the <FRAME> occurs first, and then the onLoad in the <FRAMESET>.

The behavior of onLoad for Image objects is as follows:

- onLoad occurs when the image is displayed.
- Displaying an image and loading an image are two different activities; an image is displayed when it is assigned to the src property of the Image object; an image is loaded when (for example) you use the Image() constructor.
- If you use onLoad with multi-image GIF animation, each time a new image is loaded an onLoad event is triggered.

## Examples

Listing 10.7 and Figure 10.7 demonstrate the use of onLoad. Here are a few things to notice:

- In lines 5 to 7 we create a PredatorPrey image, and assign onload (note the lowercase) and src to it.
- In whoAmI() (lines 9 to 15) we want to see the name of the image that just finished loading.
- In lines 21 to 32 we load two images, competition and PredatorPreyAgain, and assign whoAmI() to their onLoad.

- When you first load the HTML file, whoAmI() is executed for PredatorPrey. But you cannot see PredatorPrey's name from whoAmI() because the onLoad handler is a name of a function (not a call to a function; the call occurs later). You cannot pass arguments when you refer to a function by name. Thus, when PredatorPrey is loaded, its name is not displayed.

- When competition is loaded, it calls whoAmI() (line 26) and its name is displayed (lines 13 and 14).

- Finally, predatorPreyAgain is loaded, and its name is displayed (see Figure 10.7).

In case you are interested, the competition image represents a strange attractor of a mathematical model of the co-evolutionary process in a community of competing organisms. The PredatorPrey and predatorPreyAgain images represent a mathematical model of the co-evolutionary process in a community of organisms with predators and prey species. Strange attractor is a formal mathematical term.

**LISTING 10.7** Using onLoad.

```
1     <HTML>
2     </HEAD><TITLE>onLoad</TITLE>
3     <HEAD>
4     <SCRIPT>
5     PredatorPrey = new Image(50,50)
6     PredatorPrey.onload = whoAmI
7     PredatorPrey.src = "images\\StrangeAttractor3a.jpg"
8
9     function whoAmI(anImage)
10    {
11      if (anImage == null)
12       alert('An image loaded')
13      else
14       alert(anImage.name + ' loaded')
15    }
16    </SCRIPT>
17    <HEAD>
18
19    <BODY>
20    <H3>onLoad (Competition or Predator-Prey)</H3>
21    <IMG    NAME = "competition"
22            SRC = "images\\StrangeAttractor2.jpg"
```

```
23          ALIGN = "top"
24          HEIGHT = 150
25          WIDTH = 250
26          onLoad = 'whoAmI(this)'>
27   <IMG   NAME = "predatorPreyAgain"
28          SRC = "images\\StrangeAttractor3a.jpg"
29          ALIGN = "top"
30          HEIGHT = 150
31          WIDTH = 250
32          onLoad = 'whoAmI(this)'>
33   </BODY>
34   </HTML>
```

#  onMouseOut

| | |
|---|---|
| **Invoked when** | the mouse pointer leaves an area |
| **Event handler of** | Area, link |
| **See also** | **Event handlers:** onMouseOver |

## Discussion

By definition, a mouse-out event occurs when the mouse pointer leaves an area of an image in the client's window, or an area of a link in the client's window.

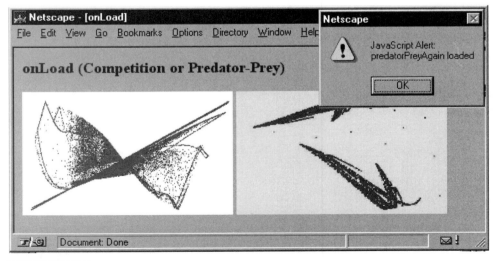

**FIGURE 10.7** Using onLoad.

Note the following:

- When the user moves the mouse cursor, `onMouseOut` (for one area) is often followed immediately by an `onMouseOver` event when the mouse remains in the client's window area.

- If you use this event handler, you must include the `HREF` attribute within the `<AREA>` tag.

- If you want `onMouseOver` to react to changes in the `status` or `defaultStatus` properties, you should return true to the `onMouseOut` event handler.

## Examples

See Listing 7.3 and Figure 7.3 in Chapter 7.

 # onMouseOver

| | |
|---|---|
| **Invoked when** | the mouse pointer moves from outside the object area to over it |
| **Event handler of** | Area, link |
| **See also** | **Event handlers:** onMouseOut |

## Discussion

By definition, a mouse-over event occurs when the mouse pointer enters an area of an image in the client's window, or an area of a link in the client's window.

Note the following:

- `onMouseOver` occurs every time the mouse pointer moves from outside to over the object area.

- Usually, `onMouseOut` from one area is followed by `onMouseOver` in another area of the client's window.

- You must include the `HREF` attribute inside the `<AREA>` tag if you use the `onMouseOver` event handler.

- If you want the `onMouseOver` to react to changes in the `status` or `defaultStatus` properties, you should return `true` to the `onMouseOver` event handler.

## Examples

See Listing 7.3 and Figure 7.3 in Chapter 7.

 # onReset

| | |
|---|---|
| **Invoked when** | a form is reset |
| **Event handler of** | form |
| **See also** | **Event handlers:** onSubmit |
| | **Methods:** reset() |
| | **Objects:** Reset |

## Discussion

By definition, a reset event occurs when the user resets a form by clicking on a Reset button. Use this event to restore a form's defaults.

## Examples

Listing 10.8 and Figure 10.8 demonstrate the use of onReset. In line 8 we set the Lawyers form. When the user clicks on the reset button (lines 15 to 17), whatever was in the text field named lawyer is reset back to the default (given in line 13). Before resetting, however, the answer to the joke is displayed in an alert window (line 9).

**LISTING 10.8** Using onReset.

```
1     <HTML>
2     <TITLE>onReset</TITLE>
3
4     <BODY>
5     <H3>onReset</H3>
6     Enter any text in the field, click on
7     "Reset for answer..." and see what happens.
8     <FORM NAME = "Lawyers"
9        onReset = "alert('A good start.')">
10    A joke:
11    <INPUT  TYPE = "text"
12         NAME = "lawyer"
13         VALUE = "What do you call 1,000 lawyers at the bottom of
                the sea?"
```

```
14          SIZE = 50><P>
15   <INPUT  TYPE = "reset"
16          VALUE = "Reset for answer..."
17          NAME = "start">
18   </FORM>
19   </BODY>
20   </HTML>
```

# ↳ onSelect

| | |
|---|---|
| **Invoked when** | text is selected in an input area of a `text` or `textarea` object |
| **Event handler of** | `text`, `textarea` |
| **See also** | **Event handlers:** `onBlur`, `onFocus` |

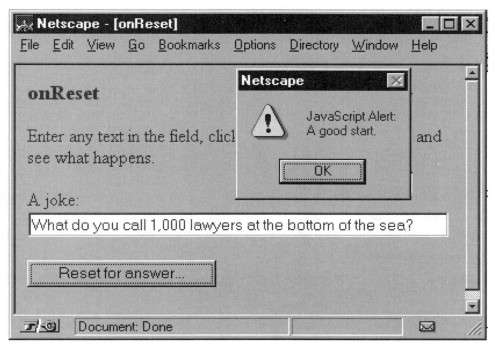

**FIGURE 10.8** Using `onReset`.

## Discussion

By definition, a select event occurs when some or all of the text in a form's text or textarea element is selected.

## Examples

Listing 10.9 and Figure 10.9 are supposed to demonstrate the action of onSelect. Presumably, when you select the text in the textarea (as shown in Figure 10.9), an alert window with the punch line should appear; it does not for me!

**LISTING 10.9** Working with onSelect (unsuccessfully).

```
1    <HTML>
2    <TITLE>onSelect</TITLE>
3
4    <BODY>
5    <H3>onSelect</H3>
6    </BODY>
7    Select any part of the text in the field
8    and see what happens.
9    <FORM NAME = "IamSupposedToWork">
10   <TEXTAREA   NAME = "JustJoking"
11          COLS = 30
12          ROWS = 3
13          WRAP = "virtual"
14          onSelect = "alert('A good start.')">
15   What do you call 1,000 lawyers at the bottom of the sea?
16   </TEXTAREA>
17   </FORM>
18   </HTML>
```

 # onSubmit

| | |
|---|---|
| **Invoked when** | the user submits a form |
| **Event Handler of** | form |
| **See also** | **Methods:** submit() |
| | **Objects:** submit |

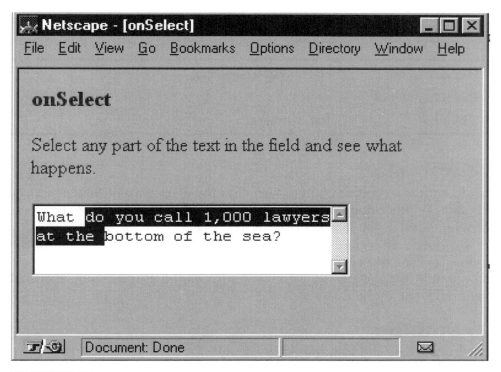

**FIGURE 10.9** Working with onSelect (unsuccessfully).

## Discussion

By definition, a submit event occurs when the user clicks on a Submit button (a submit object), or when a submit() is invoked. To submit a form conditionally, return true (or false) from the function called by the event handler. For example, if aFunction() in the statement

```
<FORM ... onSubmit = "return aFunction(arguments)"...>
```

returns false, the form will not be submitted.

## Examples

See Listing 7.36 and Figure 7.28 in Chapter 7.

 # onUnload

| | |
|---|---|
| **Invoked when** | the user exits a document |
| **Event handler of** | window |
| **See also** | **Event handlers:** onAbort, onError, onLoad |

## Discussion

By definition, an unload event occurs when the user exits a document by, say, choosing another document to load, or exiting Navigator. To use this event handler, put it in the <BODY> or <FRAMESET> tags.

If a document includes frames within a frameset, the unload event for the frames occurs before it occurs for the frameset. Thus, if you include onUnload in the <BODY> tag within a frame, expect its call to be executed before the one in the <FRAMESET> tag.

## Examples

See Listing 7.40 and Figure 7.32 in Chapter 7.

# STATEMENTS

↳ Definitions of statements
↳ Explanations of the syntax of each statement
↳ Examples for each statement

# Introduction

In using statements, note the following:

- JavaScript statements usually start with a keyword followed by code to execute (assignments, function calls, etc.).

- Keywords are a subset of reserved words (Appendix B).

- Statements can span over several lines of code.

- Nested statements should be delineated with braces, as in

```
for (...) { ... nested statements ...}
```

- If two or more statements appear on the same line, separate the statements with a semicolon (;).

In the list of available JavaScript keywords (Table 11.1), new and this are not exactly keywords (they do not define statements); the former is an operator, and the latter is a reserved word. They are traditionally included with the list of keywords. Also, some of the keywords are not in use, but are reserved for future implenentation.

**TABLE 11.1** JavaScript keywords.

| break | comment | continue | for | for...in | function | if...else |
|-------|---------|----------|-----|----------|----------|-----------|
| new | return | this | var | while | with | |

Each of the keywords is presented in this chapter in a consistent manner:

- A brief statement of its purpose
- The statement's syntax
- Related methods, objects, properties, and other keywords
- A discussion of the keyword
- Examples in which the use of the keyword is demonstrated

Most of the examples in this chapter are short and are used for illustration only. As usual, if you decide to test an example, first run it to see what it does, and then read the code.

 # break

| | |
|---|---|
| **Purpose** | Used to break out of a for or while loop. |
| **Syntax** | break |
| **See also** | **Reserved words:** continue, for, return, while |

## Discussion

When break is encountered, code execution continues from the line following the end of the loop (for or while) in which break is embedded. This reserved word is particularly useful when you intend to execute something in your code for as long as some condition is met, but you do not know when that will happen. Be sure that at some point the condition for `break` will occur; otherwise you enter the so-called (and so annoying) infinite loop.

In a JavaScript function you can break out of a loop by using a conditional `return`.

## Examples

Listing 11.1 and Figure 11.1 demonstrate the use of `while` and a few other things. Note the following:

- `validatePrompt()` is intended to validate data that is returned from the `prompt()` input (lines 4 to 15).

- In line 7 we enter an infinite `while` loop because `true` is always true.

- In line 9 we store the value returned from `prompt()` in `pInput`.

- If the value of `pInput` is not a floating number, we alert the user (lines 10 and 11) and display the prompt window again.

- If the value of `pInput` is a floating number (if line 10 is evaluated to `false`), we break out of the loop (line 13).

**LISTING 11.1** Using `break`, `while`, `if`, `else`, `prompt()`, `isNaN()`, and `parseFloat()`.

```
1    <HTML>
2    </HEAD><TITLE>break</TITLE>
3    <SCRIPT LANGUAGE = "JavaScript">
4    function validatePrompt()
5    {
6      var pInput = ""
7      while (true)
8      {
9       pInput = prompt("Enter a number:", "")
10      if (isNaN(parseFloat(pInput)))
11        alert(pInput + " is not a number")
12      else
13        break
14     }
15   }
16   </HEAD>
17   </SCRIPT>
18   <BODY>
```

```
19   <H3>break</H3>
20   Click on "Prompt..." and see what happens
21   <FORM>
22   <INPUT  TYPE = "button"
23       VALUE = "Prompt..."
24       onClick = 'validatePrompt()'>
25   </FORM>
26   </BODY>
27   </HTML>
```

A piece of advice: Use this infinite loop approach sparingly, and only in simple cases. To test this approach, you should first try something like the code snippet shown in Listing 11.2. Only after you thoroughly test the code should you replace the code in while with true.

**LISTING 11.2** Testing infinite while.

```
1    var i = 0
2    bigNumber = 10
3    while (i < bigNumber)
4    {
5      ...
6      break
```

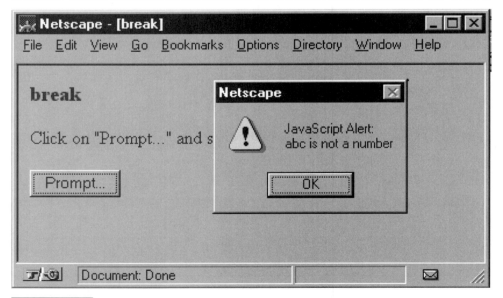

**FIGURE 11.1** Using break, while, if, else, prompt(), isNaN(), and parseFloat().

```
7      ...
8      i++
10    }
```

#  Comment

| | |
|---|---|
| **Purpose** | Used to make the code readable. |
| **Syntax** | // or the pair /* and */ |
| **See also** | **Attribute:** NOSCRIPT |

## Discussion

Use comments profusely in your code. They will remind you later of what you have done. There are two ways to comment JavaScript code:

- The double slash (//) syntax is an inline comment; JavaScript code following // is ignored to the end of line.

- If you want your comment to span multiple lines, open the comment with /* and close it with */.

## Examples

Here are some ways to embed comments in your code:

```
for (var i = 0; i < 10; i++) //This is an inline comment
for (var i = 0; i < 10; i++) /* An inline comment, close it with */
  /* Multiple-line comment starts here
     and ends here */
  for (var i = 0; i < 10; i++)
```

#  continue

| | |
|---|---|
| **Purpose** | Jump to the next iteration in a for or a while loop. |
| **Syntax** | continue |
| **See also** | **Keywords:** break, for, while |

## Discussion

Note the following:

- When continue is encountered in a for loop, execution jumps to the update expression in the loop. The update expression is that expression that appears inside the parentheses of the for statement.

- When continue is encountered in a while loop, execution jumps to the condition inside the parentheses of the while statement.

## Examples

continue is useful when you need to execute part of a loop conditionally. Take a look at Listing 11.3. In an effort to keep your caloric intake below dailyIntake, you keep track of your daily intake. You have an array of food-stuff objects, named fromFood. Each item has two properties: name and caloricContent. In line 1 you initialize the totalCalories to zero and then inside the for loop you accumulate your daily intake of calories. Because you like IceCream and CheeseCake, you decide to exclude them from the computation of your daily caloric intake.

**LISTING 11.3** Using continue.

```
1    var totalCalories = 0
2    for (var i = 0; i < dailyIntake; i++)
3    {
4      if (fromFood.name[i] == "IceCream" ||
5          fromFood.name[i] == "CheeseCake")
6        continue
7      else
8        totalCalories += fromFood.caloricContent[i]
9    }
```

 # for

| | |
|---|---|
| **Purpose** | Create loops in code. |
| **Syntax** | for ([*initial-expr*];[*condition*]; [*increment-expr*]) { [*statements*] } |
| **See also** | **Keywords:** while, for...in |

## Discussion

In the syntax above:

- *initial-expr* can be an expression that is either a statement or a variable declaration. Use this expression to initialize a counter. You can also declare the counter for the loop by using the `var` keyword.

- *condition* is evaluated on each pass through the loop. If the condition evaluates to `true`, the nested statements inside the loop are executed; otherwise, loop execution terminates and the statement following the loop is executed. If `condition` is missing, it is considered `true`.

- *increment-expr* is used to update the counter. It is evaluated for each pass through the loop.

- *statements* is one or more statements. They are evaluated each pass through the loop (that is, for as long as `condition` is true).

Note the following:

- The opening and closing braces do not have to be on separate lines; it is a matter of style.

- Indenting the block of statements inside the loop is optional, but is recommended for good style.

## Examples

Listing 11.4 demonstrates a couple of esoteric uses of `for`. I show you these just because you might encounter them in other people's code:

- The first version, in lines 6 to 11, initializes `i` to zero (line 6), and then iterates forever. To stop the iteration, we increment the value of `i` while displaying it (line 8).

- The second version (lines 13 to 18) behaves like an infinite loop.

Figuring out who is incremented when during loop execution can be confusing. Run the code and be sure to watch how the value of `i` is changing.

**LISTING 11.4** Using for.

```
1        <HTML>
2     <HEAD><TITLE>for</TITLE>
3     <SCRIPT LANGUAGE = "JavaScript">
4     function forSyntax()
5     {
6       for (var i = 0;;)
7       {
8        alert(i++)
9        if (i > 5)
10         break
11      }
12      alert(i)
13      for (;;)
14      {
15       alert(i++)
16         if (i > 10)
17           break
18      }
19    }
20    </SCRIPT></HEAD>
21
22    <BODY>
23    <H3>for</H3>
24    Click on "For..." and see what happens
25    <FORM>
26    <INPUT  TYPE = "button"
27         VALUE = "For..."
28         onClick = 'forSyntax()'>
29    </FORM>
30    </BODY>
31    </HTML>
```

# ↳ for...in

| | |
|---|---|
| **Purpose** | Iterate through all distinct properties of an object. |
| **Syntax** | `for (variable in object)`<br>`{`<br>    `[statements]`<br>`}` |
| **See also** | **Keywords:** `for`, `while` |

## Discussion

In the syntax above:

- *variable* iterates through all distinct properties of *object*.
- *statements* refer to the statements to execute for each property of *object*.

## Examples

In previous examples we introduced the idea of inspecting properties of an object. Listing 11.5 and Figure 11.2 demonstrate another implementation of this idea. In lines 7 through 9 we iterate through all the of properties theObj (window, in this case). Note that i in line 9 indicates the property name (the first i after the period), and the element in the object's array that holds the property values (the second occurrence of i on line 9).

**LISTING 11.5** Using for...in and the object inspector.

```
1    <HTML>
2    <HEAD><TITLE>for...in</TITLE>
3    <SCRIPT LANGUAGE = "JavaScript">
4    function propertiesInspector(theObj, theObjName)
5    {
6      var props = "<B>" + theObjName + " Properties:</B><BR>"
7      for (var i in theObj)
8       props +=
9          theObjName + "." + i + " = " + theObj[i] + "<BR>"
10     props += "<HR>"
11     return props
12   }
13   </SCRIPT></HEAD>
14
15   <BODY>
16   <H3>for...in</H3>
17   <P>
18   <SCRIPT LANGUAGE = "JavaScript">
19   var props = propertiesInspector(window, "window")
20   document.write(props)
21   </SCRIPT>
22   </BODY>
23   </HTML>
```

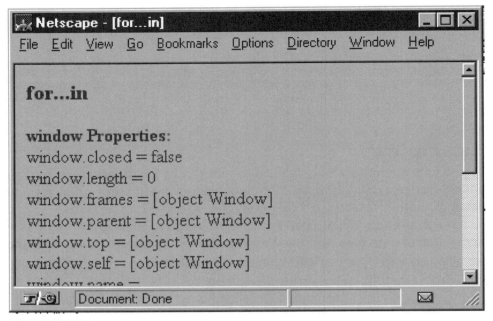

Netscape - [for...in]

File  Edit  View  Go  Bookmarks  Options  Directory  Window  Help

# for...in

**window Properties:**
window.closed = false
window.length = 0
window.frames = [object Window]
window.parent = [object Window]
window.top = [object Window]
window.self = [object Window]
window name —

Document: Done

**FIGURE 11.2**  Using `for...in` and the object inspector.

#  function

| | |
|---|---|
| **Purpose** | Create a function. |
| **Syntax** | `function name([argument1][,argument2][...,argumentN])`<br>`{`<br>    `[statements]`<br>`}` |
| **See also** | **Keywords:** `return` |
| | **Objects:** `Function` |
| | **Properties:** `arguments` |

## Discussion

The following rules apply to the `function` statement:

• Arguments can be any of the following types: string and number literals, and string, number, and object variables.

- When you call the function, you can specify fewer than the number of arguments specified in the parentheses following the `function` keyword.

- Without a statement such as `return something`, a function does not return a value.

- Functions can be recursive, but cannot be nested in another `function` statement.

- Arguments are passed to functions by value. This means that any changes a function makes to its argument values are local to the function and do not persist upon return from the function.

The last point merits some explanation. There are essentially two ways to pass arguments to a function:

- by reference or
- by value

When you pass an argument by reference—something you cannot do in JavaScript—you are actually passing to the function the address of the argument, not its value. This means that if the function changes the value of the argument in the address (the address is a physical location in memory), then that value persists even after you return from the function. For security reasons, this cannot be done in JavaScript.

When you pass an argument by value—something you can do with JavaScript—the function creates a copy of the argument in memory. You can do whatever you like to the value of the argument. As soon as the function returns, it is unloaded from memory, and changes you made to the copy of the argument are lost. To make those changes persist, you can return whatever you wish with the return statement.

## Examples

There are numerous examples of the `function` statement throughout the book. Here, I want to dwell for a moment on the issue of "passing by value"; this can cause debugging problems to novices (and experienced) programmers.

Consider the code in Listing 11.6.

- In lines 3 to 10 we define the function `noChange()`. It takes the argument `a`, prints its value, adds 5 to it, and prints its value again. So if the passed value of `a` is 1, the first `writeln()` (line 5) prints 1, and the second (line 8) prints 6.

- In lines 15 to 23 we define the function rememberThis(). Here, we set a to 1 (line 17), and write its value. Next, we call noChange() with the argument a, and then write the value of a again. Note that a = 1 after the call to noChange() (see Figure 11.3).

One more comment about the code in Listing 11.6: Because of the <PRE> tag (line 13), the function writeln() behaves as it should; without this tag, writeln() would behave just like write().

**LISTING 11.6** Passing arguments to a function by value.

```
1    <HTML><HEAD><TITLE>function</TITLE>
2    <SCRIPT LANGUAGE = "JavaScript">
3    function noChange(a)
4    {
5      document.writeln(
6       "In noChange() before adding 5 to a:  a = " + a)
7      a += 5
8      document.writeln(
9       "In noChange() after adding 5 to a:  a = " + a)
10   }
11   </SCRIPT></HEAD>
12
13   <BODY> <PRE><H3>function</H3>
14   <SCRIPT LANGUAGE = "JavaScript">
15   function rememberThis()
16   {
17     a = 1
18     document.writeln(
19      "In rememberThis(), before calling noChange(): a = " + a)
20     noChange(a)
21     document.writeln(
22      "In rememberThis(), after calling noChange(): a = " + a)
23   }
24   rememberThis()
25   </SCRIPT>
26   </PRE></BODY></HTML>
```

 # if...else

**Purpose**   Execute a block of code if a condition is true; otherwise, execute another block of code.

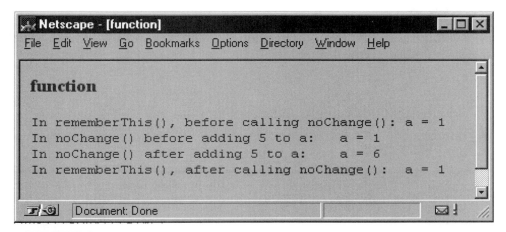

**FIGURE 11.3** Passing arguments to a function by value.

**Syntax**
```
if (condition)
{
        [statements1]
}
else
{
        [statements2]
}
```

## Discussion

In the syntax above:

- *condition* is any JavaScript expression that evaluates to `true` or `false`.

- If *condition* evaluates to `true`, *statements1* are executed and execution continues from the code line following the end of the `else` block of statements.

- If *condition* evaluates to `false`, *statements2* are executed and execution continues from the code line following the end of the `else` block of statements.

- If *statements1* is a single statement, braces are optional.

- If *statements2* is a single statement, braces are optional.

## Examples

In the following example, both `if` and `else` are redundant, because `true` always evaluates to true:

```
if (true) x = 5; else x = 6
```

 # new

| | |
|---|---|
| **Purpose** | Create an instance of a predefined object type or a user-defined object type. |
| **Syntax** | *objectName* = new *objectType*([*arg1*][,*arg2*]...[,*argN*]) |
| **See also** | **Properties:** prototype |

## Discussion

In the syntax above:

- *objectName* is the name of a new instance of the object.

- *objectType* is a pre-existing or user-defined object type. Pre-existing object types that can be created with the `new` keyword are `Array`, `Date`, `Function`, `Image`, `Option`, and `String`.

- *arg1...argN* are the *objectType* property values. These values can represent any valid JavaScript data type (numbers, strings, other objects types, and so on).

To create your own object:

- First, define a function whose name is the object type name.

- Second, create an instance of the object with `new`.

See examples below.

To add a property to a predefined object (such as `Date`) or to a user-defined object, you can:

- Simply name the new property. In this case the new property will refer to the object instance only.

- Use the prototype property. In this case the new property will be added to all instances of the object type.

See examples below.

## Examples

In Listing 11.7 we demonstrate the use of new in politics:

- First, we create a new object, named Politician with three properties: a string named affiliation, an honest scale from 0 to 10, and a photogenic scale from 0 to 10 (lines 5 to 10).

- Next, in lines 11 and 12, we create two instances of Politician, unelectable and electable, and assign values to their properties.

- Then, in lines 14 to 18, we assign the appropriate Politician object (instance) to elected.

- Finally, in line 19, we add a prototype property named whoseFault.

As lines 20 and 21 and Figure 11.4 demonstrate, whoseFault is added to all Politician objects.

**LISTING 11.7** Using new and prototype in a Politician object.

```
1     <HTML><HEAD><TITLE>new</TITLE>
2
3     <BODY> <PRE><H3>new</H3>
4     <SCRIPT LANGUAGE = "JavaScript">
5     function Politician(affiliation, honest, photogenic)
6     {
7       this.affiliation = affiliation
8       this.honest = honest
9       this.photogenic = photogenic
10    }
11    unelectable = new Politician("Republican", 8, 0)
12    electable = new Politician("Democrat", 0, 8)
13    var elected
14    if ( (unelectable.honest < electable.honest) &&
15       (unelectable.photogenic > electable.photogenic) )
16      elected = unelectable
17    else
18      elected = electable
19    Politician.prototype.whoseFault = "The People"
20    for (i in elected)
21      document.writeln("elected." + i, " = ", elected[i])
22    </SCRIPT>
23    </PRE></BODY></HTML>
```

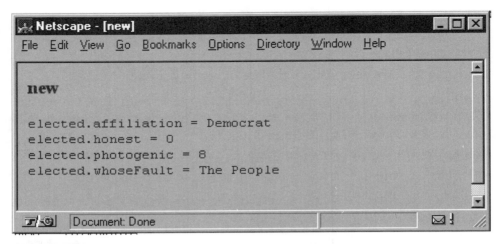

**FIGURE 11.4** Using new and prototype in a Politician object.

#  return

| | |
|---|---|
| **Purpose** | Return a value from a function. |
| **Syntax** | return *expression* |
| **See also** | **Keywords:** function |

## Discussion

In the statement

```
aVariable = aFunction()
```

the value that `aFunction()` returns is assigned to `aVariable`.

## Examples

It is important to distinguish between `undefined` and `null`:

- In `undefined`, JavaScript tells you that it knows nothing about something.
- In `null`, JavaScript tells you that it knows that something is nothing.

To understand the difference, take a look at Listing 11.8 and Figure 11.5:

- In lines 5 to 7 we define the function nothing(), which does not use return.

- In lines 8 to 11 aNull() returns the "value" null.

- Hence, politician is evaluated to undefined in line 13, and to null in line 14 (see Figure 11.5).

**LISTING 11.8** Using return, and the difference between a null and undefined politician.

```
1    <HTML><HEAD><TITLE>new</TITLE>
2
3    <BODY> <PRE><H3>new</H3>
4    <SCRIPT LANGUAGE = "JavaScript">
5    function nothing()
6    {
7    }
8    function aNull()
9    {
10      return null
11   }
12   var politician
13   document.writeln("politician = ", eval("politician=nothing()"))
14   document.writeln("politician = ", eval("politician=aNull()"))
15   </SCRIPT>
16   </PRE></BODY></HTML>
```

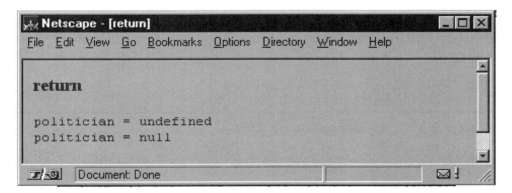

**FIGURE 11.5** Using return, and the difference between a null and undefined politician.

# this

| | |
|---|---|
| **Purpose** | Used to refer to the current object. |
| **Syntax** | this[.*propertyName*] |
| **See also** | **Properties:** name |

## Discussion

When this appears in a method, it usually refers to the object that called the method. You can use this to make your code more modular, because this refers to the current object, and is independent of the object's name.

## Examples

The code snippet

```
function aFunction(theObj)
{
  theObj.theProperty = something
}
```

can be called by the button object aButton like this:

```
<INPUT TYPE = "button" NAME = "aButton" onClick = "aFunction(this)">
```

Instead of using this in the line above, you could use 'aButton'; however, if you happen to change the value of the NAME attribute to something else, your code will be in error.

# var

| | |
|---|---|
| **Purpose** | used to declare variables |
| **Syntax** | var *variableName* [= *value*] [..., *variableName* [= *value*] ] |

## Discussion

In the syntax above:

- *variableName* is any legal identifier; it must start with a character and can include characters, digits, and underscore (_).
- You can initialize a variable or the same time that you declare it.
- You can declare more than one variable per var statement; separate the variables with commas.

The scope of the variable is as follows:

- If the variable is declared inside a function statement, the variable exists only inside the function (that is, when the function is executing).
- If the variable is declared outside a function, it is global and is recognized by all parts of the JavaScript code in the current application.
- Outside of functions, you can declare a variable without the keyword var.
- Inside a function, you must use the keyword var if a global variable of the same name exists.

## Examples

The statement

```
var politician = null
```

declares a variable named politician and assigns no value (whatsoever) to it.

 # while

| | |
|---|---|
| **Purpose** | Create a loop to execute a block of statements. |
| **Syntax** | `while (condition)`<br>`{`<br>    `[statements]`<br>`}` |
| **See also** | **Keywords:** for, for...in |

## Discussion

In the syntax above:

- *condition* is an expression that evaluates to `true` or `false`.
- *condition* is evaluated before each pass through the loop. If it evaluates to `true`, *statements* are executed; otherwise, the next statement following the braces is executed.
- *statements* execute while *condition* is `true`.
- Indentation is not required, but is a good programming practice.
- If *statements* is a single statement, braces are optional.

## Examples

See Listing 11.1 and Figure 11.1.

 # with

---

| | |
|---|---|
| **Purpose** | Establish a default object for a set of statements. |
| **Syntax** | `with (object)`<br>`{`<br>    `[statements]`<br>`}` |

---

## Discussion

In the syntax above:

- *object* is the default object.
- In *statements*, anywhere where an object name is required but does not appear, *object* is used.

## Examples

In the code snippet

```
with(Math)
{
```

```
    a = SQRT2
    b = SQRT2_1
    c = cos(PI/2)
}
```

SQRT2, SQRT1_2, and PI are properties of the Math object, and cos() is one of the object's methods. Because Math is established as the default object, there is no need to preface its constants or functions with Math (e.g., you do not need to write Math.PI).

# PART THREE

# APPLICATIONS

# THE INTERNET STORE— PRELIMINARIES

- ↳ The application design
- ↳ Goals
- ↳ Limitations of the application
- ↳ Advantages of the application
- ↳ Setting up the stereo system design

# ↳ Introduction

This is the first of three chapters that deal with the Internet store. Here and in the ensuing chapters I shall take you through the steps to build a working, full-fledged (albeit not fancy) application; you will learn how to create a store on the Internet, and how to communicate with the user without having to rely on server processing.

This chapter covers some of the more general issues of planning the software: project design, recognizing your limitations, and so on. But when it comes to software development do not put too much stock in guidelines, expert suggestions, and meticulous avoidance of pitfalls. No matter how much you plan, your plans will change as you move along. So take my advice:

Do some planning and soul-searching before you begin, but remember that at some point you should start your work. I have seen people becoming intimidated by the magnitude of this or that project to the point of paralysis. In most cases issues get resolved (for better or worse) as one proceeds. Also keep in mind that it is okay to have a few false starts. Eventually, most things take care of themselves.

# ↳ Project Design and Implementation

When thinking about a programming project, large or small, you may find the following discussion helpful. Keep in mind that developing a project (programming or otherwise) is *not* a linear process. Remember also that each of us thinks differently, and therefore should approach problem-solving in his or her unique way; straitjacket solutions often work, but they are boring and lead to unimaginative results. The steps below are loose, and they are presented in a somewhat vague order of precedence. Regardless of the order of the steps you take, you should be able at the end of the planning phase, to answer the questions of What, Why, When, and How.

## Step 1—Define the Problem

Although one cannot claim that a problem always precedes a solution, software applications are developed in answer to some tangible problems. To begin with, ask yourself questions such as:

- What are my needs?
- Are these really needs or just wishful thinking?
- If I fulfill these needs, am I likely to be happy? Frustrated? Have new needs? What are these new needs?

Trivial as they may seem, these questions are often overlooked, and failure to address them may prove costly. I wish to emphasize the second question in particular. We often embark upon projects because we fancy, rather than need, them. For example, many of us think that the Internet is a wonderful development. We then try to squeeze inappropriate and often unnecessary solutions into it. A store owner may take a fancy to the Internet and would like to set up a shop on it. Does she really need an on-line shop? Will such a shop attract more customers than she already has? Is she being oversold on the idea by herself, friends, business associates, and media hype?

Once you define the problem loosely (no need to define it precisely right from the outset), move on to Step 2.

## Step 2—Determine What Constitutes a Solution

Comprehending the problem is an important first step. In Step 2 you need to think about what constitutes a satisfactory solution. If you are a store owner, for example, you should ask yourself questions such as: "Given my understanding of the problem, would I need an interface that connects the user directly with my database? Can a small database satisfy my needs? Do I need to automate stock update as soon as a customer places an order?"

These questions will help you delineate the scope of the solution.

For example, you may decide that you need to create a large database that stores data about your merchandise items, the number available in stock, item specifications, and so on, and then interact with your home page customer via the database. Or, you may decide that the database can be small, and updated manually. In the former case you will need more than just standard access to a server; you may even need your own server. You will also need to use CGI or (preferably) Java code to negotiate interactions between JavaScript and the database. If you decide to stick with a small database and manual update, JavaScript alone, with simple Internet access (through a home page), will suffice.

Scope is important; if you are not sure about the boundaries of the solution, you will wind up trying to implement more and more as time goes on, and never reach a satisfactory solution to your problem. As I pointed out, these steps are not linear. It will be to your advantage to think about this step and the previous one simultaneously. Thinking about the scope of the solution will refocus your attention on the problem.

## Step 3—Determine the Tools and Methods to Be Used

Here you ask yourself the question of How. What kind of tools would you need to address the problem? Is JavaScript going to provide you with an acceptable solution? Can it? Perhaps you will need a different approach. If JavaScript is the tool, do you have access to the necessary browsers and computers to test the program? (One browser and one operating system will hardly suffice.) Can you get access to other sites on the Internet through which you can test development? Can you identify a group of users who might be willing to give you feedback while the project is evolving?

What follows are some cases where JavaScript cannot provide adequate solutions. In these cases you need to rely on tools such as Java and CGI.

- When you need direct communication between a visitor of your HTML page (a client) and a server-side database.

- When you need to read and write files both on your side (the URL of the HTML page, or the server) and on the visitor's side (the URL that accesses your HTML page, or the client).

- When you need to perform numerical calculations at high speed (as in simulations).

- When you want to build and display images on the fly (as opposed to displaying stored images in response to some user input).

- When your program is large (say more than about 1,000 lines of code).

Many of JavaScript's limitations arise largely because of the following reasons:

- Except for the rudimentary cookies mechanism, JavaScript cannot write files on the server and client machines.

- JavaScript cannot read files from the client machine (again, except for cookies).

- Being an interpreted language, computations and program execution are slow.

- It is extremely difficult (and inefficient) to control window display via pixel manipulation (see Chapter 15 for some ways around this limitation).

## Step 4—Determine Existing Expertise

Now that you have more or less determined the tools you need to use, ask yourself the next questions: "Can I do it? If not, do I need to get (pay) somebody else to do it? Where do I find that somebody else?" There is a Catch-22 here: If you do not know about available tools, how are you to know what tools to use. This is why I keep saying that you cannot approach an Internet programming project (or any project) using the one-step-at-a-time approach.

When you reach this point in your project development, you may need to pause for a while and do some reading. Start with things you know at least something about. If the material you read is good, it will contain suggestions about some other tools that may be useful to you. Read about those. There is a familiar trap here: You may wind up becoming an expert with no practical application in sight. Do not attempt to learn everything you need before you start implementing the project. Expect (and actually strive for) a few false starts; one of these may even be something you go back to later.

## Step 5—Identify Constraints

If you isolated your wishful thinking from a real need (see Step 1), you have come a long way toward identifying constraints. Project constraints emerge from a variety of sources: your expertise (how well trained are you to solve the problem), the amount of time and money you can afford to invest (compared to the anticipated return), the equipment and space you have, access to the Internet and speed of access, and so on.

You may need to go back and forth among these planning steps. For example, you may have identified constraints that will force you to modify your goals, as developed during problem definition; expertise might temper your goals, and of course capital is always an issue.

Now that we have discussed (briefly) how to approach a problem, let us chew on a real problem: the Internet store.

#  The Internet Store

Imagine yourself an owner of a stereo equipment store. You have set up a home page on the World Wide Web, and put your e-mail address on the page. On the home page, you advertise the equipment you carry, with prices, along with pictures and many other kinds of eye-candy. You are getting a lot of inquiries; people wish to buy your merchandise, and often complain that they cannot do it directly on the Internet. From the volume of e-mail you get and the number of visitors, your business sixth sense is telling you that allowing customers to shop in your store through the Internet will eventually result in a profitable percentage of them buying from you. You decide to start thinking about solutions.

By now you have almost convinced yourself that you want to set up an Internet store. But really, is this just a pipe dream? Something you fancy because you yourself surf the Internet? You are honest with yourself, and the answer is *yes*, you do need to set up an Internet store!

So, now that we know Why, we need to look at What.

## Your Goal

At this point, you are ready to formalize your goal. You want to provide visitors of your home page with the ability to browse through your merchandise, choose what they wish (build a stereo system they desire), and place an order, all through the Internet. We have now answered the What question.

Next, we move on to How.

## How to Achieve the Goal

To achieve your goal, you decide to build a form-based home page. In it, you want to provide the user with the tools to choose and order. The form is going to be built using JavaScript in an HTML page.

## Tools You Need

Here is what you need:

- A relatively fast PC (say, a Pentium or a Power Macintosh). If you plan to run a big operation (you are putting a whole department store on the Internet), you may need a more powerful computer, with a multiuser operating system, and all the security that comes with it. A good workstation running UNIX or some other multiuser operating system may satisfy your needs. Keep in mind, however, that once you get into the workstation world you will not be able to keep up with things yourself; you will need a professional (a system administrator) to handle many of the day-to-day computer operation tasks.

- Lots of memory and hard disk storage space. For example, on some machines, Netscape Navigator chews more than 7 MB of memory when started. Some word processor manufacturers will require more than 150 MB just to install their application.

- Access to the Internet, at a satisfactory speed. Customers will abandon your store if they have to wait for a picture of their favorite tuner to come up.

- Some way to get information from visitors. Perhaps use HTML forms.

So far, everything (as you have guessed by now) is telling you that you may be able to solve the problem with a good JavaScript program. But before moving on, let us first clarify to ourselves what the limitations are of the approach you wish to take.

## Limitations of the Current Solution

Once you decide on the solution, and it starts to look feasible, you need to clarify to yourself the solution's limitations. Without admitting its limitations, a solution can often be oversold, and then lead to disappointment.

Here are some of the limitations of the solution we've outlined:

- If you plan major modifications of the solution presented here, you need to become an expert in JavaScript.

- You will not be able to build a large database. To deal with large, inventory-type databases, you will need to build on the current solution by incorporating Java and/or CGI code to communicate between the server that holds the database and the client that submits the forms.

- There is a security problem: Data that are transferred via JavaScript and e-mail is not safe; they can be tampered with. You therefore do not want to implement credit card purchasing. (There are ways around this limitation, but they will not be discussed in this book.)

## Advantages of the Current Solution

The major advantage is that you are your own boss. You can control what application you build and how you build it. You will not need to rely on server-side services. The solution is probably cheap; in fact, the cost will be a fraction of the cost of other, comparable, and slightly more complex solutions.

## The Design

After reflecting on the problem, you decide to program forms. The forms should, at minimum, include:

- A list of the items you offer for sale, including their prices
- A user interface that allows the user to build her own system
- The ability for the user to modify choices and design different stereo systems
- Information about the customer

The next set of decisions to make are how to present the list of items and prices, how to allow the user to design his own stereo system, and so on. We now take a close look at these issues. To give you an idea of where we are heading, take a look at Figure 12.1. Here we are presenting the visitor with

**FIGURE 12.1** The stereo-system design form.

a selection list of stereo components. Each of the options includes the items that are available. For example, in the "Amplifiers" list we might include a list of models by brand name. (If you are adventurous, you could add, to the right of the list of selections, a button that loads a picture of a selected item when the user presses the button.)

Once the user selects a system configuration, clicking on the How much... button should inform the user about the cost of the configuration. From this step, you want to gather some information about the user (name, address, etc.), as shown in Figure 12.2. The user would then submit the form via the Submit... button.

Now that you have an idea where we are going, let us continue with the details.

# ↳ Data Design

First, we need to design the structure of the information we wish to present to the user. We thus need a convenient way to manipulate the information

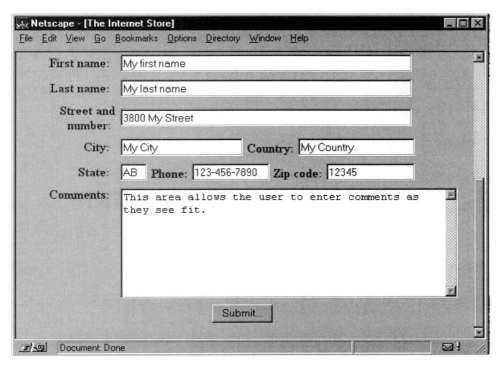

**FIGURE 12.2** The user information form.

we wish to present to the user. A natural (and intuitive) choice is to specify an object that characterizes in some way (to be defined precisely in a moment) a stereo component. Here we need to think about the common denominator of the various stereo components, and design the object based on it. We know that all stereo components (amplifiers, CD players, tape decks, etc.) have a model name, a manufacturer, and a price. We thus desire an object that has at least these three properties. The structure of the Component object is shown in Listing 12.1.

**LISTING 12.1** The Component object.

```
1    //--Component object with 3 properties
2    function Component(componentName, manufacturer, price)
3    {
4        this.componentName  = componentName
5        this.manufacturer = manufacturer
6        this.price    = price
7    }
```

Once we define the object `Component`, we can create (instantiate) different stereo components based on this object. Keep in mind that here we are not totally committed to the object structure. When we wish to add a property to the `Component` object, we can just use the `prototype` property (recall, from Chapter 9, that `prototype` defines a property that is shared by all objects of a specified type).

We next build our database.

# Specifying the Stereo Component Database

Thus far, we have defined a generic stereo component object named `Component` with three properties: `componentName`, `manufacturer`, and `price` (Listing 12.1). Next, we decide that five objects of the type `Component` suffice to represent a stereo system: an amplifier, speakers, a tuner, a CD player, and a tape deck. These are defined with the `Array()` constructor in lines 2, 12, 22, 32, and 42 of Listing 12.2, respectively.

If you decide to implement a modified version of this application, this is where you need to tinker with it most: You may need to change properties, the number of different objects of the generic type, and the number of items in each array. For example, if your Internet store sells cars instead of stereo components, you may wish to do the following:

- Define a generic car object. This object should include properties that most cars would have. Here, you can assign to your car object properties such as color, manufacturer, model, year, and an array of options.

- Then build an array of cars, each element with its specific data.

In the case of our stereo Internet store, Listing 12.2 will need to be expanded and periodically maintained. This does not require much thinking, but it does require some data entry. For each component you simply add any new elements to the end of the array. The five `Component` arrays do not have to be of equal length. They also do not need to contain elements in a consecutive order, and you do not need to keep track of the number of elements in the arrays—we shall see in a moment why. All you have to do is delete an item that is no longer available, and add new items to the appropriate array.

**LISTING 12.2** The Component database.

```
1    //—-Build the data base
2    amplifierList    = new Array(4)
3    amplifierList[0] = new Component("The Amp",
4       "Anonymous Inc.", 200)
5    amplifierList[1] = new Component("The Strongest Amp",
6       "Steroids Inc.", 180)
7    amplifierList[2] = new Component("The Noisiest Amp",
8       "Noise Inc.", 150)
9    amplifierList[3] = new Component("Don\'t buy me Amp",
10      "Bankrupt Inc.", 120)
11
12   speakersList    = new Array(4)
13   speakersList[0] = new Component("Just Speakers",
14      "Anonymous Inc.", 200)
15   speakersList[1] = new Component("Blow Out Speakers",
16      "Steroids Inc.", 250)
17   speakersList[2] = new Component("Decibel Speakers",
18      "Noise Inc.", 220)
19   speakersList[3] = new Component("Hardly Audible Speakers",
20      "Bankrupt Inc.", 280)
21
22   tunerList    = new Array(4)
23   tunerList[0] = new Component("Just a Tuner",
24      "Anonymous Inc.", 100)
25   tunerList[1] = new Component("The Biggest Tuner",
26      "Steroids Inc.", 110)
27   tunerList[2] = new Component("Static Tuner",
28      "Noise Inc.", 120)
29   tunerList[3] = new Component("One Station Tuner",
30      "Bankrupt Inc.", 130)
31
32   cdList    = new Array(4)
33   cdList[0] = new Component("CD Player",
34      "Anonymous Inc.", 100)
35   cdList[1] = new Component("Arm Twister CD",
36      "Steroids Inc.", 110)
37   cdList[2] = new Component("CD and More",
38      "Noise Inc.", 120)
39   cdList[3] = new Component("Broken CD",
40      "Bankrupt Inc.", 130)
41
42   tapeList    = new Array(4)
43   tapeList[0] = new Component("Tape Deck",
44      "Anonymous Inc.", 110)
45   tapeList[1] = new Component("Got You Tape Deck",
```

```
46        "Steroids Inc.", 120)
47    tapeList[2] = new Component("Try Again Tape",
48        "Noise Inc.", 130)
49    tapeList[3] = new Component("Oh Well",
50        "Bankrupt Inc.", 140)
```

For example, if you no longer sell the Noisiest! amplifier, but you do have a new brand—say the Quietest—upon modification, your amplifierList might look like the one shown in Listing 12.3.

**LISTING 12.3** Modified stereo components data.

```
1    amplifierList     = new Array(5)
2    amplifierList[0] = new Component("The Amp",
3        "Anonymous Inc.", 200)
4    amplifierList[1] = new Component("The Strongest Amp",
5        "Steroids Inc.", 180)
6    amplifierList[3] = new Component("Don\'t buy me Amp",
7        "Bankrupt Inc.", 120)
8    amplifierList[4] = new Component("The Quietest",
9        "Solvent Inc.", 225)
```

You can simplify the process of updating your database by including all of the array constructors in a separate file—say, sdata.js. Then use the SOURCE attribute for the <SCRIPT> tag.

If you wish to use this application only to control your stock, you can add another property to the Component object called, say, numberInStock. You will then need to find a way to automatically update this number. Although not difficult, this may be beyond your expertise.

#  Global Variables

As a rule, you should minimize the use of global variables in your application. Recall that global variables are those variables that are defined outside any function, and thus are recognized at any place in the code. If you use too many global variables, and modify them in numerous places, sooner or later you will get confused and no longer know what value of a global variable you are using. Because we use them in different functions and forms, we declare only two global variables: one to store the total price of the system, and one to store a formatted string that describes the system (see Listing 12.4).

**LISTING 12.4** Global variables.

```
1    //--Global variables
2    totalPrice = 0
3    systemDescription = ""
```

#  The Stereo Components Selection Lists

One of my objectives was to create an easily modifiable application. This generally means writing functions that are as generic as possible. The creation of a selection list is a good example of such an approach.

Because we do not know how many elements are going to be in a selection list (the number of options in a selection list is determined by the length of a component's array), we define the CreateSelectionList() function with two arguments, selectionName and selectionItems. Thus, selectionItems stores the brand name of the desired component. The selectionName argument stores the value of the NAME attribute for the appropriate Select object. For example, if we assign the value amplifier to selectionName and amplifierList to selectionItems in line 2 of Listing 12.5, then lines 5 and 6 resolve to the string

```
"<SELECT NAME = 'amplifier'>
<OPTION SELECTED>- none selected -"
```

Next, we add Options to the Select object named amplifier. How many options? As many as the number of elements in the amplifierList array. So we stumble upon lines 7 to 9 in Listing 12.5. Here we cycle through all of the elements in the selectionItems array (which is, in our example, the amplifierList array), and add options, one at a time. When we are done, we close with </SELECT> (line 10), and return the string that contains the HTML code (named selectObject) with the return statement (line 11).

**LISTING 12.5** Creating a selection list.

```
1    //--Create a selection list with name and selection items
2    function CreateSelectionList(selectionName, selectionItems)
3    {
4        var selectObject =
```

```
5            "<SELECT NAME = \"" + selectionName + "\">"
6          + "<OPTION SELECTED>- none selected -"
7        for(var i in selectionItems)
8          selectObject += "<OPTION>" +
9              selectionItems[i].componentName
10      selectObject += "</SELECT>"
11      return selectObject
12    }
```

If we use the `amplifierList` as defined in Listing 12.2, then by the time
we `return selectObject` in line 11 of Listing 12.5, we have built the equivalent of the following object:

```
<SELECT NAME = 'amplifier'>
<OPTION SELECTED>- none selected -
<OPTION> The Amp
<OPTION> The Strongest Amp
<OPTION> The Noisiest Amp
<OPTION> Don't buy me amp
</SELECT>
```

which should correspond to Figure 12.3.

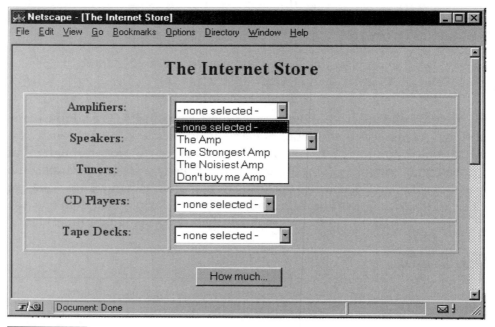

**FIGURE 12.3** The select object named amplifier.

What makes `CreateSelectionList()` in Listing 12.5 generic is that the function takes any array, and any name for the object, and creates a selection list from it. The only thing that is, perhaps, not generic in `CreateSelectionList()` is the addition of the `- none selected -` option in the `Select` object. You can easily remove this specificity by adding an item by this name to the array, or by specifying an `Option` (say, the first one) as `SELECTED`.

The function `CreateSelectionList()` will be called later from the HTML document to create as many `Selection` objects as we need on the form. In our example, we will call `CreateSelectionList()` five times, once for each of the stereo component objects (see Chapter 14 and Figure 12.1).

#  Building the Stereo System Description and Computing Its Price

The next step is to deal with the data that the user is putting together. These data will later be transmitted back to you via e-mail. To accomplish this task, we use the function `CanGetPrice()`; all it does is check if all components were specified. To keep things simple, we will force the user to choose all five components. In a more forgiving application you might want to allow the user to buy each component separately. As you will see in a moment, such a modification is quite simple.

If you want to be more sophisticated, and force the user to choose some components, but not others, add another property to the `Component` object, called `isRequired`, and assign `true` or `false` to it. Then, in your code, include the appropriate tests to see if all components whose value of `isRequired` is `true` were indeed chosen.

The function `CanGetPrice()` (Listing 12.6) sets the `totalPrice` to zero and clears the `systemDescription` (lines 4 and 5). Then, it calls each component price function: `AmplifierPrice()`, `SpeakersPrice()`, and so on (lines 7, 10, etc.). If any of these functions returns `false`, `CanGetPrice()` returns `false`. We shall see in a moment what the specific component price functions do.

**LISTING 12.6** Computing the price and building the stereo system description.

```
1    //--Were necessary data selected?
2    function CanGetPrice()
3    {
```

```
4          totalPrice = 0
5          systemDescription = ""
6
7          if(!AmplifierPrice())
8             return false
9
10         if(!SpeakersPrice())
11            return false
12
13         if(!TunerPrice())
14            return false
15
16         if(!CDPrice())
17            return false
18
19         if(!TapePrice())
20            return false
21
22         return confirm("\nYour system configuration:\n\n" +
23                 systemDescription + "\n for a total of $" +
24                 totalPrice + ".\n" + "\n Order now?")
25    }
```

If all component price functions in Listing 12.6 return `true`, we get to lines 22 to 24. Here we finalize the `systemDescription` string, and display it as shown in Figure 12.4. Take a look at line 23 of Listing 12.6 again. The bulk of the string that appears in the confirm window is stored in the global variable `systemDescription`. "Where did you store information in `systemDescription`?" you might ask. This is done in the individual component functions (called in lines 7, 10, 13, 16, and 19). Here again, the disadvantage of using global variables in the code is evident in the confusion: We are using `systemDescription` here, but populate it with data somewhere else!

The component-price functions are all similar, so I shall explain only one of them: `AmplifierPrice()` (Listing 12.7). In line 4 we assign the index of the selected item to the variable `i`. If the value of `i` turns out to be zero, it means that the current selection is - `none selected` -, and because we wish to force the user to select this item, we alert the user (line 8) and return `false`. Recall that returning `false` from here causes `CanGetPrice()` in Listing 12.6 to return `false` also.

If we happen to choose an option other than the first (that is, we choose a stereo component), we roll down to line 12. Here we need to subtract 1 from `i`. Why? Because the option zero (no component is selected) is added to the selection list when the form is built (Listing 12.5). Thus, the zero ele-

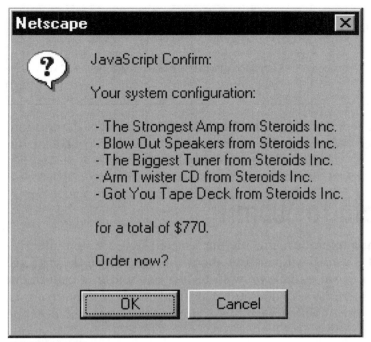

**FIGURE 12.4** Confirming user selection of a stereo system.

ment of the `amplifierList` array is in position 1 of the `Select` object. Next, we add the price of the appropriate component (an amplifier element in the `amplifierList` array, in this case) to the `totalPrice` (line 13), we add the description of the component to the `systemDescription` (line 14), and we return `true`. Returning `true` here causes `CanGetPrice()` to roll down to the next component (see Listing 12.6).

**LISTING 12.7** Component price.

```
1     //--Get the selected amplifier price
2     function AmplifierPrice()
3     {
4        var i = document.SystemForm.amplifier.selectedIndex
5
6        if(i == 0)
7        {
8           alert("\nYou must select an amplifier.\n")
9           return false
10       }
11
```

```
12        i -= 1
13        totalPrice += eval(amplifierList[i].price)
14        systemDescription += " - " + amplifierList[i].componentName +
15                   " from " + amplifierList[i].manufacturer + "\n"
16        return true
17   }
```

So far, we have seen how to build the database, the system description, and the system price. We now move on to the data we wish to get back from the user.

#  The Data to Submit

The data should, at a minimum, include the selected stereo system description, its price, and personal information about the user. Since the data are going to be sent to us via e-mail, we wish to format them in a convenient way. The function submitData() does just that. It takes one argument, a form (we shall see in a moment which form this argument refers to), and does the following, as shown in Listing 12.8:

- First, the function asks the user to confirm that he wants to submit the order (lines 3 and 4). If the user clicks on the Cancel button in the confirm dialog window (the dialog window returns false), submitData() terminates with the return value false. In this case no data are submitted (you will see why later).

- Next, we declare the variable data (line 5) and assign dataForm to it; dataForm is a form that holds the user's personal information such as first and last name (see Figure 12.2).

- Then we build a theData string, which includes the document title, its URL location, the user's personal information, the description of the stereo system the user has designed, and so on (lines 7 to 17).

- Finally, we assign the data to the value of a hidden element in the submitting form (this will be discussed shortly in line 18), and return true in line 19.

As you shall see later, submitData() is triggered from an onSubmit event handler. When submitData() returns true, the information built in the theData string is submitted via e-mail. An example of the stereo system configuration (as shown in Figure 12.1) and user personal data (as shown in Figure 12.2) is shown in the received e-mail format in Figure 12.5.

**LISTING 12.8** The data to submit.

```
1     function submitData(form)
2     {
3         if(!confirm("Are you sure?"))
4             return false
5         var data = document.dataForm
6         var theData = ""
7         theData += "Page title:\t\t" + document.title + "\n"
8         theData += "Data source:\t" + document.location + "\n\n"
9         theData += "First name:\t\t" + data.firstName.value + "\n"
10        theData += "Last name:\t\t" + data.lastName.value + "\n"
11        theData += "Street:\t\t\t" + data.street.value + "\n"
12        theData += "State:\t\t\t" + data.state.value + "\t"
13        theData += "Phone: " + data.phone.value + "\t"
14        theData += "Zip: " + data.zip.value + "\n\n"
15        theData += systemDescription + "\n\n"
16        theData += "Total = $" + totalPrice + "\n\n"
17        theData += "Comments:\n"
18        form.theData.value = theData + data.comments.value
19        return true
20    }
```

In the next chapter we tackle the important issue of data validation.

```
From:              Prof. Yosef Cohen
Sent:              Wednesday, November 20, 1996 4:14 AM
To:                yc@turtle.gis.umn.edu
Subject:           Order

Page title:        The Internet Store
Data source:       file:///C|/MINE/JS/Wiley/Listings/JS for
                   Wiley/TryStereoStore.html

First name:        My first name
Last name:         My last name
Street:            3800 My Street
State:             AB    Phone: 123-456-7890   Zip: 12345

  - The Noisiest Amp. from Noise Inc.
  - Blow Out Speakers from Steroids Inc.
  - The Biggest Tuner from Steroids Inc.
  - Arm Twister CD from Steroids Inc.
  - Got You Tape Deck from Steroids Inc.


Total = $740

Comments:
This area allows the user to enter comments as they see fit.
```

**FIGURE 12.5** The formatted e-mail order.

# CHAPTER THIRTEEN

# DATA VALIDATION

- Strategies for data validation
- Admissible and inadmissible sets
- Atomic and molecular data validation functions
- Data validation for the Internet store
- General data validation functions

 # Introduction

Data validation is one of the most important, and often difficult, issues to deal with when you gather information from users—which is why the topic was reserved for Chapter 13. It is important for at least the following reasons:

- If you wish to standardize data collection (say, for later storage in a database), the better validation you do during the data collection stage, the less work you will have to do to correct the data once it is in the database. For large databases, data correction can be a daunting task.

- Data validation makes the user interface more friendly (but only if you use the validation cleverly). For example, you can detect entry errors and "help" the user correct them.

Data validation is often difficult to deal with because, among other reasons:

- You must be able to anticipate a variety of errors that may arise, and be prepared to deal with them.

- If your data are lexically complex, you will have to program error checking with numerous permutations that may grow exponentially.

- What is and what is not an acceptable datum is often an arbitrary decision, and your initial decisions may prove inefficient later.

To make the discussion less abstract, consider a simple example. You wish to validate a telephone number entry. What are the characters you are going to allow? Possible answers are:

- The digits 0 to 9 only and the blank space character

- The above, plus the left and right parentheses and a dash

- The digits 0 to 9, left and right parentheses, a dash, and the set of characters A to Z

- The digits 0 to 9, left and right parentheses, a dash, and the set of characters a to z

- All of the above, with or without a period to separate area code

- And so on, *ad nauseam*

The problem is compounded even further if you wish to program for international (as opposed to North American) phone numbers: How many characters should you allow? What characters?

#  Strategies for Data Validation

As a working premise, let us decide that a character is any of the following:

- The digits 0 to 9

- The letters A to Z and a to z

- All punctuation marks

- A whitespace

- All special characters (\n, \t, and so on)

Let us also define the following:

- An admissible set of data validation characters is the collection of characters we decide to accept as legal for the data.

- An inadmissible set of data validation characters is the collection of characters we decide not to accept as legal for the data.

All data validation is started by answering two fundamental questions:

- What is the admissible set?

- What is the inadmissible set?

Once you determine these sets, you need to program functions that test for admissible or inadmissible data. Keep in mind that your decision about members of each of these sets will often be arbitrary.

Here are a few useful data validation strategies:

- Build your library of data validation functions from the bottom up: First test one character at a time, then a collection of characters, and so on.

- When possible, base your validation functions on testing for characters and strings, rather than for numeric quantities.

- If you can, create objects to hold the different data types.

- It is a good idea to atomize the functions that do the validation. An "atomic" validation function is one that tests for the most basic element of data (a character), and does not rely on any other validation function. For example, if your admissible set is the digits 0 to 9, then an atomic data validation function examines one character at a time and verifies that the character is a digit. Another atomic data validation function might test for letters only, and yet another for punctuation marks only.

- Code data validation functions such that each accomplishes one and only one task: for example, return `true` or `false`, but do not do anything else with the data. If you need complex data validation—for example, street address data can include some punctuation marks, digits, and letters—combine the validation atoms into validation "molecules."

- Start the names of the validation functions with a verb, and have them, as a rule, return `true` if the validation passed the test. For example, if you want to test for digits only, name the function `isDigit()`, and return `true` if the character you are testing is a digit. If the character you are testing is not a digit, return `false`. This will make the data validation logic more comprehensible.

- Whenever possible, gather data from selections the user makes, rather than from characters the user types.
- Never, never assume that you are through testing data validation functions!

It is time to stop arm waving, and get down to the business of data validation of our Internet store application. Let us go through the items of data we intend to collect from the user (see Figures 12.1 and 12.2), one at a time.

#  Validating the Stereo System Configuration

The stereo system design stage is done interactively with selection lists (Figure 12.1). Use this approach whenever you can because:

- It relieves the user from typing in data (selecting options from a list is easier than typing them).
- Data validation is done at the programming (as opposed to execution) stage.
- There is no need to anticipate possible combinations of errors.

Also, using arrays and basing selection options on these arrays simplifies (and limits) the work you need to do to maintain the data. For example, to change the items you offer in your store, just modify the appropriate arrays (see Listing 12.1). The limitation here is that very long arrays—for example, containing all the states in the United States—are poor ways to communicate with the user.

In general, though, if you choose selection lists, you make life easier for the user and for yourself.

# Validating a First Name

The admissible set of characters for first name data should include all letters (blank space, A to Z, and a to z). Note that I arbitrarily define a blank space to be a character. Some punctuation marks such as hyphen (-), comma (,) and period (.), single quote ('), and back-quote (`) should also be included in the set of admissible characters. If you use a character set other than English, you will need to add them to the admissible set.

The function `isValidName()` in Listing 13.1 implements these specifications. Let us see what it does:

- The function is called by a `form` element (such as `text`, `textarea`, `button`, and so on). It should usually be called when the user has typed in the data and is leaving the entry field by clicking on another field or window area, or by pressing the tab key; it should usually be triggered by the `onBlur` event handler.

- `isValidName()` takes two arguments; the form object that calls the function (`theForm`), and the index of the calling form element in the `elements` array (`index`).

- In lines 4 and 5, we define a `String` object, `theName` (I shall explain why this is done in a moment—it is important!) and assign to it the data stored in the `value` property of the calling form element. The `value` is a string, not necessarily a `String` object. Recall that a string is a collection of characters (a data type), while a `String` is an object that has properties and methods that we shall make use of later.

- In line 6 we define a variable, `theChar`. This variable will hold each character of the data `String`, one character at a time.

- In lines 7 through 26 we cycle through each of `theName` characters.

- In line 9 we assign a character from `theName` to `theChar`. Note the use of the `String` method `charAt()`. This is one reason why we want to convert the string we are testing for to a `String` object.

- In line 11 we test that `theChar` is a letter; `isLetter()` is our first atomic data validation function. If `theChar` is a letter, `isLetter()` returns `true`, and `!isLetter()` resolves to `false`. Thus, the code between lines 12 and 25 is not executed, and we are done with the character. Execution moves on to the next character in `theName` (back to line 7).

- If, in line 11, `isLetter()` returns `false` (`theChar` is not a letter), then we need to do some more testing (lines 14 to 18).

- In lines 14 to 18 we check that `theChar` is a hyphen, a period, a comma, a single quote, or a back-quote (these and letters are allowed as part of a name). If `theChar` is none of these, then we have an illegal character, which makes `theName` illegal data, and we must tell the user that the name contains invalid characters (lines 20 to 23).

- To make the application more user-friendly, if we have illegal data we first alert the user (line 20), then return focus by moving the cursor back to the offending field (line 21), select the data in the field (line 22), and return `false`. The effect of these actions is to allow the user to type in new data with a minimum number of keystrokes.

As you can see, `isValidName()` is a molecular data validation function. It is based on one atomic data validation function, `isLetter()`, and some additional characters that we are willing to accept. Before we discuss how `isLetter()` works, I owe you an explanation.

Recall that we force the string data into a `String` object (lines 4 and 5 in Listing 13.1) named `theName`. There are three reasons for going through this extra step, rather than dealing with the data as a string.

- First, it turns out that cycling through characters in a string is not consistent, and can lead to irritating bugs. For example, instead of forcing `theName` into a `String` object and using the `charAt()` method in line 9, I tried one of the following approaches:

```
theChar = theForm.elements[index].value[i]
```

or

```
theName = theForm.elements[index].value
```

(without using lines 4 and 5 first) and then

```
theChar = theName[i]
```

None of these approaches worked.

- Second, when you change a string to a `String` object (as we do in lines 4 and 5 of Listing 13.1) you can safely use the properties and methods that are available for the `String` object, such as `charAt()`, `indexOf()`, `split()`, `substring()`, and so on (see the appropriate sections of Chapters 7 and 8).

- Third, if you change your data to an appropriate object, your code will most probably remain compatible with future releases of JavaScript, and you will be able to easily upgrade it (in case, for example, new methods and properties are added to the object type you are using).

LISTING 13.1 Validating first name.

```
1    //Name is characters and , . ' ` -
2    function isValidName(theForm, index)
3    {
4      var theName =
5       new String(theForm.elements[index].value)
6      var theChar
7      for (var i = 0; i < theName.length; i++)
8      {
9       theChar = theName.charAt(i)
10      //is it not a character?
11      if ( !isLetter(theChar) )
12      {
13        //is it not one of the allowed punctuation?
14        if ( !(      (theChar == '-') ||
15                     (theChar == '.') ||
16                     (theChar == ',') ||
17                     (theChar == '\'') ||
18                     (theChar == '`') ) )
19        {
20          alert("Use only letters and these characters:
    - . , \ ' ` ; try again")
21          theForm.elements[index].focus()
22          theForm.elements[index].select()
23          return false
24        }
25      }
26      }
27      return true
28    }
```

# ↳ Validating Letter Data

In the previous section we used isLetter(), an atomic data validation function, to test data for characters (Listing 13.1, line 11). This function is given in Listing 13.2. The function takes a single character, theChar, as its argument (line 2), and then cycles through all of the letters that we wish to define as such (lines 13 to 15). If theChar equals any of the characters in charArray, we return true (line 15). Otherwise we return false (line 16).

You may wonder why I use an explicit array of characters, charArray, for validation (lines 5 to 11). "You could," you may point out, "use functions such as `escape()` and `unescape()` to deal with the numerical values of these characters, instead of cycling through characters in the `charArray` array." True, but I do not want to, for two reasons:

- From my experience, `escape()` and `unescape()` do not behave consistently according to (at least my) expectations. Take a look at Listings 8.18 and 8.22, and Figures 8.14 and 8.18. There, for example, JavaScript refused to print the letter 'z' for some reason.

- You may wish to define your own set of letters. For example, I decided, arbitrarily, to include the space character in the set of admissible letters. The French, as tradition goes, might want to go their own way, and so on. The sacrifice of a little storage space (for the `charArray`), and no sacrifice of speed of execution, is worth this simple but effective approach.

**LISTING 13.2** Validating a letter.

```
1    //theChar includes letters only
2    function isLetter(theChar)
3    {
4      //Blank space is considered a character
5      var charArray = new Array(
6       ' ', 'A', 'B', 'C', 'D', 'E', 'F', 'G', 'H',
7       'I', 'J', 'K', 'L', 'M', 'N', 'O', 'P', 'Q',
8       'R', 'S', 'T', 'U', 'V', 'W', 'X', 'Y', 'Z',
9       'a', 'b', 'c', 'd', 'e', 'f', 'g', 'h', 'i',
10      'j', 'k', 'l', 'm', 'n', 'o', 'p', 'q', 'r',
11      's', 't', 'u', 'v', 'w', 'x', 'y', 'z')
12
13      for (j = 0; j < charArray.length; j++)
14        if (theChar == charArray[j])
15          return true
16      return false
17   }
```

 # Validating a Last Name

Last name data are validated exactly like first name data (see Listing 13.1).

 # Validating a Street Address

The admissible set for a street address should be all of the letters (see lines 5 to 11 in Listing 13.2), the digits 0 to 9, and some punctuation marks (comma, period, single quote, backslash, hyphen and back-quote). The function `isValidStreet()` does it for us (Listing 13.3); let us see how:

- In lines 4 and 5 we define a new `String` object, `theStreet`, and assign to it the string we wish to test. The latter comes from an element on `theForm`, whose index in the `elements` array is `index` (see line 2).

- Next, just as we did in validating a first name (Listing 13.1), we cycle through all of the characters in the object `theStreet`, one at a time (lines 7 to 28).

- In line 9 we assign the character at position `i` in `theStreet` object to `theChar` with the `String` method `charAt()`.

- In line 11 we test `theChar` to see if it belongs to part of the admissible set. We call this subset the alphanumeric set. The latter includes all of the letters and the digits 0 to 9.

- The `isAlphaNumeric()` function tests if a character is alphanumeric. (We discuss this function in detail in the next section.)

- If `theChar` is alphanumeric, `isAlphaNumeric()` evaluates to `true`, `!isAlphaNumeric()` resolves to `false`, and we fall to lines 27, 28, and back to the next character (line 7).

- If `theChar` is not alphanumeric, then we are not done; we need to see if it is one of the punctuation marks that belong to the admissible set. This test is done in lines 14 to 20.

- The logic in lines 14 to 20 works like this: if `theChar` is a period, or a comma, or a single quote, or a backslash, or a hyphen, then the test in lines 15 to 20 returns `true`, its negation (!) in line 14 causes the expression in the `if` parenthesis to evaluate to `false`, and we fall to lines 26, 27, 28, and back to line 7 for the next character in `theStreet`. If `theChar` is none of these, we process the error in lines 20 to 23.

- To process the fact that a street data contain an invalid character we alert the user that the data are invalid (line 22), set the focus on the offending field in the form (line 23), select the text in the offending field (line 24), and return `false` (line 25). The sequence of these statements minimizes the number of keystrokes for the user.

Note that `isValidStreet()` is a "molecular" data validation function: It relies on another function, `isAlphaNumeric()`, and some of its own testing for the punctuation marks. Next, we take a look at `isAlphaNumeric()`.

**LISTING 13.3** Validating a street address.

```
1    //Street is alpha-numeric and , . ' ` \ -
2    function isValidStreet(theForm, index)
3    {
4      var theStreet =
5       new String(theForm.elements[index].value)
6      var theChar
7      for (var i = 0; i < theStreet.length; i++)
8      {
9       theChar = theStreet.charAt(i)
10      //is it not a character or a digit?
11      if ( !isAlphaNumeric(theChar) )
12      {
13        //is it not one of the allowed punctuation?
14        if ( !(
15           (theChar == '.') ||
16           (theChar == ',') ||
17           (theChar == '\'') ||
18           (theChar == '`') ||
19           (theChar == '\\') ||
20           (theChar == '-' ) ) )
21        {
22          alert("Use only letters and these characters: . , \ ' `
     \\ -; try again")
23          theForm.elements[index].focus()
24          theForm.elements[index].select()
25          return false
26        }
27      }
28    }
29    return true
30  }
```

#  Validating Alphanumeric Data

Alphanumeric character is a character that is any of the following: a letter of the alphabet (and by our arbitrary definition, the space character), or a digit 0 to 9. The function isAlphaNumeric() in Listing 13.4 tests for such data. It is a molecular data validation function, relying on two other functions, isDigit(), and isLetter(). The latter is explained in the discussion of Listing 13.2. The function isDigit() will be explained shortly.

Here is how isAlphaNumeric() works:

- theChar, the character we are testing for, is passed to isAlphaNumeric() as an argument (line 2).

- In line 3 we test for a digit. If theChar is a digit, isDigit() returns true, and !isDigit() resolves to false. Execution then continues from line 7, and isAlphaNumeric() returns true.

- If theChar is not a digit, we test if it is a letter (line 5). If it is a letter, !isLetter() resolves to false, and execution continues from line 7; again, isAlphaNumeric() returns true.

isAlphaNumeric() relies on isDigit() for its testing, so we discuss the latter next.

**LISTING 13.4** Validating alphanumeric data.

```
1    //Characters and digits
2    function isAlphaNumeric(theChar)
3    {
4      if ( !isDigit(theChar) )
5       if ( !isLetter(theChar) )
6          return false
7      return true

8    }
```

#  Validating a Digit

The admissible set for a digit is the digit characters 0 to 9. The test for a digit (Listing 13.5) is very much like the test for a letter (Listing 13.2). It is done this way:

- The argument to isDigit() is theDigit (line 2).

- In lines 4 and 5 we specify the admissible set and assign it to digit Array.

- In lines 7 to 9 we cycle through the admissible set, testing one element at a time against theDigit.

- If theDigit does not equal digitArray[j], we go back to line 7 and test for the next digit in digitArray.

- If theDigit equals digitArray[j], then theDigit belongs to the set of digits, and we can safely return from isDigit() with true (line 9).

- If we have cycled through all of the digits in `digitArray` without returning from the function, then `theDigit` does not belong to the set of digits, and `isDigit()` must return `false` (line 10).

A few comments. First, note that `isDigit()` is an atomic data validation function, and we make use of it in `isAlphaNumeric()` (Listing 13.4). Second, note that if you choose atomic data validation functions cleverly, then testing for more complicated data becomes simple (see Listing 13.3). Finally, I could simplify (presumably) the testing by using a statement like this:

```
if(theDigit <= 9 && theDigit >= 0)
```

For reasons discussed along with the explanation of `isLetter()`, I chose to specify my own admissible set. This, in my opinion, is much simpler.

**LISTING 13.5** Validating a digit.

```
1    //Digit is one of the characters 0, 1, ..., 9
2    function isDigit(theDigit)
3    {
4      digitArray = new Array('0','1','2','3','4',
5        '5','6','7','8','9')
6
7      for (j = 0; j < digitArray.length; j++)
8        if (theDigit == digitArray[j])
9          return true
10     return false
11
12   }
```

While we are at it, let me add a few more data testing functions that, although not used in the Internet store application, may be handy in the future.

#  Validating a Positive Integer

Listing 13.6 shows how to validate a positive integer. The argument to `isPositiveInteger()` is a string (`theString` in line 2). For reasons discussed above, we type-cast it into a `String` object named `theData` (line 4), and then work with it. Here is what we do:

- In line 6 we test for the first character of `theData`. If it is not a digit (line 6), it may be a + (we want to allow the user to enter a positive integer with the unary operator +). We test for a + in line 7. If the first character is neither a digit nor a +, isPositiveInteger() returns false (line 8).

- In lines 10 through 12 we cycle through the remaining characters in theString. Here we allow no character other than the digits 0 to 9. If any of the characters does not belong to the admissible set, we return with false (line 12).

- If we are done testing for all characters, it means that they all met our criterion for a digit, and isPositiveInteger() returns true (line 13).

Note that since we already have the atomic data validation function isDigit(), it is a trivial task to create a test for a positive integer.

**LISTING 13.6** Validating a positive integer.

```
1    //Any digit, and + at location 0
2    function isPositiveInteger(theString)
3    {
4      var theData = new String(theString)
5
6      if (!isDigit(theData.charAt(0)))
7       if (!(theData.charAt(0)== '+')
8         return false
9
10     for (var i = 1; i < theData.length; i++)
11      if (!isDigit(theData.charAt(i)))
12        return false
13     return true
14   }
```

# Validating a Negative Integer

Testing for a negative integer is done exactly as shown in Listing 13.6, except that in line 7 we replace the + with a -. For the sake of completeness, the function isNegativeInteger() is given in Listing 13.7.

**LISTING 13.7** Validating a negative integer.

```
1    //Any digit, and - at location 0
2    function isNegativeInteger(theString)
3    {
```

```
4      var theData = new String(theString)
5
6      if (!isDigit(theData.charAt(0)))
7       if (!(theData.charAt(0)== '-')
8        return false
9
10     for (var i = 1; i < theData.length; i++)
11      if (!isDigit(theData.charAt(i)))
12       return false
13    return true
14   }
```

# Validating an Integer

To test for an integer, use the built-in JavaScript function parseInt(), along with the function isNaN() (see Listing 8.36 and Figure 8.31 and Listing 8.29 and Figure 8.24, respectively). You can skip the test with isNaN(), but I do not recommend it.

Listing 13.8 shows how to test for an integer. The function takes a single argument, theData. Here, theData can be a string or an integer. In line 4 we parse theData. If theData is not an integer, parseInt() returns a value named NaN (not a number). We then test if the value returned from parseInt() is NaN. If it is, isInteger() returns false. Otherwise it returns true.

**LISTING 13.8** Validating a floating-point number.

```
1    //test for an integer
2    function isInteger(theData)
3    {
4      if (isNaN(parseInt(theData)))
5       return false
6      else
7       return true
8    }
```

# Validating a Floating-Point Number

To test for a floating-point number, use the built-in JavaScript function parseFloat(), along with the function isNaN() (see Listing 8.35 and Figure

8.30 and Listing 8.29 and Figure 8.24 respectively). You can skip the test with isNaN(), but I do not recommend it.

Listing 13.9 shows how to test for a float. The function takes a single argument, theData. Here, theData can be a string or a number. In line 4 we parse theData. If theData is not a float, parseFloat() returns a value named NaN (not a number). We then test if the value returned from parseFloat() is NaN. If it is, isFloat() returns false. Otherwise it returns true.

**LISTING 13.9** Validating a floating-point number.

```
1    //test for a float
2    function isFloat(theData)
3    {
4      if (isNaN(parseFloat(theData)))
5       return false
6      else
7       return true
8    }
```

 # Validating a Number Less Than a Maximum Number

The function isLessThan() in Listing 13.10 takes two arguments (line 2): theNumber and maxNumber. Because we usually validate input data, and because input data are usually strings, isLessThan() does not care what data type theNumber is; it can be either a string or a number (integer or float). However, maxNumber must be a number (integer or float).

In line 4 we verify that theNumber is a float or an integer (this means that we can use isLessThan() to test theNumber directly as we read it from the input, without having to test that it is a number first). If it is neither, we return false. If theNumber is a number (a float or an integer), we test (in line 7) if the number is >= maxNumber. If it is, we return false. If theNumber passes the tests in lines 4 and 7, isLessThan() returns true.

The advantage of using this function (over conventional testing) is that isLessThan() does not care what theNumber is: It can be a number, a string that resolves to a number, or a string that does not resolve to a number. You can thus test your input directly with isLessThan(). Because JavaScript is a permissive language (it does not do strong type-checking), you can bypass this function, and use an if statement directly to validate your data. However, you will first have to verify that theNumber is indeed a number, and this is what we essentially do with isLessThan().

**LISTING 13.10** Validating a number smaller than a maximum value.

```
1    //test for theNumber < maxNumber
2    function isLessThan(theNumber, maxNumber)
3    {
4      if (!isFloat(theNumber))
5       return false
6      else
7       if (parseFloat(theNumber) >= maxNumber)
8         return false
9      return true
10   }
```

#  Validating a Number Greater Than a Minimum Number

Testing for a number greater than a specified value can be done exactly as shown in Listing 13.10, except that in line 7 you should replace >= with <=. For the sake of completeness, the function isGreaterThan() is given in Listing 13.11. The advantage of using this function (over conventional testing) is that isGreaterThan() does not care what theNumber is: It can be a number, a string that resolves to a number, or a string that does not resolve to a number. You can thus test your input directly with isGreaterThan() (see also the discussion of isLessThan()).

**LISTING 13.11** Validating a number greater than a minimum value.

```
1    //test for theNumber > minNumber
2    function isGreaterThan(theNumber, minNumber)
3    {
4      if (!isFloat(theNumber))
5       return false
6      else
7       if (parseFloat(theNumber) <= minNumber)
8         return false
9      return true
10   }
```

# Validating a Number Less Than or Equal to a Maximum Number

The function `isLessEqual()` in Listing 13.12 works much like `isLessThan()`. It takes two arguments (line 2): `theNumber` and `maxNumber`. Because we usually validate input data, and because input data are usually strings, `isLessEqual()` does not care what data type `theNumber` is; it can be either a string or a number (integer or float). However, `maxNumber` must be a number (integer or float).

In line 4 we verify that `theNumber` is a float or an integer (this means that we can use `isLessEqual()` to test `theNumber` directly as we read it from the input, without having to test that it is a number first). If it is neither, we return `false`. If `theNumber` is a number (a float or an integer), we test (in line 7) if the number is > `maxNumber`. If it is, we return `false`. If `theNumber` passes the tests in lines 4 and 7, `isLessEqual()` returns `true`.

The advantage of using this function (over conventional testing) is discussed in the section that explains `isLessThan()`.

**LISTING 13.12** Validating a number smaller than or equal to a maximum value.

```
1    //test for theNumber < maxNumber
2    function isLessThan(theNumber, maxNumber)
3    {
4      if (!isFloat(theNumber))
5        return false
6      else
7        if (parseFloat(theNumber) > maxNumber)
8          return false
9      return true
10   }
```

 # Validating a Number Greater Than or Equal to a Minimum Number

Testing for a number greater than or equal to a specified value is done much like testing for greater than (see Listing 13.11), except that in line 7 you should replace <= with <. For the sake of completeness, the function `isGreaterEqual()`

is given in Listing 13.13. The advantage of using this function (over conventional testing) is that isGreaterEqual() does not care what theNumber is: It can be a number, a string that resolves to a number, or a string that does not resolve to a number. You can thus test your input directly with isGreaterEqual() (see also the discussion of isGreaterThan() and Listing 13.11).

**LISTING 13.13** Validating a number greater than or equal to a minimum value.

```
1    //test for theNumber > minNumber
2    function isGreaterEqual(theNumber, minNumber)
3    {
4      if (!isFloat(theNumber))
5       return false
6      else
7       if (parseFloat(theNumber) < minNumber)
8          return false
9      return true
10   }
```

# ⮥ Validating a Number in a Range

Listing 13.14 validates that theNumber is between minNumber, maxNumber, including the boundaries. It makes use of isGreaterEqual() and isLessEqual(). The advantage of using this function (over conventional testing) is that isInRange() does not care what theNumber is: It can be a number, a string that resolves to a number, or a string that does not resolve to a number. You can thus test your input directly with isInRange(). Note that the arguments minNumber and maxNumber must resolve to numbers.

**LISTING 13.14** Validating for a number in a range.

```
1    //test for minNumber < theNumber < maxNumber
2    function isInRange(theNumber, minNumber, maxNumber)
3    {
4      if ( isGreaterEqual(theNumber, minNumber) &&
5        isLessEqual(theNumber, maxNumber) )
6       return true
7      else
8       return false
9    }
```

# Validating a Phone Number

We now return to the Internet store application. For phone number data, the members of the admissible set (by my definition) are the digits 0 to 9, the left and right parentheses, and the dash character.

Listing 13.15 shows how to validate a phone number; let us examine it:

- Like the functions that validate data of other form elements, isValidPhone() takes two arguments: theForm to which the element belongs and the index of the element in the elements array of theForm (line 2).

- For reasons discussed above (in "Validating a First Name"), we cast the data to a String object and assign the object to thePhone (lines 4 and 5).

- In lines 8 to 26 we cycle through thePhone, one character at a time.

- First, we isolate a character in thePhone using charAt() and assign it to theChar (line 10).

- Next, we test with isDigit(). If theChar is a digit, isDigit() returns true, and !isDigit() resolves to false. This causes execution to go back to the head of the loop and iterate to the next character of thePhone (line 8).

- If theChar is not a digit, !isDigit() resolves to true, and we need to test for the other members of the admissible set.

- In lines 15 to 18 we test if theChar is of any of the admissible characters (left parenthesis, right parenthesis, or dash). If theChar is one of these, then the ! in line 15 causes the statements in lines 15 to 18 to resolve to false, and we move on to the next character (line 8).

- If theChar does not equal any the admissible characters in lines 16 to 18, then if evaluates to true (because of the ! in line 15), and lines 20 to 23 are executed.

- In line 20 we alert the user that the data are invalid, then we set the focus back to the offending field (line 21), select the text in it (line 22), and return false. This sequence of methods minimizes the number of keystrokes the user needs to enter to correct the data.

If you are going to allow the user to enter letters as part of a phone number, include those in the admissible set, and instead of testing for a digit with isDigit(), test with isAlphaNumeric(). If your store is for U.S. and Canadian customers only, you can also test for a fixed number of characters in the input string (we will discuss how to test for a number of characters in a string when we validate the state data entry, below).

**LISTING 13.15** Validating a phone number.

```
1    //Phone is digits and ( - )
2    function isValidPhone(theForm, index)
3    {
4      var thePhone =
5       new String(theForm.elements[index].value)
6      var theChar
7
8      for (var i = 0; i < thePhone.length; i++)
9      {
10      theChar = thePhone.charAt(i)
11      //is it not a character or a digit?
12      if ( !isDigit(theChar) )
13      {
14        //is it not one of the allowed punctuation?
15        if ( !(
16           (theChar == '(') ||
17           (theChar == ')') ||
18           (theChar == '-') ) )
19        {
20         alert("Invalid phone; try again")
21         theForm.elements[index].focus()
22         theForm.elements[index].select()
23         return false
24        }
25      }
26      }
27      return true
28    }
```

# ↳ Validating a State

There are three approaches to validating a state datum: You can use a selection list that includes the two-letter postal codes of all states, you can create an array of two-letter codes and designate the array as your admissible set, or you can simply verify that the user includes two characters, both letters, in the field. Since I do not want the Internet store application to be limited to U.S. users only, I chose the last approach (the first approach is discussed later in this chapter). Here is how it works:

- In line 2 of Listing 13.16 we use the usual arguments to `isValid State()`: `theForm` in which the data field resides, and the `index` of this field in the `form`'s `elements` array.

- For reasons discussed in "Validating a First Name," we cast the data to a `String` object, and assign it to `theState` (lines 4 and 5).

- In lines 8 to 14 we test that `theState` contains two characters only. Here we use `isLength()` (discussed below). If `theState` does not include exactly two characters, `isLength()` returns `false`, `!isLength()` resolves to `true`, and we use the usual approach: alert the user (line 10), focus on the field (line 11), and select the data in it (line 12).

- If we pass the first test (the state data include two characters only), we move on to the next test: cycling through all of the characters, one at a time, and verifying that they are all letters. Note that by the time we reach line 16, we know that `theState` is two characters long. Yet, I chose to cycle through `theState.length` characters. This conforms to the standard we use for most of the data validation routines, and will allow you to generalize the approach to other strings for which you want to test for both exact length and letters.

- In lines 16 to 27 we cycle through the state characters. First we isolate the character at position `i` and assign it to `theChar` (line 18). Next, we use the atomic data validation function `isLetter()` (line 20). If `theChar` is not a letter, `isLetter()` returns false, `!isLetter()` resolves `true`, and we handle the error exactly as we did in lines 10 to 13.

- Finally, if all the tests are passed, `isValidState()` returns `true`.

**LISTING 13.16** Validating a state.

```
1    //2 letters only
2    function isValidState(theForm, index)
3    {
4      var theState =
5       new String(theForm.elements[index].value)
6      var theChar
7
8      if (!isLength(theState,2))
9      {
10       alert("2 characters please")
11       theForm.elements[index].focus()
12       theForm.elements[index].select()
```

```
13      return false
14    }
15
16    for (var i = 0; i < theState.length; i++)
17    {
18     theChar = theState.charAt(i)
19     //is it not a character?
20     if ( !isLetter(theChar) )
21     {
22        alert("Invalid state; try again")
23        theForm.elements[index].focus()
24        theForm.elements[index].select()
25        return false
26     }
27    }
28    return true
29  }
```

Listing 13.16 makes use of isLength(), so we discuss it next.

 # Validating an Exact Number of Characters in a String

Listing 13.17 implements a test of an exact string length. The function isLength() takes two arguments: aString, and its length (aLength); the former is a string and the latter is an integer. It then verifies that aString's length is <= a maximum length (in line 4) and that it is >= a minimum length (line 5). If both are true, aString's length equals aLength, and we return true (line 6); otherwise, we return false (line 8). The functions isMaxLength() and isMinLength() are explained next.

**LISTING 13.17** Validating an exact string length.

```
1    //--Test that aString is exactly aLength
2    function isLength(aString, aLength)
3    {
4      if (isMaxLength(aString, aLength) &&
5         isMinLength(aString, aLength))
6      return true
7      else
8        return false
9    }
```

# Validating a Maximum Number of Characters in a String

Listing 13.18 implements a test for a maximum string length. The function isMaxLength() returns true if aString's length is <= maxLength and false otherwise. The arguments are a string (aString) and an integer (maxLength).

**LISTING 13.18** Validating a maximum string length.

```
1    //—-Test that aString is no longer than maxLength
2    function isMaxLength(aString, maxLength)
3    {
4            if (aString.length <= maxLength)
5      return true
6      else
7        return false
8    }
```

 # Validating a Minimum Number of Characters in a String

Listing 13.19 implements a test for a minimum string length. The function isMinLength() returns true if aString's length is >= minLength and false otherwise. The arguments are a string (aString) and an integer (minLength).

**LISTING 13.19** Validating a minimum string length.

```
1    //—-Test that aString is no shorter than minLength
2    function isMinLength(aString, minLength)
3    {
4            if (aString.length >= minLength)
5      return true
6      else
7        return false
8    }
```

# An Alternative to Validating State

As discussed in the "Validating a State" section, there are two additional ways to validate a state. One is to simply create a Select object with the appropriate number of Option objects and allow the user to choose her own state. Once an Option is chosen, you will need to process it. How to determine which option is selected is discussed in Chapters 7 and 9 (see the Select and Option objects in Chapter 7 and the defaultSelected and selected properties in Chapter 9).

Listing 13.20 shows how to validate a state by this method. Figure 13.1 illustrates the result.

**LISTING 13.20** Validating a state via Select and Option objects.

```
1    <HTML>
2    <TITLE>Validating State</TITLE>
3    <BODY>
4    <B>Validating State</B>
5    <P>
6    <FORM>
7      <SELECT NAME="state" SIZE="1">
8      <OPTION VALUE="">Not Selected
9      <OPTION VALUE="AL">Alabama
10     <OPTION VALUE="AK">Alaska
11     <OPTION VALUE="AZ">Arizona
12     <OPTION VALUE="AR">Arkansas
13     <OPTION VALUE="CA">California
14     <OPTION VALUE="CO">Colorado
15     <OPTION VALUE="CT">Connecticut
16     <OPTION VALUE="DE">Delaware
17     <OPTION VALUE="DC">District of Columbia
18     <OPTION VALUE="FL">Florida
19     <OPTION VALUE="GA">Georgia
20     <OPTION VALUE="HI">Hawaii
21     <OPTION VALUE="ID">Idaho
22     <OPTION VALUE="IL">Illinois
23     <OPTION VALUE="IN">Indiana
24     <OPTION VALUE="IA">Iowa
25     <OPTION VALUE="KS">Kansas
26     <OPTION VALUE="KY">Kentucky
27     <OPTION VALUE="LA">Louisiana
28     <OPTION VALUE="ME">Maine
29     <OPTION VALUE="MD">Maryland
30     <OPTION VALUE="MA">Massachusetts
```

```
31      <OPTION VALUE="MI">Michigan
32      <OPTION VALUE="MN">Minnesota
33      <OPTION VALUE="MS">Mississippi
34      <OPTION VALUE="MO">Missouri
35      <OPTION VALUE="MT">Montana
36      <OPTION VALUE="NE">Nebraska
37      <OPTION VALUE="NV">Nevada
38      <OPTION VALUE="NH">New Hampshire
39      <OPTION VALUE="NJ">New Jersey
40      <OPTION VALUE="NM">New Mexico
41      <OPTION VALUE="NY">New York
42      <OPTION VALUE="NC">North Carolina
43      <OPTION VALUE="ND">North Dakota
44      <OPTION VALUE="OH">Ohio
45      <OPTION VALUE="OK">Oklahoma
46      <OPTION VALUE="OR">Oregon
47      <OPTION VALUE="PA">Pennsylvania
48      <OPTION VALUE="RI">Rhode Island
49      <OPTION VALUE="SC">South Carolina
50      <OPTION VALUE="SD">South Dakota
51      <OPTION VALUE="TN">Tennessee
52      <OPTION VALUE="TX">Texas
53      <OPTION VALUE="UT">Utah
54      <OPTION VALUE="VT">Vermont
55      <OPTION VALUE="VA">Virginia
56      <OPTION VALUE="WA">Washington
57      <OPTION VALUE="WV">West Virginia
58      <OPTION VALUE="WI">Wisconsin
59      <OPTION VALUE="WY">Wyoming
60      <OPTION VALUE="Alberta">Alberta
61      <OPTION VALUE="British Columbia">British Columbia
62      <OPTION VALUE="Manitoba">Manitoba
63      <OPTION VALUE="New Brunswick">New Brunswick
64      <OPTION VALUE="Nova Scotia">Nova Scotia
65      <OPTION VALUE="Newfoundland">Newfoundland
66      <OPTION VALUE="N.W.T.">N.W.T.
67      <OPTION VALUE="Ontario">Ontario
68      <OPTION VALUE="Quebec">Quebec
69      <OPTION VALUE="Prince Edward Island">Prince Edward Island
70      <OPTION VALUE="Saskatchewan">Saskatchewan
71      <OPTION VALUE="Yukon">Yukon
72      <OPTION VALUE="PR">Puerto Rico
73      <OPTION VALUE="VI">Virgin Island
74      <OPTION VALUE="MP">Northern Mariana Islands
75      <OPTION VALUE="GU">Guam
76      <OPTION VALUE="AS">American Samoa
77      <OPTION VALUE="PW">Palau
```

```
78      </SELECT>
79    </FORM>
80    </BODY>
81  </HTML>
```

# ↳ Validating a Zip Code

The last item we wish to verify in our application is the zip code (Figure 12.2). Listing 13.21 implements the validation.

- The function isValidZip() takes two arguments: theForm in which the data element resides, and the index of the data element in the form's elements array (line 2).

- For reasons explained in "Validating a First Name," we cast the data to a String object (line 4). Next, we assign the data to theZip.

- In lines 7 to 23 we cycle through theZip, one character at a time.

- First, we extract the i-th character from theZip using charAt(), and assign it to theChar.

- Next, we test if theChar is alpha numeric (part of the admissible set). If it is not, isAlphaNumeric() returns false, !isAlphaNumeric() resolves to true, and we test if theChar is a dash (line 15). If it is a dash, line 15

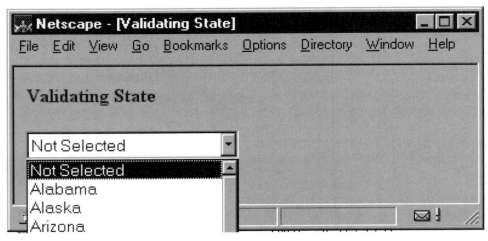

**FIGURE 13.1** Validating a state via Select and Option objects.

evaluates to `true`, and lines 14 and 15 resolve to `false`, in which case we move on to the next character in `theZip` (line 7).

- If `theChar` is neither alpha numeric nor a dash, we process the error in lines 17 to 20: We alert the user, set the focus to the field, select the data, and return `false`.

- If everything goes well (we tested all the characters in `theZip` and were not bumped out of the function), then `isValidZip()` returns `true` (line 24).

**LISTING 13.21** Validating a zip code.

```
1    //Zip is alphanumeric and includes -
2    function isValidZip(theForm, index)
3    {
4      var theZip =
5       new String(theForm.elements[index].value)
6      var theChar
7      for (var i = 0; i < theZip.length; i++)
8      {
9       theChar = theZip.charAt(i)
10      //is it not a character or a digit?
11      if ( !isAlphaNumeric(theChar) )
12      {
13        //is it not one of the allowed punctuation?
14        if ( !(
15          (theChar == '-') ) )
16        {
17         alert("Invalid Zip; try again")
18         theForm.elements[index].focus()
19         theForm.elements[index].select()
20         return false
21        }
22      }
23      }
24      return true
25   }
```

# ↳ Validating a Date

Validating that a string specifies a date is tough, particularly if you wish to cater to a global market: Europeans specify the day first, then the month, while Americans the month first, then the day. To deal with date validation strategically, simply set selection lists in your form for the day, month, and year (just as is done for the state in Listing 13.20 and Figure 13.1), so that the user can only select, not type, the date. For February, make sure that you are allowing the user to choose 29 as the lost day of the month.

We next discuss how to lay out the stereo system design form, and how to communicate with the user.

# THE INTERNET STORE— COMMUNICATING WITH THE USER

⤷ The forms that determine the look and feel of the application

⤷ Integrating all of the program modules into a single program

⤷ Strategies for quality control: software testing and debugging

# ⤷ Communicating with the User

Recall that in developing the application we have two important goals:

- We want to collect information from the user: the stereo system the user designed and some personal information.

- We also want to be independent of a server; we wish to be responsible for all of the information on our own.

To accomplish these goals, the application design calls for three forms: the stereo system design form (Figure 12.1), the user information form (Figure 12.2), and the data submission form. These forms are discussed in the following three sections.

# The Stereo System Design Form

Listing 14.1 details the stereo system design form. I am not going to dwell on the HTML tags and their attributes—use Figure 12.1 to see the outcome of the listing. Here I just want to point out the following:

- In lines 9 to 11 we place the amplifier Selection object in the appropriate table cell on the form. Here we call CreateSelectionList() with the object name, amplifier, and with the array that determines the number and content of the Option objects in the Selection object. Recall that this array is named amplifierList (Listing 12.2). See Listing 12.4 and its accompanying discussion for an explanation of CreateSelectionList().

- This approach, of creating Selection and Option objects via JavaScript, endows us with a certain amount of flexibility: When we want to add, delete, or modify the list of amplifiers we offer, we mess around with the amplifierList only!

- The same approach is used in creating the choice of speakers (lines 17 to 19), tuners (lines 25 to 27), CD players (lines 33 to 35), and so on.

- Finally, we place the compute button in the SystemForm (lines 48 to 51). The onClick event handler in line 51 triggers CanGetPrice(), which checks that the system price can be calculated (see Listing 12.6 and Figure 12.4). If we can calculate the system price, that is, CanGetPrice() returns true, we tell the user to fill in the personal information (see Figure 12.2); otherwise we do nothing.

**LISTING 14.1** The stereo system design form.

```
1    <FORM NAME = "SystemForm">
2    <CENTER>
3    <TABLE WIDTH = 99%
4        CELLPADDING = 4
5        BORDER>
6      <TR>
7       <TH VALIGN = TOP>Amplifiers:</TH>
8       <TD>
9         <SCRIPT LANGUAGE = "JavaScript">
10          document.write(CreateSelectionList("amplifier",
     amplifierList) + "<BR>")
```

```
11          </SCRIPT>
12       </TD>
13      </TR>
14      <TR>
15       <TH VALIGN = TOP>Spkeakers:</TH>
16       <TD>
17         <SCRIPT LANGUAGE = "JavaScript">
18          document.write(CreateSelectionList("speakers",
   speakersList) + "<BR>")
19         </SCRIPT>
20       </TD>
21      </TR>
22      <TR>
23       <TH VALIGN = TOP>Tuners:</TH>
24       <TD>
25         <SCRIPT LANGUAGE = "JavaScript">
26          document.write(CreateSelectionList("tuner", tunerList) +
   "<BR>")
27         </SCRIPT>
28       </TD>
29      </TR>
30      <TR>
31       <TH VALIGN = TOP>CD Players:</TH>
32       <TD>
33         <SCRIPT LANGUAGE = "JavaScript">
34          document.write(CreateSelectionList("CDPlayer", cdList) +
   "<BR>")
35         </SCRIPT>
36       </TD>
37      </TR>
38      <TR>
39       <TH VALIGN = TOP>Tape Decks:</TH>
40       <TD>
41         <SCRIPT LANGUAGE = "JavaScript">
42          document.write(CreateSelectionList("tapeDeck", tapeList) +
   "<BR>")
43         </SCRIPT>
44       </TD>
45      </TR>
46   </TABLE>
47    <BR>
48 <INPUT    TYPE = button
49          NAME = "compute"
50          VALUE = "How much..."
51          onClick = "if(CanGetPrice()) confirm('Please fill
   mailing information below')">
52   </FORM>
```

# The User Information Form

The user information form, named dataForm, is also placed in a table, to allow us to present the information in a nice format (Listing 14.2). Again, I am not going to dwell on the HTML code here (refer to Figure 12.2), but rather point out the event handlers that trigger data validation:

- The text object named firstName (Listing 14.2) accepts the user's first name. Here we use two event handlers. onBlur triggers isValidName() (see Listing 13.1) with two arguments: the dataForm object (which is specified as this.form in line 7), and the index of the firstName text element in the elements array of dataForm (zero, in line 7). This means that when the user leaves the firstName field, the user's first name is validated (for legal data). To ease editing, whenever the user enters the firstName field (brings it to focus), we select the data in it with the onFocus event handler that triggers this.select() (line 8).

- A similar approach is taken for the remaining fields (shown in Figure 12.2): For each we use onBlur to trigger the appropriate data validation function (as explained in Chapter 13), and onFocus to select the text in the field.

- Note that we must keep track of the index of each element in the elements array because all calls to the data validation functions follow the same pattern: the first argument is this.form, and the second is the index that specifies the location of the item in the elements array of this.form.

- Finally, we insert the textarea object named comments in the dataForm (lines 63 to 67). Refer to Chapter 7 a for full discussion and examples of this important object.

**LISTING 14.2** The user information form.

```
1    <TABLE>
2      <FORM NAME = "dataForm">
3        <TR>
4          <TH ALIGN = right>First name:
5          <TD><INPUT TYPE = "text"
6                     NAME = "firstName"
7                     onBlur = 'isValidName(this.form,0)'
8                     onFocus = 'this.select()'
9                     SIZE = 50>
```

```
10      </TR>
11      <TR>
12        <TH ALIGN =right>Last name:
13        <TD><INPUT TYPE = "text"
14                  NAME = "lastName"
15                  onBlur = 'isValidName(this.form,1)'
16                  onFocus = 'this.select()'
17                  SIZE = 50>
18      </TR>
19      <TR>
20        <TH ALIGN =right>Street and number:
21        <TD><INPUT TYPE = "text"
22                  NAME = "street"
23                  onBlur = 'isValidStreet(this.form,2)'
24                  onFocus = 'this.select()'
25                  SIZE = 50>
26      </TR>
27      <TR>
28        <TH ALIGN =right>City:
29        <TD><INPUT TYPE = "text"
30                  NAME = "city"
31                  onBlur = 'isValidName(this.form,3)'
32                  onFocus = 'this.select()'
33                  SIZE = 20>
34        <B>Country:</B>
35        <INPUT    TYPE = "text"
36                  NAME = "country"
37                  onBlur = 'isValidName(this.form,4)'
38                  onFocus = 'this.select()'
39                  SIZE = 19>
40      </TR>
41      <TR>
42        <TH ALIGN =right>State:
43        <TD><INPUT TYPE = "text"
44                  NAME = "state"
45                  onBlur = 'isValidState(this.form,5)'
46                  onFocus = 'this.select()'
47                  SIZE = 3>
48        <B>Phone:</B>
49        <INPUT    TYPE = "text"
50                  NAME = "phone"
51                  onBlur = 'isValidPhone(this.form,6)'
52                  onFocus = 'this.select()'
53                  SIZE = 12>
54        <B>Zip code:</B>
55        <INPUT    TYPE = "text"
56                  NAME = "zip"
57                  onBlur = 'isValidZip(this.form,7)'
```

```
58                    onFocus = 'this.select()'
59                    SIZE = 14>
60      </TR>
61      <TR>
62        <TH ALIGN = right VALIGN = top>Comments:
63        <TD><TEXTAREA NAME = "comments"
64                      COLS = 50
65                      ROWS = 8
66                      WRAP = virtual>
67          </TEXTAREA>
68      </TR>
69      </FORM>
```

## Submitting the Data: submitForm

We are now ready to submit the data. Be sure to submit the data via a hidden object that resides in a form different from others (where the data are entered). If you neglect to do this, the e-mail information will include attachments (one for each element on the form), and that is not what you want.

By receiving the user information via e-mail you bypass server activity that is normally associated with data processing. The data from the dataForm (Listing 14.2) is returned by e-mail directly to you as soon as the user clicks on the Submit... button (see Listing 14.3) without server intervention, and you can process the e-mail message in any way you wish. Keep in mind however, that sending and receiving e-mail messages involves mail server activity, but this does not require any special server programming on your part.

You need to collect and format the data before sending it. Because you do not need to show the formatted data to the user, you format it in a string, and assign it to the value property of a hidden object (see Listing 12.8) . It is this value that you e-mail. The submit button object submits data that is stored in all of the input elements on a form. Because you have already collected all of the data in the value property of a hidden object, that is the only form element you need to submit. You therefore isolate the hidden and submit objects in a form separate from the user input form. This is what we do in the submitForm, which we discuss next.

In the submitForm (Listing 14.3) we do the following:

- We set the ACTION tag to mailto: (see discussion of the form object in Chapter 7, and the mailto property in Chapter 9).

- We supply an e-mail address to which data are to be sent. If you want the user choice of the stereo system and personal information (as shown in Figure 12.5) sent to you, replace `name@address` in line 3 with your e-mail address.

- We supply a message subject for the e-mail: `Order`. You can substitute a message of your choice; just be sure not to leave any spaces on both sides of the equal sign in line 3.

- To get the message in the format we want (Figure 12.5), we set METHOD to `post` (line 4), and ENCTYPE to `multipart/form-data` (line 5).

- We use the `onSubmit` event handler (line 6) to trigger `submitData()` with the `submitForm` as its argument.

- Recall from the discussion accompanying Listing 12.8 that `submitData()` gathers the information from the other forms (`SystemForm` and `dataForm`), builds and formats the e-mail message, and asks the user, for the last time, if she is sure she wants to send the data.

- The data we e-mail is assigned to the `value` of the hidden object named `theData` in the `submitData()` function.

**LISTING 14.3** submitForm

```
1    <FORM NAME = "submitForm"
2       ACTION =
3         "mailto:name@address?subject=Order"
4       METHOD = "post"
5       ENCTYPE = "multipart/form-data"
6       onSubmit = "return submitData(this)">
7    <INPUT        TYPE = "hidden"
8                  NAME = "theData"
9                  VALUE = "">
10   <TR>
11   <TD COLSPAN = 2
12     ALIGN = center>
13   <INPUT  TYPE = "submit"
14         VALUE = "Submit...">
15   </TR>
16   </FORM>
```

We are done! Time to wipe your forehead and take a rest. In the next section we present nothing new—we just put everything together.

# ↳ Putting It All Together

Rather than repeat all of the code here (the complete code is given on the accompanying CD), I shall just show you where the code fits in the general scheme, pointing out the appropriate listing to insert (Listing 14.4). In places where no corresponding listing exists, I added the necessary code (see, for example, lines 39 to 104).

To summarize the structure of the code (Listing 14.4):

- We start by including the commonf.js file, which includes common functions (lines 4 to 5). Although the application's code is independent of code in commonf.js, I include this JavaScript source file because this is what I did during the application development, and because I want to remind you that you can put functions (common or not) somewhere else, and thus reduce the code clutter.

- Then comes the section of the code that includes all of the JavaScript functions we need (lines 6 to 185). Each of the functions the application relies on is mentioned by name (along with the necessary arguments), and its corresponding listing is given (see, for example, line 11).

- In line 188 we start the document body and form layout.

- The SystemForm is laid out first (line 189; see Figure 12.1), then the dataForm (line 194; see Figure 12.2), and finally the submitForm (line 197; see Figure 12.2).

**LISTING 14.4** The Internet store application.

```
1     <HTML>
2     <HEAD>
3     <TITLE>The Internet Store</TITLE>
4     <SCRIPT LANGUAGE = "JavaScript" SRC = "commonf.js">
5     </SCRIPT>
6     <SCRIPT LANGUAGE = "JavaScript">
7
8     //--Component object with 3 properties
9     function Component(componentName, manufacturer, price)
10    {
11    ...See Listing 12.1
12    }
13
14    //--Build the data base
```

```
15   ...See Listing 12.2
16
17   //—-Global variables
18   ...See Listing 12.4
19
20   //—-Create a selection list with name and selection items
21   function CreateSelectionList(selectionName, selectionItems)
22   {
23   ...See Listing 12.5
24   }
25
26   //—-Were necessary data selected?
27   function CanGetPrice()
28   {
29   ...See Listing 12.6
30   }
31
32   //—-Get the selected amplifier price
33   function AmplifierPrice()
34   {
35   ...See Listing 12.7
36   }
37
38   //—-Get the selected speakers price
39   function SpeakersPrice()
40   {
41     var i = document.SystemForm.speakers.selectedIndex
42
43     if(i == 0)
44     {
45      alert("\nYou must select speakers. \n")
46      return false
47     }
48
49     i -= 1; totalPrice += eval(speakersList[i].price)
50     systemDescription  += " - " + speakersList[i].componentName +
51         " from " + speakersList[i].manufacturer + "\n"
52     return true
53   }
54
55   //—-Get the selected tuner price
56   function TunerPrice()
57   {
58     var i = document.SystemForm.tuner.selectedIndex
59
60     if(i == 0)
61     {
```

```
62      alert("\nYou must select a tuner. \n")
63      return false
64      }
65
66      i -= 1; totalPrice += eval(tunerList[i].price)
67      systemDescription += " - " + tunerList[i].componentName +
     " from "
68            + tunerList[i].manufacturer + "\n"
69      return true
70   }
71
72   //--Get the selected CD price
73   function CDPrice()
74   {
75     var i = document.SystemForm.CDPlayer.selectedIndex
76
77     if(i == 0)
78     {
79      alert("\nYou must select a CD Player. \n")
80      return false
81     }
82
83      i -= 1; totalPrice += eval(cdList[i].price)
84      systemDescription += " - " + cdList[i].componentName +
85         " from " + cdList[i].manufacturer + "\n"
86      return true
87   }
88
89   //--Get the selected tape deck price
90   function TapePrice()
91   {
92     var i = document.SystemForm.tapeDeck.selectedIndex
93
94     if(i == 0)
95     {
96      alert("\nYou must select a tape deck. \n")
97      return false
98     }
99
100    i -= 1; totalPrice += eval(tapeList[i].price)
101    systemDescription += " - " + tapeList[i].componentName +
102        " from " + tapeList[i].manufacturer + "\n"
103    return true
104  }
105
106  //--Builds a formatted string containing the data
107  //  to be submitted
```

```
108  function submitData(form)
109  {
110  ...See Listing 12.8
111  }
112
113  //—-Test that aString is no longer than maxLength
114  function isMaxLength(aString, maxLength)
115  {
116  ...See Listing 13.8
117  }
118
119  //theChar includes letters only
120  function isLetter(theChar)
121  {
122  ...See Listing 13.2
123  }
124
125  //Digit is the characters 0, 1, ..., 9
126  function isDigit(theDigit)
127  {
128  ...See Listing 13.5
129  }
130
131  //Characters and digits
132  function isAlphaNumeric(theChar)
133  {
134  ...See Listing 13.4
135  }
136
137  //Name is letters and , . ' `
138  function isValidName(theForm, index)
139  {
140  ...See Listing 13.1
141  }
142
143  //Street is alpha-numeric and , . ' `
144  function isValidStreet(theForm, index)
145  {
146  ...See Listing 13.3
147  }
148
149  //—-Test that aString is no longer than maxLength
150  function isMaxLength(aString, maxLength)
151  {
152  ...See Listing 13.18
153  }
154
```

```
155  //--Test that aString is no shorter than minLength
156  function isMinLength(aString, minLength)
157  {
158  ...See Listing 13.19
159  }
160
161  //--Test that aString is exactly aLength
162  function isLength(aString, aLength)
163  {
164  ...See Listing 13.17
165  }
166
167  //2 letters only
168  function isValidState(theForm, index)
169  {
170  ...See Listing 13.16
171  }
172
173  //Phone is digits and ( - )
174  function isValidPhone(theForm, index)
175  {
176  ...See Listing 13.15
177  }
178
179  //Zip is alphanumeric and includes -
180  function isValidZip(theForm, index)
181  {
182  ...See Listing 13.21
183  }
184
185  </SCRIPT>
186  </HEAD>
187
188  <BODY BGCOLOR = 'lightblue'>
189  <FORM NAME = "SystemForm">
190  ...See Listing 14.1
191  </FORM>
192
193  <TABLE>
194    <FORM NAME = "dataForm">
195    ...See Listing 14.2
196    </FORM>
197    <FORM NAME = "submitForm">
198    ...See Listing 14.3
199    </FORM>
200  </TABLE>
201  </BODY>
202  </HTML>
```

# Suggestions for Extensions

By the time you are done analyzing the code for the Internet store application, you should be able to figure out how to modify the code to fit your own needs. Below are some suggestions.

## A Video or Car Dealership Store

Whatever modifications you wish to implement, think first about the structure of objects you wish to work with. If, for example, you are modifying the application to build a video rental store, you may want to design your prototype object along the lines of the one shown in Listing 14.5.

**LISTING 14.5** An object structure for a video store.

```
1    function Video(title, located, numberOfCopies,
2      starring, director, abstract)
3    {
4      this.title = title
5      this.located = located
6      this.numberOfCopies = numberOfCopies
7      this.starring = starring
8      this.director = director
9      this.abstract = abstract
10   }
```

Next, you need to start building your array of video movies, one object instance at a time, as shown in Listing 14.6. From here on, you implement your application in much the same way as in Listing 14.4.

**LISTING 14.6** A Video object.

```
1    movieArray = new Array()
2    movieArray[0] = new Video(
3      "Mr. Smith Goes to Washington",
4      "Aisle 4", 100,
5      "James Stuart",
6      "Frank Capra",
7      "A young and naive senator takes on the Senate, the
     Washington lobby, and currupt politicians"
8    movieArray[1] = ...
```

If you are into visual effects, you can add a property to your objects, call it (for example) imageInFile, and assign to it the name (and location) of a file that includes an image of the object. Then, include in your document, in addition to some of the object's properties, a URL (anchor) to the location of an HTML file that contains (or loads) the image. In this HTML file you want to provide a button that allows the user to return to the store listing. See, for example, the discussion of the Image object in Chapter 7 and its properties in Chapter 8.

If you want to design a car dealership, design a Car object, much like the Video in Listing 14.6, with properties such as model, year, make, and other information (do not forget to include the price).

## Creating a User Survey Form

If, instead of selling over the Internet, you are interested in user surveys, you can remove the SystemForm from the application (Listing 14.4), and add objects to the dataForm such as checkboxes, radio buttons, selection lists, and options. Then gather the data from the survey and e-mail it to yourself. In the appropriate sections of Chapters 7 to 10 you will find examples to get you started.

## Including the Data in Your Database

If, after developing your application, you are still excited about it, and still insist upon independence from a server, you can do the following:

- Format the e-mail message you receive such that you can easily parse the data into a database.

- Set the subject of the message to a recognizable and distinct name.

- Use an e-mail program that allows you to use filters (on message subjects, for example) and macros that will recognize a message by its subject and save it as a file.

- Write a program in your database to parse the information in the file, and input it to the database.

These tasks are not trivial; you will need to learn a few things in the process. The work may be even more complicated than using CGI or Java, for example, but it will free you from dependence on a server. You may also want to learn Java; it will allow you to implement some powerful ideas without relying on a server.

#  Testing and Debugging the Application

Testing and debugging, like data validation, is complicated, and can be very difficult. Suggestions for debugging strategies are sprinkled throughout the book. Here I want to discuss overall strategies for testing and debugging applications; these can be applied to the Internet Store application as well as any other applications you develop.

## Strategies for Debugging

I want to summarize suggestions for debugging strategies. Specifically, I will discuss strategies for defensive programming, functions design, how to simplify program logic, and using the `alert` dialog window for debugging.

### Defensive Programming

Defensive programming will go a long way toward reducing the burden of debugging. By defensive programming I mean the following:

- Cut your program into slices (modules) as small as possible.

- Make sure these slices are as independent of others as possible.

- Design these slices such that they have minimal side effects; i.e., they change as few values of global variables as possible.

- Test each slice as soon as it is done and then incorporate it into the program.

- Test the program with the slices added incrementally.

### Designing Functions

In most cases, functions can constitute program slices. When you design a function, follow these suggestions:

- Have the function accomplish one task.

- Make the function as small as possible.

- Make it as flat as possible (do not call a function from a function from a function).

- Give the function a descriptive name, with active verbs.

There is often a contradiction between making functions flat and making them short. While you will have to find the solution that is optimal for you.

## Simplifying Program Logic to Avoid Logical Errors

Logical errors are often very difficult to pinpoint, and may come up only after the program reaches the user. This is so because it is difficult to test all possible combinations of program branches, but with a variety of users some untested combinations will inevitably occur.

To avoid logical errors, follow these suggestions:

- Minimize the number of conditions in an `if` statement.

- Avoid cascading `if` statements. For example, the logic in the code

```
if (...)
   if (...)
    if (...)
```

will be hard to debug. To circumvent this problem, you can do something like this:

```
if (...)
   go somewhere so that you do not reach the next if
if (...)
   go somewhere so that you do not reach the next if
if (...)
   and so on
```

This is a common approach taken in the design of functions. When your first `if` in a function is `true`, `return` from the function. If it is `false`, the next `if` will be executed, and so on.

- When testing logic, avoid double negatives. For example, the logic of `if(!(false))` is sometimes hard to decipher; use `if(true)` instead.

- Unless you are in the business of making an impression (on the wrong people), there is no need to be overly terse in your code. For example, instead of using statements like this:

```
if ( !(aVariable = aFunction()))
   use aVariable
```

use code like this:

```
aVariable = aFunction()
if (aVariable)
   use aVariable
```

### Using `alert()`

As you test your program, use alert dialog windows profusely. Be careful not to put these alert messages in long (or infinite) loops. In the alert message, put information such as the name of the function in which the alert resides, the value of the iteration index (if the alert is embedded in a loop), values of object properties that may cause errors, and so on. We use this technique in many places throughout the book.

## Testing the Code

In testing the code, you want to create all possible permutations of program logic. This will force execution of all parts of the program. For example, for the code

```
if (condition1)
   do something
if (condition2)
   do something else
```

you must ensure that `condition1` is `true` at least once, and do the same for `condition2`; otherwise, if the code corresponding to `do something` or `do something else` includes an error, you will not detect it until a user creates conditions that cause `condition1` or `condition2` to resolve to `true`.

To make sure that you test as many permutations as possible (the number can be astronomical if your program is large and complicated), draw a flow chart of your testing procedure. In the flow chart list the specific data that need to be entered in order to execute the code. For example, you can draw a flow diagram of the whole program, and next to each `if` branch list all possible conditions that will produce `true` or `false` for the `if`, along with the data that are necessary to produce these.

There is a vast literature on code testing and software quality control; this difficult and complicated subject is beyond the scope of this discussion. Even with the most sophisticated software quality control approaches, consumers still get software with bugs from giants like Microsoft, Netscape, and many other software companies.

## Testing the Internet Store Application

To make things less abstract, here is a partial checklist for testing the Internet store application:

- To test the stereo system design portion of the application, choose all possible combinations of stereo components. This will ensure that functions such as `CanGetPrice()`, `AmplifierPrice()`, `SpeakersPrice()`, and so on (see Listing 14.4) will all be tested. For example, when I first coded the application, I forgot that there is a discrepancy between the index of a component in the component array and its index in the `Select` list because of the addition of `--non selected--`. Thus, I neglected to include the `i -= 1` in each of the appropriate functions (see, for example, lines 49, 66, 83, 100 in Listing 14.4). If you test the code on the first three components of the selection (see Figure 12.1), but not on the last one, the application will not complain! Can you figure out why?

- Compute, by hand, the cost of various system combinations, and then create those with the software. Did your computations correspond to those produced by the program?

- To test that the validation functions for the user information part of the form (shown in Figure 12.2) all work as expected, test each field with characters from the admissible and inadmissible sets. For the state field, for example, you need to do the following: try to enter one letter, then three letters, than one letter and one digit, and finally, two letters.

- To test the e-mail message part of the application, change the e-mail address in the `mailto:` action in the `submitForm` (line 3 in Listing 14.3) and read the message received. Is the message what you expected?

# DRAWING WITH JAVASCRIPT — A BAR GRAPH

↳ How to implement drawings in JavaScript
↳ How to construct a bar graph

 # Introduction

In this, the last chapter of the book, I wish to show you how to use JavaScript for drawing. By now you should be a JavaScript expert, and I will therefore keep things short. The trick to drawing with JavaScript is to construct an image file that includes a single pixel. One such file is black.gif (see Listing 15.1, page 651, line 13). If you wish to draw with colors, you can create an image file for each color you wish to work with. Each file should contain a single pixel with the color of your choice. To manipulate gif files, use your favorite graphics file editor. These images are then placed and sized (using HEIGHT and WIDTH).

The bar graph drawing application (Listing 15.1) draws a bar graph of data you supply (Figure 15.1). Run it and see what it does. Then, go over the sections in this chapter that explain how the application works.

#  Global Variables

Although not advisable, I chose to declare both the plot data and some plot parameters as global variables. Do not follow this practice if your application is long (that is, if it includes many lines of code and many functions).

## The Data

Lines 6 to 10 of Listing 15.1 (page 651) are the only places where you need to make changes if you wish to create your own bar graph as shown in Figure 15.1. You will need to specify an array of your data. The xData array contains the names of the categories for the bar graph. The elements of this array do not have to be numbers; they can also be strings. The x data will appear on the right side of the graph (see Figure 15.1).

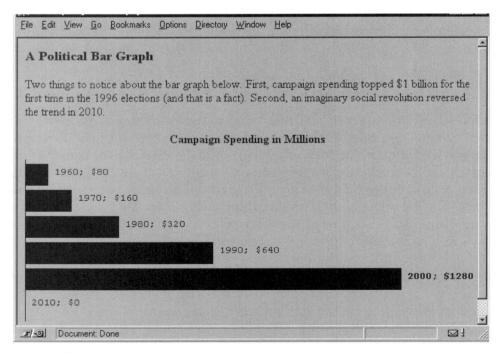

**FIGURE 15.1** A bar graph application.

The yData array (line 8) specifies the values for which bars are going to be plotted. To avoid difficulties, be sure to verify that xData and yData have the same number of elements. Next, the number of elements in both arrays is assigned to nBars. Finally, the plot's title is defined by assigning a string literal of your choice to plotTitle.

## Plot Parameters

In lines 12 to 17 of Listing 15.1 we set up the following global plot parameters:

- blackPen stores the part of the IMG tag that we will use repeatedly later. This, as you will see momentarily, simplifies coding. The image we use is a single black pixel, stored in the file black.gif, in the images directory. The images directory is a subdirectory of the directory in which the application (Listing 15.1) resides. Note the use of the align attribute in line 13. To see how it works, try other alignments (see the Image object section in Chapter 7).

- In line 14 we define the plotWidth in pixels. Our bar graph is horizontal, and as you will see momentarily, the maximum of the yData array will be scaled to plotWidth.

- In line 15 we define the barHeight and assign a convenient number of pixels to it. Keep in mind that bar widths reflect data values, while the bar height is a constant value—the thickness of the bar.

- In line 16 we define barGap as a fraction of barHeight. This will set up the gaps between the bars. If you set its value to zero, then the bars will have no gaps between them.

- Finally, in line 17 we set up an array of barWidths, which reflects data values.

# The maxOfArray() and minOfArray() Functions

In lines 19 to 27 of Listing 15.1 we determine the maximum value of an array. This will allow us later to scale the data to the plotWidth. The function takes two arguments: theArray and itsLength. Then in line 21 we set some minimum value. In the unlikely event that your data involves very small numbers, change -1e-20 in line 21 to a smaller number. If your data does deal with small numbers, I suggest you scale the data before working with them in the first place.

Next, in lines 22 through 24 we cycle through all of theArray elements. If we find an element larger than maxArray, we assign that element value to maxArray. When done, we return the value of maxArray.

If you are a keen observer, you might ask: "With long arrays, wouldn't it be faster to simply copy the array, sort it in descending order, and then assign the first element to maxArray?" Yes, of course. However, recall that when you make a copy of an array, you are not copying the array's data; you are just giving the array another name. For example, if you have a descending-order sorting function named sort(), you can write something like this:

```
var A = new Array(1, 2, 4, 3)
var B = A
sort(B)
maxArray = B[0]
```

but then both A and B will have their elements ordered as 4, 3, 2, 1, and you will lose the order of the data. This, in the case of graphing, is not something you want to do.

To bypass this difficulty, you can build an array of elements that have two properties: the data value and the element's location in the data array. Then, when you do sorting or manipulate array elements in any other way, these two properties stick together and you can always recover the natural order of the data.

In lines 30 to 37 we calculate the value minOfArray(). Here we first assign a large value to the minArray variable (line 31), and then cycle through all of theArray elements. If we find an element whose value is smaller than minArray, we assign that value to minArray (lines 33 and 34), and then we return minArray (line 36).

 # The computeBarWidths() Function

In lines 39 to 45 of Listing 15.1 we scale the bar widths. This is done as follows:

- We determine maxData and minData for the yData array (lines 41 and 42), and then calculate the dataRange (line 43).

- Next, we cycle through each element of the yData, scale each element to a value between zero and 1, multiply by the plotWidth, and assign an integer to barWidths[i].

#  The doBar() Function

In the doBar() function (lines 49 to 71 of Listing 15.1) we draw the bars. In lines 51 and 52 we display the plot title (see Figure 15.1). Then we computeBarWidths() (line 54). Next, we repeat the following for each element in the barWidths array:

- In lines 59 and 60 we build the HTML code

```
<pre><img src='images\\black.gif'
    align='middle' height=7.5 width=1><br>
```

Note that barGap = barWidth/4 = 7.5.

- In lines 61 and 62 we build the HTML code

```
<pre><img src='images\\black.gif'
    align='middle' height=30 width=x>
```

where x is the width of the i-th bar.

- In line 65 we put to the right of the i-th bar the value of xData[i] and yData[i].

- In lines 69 and 70 we again build the HTML code that we built in lines 61 and 62.

In brief, to draw the bar graph in a window, we scale the data and then insert the single-pixel image in the document with the appropriate values for HEIGHT and WIDTH attributes of the IMG HTML tag.

**LISTING 15.1** A bar graph application.

```
1   <HTML>
2   <HEAD>
3   <TITLE>A Bar graph</TITLE>
4   <SCRIPT LANGUAGE = JavaScript>
5   //Plot data; this is the only thing
6   //you need to change:
```

```
7    var xData = new Array(1960,1970,1980,1990,2000,2010)
8    var yData = new Array(80,160,320,640,1280,0)
9    var nBars = 6
10   var plotTitle = "Campaign Spending in Millions"
11
12   //Plot parameters
13   var blackPen = "<img src='images\\black.gif' align='middle'
     height="
14   var plotWidth = 500
15   var barHeight = 30
16   var barGap = barHeight/4
17   var barWidths = new Array(nBars)
18
19   function maxOfArray(theArray, itsLength)
20   {
21     var maxArray = -1e-20
22     for (var i = 0; i < itsLength; i++)
23      if (theArray[i] > maxArray)
24        maxArray = theArray[i]
25
26     return maxArray
27   }
28
29   function minOfArray(theArray, itsLength)
30   {
31     var minArray = 1e20
32     for (var i = 0; i < itsLength; i++)
33      if (theArray[i] < minArray)
34        minArray = theArray[i]
35
36     return minArray
37   }
38
39   function computeBarWidths()
40   {
41     var maxData = maxOfArray(yData, nBars)
42     var minData = minOfArray(yData, nBars)
43     var dataRange = maxData - minData
44     for (var i = 0; i < nBars; i++)
45      barWidths[i] = Math.floor(
46        (yData[i]-minData) / maxData * plotWidth )
47   }
48
49   function doBar()
50   {
51     document.write("<CENTER><B>"+plotTitle+
52      "</B></CENTER><P>")
53
```

```
54     computeBarWidths()
55
56     var i, j
57     for (i = 0; i < nBars; i++)
58     {
59      document.write("<pre>" +
60         blackPen + barGap + " width=1><br>")
61      document.write(blackPen + barHeight +
62         " width=" + parseFloat(barWidths[i])+">")
63      if (yData[i] > 1000)
64         document.write("<B>")
65      document.write(" "+ xData[i]+"; $"+yData[i]+"<br>")
66      if (yData[i] > 1000)
67         document.write("</B>")
68     }
69     document.write(blackPen + barGap +
70       " width=1><br></pre>")
71    }
72
73    </SCRIPT>
74    </HEAD>
75
76    <BODY>
77    <H3> A Political Bar graph </H3>
78    Two things to notice about the bar graph below. First,
79    campaign spending topped $1 billion for the first
80    time in the 1996 elections (and that is a fact). Second,
81    an imaginary social revolution reversed the trend in 2010.
82    <P>
83    <SCRIPT LANGUAGE = JavaScript>
84    doBar()
85    </SCRIPT>
86    </BODY>
87    </HTML>
```

# ↳ Some Extensions

As I've mentioned, you can define as many one-pixel image files as you wish, and then use them for drawing in colors. You can create small multi pixel graphics objects such as circles, squares, and so on, and then manipulate them with the IMG HEIGHT and WIDTH attributes—just as we did in Listing 15.1.

To show you what I mean, let us take a look at Listing 15.2 and Figure 15.2. Here we define two image files, black.gif and white.gif (lines 7 and 8), and two corresponding pens: blackPen and whitePen. We then define plotWidth (line 9).

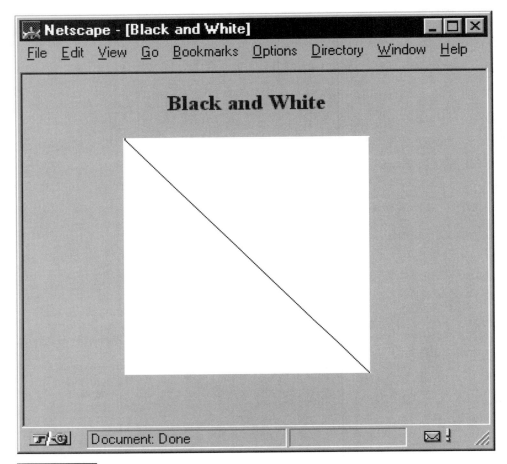

**FIGURE 15.2**  Drawing a line.

Next, in lines 11 through 24 we `doBlackAndWhite()`:

- For the `plotWidth`, we define an image width for each `i` (line 17), and draw it with `whitePen`.

- Then we draw a single pixel with `blackPen` (line18).

- Next, we draw with `whitePen` the remaining width of the plot (lines 19 and 20).

Note that without `eval()` in line 20 we would not be able to draw; the `document.write()` calls produce HTML code from JavaScript, and you cannot put a JavaScript evaluation in an HTML tag unless it is with a call to an event handler or related activity. Using `eval()` produces a literal that HTML can work with.

**LISTING 15.2** Drawing a line.

```
1    <HTML>
2    <HEAD>
3    <TITLE>Black and White</TITLE>
4    <SCRIPT LANGUAGE = JavaScript>
5
6    //Plot parameters
7    var blackPen = "<img src='images\\black.gif' height=1 "
8    var whitePen = "<img src='images\\white.gif' height=1 "
9    var plotWidth = 200
10
11   function doBlackAndWhite()
12   {
13     var i
14     document.write("<CENTER>")
15     for (i = 0; i < plotWidth; i++)
16     {
17      document.write(whitePen + " width = " + i + ">")
18      document.write(blackPen + " width = 1>")
19      document.write(whitePen + " width = "+
20        eval(plotWidth-i-1)+">")
21      document.write("<BR>")
22     }
23     document.write("</CENTER>")
24   }
25
26   </SCRIPT>
27   </HEAD>
28
29   <BODY>
30   <CENTER><H3>Black and White</H3></CENTER>
31   <SCRIPT LANGUAGE = JavaScript>
32   doBlackAndWhite()
33   </SCRIPT>
34   </BODY>
35   </HTML>
```

You could modify the program (Listing 15.1) to draw vertical bars rather than horizontal ones. You could also (if you insist) modify Listing 15.2 to generate scatter plots, lines, diagrams, and so on. Yet, I do not recommend using JavaScript for such tasks. You might as well use that investment of time and effort to learn Java. Dealing with Java is reserved for my next book.

# PART FOUR

# APPENDICES

# GLOSSARY

**argument** A variable that appears in a function declaration. When the function is called, data for the variable is supplied with the call. For example, `function f(a1, a2){...}` is declared with two arguments, `a1` and `a2`. A call to `f` may look like this: `f(1, 2)`. In this example, `a1` and `a2` will be recognized in `f`, and will have the values `1` and `2`, respectively.

**array** An indexed collection of values such as numbers and strings. Each element is identified by its location. The location position of an element is called the index.

**ASCII file** A simple computer file that contains alphabetic and numeric characters, punctuation marks, spaces, and tabs only.

**Boolean** A data type that takes on two values only: true or false.

**browser** The software that allows you, the user, to navigate through the Internet, build your own Internet home page, and accomplish other Internet-related tasks.

**bug** In programming jargon, a programming error.

**button** An active rectangular area in an HTML page, with a word or two in it. When the user clicks on it, some action is taken by the program that created it.

**C** A procedural (function)-oriented programming language.

**C++** An object-oriented programming language. A descendant of C.

**CGI** Common Gateway Interface. A kind of scripting that is usually used to communicate between documents and user interface elements in the document and the server. Many server management tasks are accomplished by using CGI.

**class** A collection of properties (variables) and methods that are designed to accomplish some task(s) in a program. In a programming language context, a class defines a data type (see object).

**Compile** The process of translating a text file into a binary file that is "understood" by the central processor as a set of instructions to execute. Compilation produces an object file.

**constructor** A method that bears the name of a class. The method creates an instance (object) of the class, and initializes property values if necessary. For example, `a = new Array(2)` creates a two-element `Array` object `a`.

**CPU** Central processing unit. The "heart" of the computer. Here the instructions to perform computations are executed.

**data tainting** For security reasons, scripts on one server are normally prevented from accessing properties of documents on a different server. In some cases (e.g., "navigation helper"), this restriction is undesirable. The data tainting mechanism allows JavaScript in one window to see properties of another window, no matter what server the other window's document was loaded from.

**event handlers** Trigger code that is executed when an event occurs.

**events** Actions that occur as a result of something the user does. For example, when a button is clicked, an event (`onClick`) occurs.

**executable** A file that can be executed by the operating system. Software usually comes in the form of executable files.

**expression** A set of valid literals, variables, and operators that evaluate to a single value.

**function** A collection of statements that performs some task. This collection is isolated from the rest of the code, and thus can be called from different places in the JavaScript.

**GUI** Graphical User Interface. The graphical presentation through which the user interacts with the operating system or software. Data are displayed in windows that can be sized, moved, and scrolled. The user can make choices using the mouse, by clicking on buttons, checkboxes, menus, and so on. MacOS, Solaris, and Windows95 are examples of GUI-based operating systems. In contrast, in character-based operating systems and software like DOS and plain-vanilla UNIX, the user interface is a command line, and the user input must be typed.

**HTML** Hypertext Markup Language. The language that is used to create Web pages. It consists of predefined constructs (markers) that highlight words, tag areas in the document that respond to user input, format the document, load graphics files into specified areas in the document, structure the document, and so on.

**index** An integer that specifies the location of an element in an array.

**inheritance** The process by which a class is extended and reused. A daughter class inherits properties and methods of a parent class, and then adds its own properties and methods.

**interpreter** A program that recognizes script statements and knows what to do with them.

**Java** An object-oriented programming language.

**JavaScript** The JavaScript language. Code embedded in an HTML document that performs a variety of useful tasks.

**keyword** A word (string) that has a built-in meaning assigned to it in a computer language.

**layout** The process of placing HTML elements on the page. Layout is specified by HTML tags, and is read by the browser sequentially from the top of the HTML file down.

**link** In programming, to combine several object files into a single executable file.

**literals** In JavaScript, fixed values that literally represent the value that you provide. For example, `"Hello"`, `2`, and `4.6` are all literals.

**methods** The collection of functions in an object that, with the properties, make the object behave in a certain way.

**modal** A modal dialog window remains in focus (the top window) until the user takes some action that removes the window.

**object** A programming construct that includes properties and methods. An instance of a class.

**object file** A binary file (it contains zeroes and ones only) that is produced by the compilation process.

**object-oriented programming** An approach to programming that is object-based.

**program control structures** A small set of programming constructs that allows the programmer to execute statements conditionally, execute statements multiple times, etc. For example, `if a = b then do something else` is a control structure.

**properties** The various data items that an object possesses. Properties usually define data that characterize the object.

**scope** Variable scope refers to the parts of the script in which the variable name is recognized.

**script** In this book, a script that denotes a collection of JavaScript programming statements that reside in an HTML page, and is designed to accomplish some Internet-related task.

**string** A sequence of characters, enclosed in single or double quotes, and recognized as a constant value.

**text file** See ASCII file.

**URL** Universal Resource Locator. The convention by which locations on the Internet are located and searched.

# JAVASCRIPT RESERVED KEYWORDS

The following keywords have assigned meanings in JavaScript and cannot be used as variables, functions, methods, or object names:

| | | | |
|---|---|---|---|
| abstract | boolean | break | byte |
| case | catch | char | class |
| const | continue | default | do |
| double | else | extends | false |
| final | finally | float | for |
| function | goto | if | implements |
| import | in | instanceof | int |
| interface | long | native | new |
| null | package | private | protected |
| public | return | short | static |
| super | switch | synchronized | this |
| throw | throws | transient | true |
| try | var | void | while with |

# COLOR NAMES AND VALUES

Use the table below to set colors and the `fontcolor` method for the following JavaScript properties: `alinkColor`, `bgColor`, `fgColor`, `linkColor`, and `vlinkColor`. You can use these string literals (under the column heading Color Literal) wherever colors are set as attributes of HTML tags. The RGB equivalents are given as hexadecimal values.

| Color Literal | Hexadecimal Values | | |
|---|---|---|---|
| | Red | Green | Blue |
| aliceblue | F0 | F8 | FF |
| antiquewhite | FA | EB | D7 |
| aqua | 00 | FF | FF |
| aquamarine | 7F | FF | D4 |
| azure | F0 | FF | FF |
| beige | F5 | F5 | DC |
| bisque | FF | E4 | C4 |
| black | 00 | 00 | 00 |
| blanchedalmond | FF | EB | CD |
| blue | 00 | 00 | FF |
| blueviolet | 8A | 2B | E2 |
| brown | A5 | 2A | 2A |
| burlywood | DE | B8 | 87 |

| Color Literal | Hexadecimal Values | | |
|---|---|---|---|
| | Red | Green | Blue |
| cadetblue | 5F | 9E | A0 |
| chartreuse | 7F | FF | 00 |
| chocolate | D2 | 69 | 1E |
| coral | FF | 7F | 50 |
| cornflowerblue | 64 | 95 | ED |
| cornsilk | FF | F8 | DC |
| crimson | DC | 14 | 3C |
| cyan | 00 | FF | FF |
| darkblue | 00 | 00 | 8B |
| darkcyan | 00 | 8B | 8B |
| darkgoldenrod | B8 | 86 | 0B |
| darkgray | A9 | A9 | A9 |
| darkgreen | 00 | 64 | 00 |
| darkkhaki | BD | B7 | 6B |
| darkmagenta | 8B | 00 | 8B |
| darkolivegreen | 55 | 6B | 2F |
| darkorange | FF | 8C | 00 |
| darkorchid | 99 | 32 | CC |
| darkred | 8B | 00 | 00 |
| darksalmon | E9 | 96 | 7A |
| darkseagreen | 8F | BC | 8F |
| darkslateblue | 48 | 3D | 8B |
| darkslategray | 2F | 4F | 4F |
| darkturquoise | 00 | CE | D1 |
| darkviolet | 94 | 00 | D3 |
| deeppink | FF | 14 | 93 |
| deepskyblue | 00 | BF | FF |
| dimgray | 69 | 69 | 69 |
| dodgerblue | 1E | 90 | FF |
| firebrick | B2 | 22 | 22 |
| floralwhite | FF | FA | F0 |
| forestgreen | 22 | 8B | 22 |
| fuchsia | FF | 00 | FF |
| gainsboro | DC | DC | DC |
| ghostwhite | F8 | F8 | FF |

| Color Literal | Hexadecimal Values | | |
|---|---|---|---|
| | Red | Green | Blue |
| gold | FF | D7 | 00 |
| goldenrod | DA | A5 | 20 |
| gray | 80 | 80 | 80 |
| green | 00 | 80 | 00 |
| greenyellow | AD | FF | 2F |
| honeydew | F0 | FF | F0 |
| hotpink | FF | 69 | B4 |
| indianred | CD | 5C | 5C |
| indigo | 4B | 00 | 82 |
| ivory | FF | FF | F0 |
| khaki | F0 | E6 | 8C |
| lavender | E6 | E6 | FA |
| lavenderblush | FF | F0 | F5 |
| lawngreen | 7C | FC | 00 |
| lemonchiffon | FF | FA | CD |
| lightblue | AD | D8 | E6 |
| lightcoral | F0 | 80 | 80 |
| lightcyan | E0 | FF | FF |
| lightgoldenrodyellow | FA | FA | D2 |
| lightgreen | 90 | EE | 90 |
| lightgrey | D3 | D3 | D3 |
| lightpink | FF | B6 | C1 |
| lightsalmon | FF | A0 | 7A |
| lightseagreen | 20 | B2 | AA |
| lightskyblue | 87 | CE | FA |
| lightslategray | 77 | 88 | 99 |
| lightsteelblue | B0 | C4 | DE |
| lightyellow | FF | FF | E0 |
| lime | 00 | FF | 00 |
| limegreen | 32 | CD | 32 |
| linen | FA | F0 | E6 |
| magenta | FF | 00 | FF |
| maroon | 80 | 00 | 00 |
| mediumaquamarine | 66 | CD | AA |
| mediumblue | 00 | 00 | CD |

| Color Literal | Hexadecimal Values | | |
|---|---|---|---|
| | Red | Green | Blue |
| mediumorchid | BA | 55 | D3 |
| mediumpurple | 93 | 70 | DB |
| mediumseagreen | 3C | B3 | 71 |
| mediumslateblue | 7B | 68 | EE |
| mediumspringgreen | 00 | FA | 9A |
| mediumturquoise | 48 | D1 | CC |
| mediumvioletred | C7 | 15 | 85 |
| midnightblue | 19 | 19 | 70 |
| mintcream | F5 | FF | FA |
| mistyrose | FF | E4 | E1 |
| moccasin | FF | E4 | B5 |
| navajowhite | FF | DE | AD |
| navy | 00 | 00 | 80 |
| oldlace | FD | F5 | E6 |
| olive | 80 | 80 | 00 |
| olivedrab | 6B | 8E | 23 |
| orange | FF | A5 | 00 |
| orangered | FF | 45 | 00 |
| orchid | DA | 70 | D6 |
| palegoldenrod | EE | E8 | AA |
| palegreen | 98 | FB | 98 |
| paleturquoise | AF | EE | EE |
| palevioletred | DB | 70 | 93 |
| papayawhip | FF | EF | D5 |
| peachpuff | FF | DA | B9 |
| peru | CD | 85 | 3F |
| pink | FF | C0 | CB |
| plum | DD | A0 | DD |
| powderblue | B0 | E0 | E6 |
| purple | 80 | 00 | 80 |
| red | FF | 00 | 00 |
| rosybrown | BC | 8F | 8F |
| royalblue | 41 | 69 | E1 |
| saddlebrown | 8B | 45 | 13 |
| salmon | FA | 80 | 72 |

| Color Literal | Hexadecimal Values | | |
|---|---|---|---|
| | Red | Green | Blue |
| sandybrown | F4 | A4 | 60 |
| seagreen | 2E | 8B | 57 |
| seashell | FF | F5 | EE |
| sienna | A0 | 52 | 2D |
| silver | C0 | C0 | C0 |
| skyblue | 87 | CE | EB |
| slateblue | 6A | 5A | CD |
| slategray | 70 | 80 | 90 |
| snow | FF | FA | FA |
| springgreen | 00 | FF | 7F |
| steelblue | 46 | 82 | B4 |
| tan | D2 | B4 | 8C |
| teal | 00 | 80 | 80 |
| thistle | D8 | BF | D8 |
| tomato | FF | 63 | 47 |
| turquoise | 40 | E0 | D0 |
| violet | EE | 82 | EE |
| wheat | F5 | DE | B3 |
| white | FF | FF | FF |
| whitesmoke | F5 | F5 | F5 |
| yellow | FF | FF | 00 |
| yellowgreen | 9A | CD | 32 |

# INTERNET RESOURCES

Below is a list of sites that you can access to obtain more information about JavaScript. The list is, as all Internet resources are, subject to change. Once you locate one or two sites, you can follow their links to yet other sites.

- comp.lang.javascript is a newsgroup to which you can subscribe. Use this group to read questions from other users, and advice, and the latest news about JavaScript. You can also submit your own questions.

- A listserv dedicated to JavaScript is available at majordomo@obscure.org; send a message to the server with the text `subscribe javascript` *name*, where *name* stands for your name. You can instead get a digest of the information on this listserv if you send a message with the text `subscribe javascript-digest` *name*, where *name* is your name.

- The major www JavaScript site is Netscape's http://home.netscape.com. This site will lead you to other sites.

As you surf on the Internet, you will undoubtedly come across numerous sites that use JavaScript extensively. Use your browser to view these HTML documents in a source mode. Copy and paste into your own documents. You will learn much from good (and bad) JavaScript scripters.

For examples and JavaScript tips, visit the following sites (and the links therein):

http://www.c2.org/~andreww/javascript/

http://acwww.bloomu.edu/~mpscho/jsarchive/

http://webreference.com/javascript/

For JavaScript resources, visit one of the following:

http://home.netscape.com/comprod/products/navigator/version_2.0
/script/script_info/index.HTML

http://www.inquiry.com/techtips/js_pro/

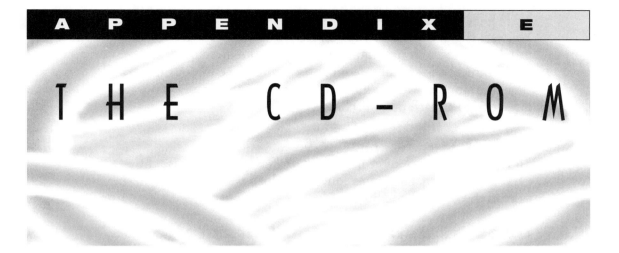

# THE CD-ROM

The CD-ROM contains all of the source code listings described in the book. It is organized according to the following structure:

**Root Directory** Contains all of the book's listings, organized by chapter. Each chapter has its own directory. The listings are named according to their corresponding listing number, as found in the text.

`iss.htm` This file is the complete code of the Internet Store application that was explained in Chapters 12 through 14.

`bar.html` This file contains the bar graph application from Chapter 15.

`commonf.js` Common JavaScript functions are collected here. Use this file with the `SOURCE` attribute of the `<SCRIPT>` tag.

`toc.html` Use this file to quickly navigate to a listing of interest. This file also includes some other information that relates to the listings.

`chapters.html` Used by toc.html.

## Hardware Requirements

To run the included listings and the Internet store application you need MacOS, Windows 3.11 (32-bit mode), Solaris, or any other platform that runs Netscape Navigator 3.0 and up.

## Installing the Software

You can run the HTML files directly from the CD-ROM. If you wish to install the files in your computer, just copy the directory `listings` and all of its subdirectories and files to an appropriate place in your hard disk.

For example, with Windows 95 or MacOS, simply drag the `listings` directory to a place of your choice.

## Using the Software

To run any of the chapter listings, start Navigator, and use the `File | Open File in Browser...` menu-sequence to load the listing you desire. Be sure to read the notes in toc.html.

## User Assistance and Information

The software accompanying this book is being provided as is without warranty or support of any kind. Should you require basic installation assistance, or if your media is defective, please call our product support number at (212) 850-6194 weekdays between 9 AM and 4 PM Eastern Standard Time. Or, we can be reached via e-mail at: **wprtusw@wiley.com**.

To place additional orders or to request information about other Wiley products, please call (800) 879-4539.

If you need help with the program listings, or have comments or questions, you may contact the author via e-mail (yc@turtle.gis.umn.edu), or the author's home page (http://turtle.gis.umn.edu).

# INDEX

## A

abs(*number*), 285
acos(*number*), 285-287
action, 424-426
Address, validating, 608-610
alert(), using, 645
alert([*argument*]), 287-289
alert (*aString*), 87
Alert dialog window, 23-25, 52, 645
  error displayed, 69
alinkColor, 102, 426-428
Alphanumeric data, validating, 610-611
anchor, 102, 163-167
anchor(*anchorNameAttribute*), 289-290
anchors, 102, 163-167, 428-429
appCodeName, 430-431
applet, 167-170
Applet, 102-103
applets, 103
appName, 431-433
appVersion, 433-434
Area, 103, 149, 170-173
arguments, 435-436
Arithmetic operators, 125-126
Array, 157, 173-176
Array of objects, populating, 49
Arrays, 62
  dealing with, 48-50
asin(*number*), 290-291
Assignment operators, 124-125
Assignments, 28
atan(*number*), 292-293
atan2(*xCoordinate,yCoordinate*), 293-295

## B

back(), 295, 331-332
Bar graph:
  computeBarWidths(), 650-651
  data, 648-649
  doBar(), 651-653
  maxOfArray() and minOfArray(), 649-650
  plot parameters, 649
bgColor, 103, 436-439
big(), 295-296
blink(), 296-297
blur(), 87-88, 297-300
bold(), 300
Boolean data type, literals, 121
border, 439-441
Braces, 142-143
break, 138-139, 558-561
Browsers, downloading, 12-13
button, 112, 176-179

Button, 23-25, 67
  clicking on, 76-77
  properties, 65-67

## C

Calculator, events and event handlers, 40-41
CD-ROM, 673-674
ceil(*number*), 300-301
Characters, validating:
  exact number in a string, 622
  maximum number in a string, 623
  minimum number in a string, 623
charAt(*position*), 301-303
checkbox, 112, 179-184
checked, 307-308, 440-443
Class, 58-59
  hierarchy, 58
clearTimeout(*idFrom_set Timeout*), 303-305
clearTimeout (*timeOutID*), 88
click(), 305-308
close(), 88, 92-93, 105, 308-311
Color names and values, 665-669
comment, 561
Comments, in JavaScript code, 21
Comment statements, 142
Comparison operators, 126-127
complete, 444-446
computeBarWidths(), 650-651
Conditional statement, 134-135
confirm([*argument*]), 311-313
confirm (*aString*), 88-90
Constructor, 48
continue, 139, 561-562
cookie, 103, 445-451
cos(*angle*), 314-315
createWindow function, 93-94

## D

Data design, 589-590
Data tainting, 147-149
Data types, 117-120
Data validation, 601-628
  alphanumeric data, 610-611
  date, 627-628
  digit, 611-612
  exact number of characters in a string, 622
  first name, 604-607
  floating point number, 614-615
  integer, 614
  last name, 608
  letter data, 607-608
  maximum number of characters in a string, 623
  minimum number of characters in a string, 623
  negative integer, 613-614
  number is greater than a minimum number, 616
  number is greater than or equal to a minimum number, 617-618
  number is in a range, 618
  number less than a maximum number, 615-616
  number less than or equal to a maximum number, 617
  phone numbers, 619-620
  positive integer, 612-613
  state, 620-622, 624-626
  strategies, 602-604
  stereo system configuration, 604
  street address, 608-610
  zip code, 626-627
Date, 184-186
Date, validating, 627-628

Daughter object, 62
Debugging, strategies, 643-645
`defaultChecked`, 449-453
`defaultSelected`, 452-455
`defaultStatus`, 79-81, 86-87, 456-457
`defaultValue`, 457-460
Defensive programming, 643
`description`, 459-462
Digit, validating, 611-612
`doBar()`, 651-653
`document`, 79
`document` object, 99-106, 187-191
   event handlers, 100
   hierarchy, 101
   methods, 100, 105-106
   properties, 100, 102-105
`document.write`, 21-22, 36
Dot notation, 62
Drawing:
   line, 653-655
   *see also* Bar graph

## E

`elements`, 191-193, 462-463
`embeds` array, 103, 242-243
`enabledPlugin`, 463-465
`encoding`, 465-467
Error, displayed in alert window, 69
`escape(aString)`, 315-317
`eval(aString)`, 317-320
`eventHandler`, 44
Event handlers, 38-42, 76
   canceling action of, 153-154
   listing, 46
   new or modified, 151-154
   resetting, 152-153
   `window` object, 97
Events, 38-42
   applicable HTML tags, 47

   listing, 46
   new or modified, 151-154
Expressions, 122-123
`exp(x)`, 320-322

## F

`fgColor`, 103, 438-439, 468
`file`, 112-113
`filename`, 468-470
File transfer Protocol. *See* FTP
`fileUpload`, 193-195
`fixed()`, 322-323
Floating point literals, 121
Floating point number, validating, 614-615
`floor(number)`, 323-324
`focus()`, 90, 324
`fontcolor(color)`, 325-329
`fontsize(integer)`, 329-330
`for ... in`, 139-141, 564-566
`for` loop, 68, 135-138, 562-564
`form`, 106-108, 196-197
Form elements, new or modified, 151
`forms`, 103-104, 470-472
Forms, 42
   new or modified, 151
`forms` array, 106-108, 196-197
`forward()`, 330-332
`frame`, 97-99, 198-204
`frames`, 79-80, 198-204, 472-473
FTP, 13
FTP sites, to download Internet browsers, 14
FTP software, 13
`Function`, 149, 205-209
Function arguments, 33
Function call, 33, 35
Function definition, 33, 35
   in `HEAD`, 56

syntax, 33
Functions, designing, 643
function statement, 566-568

## G

getDate(), 332-333
getDay(), 334
getHours(), 334-335
getMinutes(), 335
getMonth(), 335-336
getSeconds(), 336
getTime(), 336-337
getTimezoneOffset(), 337-338
getYear(), 338-339
Glossary, 659-662
go(), 331-332
go(*relativePosition* | *"url"*), 339-340

## H

Hardware, 12
hash, 473
HEAD, defining functions, 56
height, 474-475
"Hello World" example, 15-25
    with button and alert window, 23-25
    comments, 21
    document.write function, 21-22
    embedding a string within a string, 22-23
    LANGUAGE keyword, 21
    <NOSCRIPT> tag, 19-21
    <SCRIPT> tag, 18
hidden, 114, 209-212
history, 104, 212-214
host, 475-477
hostname, 478
href, 479
hspace, 480
HTML attributes:
    new, 154-157
    value, referring to JavaScript entities, 154-156
HTML document:
    browser identification, 10
    form object, 42
HTML page:
    automatically created objects, 63
    how to use JavaScript, 25-26
    layout, 72-74
    updating, 55-56
HTML tags:
    applicable events, 47
    new, 154-157

## I

IDE, 15
if ... else, 42, 568-570
if statement, 134-135
image, 104
Image, 149, 215-221
images array, 104, 215-221
Indentation levels, 32
index, 480-485
Index, 48
Indexing, properties, 150-151
indexOf(*searchForString* [, *startFrom*]), 340-343
Inheritance, 58-59
Integers, 121
    validating, 614
Internet resources, 671-672
Internet store:
    advantages of current solution, 587
    building stereo system description and computing prices, 595-598
    code structure summary, 636-642
    communicating with user, 629-635
    data design, 589-590
    data to submit, 598-599

debugging application, 643-645
design, 587-589
formalizing goal, 586
global variables, 592-593
how to achieve goal, 586
including data in your database, 642
limitations of current solution, 587
specifying stereo component database, 590-592
stereo components selection lists, 593-595
stereo system design form, 630-631
submitting data, 634-635
testing application, 645-646
testing code, 645
tools needed, 586
user information form, 632-634
user survey form, 642
validating stereo system configuration, 604
*see also* Project design and implementation
Interpreter, 5, 8
isNaN(*aValue*), 343-345
isValidName(), 605-607
italics(), 345-346

## J

Java:
history, 4-6
versus JavaScript, 7-9
javaEnabled(), 346-348
JavaScript:
added and modified language features, 157-158
definition, 6-7
entity, referring to HTML attribute values, 154-156
history, 4-6
versus Java, 7-9
LiveConnect communication with Java, 147
new and changed features, 146
reasons for using, 9-10
using in HTML page, 25-26
join(), 348-349
JScript, 7

## K

Keywords, 558
reserved, 663

## L

LANGUAGE keyword, 21
lastIndexOf(*searchForString [, startFrom]*), 349-351
lastModified, 28, 483, 485
"Last Modified" example, 26-28
Layout, 72-74
length, 78, 485-486
Letter data, validating, 607-608
Line, drawing, 653-655
link, 104, 221-227
linkColor, 104, 486-488
link(*hrefAttribute*), 352
links, 104, 221-227, 488-489
Literals, 121-122
LiveConnect, 147
LN2, 489
LN10, 489-490
location, 78, 227-230, 490
log(), 352-353
LOG2E, 490-491
LOG10E, 491
Logical errors, simplifying program logic to avoid, 644
Logical operators, 127-128
Loop statements, 68, 135-138, 562-564
lowsrc, 491-493

## M

Math, 157, 230-231
maxOfArray(), 649-650
max(x1, x2), 353
method, 494
Methods, 54, 62, 76
    document object, 105-106
    new or modified, 151
    window object, 87-96
mimeTypes, 232-234
minOfArray(), 649-650
min(x1, x2), 353-354
Modal dialog windows, 54-55

## N

name, 78, 494-496
Name, validating, 604-608
navigator, 234-237
Negative integer, validating, 613-614
Netscape Navigator:
    JavaScript, new features, 147-149
    object hierarchy, 59-60
new, 48, 570-572
<NOSCRIPT> tag, 19-21
Notation conventions, xvii-xix
NOYB, 442-443
Number, 119
    validating that it is greater than a minimum number, 616
    validating that it is greater than or equal to a minimum number, 617-618
    validating that it is in a range, 618
    validating that it is less than a maximum number, 615-616
    validating that it is less than or equal to a maximum number, 617

## O

Oak, 4-5
Object hierarchy, 57-62

dot notation, 62
first to third generation, 60
Netscape Navigator, 59-60
third to fifth generation, 61
Object inspector, 565-566
Object manipulation statements, 139-142
Object names, 145-146
Object properties, 75
    examining, 63-67
    ways to index, 150-151
    see also specific properties
Objects:
    automatically created, 62-74
    availability for use in JavaScript, 72-74
    defining, 49
    methods, 54
    new, 149
    user-interface, 108-115
onAbort, 151, 536-537
onBlur, 97, 151, 537-539
onChange, 539-540
onClick, 540-542
    canceling, 153-154
onError, 97, 152, 542-546
onFocus, 97, 151, 546-547
onLoad, 97, 548-550
onMouseOut, 152, 550-551
onMouseOver, 551-552
onReset, 152, 552-553
onSelect, 553-554
onSubmit, 554-555
onUnload, 97, 556
open(), 90-94, 309-311
opener, 80, 149, 496-497
open([mimeType]), 105-106, 354-355
open([URL, windowName[, windowFeatures]]), 355-357
Operating systems, 12
Operators, 123-133
    arithmetic, 125-126

assignment, 124-125
comparison, 126-127
logical, 127-128
precedence, 130-133
typeof, 128-129
void, 129-130
option, 114
Option, 237-239
Option(), 481-485
options array, 253-259, 498

## P

parent, 80, 85-86, 498-499
parse(aDate), 357-359
parseFloat(aString), 359-361
parseInt(aString[, radix]), 361-363
password, 114, 239-241
pathname, 499-500
Phone number, validating, 619-620
PI, 500-501
Plot parameters, 649
plugin, 105, 242-243
Plug-ins, determining installed, 147
plugins array, 243-246
port, 501-502
Positive integer, validating, 612-613
pow(base, exponent), 364-365
Program logic, simplifying to avoid logical errors, 644
Programming:
   defensive, 643
   discipline, 31-33
Project design and implementation, 582-585
   defining problem, 582-583
   determining what constitutes a solution, 583
   existing expertise, 584-585
   identifying constraints, 585

tools and methods to be used, 583-584
prompt([argument][, defaultArgument]), 365-366
prompt (aString[, defaultValue]), 94
Properties, 28, 62
   document object, 102-105
   new, 149-150
   referring to wrong, 64
   see also Object properties; specific properties
protocol, 502
prototype, 150, 503-505

## Q

Quotes, using, 56

## R

radio, 114, 246-249
random(), 367-371
referrer, 105, 505-507
reload([true]), 372-374
replace(URL), 374-375
Reserved word, 53
reset, 114, 249-253
reset(), 375-377
return, 572-573
reverse(), 377-379
round(x), 380-381
Run-time error, 36

## S

Scope, 93
Scripts, 8
<SCRIPT> tag, 18
   SRC attribute, 156-157
scroll(x, y), 96, 381-384
search, 508
select, 115, 253-259
select(), 384-385

selected, 454-455, 508-509
selectedIndex, 481-485, 509-510
Selection list, creating, 593-595
self, 81, 510-511
setDate(*dayOfTheMonth*), 385-386
setHours(*hourOfTheDay*), 386-388
setMinutes(*minuteOfTheHour*), 388-390
setMonth(*monthOfTheYear*), 390-391
setSeconds(*secondOfTheMinute*), 391-393
setTime(*millisecondsSinceEpoch*), 393-394
setTimeout(*expression, milliseconds*), 395
setTimeout ("*expression*", *millisecondsToWait*), 96
setYear(*yearInteger*), 395-396
sin(*angle*), 314-315, 397
small(), 397-398
Software, needed, 12-14
sort([*sortOrderFunction*]), 398-400
Special characters, 119, 122
split([*separator*]), 400-402
SQRT1_2, 511
SQRT2, 511-512
sqrt((*aNumber*), 402-403
src, 492-493, 512
SRC attribute, <SCRIPT> tag, 156-157
State, validating, 620-622, 624-626
Statements:
   break and continue, 138-139
   comment, 142
   conditional, 134-135
   loop, 135-138
   object manipulation, 139-142
status, 81, 86-87, 456-457, 513
strike(), 403-405

String, 259-262
String addition, 28
String data type, literals, 121-122
String object, 157
Strings, 119
   creation, 52
   dealing with, 50-51
   embedding within a string, 22-23
sub(), 405-406
submit, 115, 263-267
submit(), 406
submitData(), 598-599
submitForm, 634-635
substring([*beginIndex*][, *endIndex*]), 406-408
suffixes, 513-514
sup(), 408-409
Syntax error, 36

## T

taint(), 148-149
taint(*aProperty*), 409
tan(*anAngle*), 409-411
target, 514-515
text, 115, 268-270, 515-517
Text, properties, 65-67
textarea, 115, 271-277
Text editor, 15
theForm.expression, 42-43
this, 141, 574
title, 105, 517-518
toGMTSTring(), 411-412
toLocaleString(), 412-413
toLowerCase(), 413-414
top, 81, 519
toString([*radix*]), 414-417
toUpperCase(), 417-418
type, 149, 519-521
typeof operator, 128-129

# U

unescape(), 418
untaint(), 148-149, 418-419
Updating, HTML page, 55-56
URL, 105, 521-522
userAgent, 522-524
User-interface objects, 108-115
UTC(), 419-420

# V

value, 482-485, 524-529
var, 574-575
Variables, 28
  global, 648-649
  names, 32, 53, 119-120
  scope, 93, 120
VBScript, 7
Visual Basic Scripting Edition, 7
vlinkColor, 105, 529-531
void operator, 129-130
vspace, 531

# W

while, 138, 575-576
width, 531-532
window, 277-282, 532-533
window object, 77-97
  defaultStatus, 79-81
  document, 79
  event handlers, 77, 97
  frames, 79-80
  frames and windows example, 82-85
  length, 78
  location, 78
  methods, 77, 87-96
  name, 78
  opener, 80
  parent, 80, 85-86
  properties, 77, 79-81
  self, 81
  status, 81
  status and defaultStatus example, 86-87
  top, 81
  using properties, 82-87
  window property, 81
Window properties, examining, 70-72
window property, 81
Windows 95, organizing work, 14-15
with, 141-142, 576-577
write(), 420-421
write (["aString"]), 106
writeln(), 421-422
writeln (["aString"]), 106

# Z

Zip code, validating, 626-627